THE EPISCOPATE IN THE KINGDOM OF LEÓN IN THE TWELFTH CENTURY

by

R. A. FLETCHER

OXFORD UNIVERSITY PRESS
1978

Oxford University Press, Walton Street, Oxford OX2 6DP

OXFORD   LONDON   GLASGOW
NEW YORK   TORONTO   MELBOURNE   WELLINGTON
IBADAN   NAIROBI   DAR ES SALAAM   LUSAKA   CAPE TOWN
KUALA LUMPUR   SINGAPORE   JAKARTA   HONG KONG   TOKYO
DELHI   BOMBAY   CALCUTTA   MADRAS   KARACHI

ISBN 0 19 821869 9

©*R. A. Fletcher 1978*

Set by Hope Services, Wantage
and printed in Great Britain by
Billing & Sons Ltd.,
Guildford, Worcester and London

PREFACE

The scope and limitations of the essay which follows are set out in its first chapter. Of its shortcomings it will be for others to speak. I am sensible that it has many. There would have been more had it not been for the assistance and advice which have been so generously offered to me at every stage of the enterprise.

I am grateful to the Consejo Superior de Investigaciones Científicas for the grant of a scholarship in the academic year 1966-7; to the University of Oxford for awarding me the Duque de Osma Studentship in 1968; and to the University of York for contributing to my expenses in Spain in 1972.

The thesis upon which the present book is based was supervised by Miss E.S. Procter, and I owe much to her watchful criticism, especially where legal and institutional matters are concerned. I hope that I have also profited from the criticisms of my examiners, Professor P.E. Russell and Dr. P. Chaplais. I also received much useful advice at an early stage from Dr. (now Professor) D.W. Lomax.

I was happily enabled to benefit from the experienced counsel of Dr. P.A. Linehan, who had completed a *viaje de investigación* round the cathedral archives shortly before I began my own; with these practical matters, as with others, his help was invaluable. Professor Russell furnished me with an introduction which made my visit to Avila agreeable as well as profitable. In Spain it is however to Don Antonio García y García, of the Universidad Pontificia de Salamanca, that I am most deeply indebted: he supplied me with introductions to all the ecclesiastical archives of his native Galicia; he unstintingly lent me books from his own library, and brought to my notice others of which I would have remained ignorant; he plied me lavishly with food and drink on the occasions of my visits to Salamanca. To his scholarship and liberality I owe a great debt.

Dr. Chaplais guided my first steps in the science of Diplomatic and kindly read and commented upon early drafts of chapter 3. Professor the Reverend Colin Morris, of the University of Southampton, with great generosity read the whole

of my thesis and made a number of suggestions which have
been of the utmost value to me in my revision of the text.
Mr. Bernard Barr, of York Minster Library, put at my disposal his extensive knowledge of medieval Latin, and scrutinized
the curious and sometimes bizarre language of the documents
printed in the appendix: I am grateful to him for the correc-
tion of errors and for some conjectural readings where the
originals were damaged or illegible.

Fulford, York
April 1976

CONTENTS

LIST OF TEXT FIGURES & PLATE

ABBREVIATIONS

AC	Archivo de la Catedral de
AD	Arquivo Distrital de
AEM	*Anuario de Estudios Medievales*
AHD	Archivo Histórico Diocesano de
AHDE	*Anuario de Historia del Derecho Español*
AHN	Archivo Histórico Nacional, sección de clero.
AHN cód.	Archivo Histórico Nacional, sección de códices.
AHRG	Archivo Histórico del Reino de Galicia
ANTT	Arquivo Nacional da Torre do Tombo
ap.	apéndice *or* appendix
BCM Lugo	*Boletín de la Comisión Provincial de Monumentos de Lugo*
BCM Orense	*Boletín de la Comisión Provincial de Monumentos de Orense*
BN	Biblioteca Nacional
BRAH	*Boletín de la Real Academia de la Historia*
CAI	*Chronica Adefonsi Imperatoris,* ed. L. Sánchez Belda (Madrid, 1950)
CHE	*Cuadernos de Historia de España*
DHGE	*Dictionnaire d'histoire et de géographie ecclésiastiques*
DMP	*Documentos Medievais Portugueses: Documentos Regios,* vol. I (Lisbon, 1958)
Docs. Galicia	L. Sánchez Belda, *Documentos Reales de la Edad Media referentes a Galicia* (Madrid, 1953)
Docs. Oviedo	*Colección de Documentos de la Catedral de Oviedo,* ed. S. García Larragueta (Oviedo, 1962)
EEMCA	*Estudios de la Edad Media de la Corona de Aragón*
Escalona, *Sahagún*	R. Escalona, *Historia del Real Monasterio de Sahagún* (Madrid, 1782)
ES	*España Sagrada,* ed. E. Flórez, M. Risco, and others (Madrid, 1747–1879)
GAL	J. González, *Alfonso IX de León* (Madrid, 1944)
GRC	J. González, *El Reino de Castilla en la época de Alfonso VIII* (Madrid, 1960)
GRF	J. González, *Regesta de Fernando II* (Madrid, 1943)

HC	*Historia Compostellana,* ed. E. Flórez (Madrid, 1765) (= *ES* vol. XX)
JL	*Regesta Pontificum Romanorum,* ed. P. Jaffé, revised by S. Loewenfeld and others, (Leipzig, 1885)
leg.	legajo
LFH	A. López Ferreiro, *Historia de la S.A.M. Iglesia de Santiago de Compostela* (Santiago de Compostela, 1898–1911)
Mansi, *Concilia*	*Sacrorum Conciliorum Nova et Amplissima Collectio,* ed. J. D. Mansi (Florence, 1759–)
MHV I	*Monumenta Hispaniae Vaticana, Registros,* vol. I, *La Documentación Pontificia hasta Inocencio III,* ed. D. Mansilla (Rome, 1955)
MHV II	*idem,* vol. II, *La Documentación Pontificia de Honorio III,* ed. D. Mansilla (Rome, 1965)
PUP	*Papsturkunden in Portugal,* ed. C. Erdmann (Göttingen, 1927)
Rassow	P. Rassow, 'Die Urkunden Kaiser Alfons' VII von Spanien', *Archiv für Urkundenforschung* x (1928), 328–467 and xi (1930), 66–137
Rodrigo, *De Rebus Hispaniae*	Rodrigo Ximénez de Rada, *De Rebus Hispaniae,* ed. J. de Lorenzana (Toledo, 1793)
S de C	Santiago de Compostela
Note:	Place-names in italic are those that I have not identified on the modern map.

1

THE SETTING

In the course of the years which elapsed between about 1050 and about 1200 western Spain entered upon the fullness of a European inheritance in which she had shared but faintly and uncertainly during the preceding three centuries. The process was long and not without pain. No historian has yet attempted to describe it; too many have been seduced by the flashy glamour of the *Reconquista* into a neglect of what went on behind its lines, into the mischievous error that the history of the *Reconquista* is the history of medieval Spain. If and when this different history comes to be written it will be less spectacular than the story of the *Reconquista*, but no less harsh, no less sad and no less squalid. For the peoples of western Spain did not enter rejoicing upon their new inheritance. Changes were forced upon them, often brutally, and by men who were lacking in scruple; much that had answered well—wayward, peculiar, as it may have been—had ruthlessly to be destroyed; and the bewilderment and resentment that were generated have proved in the centuries which followed to be forces complex, unyielding, intractable. The time is not yet at hand for a systematic account of what occurred; too many facets remain unworked. Yet something of what was involved in this process of change may, it is hoped, be gauged from the essay which follows. Its scope is narrow, being restricted to the doings of the bishops of the north-western quarter of the Iberian Peninsula, the kingdom of León, in the course of the twelfth century.

The kingdom of León originated early in the tenth century, when the Christian rulers of the little Asturian kingdom moved their principal residence south from Oviedo, between the Cantabrian mountains and the Bay of Biscay, down to León, on the *meseta* of central Spain. They regarded themselves as the heirs of the Visigothic kings who had once ruled all Spain from Toledo, and during the tenth century they began to call themselves emperors; claims and pretensions which sat oddly upon the realities of their puny monarchy.

The kingdom was fissile. The county of Castile emancipated itself from Leonese rule during the first half of the century; on occasion the north-west threatened to go the same way. Wrangling between Castilians and Leonese was the most obvious feature of the confused political history of the later tenth and early eleventh century, and it exposed the two principalities to predatory intervention from without. Sancho the Great of the Pyrenean kingdom of Navarre (1004-35) absorbed Castile in the 1020s, and León—though not Galicia —in the last year of his life. In the division of lands which followed his death his son Fernando succeeded to the county of Castile. Two years later, in 1037, he conquered León and Galicia. For nearly thirty years, until his death in 1065, he ruled over a combined kingdom of León-Castile.

No one who is conversant with the history of Spain at any period will be surprised to learn that the kings' main task in the tenth century had been to make their kingdom cohere. Neither will he be surprised to learn that they failed in it. It was only partly their fault. True, they never displayed that creative power of shaping institutions to their purposes which their contemporaries of the house of Wessex possessed in so high a degree. They lacked the wealth the task demanded. They lacked—despite their high claims—traditions of government, access to an intellectual culture which could be harnessed to practical ends. Above all, the facts of geography were against them. A line drawn between León and Burgos marks the northern frontier of the Tierra de Campos, the high, rich, dreary arable land of northern Spain; its southern boundary would be marked by a line drawn from Salamanca to Segovia. This table-land, the *meseta*, is as it were the pit of an amphitheatre formed by a gigantic ring of mountains. The Cordillera Cantábrica, in the north, divides the Asturias from the *meseta*. The range is continued towards the south-west by the Montes de León, the Sierra de la Cabrera, the mountains of what is now the province of Tras os Montes in northern Portugal, and finally the Serra da Estrêla, before it petres out in the basin of the lower Tagus. This formidable barrier shuts off Galicia and northern Portugal, the whole Atlantic littoral, from the plain of León. To the east the plain is closed by the Sierra de la Demanda and its associated ranges;

it was here, to the east of Burgos, the area of Belorado, Salas de los Infantes, Covarrubias and Silos, that the county of Castile was born. To the south, the huge slanting barrier of the Sierra de Guadarrama and the Sierra de Gredos close the square. The areas to the north and west of the mountain chain, the Asturias, Galicia and northern Portugal, differ from the *meseta* in their relief, climate and vegetation. They differed in the early Middle Ages, as to a great degree they still do, in their agrarian practice and their social institutions. Communication between the two halves of the kingdom of León was difficult and slow, owing to the height and extent of the ranges which divide them. Nature here placed more blunt obstacles in the way of the wielders of authority, whether secular or ecclesiastical, than she placed anywhere else in western Christendom.

The society of the north-west has been aptly characterized by Claudio Sánchez Albornoz:[1]

'Galica was the region of the old Asturian and Leonese kingdom where large landed estates were first formed, where big episcopal, abbatial and lay lordships emerged earlier than anywhere else, and where the peasants became more quickly and more completely subject than they did elsewhere. From an early date the cities of Galicia were under the lordship of the bishops, and the countryside was shared out between the cathedrals, the abbeys and the secular aristocracy'.

What was true of Galicia was also true of the Asturias. But a quite different society existed on the plains. Here the settlers —*repobladores*—of the ninth and early tenth centuries had been freemen from the Asturian kingdom and Mozarabs departing from al-Andalus. Offered generous terms by kings whose most pressing need was manpower, they had created a society whose most characteristic member was the free peasant proprietor who was also a soldier, the *caballero villano*; and where the most common form of social relationship was not, as in Galicia, serfdom, but commendation, the contract of *behetría*. The inhabitants of the kingdom of León acknowledged one king and observed one Visigothic law. But the rulers of the kingdom could never forget that their subjects

[1] C. Sánchez Albornoz, *Estudios sobre las Instituciones Medievales Españolas* (Mexico City, 1965), pp. 144–5 (my translation).

formed two societies, distinguished one from the other in their social organization and custom.

These were not wealthy societies. The armies which the kings of León could put into the field were small. The churches which their clergy served were modest. The wills of their aristocracy display no great bulk of movable posessions. We have few references to any industry apart from agriculture, and those tell only of activities, like salt-making and iron-smelting, closely tied to the primary needs of rural communities. Exchange seems to have been sluggish; the kings issued no coinage; and the only town worthy the name was León itself. Our sources are too meagre to allow of any exercise more disciplined than the forming of impressions. But poverty is a relative term, and we can say with confidence that early Leonese society was poor by comparison with its neighbour to the south, the society of Moslem Spain, of al-Andalus.

The caliphate of Córdoba embodied in the tenth century the richest economy, the most sophisticated civilization and the most imposing political system in'the western world. It reached its apogee in the tenth century under three great rulers: the first Caliph, Abd-al-Rahman III (912-61), his son al-Hakam II (961-76) and Ibn Abi Amir, more familiar under the name Almanzor (al-Mansur, 'the Victorious') the adventurer who ruled the caliphate in all but name from 981 to 1002. Contemporaries were flabbergasted by it. The geographer Ibn Hawkal, who visited al-Andalus in 948, became positively lyrical when he described its flourishing cities, its great variety of exotic crops, the amount of money in circulation, the many mineral industries, the wondrous textiles, the great range and bulk of commerce. The society of al-Andalus has been superlatively described by Lévi-Provençal,[1] and we need not linger over it here. Before we leave it, however, a few comparisons will drive home the contrast with the Christian north. The town of León had a population of perhaps 8-10,000 in the mid-tenth century; Córdoba's population probably approached a quarter of a million. Leonese rulers were pleased to be able to get together an army of a

---

[1] Especially in his *Histoire de l'Espagne musulmane* (Paris, 1950-5).

few hundred men; Abd-al-Rahman III had a standing army of about 30,000 men, which was increased under Almanzor to some 60,000–70,000. The caliphs had at their disposal a large and efficient bureaucracy; the kings of León, a handful of household officials and priests.

Early Leonese society was isolated as well as poor. The inhabitants of the north-west did not venture upon the Atlantic —the dark ocean, as Idrisi called it in the twelfth century, where navigation was hindered by the huge waves, the frequent storms, the violent winds, the all-pervading darkness and the variety of sea-monsters. The Vikings braved it; but their raids, recorded from time to time in the ninth, tenth, and eleventh centuries, can only have given the Asturians and Galicians further inducement to stay at home. When the archbishop of Santiago de Compostela wanted to build a fleet early in the twelfth century it was to Genoese shipwrights that he turned. Neither was there much, if any, contact between León-Castile and the outside world overland. The eighth-century Asturian princes had had relations with the court of Charlemagne, but their tenth-century successors indulged in no such far-flung diplomatic exchanges. Otto I sent embassies to Córdoba, but none to León: why should he ever have thought to do so? The churchmen of León had no contact (as we shall see) with the popes, nor with the churches of southern France, nor even, before the reign of Sancho the Great, with those of eastern Spain. The movement of monastic revival associated with the name of St. Rosendo (d. 977) occurred in complete independence of similar contemporary movements in France, Germany and England. The books which were copied in Leonese *scriptoria* (in the peculiar Visigothic script) form a particularly revealing index of the intellectual isolation and conservatism of these churchmen; the learning is there, but it is the learning of an earlier day, the Fathers, the great luminaries of the seventh century, Isidore, Braulio, Ildefonso, Julian, untouched, unfertilized by the movement of thought we call the Carolingian renaissance. Leonese merchants did not trade beyond the Pyrenees. Some foreign traders did come to Spain—the slavers of Verdun, for example, of whom Liudprand tells—but their business was with Córdoba, and we may think it more probable that their

route lay through the Spanish March and eastern Spain than
through the Basque country of the western Pyrenees, about
whose savage people with their incomprehensible tongue
Aimery Picaud had such chilling stories to tell two centuries
later. Leonese chroniclers showed no interest in what was
happening beyond the Pyrenees. A very few French chroniclers had something to say about Spain—Adémar of Cha-
bannes had seen captive Moors at Limoges, and he knew
something of Sancho the Great—but in general they displayed
no interest in Spanish affairs.

This Christian society of the north-west, so poor in the
tenth and early eleventh centuries, suddenly became rich beyond the dreams of avarice in the period after about 1050.
This development, so strange, so unexpected, brought far-
reaching consequences in its train, which underlay much of
the history of the twelfth century; so we should seek to
examine it rather carefully. It sprang essentially from the
political troubles of the caliphate. During the latter part of
the reign of Abd-al-Rahman III and throughout most of the
reign of his son al-Hakam II the rulers of León had been, in
effect, the tributaries of the caliphs. In the last twenty years
of the tenth century Almanzor had subjected the whole of
Christian Spain to a series of raids and had inflicted upon its
rulers a number of severe military defeats. But early in the
eleventh century the tables were turned. A political malaise
whose causes are still not wholly understood afflicted the
caliphate; the whole imposing structure crumbled and fell
apart; and in its place emerged during the 1020s and 1030s a
number of successor states, known to historians as the *reinos
de taifas*. The number of such kingdoms fluctuated. At first
there were at least twenty of them, but by the middle of the
century, after a good deal of intricate diplomatic and military
manoeuvring, this had been reduced to a smaller number, of
which the most important were the *taifa* principalities of
Seville, Badajoz, Toledo, Zaragoza, Albarracín, Valencia,
Almería and Granada. Heirs to the wealth of the caliphate,
they were rich; a prey to internal political instability and in a
state of endemic hostility with their neighbours, they were
vulnerable.

If the Christian princes of Spain had had before their eyes

the ideal of a Christian Spain, wrought out of a military *Reconquista*, this was the time for them to have acted. Wisely perhaps—or simply because they did not have such an ideal— they chose instead to turn the *taifas* into a source of profit for themselves. The Moslem princes became the clients of the Christians. Their clientage was expressed in the payment of tributes known as *parias*; and it was the payment of *parias* which formed the most characteristic mode of relations between Christian and Moslem between about 1050 and 1100. The rulers of eastern Spain, the counts of Barcelona and the kings of Aragon, may have been the first to exact *parias* in any systematic way. In western Spain Fernando I of León-Castile was the first ruler to do so' Our sources leave much to be desired, but there is some reason to suppose that during the last five years of his reign—perhaps during the last ten— Fernando I was regularly receiving *parias* from the *taifas* of Zaragoza, Toledo and Seville, possibly also from Valencia and Badajoz. When he died in 1065 he divided his empire—the territories and the income from *parias*—between his three sons Sancho, García and Alfonso. After a period of confused fratricidal strife, Alfonso re-united the inheritance and ruled the undivided kingdom of León-Castile from 1072 until his death in 1109. To the income from *parias* enjoyed by his father he added a further *paria* from Granada.

Gigantic sums were involved. The tributes were paid in the gold coins (*dinars* or *mithqals*) which were current in al-Andalus. The *vetus paria* paid by Zaragoza to the king of Aragon, which Fernando I succeeded in diverting to himself in about 1060, stood probably at 10,000 *aurei* per annum. When in his turn the king of Navarre managed to divert the payment to himself, at a slightly later date, he stipulated for 12,000 *numos de auro* per annum. Alfonso VI raised 30,000 *mithqals* from the ruler of Granada in about 1075. This amount, which was reached only after a good deal of haggling, included arrears for probably two years, so it would seem that Granada was paying at something like the same rate as Zaragoza. The most skilful operator in this field was Alfonso's most famous subject, Rodrigo Díaz, El Cid. He contrived to pick up for himself from the *taifas* of eastern Spain in the years 1089–91 the astounding sum of 146,000 *dinars*. We should remember, too, that payment of cash was usually accompanied by the giving of presents of carpets, silks, ivories, plate, etc. What do these figures mean? We are so ill-informed about the value of money in Spain at this date that we cannot answer this question with any precision. Noblemen could be ransomed for sums in the range of 500–1,000 *aurei* at this period. In Córdoba in the 1060s 10,000 *mithqals* would have bought 400 horses or about 70 slaves. We can only say helplessly that the *parias* made their recipients extraordinarily wealthy.

Where did the money go to? In the first instance it went to the Christian kings. From being among the poorest rulers in Europe they quickly became among the richest. Some of it was passed on to the cathedral churches and monasteries of León-Castile, some of it to the aristocracy. Some of it went— and this is most significant for our purposes—to destinations outside Spain. The most famous such instance is to be found in the annual *census* paid to the monastery of Cluny, established by Fernando I at an unknown date between 1053 and 1065, re-established by Alfonso VI in 1077, and confirmed by him in 1090. The sum was fixed at 1,000 *aurei* by Fernando I, and doubled by Alfonso VI in 1090. For Cluny, the sum was clearly enormous; it was 'the biggest donation that Cluny ever received from king or layman, and it was never to be surpassed';[1] Henry I of England's annual grant of 100 marks—silver, of course, not gold—from 1131 looks puny in comparison. The Alfonsine census enabled Abbot Hugh to undertake the building of the huge third abbey church of Cluny; and when, later on, payment lapsed, this was among the most important factors in bringing about the financial difficulties, deepening into crisis, which crippled the Cluniacs during the abbacies of Pons and Peter the Venerable. But that is another story. What is important for us is that the export of gold from Spain publicized the new-found riches of the Spanish Christians. The kingdom of León-Castile, in particular, acquired a reputation for inexhaustible wealth during the second half of the eleventh century. What Mexico was to the

---

[1] C. J. Bishko 'Fernando I y los orígenes de la alianza castellano-leonesa con Cluny', *CHE* xlvii–xlviii (1968), 107.

Europeans of the sixteenth century, Spain was to their ancestors of the eleventh and early twelfth; especially to those
nearest at hand, the French. They wanted to join in and share
it, and they were none too scrupulous about how they did so.

The forces which dragged western Spain out of her isolation were compounded of strands of both piety and self-
seeking. The piety found expression in the pilgrimages to
Santiago de Compostela. At some point (which cannot be
exactly established) in the early ninth century a tomb which
was believed to be that of St. James the Greater—Sant 'Iago,
Santiago—was discovered in the diocese of Iria in the extreme
north-west of the Asturian kingdom. What was actually
found we shall never know, and perhaps it does not matter.
What we should very much like to know, but which our
sources are too meagre, discreet or untrustworthy to tell us,
is something of the means by which the local cult of the saint
which grew up in Galicia was transformed into an international cult drawing pilgrims from distant parts of Christendom. The earliest recorded pilgrims from beyond the Pyrenees
visited the shrine in the middle of the tenth century, but it
would seem that it was not until a century later that pilgrims
from abroad were journeying there regularly and in large
numbers. (The first recorded pilgrims from England, we may
note in passing, made the journey between 1092 and 1105).
By the early twelfth century the pilgrimage was a highly
organized affair. Four established pilgrim-roads ran from
starting-points in France and converged in the western Pyrenees, thence to run through northern Spain—by Burgos,
Carrión, Sahagún, León, Astorga and Lugo—to their goal. The
diverse needs of the pilgrims were met by a series of caravan-
serais along the way; by royal protection of so potentially
lucrative a source of revenue; by the evolution of a type of
ecclesiastical architecture designed to cope with large parties
of the devout; by sellers of badges and souvenirs; by the remarkable guide-book put together in about 1140; in short by
the usual paraphernalia of tourism. The most important
social effect of the pilgrimage lay in the opening-up of western Spain to outside influences, and in particular to the influence of France, whence the great majority of pilgrims always came. Its most striking manifestation was the settlement

of Frenchmen in the towns which lay along the pilgrimage route, towns whose size, appearance and economic concerns were transformed by the settlers.

If devotion brought such men to Spain, self-interest kept them there. There were opportunities to hand, which were grasped eagerly. Some came to Spain avowedly to make their fortunes. Warriors came to fight. Two such were Raymond of Burgundy and his cousin Henry. They belonged to the comital house of Burgundy and were thereby highly-placed among the feudal aristocracy of France. Their family had links with the monastery of Cluny and distinguished connections in the secular church, for Raymond's brother was Guy, archbishop of Vienne, who later became pope as Calixtus II. There were already dynastic connections between Burgundy and León-Castile, for Henry's aunt Constance had married Alfonso VI in about 1079. It was some years later that the cousins followed her to Spain. They did very well for themselves. Raymond married the king's legitimate daughter Urraca, probably in 1092, Henry an illegitimate daughter Teresa in 1096. Raymond received a vast Luso-Galician-Leonese honour from the king perhaps as early as 1087, and a county of Portugal was carved out of this for Henry in 1095.[1] Raymond predeceased his father-in-law in 1107; his widow reigned over León-Castile from 1109 to 1126, and their son Alfonso VII, the last of the emperors, from 1126 to 1157. Henry died in 1112; his son, Afonso Henriques, was the first king of independent Portugal. (The pedigree (p. 11) which is much simplified—is intended to make clear some of the relationships mentioned in this chapter.)

Not all who came were of such exalted rank, neither could all hope to be so successful. Some left an unsavoury reputation behind them. Such a one was William 'the Carpenter', viscount of Melun, who led a contingent to fight for Alfonso VI in 1087; his conduct in Spain was alluded to by the author of the *Gesta Francorum* when recounting his attempt to

---

[1] For a discussion of these difficult chronological problems, see B. F. Reilly, 'Santiago and Saint Denis: the French presence in eleventh-century Spain', *Catholic Historical Review* liv (1968), 467–83. On the whole question of French influence in Spain, see the fine study of M. Défourneaux, *Les Français en Espagne aux XIe et XIIe siècles* (Paris, 1949).

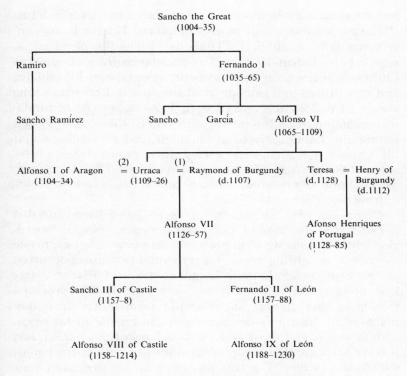

Sancho the Great
(1004–35)

Ramiro

Fernando I
(1035–65)

Sancho Ramírez

Sancho   García   Alfonso VI
(1065–1109)

Alfonso I of Aragon
(1104–34)

(2)
= Urraca
(1109–26)

(1)
= Raymond of Burgundy
(d.1107)

Teresa   = Henry of
(d.1128)   Burgundy
                (d.1112)

Alfonso VII
(1126–57)

Afonso Henriques
of Portugal
(1128–85)

Sancho III of Castile
(1157–8)

Fernando II of León
(1157–88)

Alfonso VIII of Castile
(1158–1214)

Alfonso IX of León
(1188–1230)

Genealogical Table of the Leonese-Castilian Dynasty

desert from the army of the First Crusade in 1098.[1] Others
came to Spain with different qualifications, for different
tasks. Settlers were needed to colonise the sparsely-populated
land. Clergy were needed to supervise the spiritual life of the
colonists. We shall have more to say of the clergy later, so let
one example suffice for the moment—Bernardo of Toledo.
Born near Auch, he entered the nearby Cluniac priory of St.
Orens and later moved to Cluny itself; in 1080 or 1081 he
was sent by Abbot Hugh to replace Robert—another Frenchman—abbot of the Cluniac house of Sahagún. After a short

[1] *Anonymi Gesta Francorum et aliorum Hierosolymitanorum*, ed. R. Hill (Edinburgh, 1962), pp. 33–4; *Chronicon Sancti Maxentii Pictavensis s.a.* 1087, in
Chroniques des Eglises d'Anjou, ed. P. Marchegay and E. Mabille (Paris, 1869),
p. 411.

but active abbacy Bernardo was appointed by Alfonso VI to the archiepiscopal see of newly-conquered Toledo, being consecrated late in 1086. In 1088 he visited the papal curia, where Pope Urban II—an old acquaintance from his days at Cluny—confirmed his appointment, granted him his pallium and constituted him primate of all the Spains. Bernardo's long tenure of office—he survived until 1124—was to be of fundamental importance for the organization of the secular church within the Leonese-Castilian kingdom, and we shall see that his chosen servants were ecclesiastics drawn from southwestern France, all of whom rose to high office in Spain.[1] Throughout this period, French monastic houses were acquiring dependencies in Spain.[2]

Colonists, whether secular or ecclesiastical, were needed because the kingdom of León was becoming bigger. Expansion provoked (as we shall presently see) new enmities; hence the need for fighting men. This territorial expansion occurred at the expense of the *taifa* kingdoms whom Christian rulers had hitherto been content to leave unmolested, provided they paid their *parias*. But it would seem that a shift took place in Alfonso VI's designs about the middle of his reign. This is one of the most delicate problems of this period, and it is unfortunate that it cannot be discussed here at the length which it deserves. Crudely put, it may be suggested that Alfonso moved from being the patron of his client Moslem neighbours, the patron who exploited even as he 'protected' them, to being the enemy whose aim was to conquer them and to incorporate their dominions in his own. With this shift a new mood came into being. The *Reconquista* as it is normally understood began in the latter part of the reign of Alfonso VI. The change of emphasis was partly the result of circumstance. Compelled to intervene in the disturbed internal politics of the client kingdom of Toledo, he was finally compelled to conquer its capital city, which surrendered to him on 6 May 1085; Toledo conquered, the territories depending on it had to be settled and defended; a Christian es-

---

[1] The best account of Bernardo is to be found in J. F. Rivera Recio, *La Iglesia de Toledo en el siglo XII* (Rome–Madrid, 1966), especially ch. 3.
[2] See, for example, C. Higounet, 'Un mapa de las relaciones monásticas transpirenáicas', *Pirineos* vii (1951), 543–53; M. Cocheril, *Etudes sur le monachisme en Espagne et au Portugal* (Paris-Lisbon, 1966).

tablishment had to be introduced. A certain course of action —a novel one—was forced upon the king. But there were ideas as well as circumstances at work. Alfonso seems gradually to have arrived at a new view of what a Christian ruler faced by Moslems ought to be doing. In the nature of the case we cannot trace these vague, unformulated notions to their obscure roots, but that these lay outside Spain is certain. The aristocratic circles (lay and clerical) of northern and eastern France, the papal curia of Humbert and Gregory VII, conceivably the Cluny of St. Hugh, were the communities wherein crusading ideals took shape in the generation before the council of Clermont. Influences from each of these quarters can be shown to have played upon the court of Alfonso VI of León-Castile.

The decision to turn to the way of violence, to military reconquest, was disastrous in its effects. It drove the *taifa* kings into the arms of a dangerous ally, whose help proved mortal to them—Yūsuf ibn-Tāshufin, Almoravide ruler of Morocco. The Almoravide movement originated in the teaching of a Malikite jurist, Ibn-Yāsin, among the tribes of the basins of the Senegal and upper Niger rivers; the name of the movement is derived from the *ribāt* which he founded about 1040. Militant expansion among the neighbouring tribes began shortly afterwards, and the Almoravide interpretation of the Islamic faith was imposed at the point of the sword. 'If (the tribes) persist in their errors and infidelity, let us invoke the aid of God against them and make war upon them until God decides the issue between us'.[1] It appeared that God favoured the Almoravides, for the movement was successfully diffused up and down the African coast. After Ibn-Yāsin's death in 1059, the leadership passed into the hands of Abū Bakr ibn-Ūmar. Shortly afterwards the need for simultaneous military expansion on two fronts led him to share his authority, and he delegated a northern command to his kinsman Yūsuf ibn-Tāshufin. Abū Bakr moved south and conquered the kingdom of Gāna in 1076. Yūsuf overran Morocco and founded a northern capital for himself at Marrakesh in 1062.

Yūsuf was a bold leader and his troops were good fighters.

---

[1] Quoted by J.S. Trimingham, *A History of Islam in West Africa* (Oxford, 1962), pp. 23-4.

His progress was watched with interest tinged with apprehension by the *taifa* kings of al-Andalus. After Alfonso VI's conquest of Toledo the rulers of Seville, Badajoz and Granada decided with some misgivings to seek his aid against the Christians. Yūsuf accepted their invitation, crossed the straits with an army, and inflicted a shattering defeat upon the forces of Alfonso VI at Sagrajas, a little to the north of Badajoz, in October 1086. In 1088 and 1090 he carried out further operations against the Christians. But this was not all. After an unsuccessful attack upon Toledo, probably in July of 1090, he turned upon his employers, accusing them of failing to give him adequate support and of playing him false: he alleged, apparently with some truth, that they had opened negotiations behind his back with Alfonso VI. In revenge, he occupied the *taifa* kingdom of Granada in September 1090.

Deeper issues were at stake than a squabble between a mercenary captain and his paymasters. The Almoravide version of Islam was exclusive. Orthodox and fundamentalist, they were fiercely conscious of their 'purity' as a 'chosen people', whose mission was to restore the simplicity and the fervour of the early days of Islam, and to extend the range of the faith by *jihād*.[1] Moreover, they professed political loyalty to the rightful caliphs, the Abbasids of Baghdad. Yūsuf and his followers were shocked by what they found in al-Andalus and considered that the *taifa* kings had betrayed the Prophet's ideals. Observance of the precepts of the Law was slack; nothing was being done to extend the frontiers of the Faith; the caliph's authority was not acknowledged. Yūsuf told them what he thought of them. Unfortunately, they paid him back in the same coin. To these cultivated men Yūsuf was a fanatic from the desert; he dressed in skins, smelt of camels and could not speak Arabic. Incomprehension deepened into distrust and distrust became hostility. The seizure of Granada was only a beginning. By the time of Yūsuf's death in 1106 most of al-Andalus had fallen into his hands; his son Ali (1106–43) finished the job with the conquest of the last *taifa* kingdom, Zaragoza, in 1110.

Almoravide expansion had far-reaching consequences. It

[1] This is usually translated 'Holy War': but see the comments of W. M. Watt, *The Influence of Islam on Medieval Europe* (Edinburgh, 1972), p. 6.

united al-Andalus once more, as in the great days of the caliphate of Córdoba, but now under an intolerant, a fighting faith. It inspired terror among the Spanish Christians, leading them to appeal for help from beyond the Pyrenees, which brought Raymond and Henry of Burgundy, among others, to Spain, and which caused Popes Urban II and Paschal II to look on Spain as a battleground upon which Christianity was being tried by ordeal. It injected a new strain of religious hatred into relations between Christian and Moslem. Above all, it cut off the supply of *parias*. The flood of gold to the north had dwindled to a trickle by the year 1100; shortly afterwards it dried up altogether. The Cluniacs experienced an abrupt decline in their income, from which they were never to recover. The rulers of León-Castile lost what had been the major part of their revenues for fifty years. It is not too much to say that this crippled their actions throughout the twelfth century.

The economic crisis which faced the rulers of León-Castile in the early twelfth century was combined with a political crisis. In May 1108 a Christian army had been defeated by the Almoravides at Uclés. The *infante* Sancho, Alfonso VI's only son and heir, was killed. The king was an old man and had already been stricken in November 1107 with the illness which was to prove his last. He decided to make his daughter Urraca his heir. As we have seen, Urraca had married Raymond of Burgundy. Raymond had died late in 1107, leaving his widow with a young son, Alfonso Raimúndez, later to be Alfonso VII of León-Castile. In 1108 the latter was an infant three years old. Alfonso VI conceived the plan of marrying Urraca to his namesake Alfonso I of Aragon (1104–34), known to history as Alfonso *el Batallador*. By this marriage the defence of the kingdom would be secured in this moment of military crisis—for the king of Aragon was already known as a highly successful general—and the Leonese-Castilian kingdom would not be left under the rule of a woman, for which there existed no precedent. The time-factor was all-important for clearly Alfonso VI had not long to live. From the sources at our disposal we cannot reconstruct the hectic negotiations which must have taken place in the year which elapsed between the battle of Uclés and the death of Alfonso VI on

1 July 1109: but we do know that the king had his way; Urraca and Alfonso of Aragon were married either just before or, perhaps more probably, shortly after his death. But the succession problem was not to be solved so easily. In the first place the Aragonese were the traditional enemies of the Castilians, Alfonso I was personally disliked in León-Castile, and he and his new wife were temperamentally unsuited to one another. Secondly, the royal couple were related by their common descent from Sancho the Great of Navarre; the marriage was condemned as incestuous by Pope Paschal II and by the bishops of León-Castile under Archbishop Bernardo of Toledo (who seems to have led opposition to it before it took place). Thirdly, there existed a rival claimant who was determined to draw a profit for himself from Urraca's difficulties. Henry of Burgundy, count of Portugal, had married Alfonso VI's illegitimate daughter Teresa. In circumstances that still remain obscure he had intrigued with his cousin Raymond to share out the kingdom after the old king's death. He was unwilling to accept the solution to the succession-question engineered by Alfonso VI, and was astute enough to take initiatives which left him in a position of *de facto* independence. He died in 1112, but his widow Teresa inherited his ambitions and prosecuted them with energy until her death in 1128. Their son Afonso Henriques was soon to style himself king of Portugal—a title which his cousin Alfonso VII was to be forced to recognize.

The secession of Portugal from León-Castile was occasioned by the circumstances of the early twelfth century (though it had its social roots in a distant Suevic and Luso-Roman past) but it was not the only feature which made the reign of Urraca so unhappy. War broke out between the queen and her husband, as a result of which parts of eastern Castile passed under Aragonese control. The partisans of the young Alfonso Raimúndez opposed her, and she was ultimately forced to partition her kingdom and hand over to him authority over Toledo, Extremadura and Galicia. The Almoravides were pressing hard at the southern frontier. And throughout this troubled time the government was desperately poor, for reasons already outlined, and compelled to turn to the only source of revenue left to hard-pressed rulers—spoliation of the church. Urraca's reputation among the clerical writers upon whom we depend for our knowledge of events was consequently low; and it is difficult to cut through the barrier of their vituperation or contempt and grasp what was really happening and what the queen was trying to do about it. Modern historians have been as unsympathetic as their medieval precursors. We still lack an authoritative account of the reign of Urraca, despite the fact that the sources are, by Spanish standards, abundant.

The reign of her son Alfonso VII, the last of the king-emperors of León-Castile, was superficially more successful and was later looked back upon as a golden age. That we still think of it in this way is largely because the chroniclers want us to. Ecclesiastical circles approved of Alfonso VII. His uncle Pope Calixtus II had watched over his early days with a kinsman's indulgence. He kept on good terms with most of his bishops. He and his pious sister Doña Sancha were famed as patrons of monasteries, especially of Cistercian monasteries. He promoted several monks to bishoprics. A contemporary panegyric, the *Chronica Adefonsi Imperatoris*,[1] celebrated his wars in al-Andalus in language which recalled that of the Old Testament, so that Alfonso was made to look like an Israelite king leading a chosen people to the fulfilment of God's holy task. The wars provided him with an income too, which meant that he had no need to tap those sources of revenue near at hand, in the churches of his kingdom, to which his mother had had to resort.

The political affairs of al-Andalus underwent rapid change during the reign of Alfonso VII. The Almoravide conquerors had not been popular with their Hispano-Moslem subjects, who objected to being ruled harshly and taxed heavily as the colony of an empire based on Marrakesh. The Berbers who made up the Almoravide élite were riddled with inter-tribal rivalries. So the Almoravide grip on al-Andalus was, after the frantic successes of the first few years, only a shaky one. More importantly, however, al-Andalus succeeded, as so often before, in subduing her conquerors, and the Almoravides came to appreciate and to emulate the sophisticated culture which Yūsuf had so despised, and to introduce it to

[1] Ed. L. Sánchez Belda (Madrid, 1950); hereafter referred to as *CAI*.

Morocco. Once again there were those who were prepared to point this out and to act on their convictions.

In 1118 a Berber from Morocco named Ibn-Tūmart returned to the Maghrib from a long course of study in the east which had convinced him that he had a religious mission to perform. He believed that it was his task to reform the doctrine and mores of the corrupted Almoravides and to bring them back to the straight path of Islamic orthodoxy. In 1121 he was proclaimed Mahdi by his followers and began guerilla attacks upon the local Almoravide forces. Thus was the Almohade movement born. The similarities between Almoravide and Almohade sects are only superficial. The Almoravides were wild men from the desert: their ideas were crude and their energies were soon dissipated among the flesh-pots of Andalusia. The Almohades had a coherent and sophisticated religious philosophy deriving directly from the intellectual vitality of the heartlands of Islam. Theirs was not the fanaticism of the uncouth, but the zealous conviction of those who believed they had found a—or rather the—divinely inspired and guided leader, the Mahdi. The empire they founded had a far longer and more interesting life than the short-lived desert empire of the Almoravides whom they displaced. But its growth was slow at first. Ibn-Tūmart was killed in battle in 1130. His successor Abd al-Mū'min (1130–63) was to carry the movement across the straits to al-Andalus. The circumstances in which he did so bear some resemblance to those which had brought Yūsuf to Spain at the end of the previous century. In the years 1144–6 a series of rebellions against Almoravide rule broke out in al-Andalus. The rebels appealed for help to the Almohades, who came as allies and then turned into conquerors. At this time Abd al-Mū'min was less interested in conquest in Spain than in eastward expansion along the coast of north Africa. So although Almoravide authority had been shattered in Spain, it had not been replaced by Almohade rule, except in parts of the Algarve and the Guadalquivir valley. So, as in the early eleventh century, political authority disintegrated and a number of small principalities emerged—known to historians as the second *taifas*—which formed the political society of Moslem Spain for some twenty years after 1145. At the end of his life Abd al-Mū'min turned from north Africa to Spain and prepared a large expedition in 1162–3 to conquer it. Death cut short his plans, but they were inherited by his son and successor Abu-Ya'qub Yūsuf (1163–84), who brought the whole of al-Andalus under Almohade authority in the years 1171–3.

The Christian rulers of Spain had profited from the Andalusian anarchy of the 1140s and the weakness of the little principalities which grew out of it. Alfonso VII had reconstituted the kingdom of León-Castile as it had been in his grandfather's day—ultimately reconciling himself to the loss of Portugal—and had had himself crowned emperor in 1135. His raids to the south took on the character of crusading wars of conquest, and by a combination of diplomacy and force he built up a large, sprawling 'empire' to the south of his patrimonial lands, beyond the barrier of the Sierra Morena. Córdoba he acquired by assisting the rebels against the Almoravides in 1146; Almería he conquered in 1147 with the help of troops from southern France and a Genoese navy; in 1151 he had designs on Seville. But his empire was short-lived. He had neither time nor resources for following up the conquests with the colonization—*repoblación*—of the conquered territories, and even before his death the ramshackle structure had begun to fall apart. He died, indeed, while on his way back to Toledo after vainly attempting to force an Almohade army to raise a siege of Almería which shortly afterwards achieved its end. The buoyant optimism of the middle years of the century withered into a mood of uncertainty and this, as Almohade power reached its zenith in the last quarter of the century, turned into panic.

On the death of Alfonso VII the kingdom of León-Castile was divided between his two sons Sancho and Fernando, to the former going Castile and to the latter León. The decision to divide the inheritance, seemingly so foolish, had not been a hasty one; it had certainly been made by 1143.[1] Its effect was to keep León and Castile apart, and frequently at war with one another, for some seventy years. They were finally reunited, this time for ever, by Fernando III in 1230.

It so happens that the sources at the disposal of the historian,

---

[1] A document from the Galician monastery of Sobrado dated 1 March 1143 shows that the dispositons had been made by that date: AHN 526/11.

never abundant in twelfth-century Spain, are specially meagre for this the last age of the independent kingdom of León. We have, for example, not a single contemporary Leonese chronicle from this period. The royal charters have been assembled and the reigns of the last two kings of León studied in their light;[1] but it is hard satisfactorily to reconstruct the history of a reign from charter-evidence alone. It seems beyond doubt, however, that these were difficult years. Fernando II (1157-88) had to contend not only with a powerful Almohade state upon his southern marches but also with Christian enemies. To the east, his rash interventions in Castilian affairs during the minority of his nephew Alfonso VIII (1158-1214) made an enemy of that able ruler. In the west, territorial rivalries with Portugal, especially in Galicia and Extremadura, gave rise to a state of smouldering hostility, sometimes flaring into open warfare, between Fernando and the long-lived Afonso Henriques (1128-85). León could not afford wars. Fernando II himself was a man of reckless extravagance. His son Alfonso IX tactfully referred to his father's *superabundans liberalitas* and his *immensa benignitas* and laid the blame for what happened upon the unscrupulous *familiares* with whom he had surrounded himself: but he makes the consequences clear; by the end of the reign the government was virtually bankrupt.[2]

Alfonso IX (1188-1230) inherited other ills besides an empty treasury. He had a rival to the throne in the person of an illegitimate son of Fernando II whose claims were supported by the Haro family, the powerful noble house from which the mother had come. To gain resources and to rally support the king was led to make far-reaching constitutional concessions early in his reign, which weakened such authority as he might have hoped to wield. Caught between Portugal and Castile, he sought a truce with the Almohades to the south. It was a prudent step but it did him no good. The fall of Jerusalem in 1187 had served to alert western opinion to the vulnerability of the Christian states of Spain at the opposite end of the Mediterranean. The worst fears were confirmed

[1] J. González, *Regesta de Fernando II* (Madrid, 1943) and *Alfonso IX de León* (Madrid, 1944); hereafter referred to as respectively *GRF* and *GAL*.
[2] *GAL* no. 5.

when at Alarcos in 1195 the Almohades inflicted a decisive defeat upon the Castilians. Clement III, Celestine III and finally Innocent III exerted themselves to the utmost to organize a crusade in Spain. Alfonso IX, by sticking obstinately to his Almohade alliance, seemed to be a traitor to Christendom. He was already in trouble over his marriages: two successive marriages, essential to the conduct of his diplomacy, were wiith brides to whom he was related within the prohibited degrees. When the crusade was finally launched in 1212 the king of León stood aside. When it was spectacularly successful at Las Navas de Tolosa he reaped no territorial harvest from the victory. He preserved his kingdom's integrity; he even enlarged its area slightly by the conquest of Cáceres in 1227. He was a more prudent husbandman of the royal resources than his father had been. But he never aimed high, and his achievements were correspondingly modest.

It is with the bishops who presided over the spiritual life of the kingdom of León that this book is concerned. There were twelve dioceses.[1] Fiva lay in Galicia—Santiago de Compostela, Mondoñedo, Lugo, Orense and Tuy. Oviedo was in the Asturias, tucked between the Cantabrian mountains and the sea, and to the south of it, on the *meseta*, were situated León and nearby Astorga. Zamora was further south again, on the Duero, and beyond the Duero, in Extremadura, were Salamanca, Ciudad Rodrigo and Coria. This pattern of ecclesiastical organization was very old. Few scholars would now believe that the origins of Christianity in western Spain are to be sought in the apostolic age. But there was certainly a patristic church there, and the lines of its organization were drawn upon the Roman administrative framework, inherited in the course of time by Suevi and Visigoths and then by the Mozarabs, the Christians who preserved their faith under Islamic rule. Of the twelve dioceses of the twelfth century, eight had existed in the Visigothic period—Iria (the transfer of the seat of the bishopric to Santiago de Compostela was ratified only in 1095[2]), Lugo, Orense, Tuy, Astorga, Salamanca, Coria and possibly Ciudad Rodrigo. Mondoñedo ori-

[1] See the map on p. 22. [2] JL 5601.

The dioceses of Western Spain and Portugal in the Twelfth Century

ginated as a bishopric based upon he monastery of Bretoña (*Britonia*) for the Celtic migrants who had settled on the north coast of Spain during the sixth century. It was this ancient pattern which the authorities of the eleventh and twelfth centuries wished to revive.

'The ecclesiastical restoration which occurred in the course of the Reconquest had as its controlling notion the revival of the ecclesiastical organization of the Visigoths. For the Christian conquerors the land recovered from the Moors was as it were a palimpsest, whose earlier script—faint, erased, sometimes quite invisible—it was essential to restore.'[1]

This was easier said than done. Sometimes, revival presented no problems—the restoration of the see of Coria in 1142, for example, was effected smoothly. The trouble was that changes had occurred in the framework and were continuing to occur: what had been suitable in the conditions of the seventh century was not necessarily suitable four or five centuries later. Oviedo and León had become episcopal sees because they were centres of royal government. Zamora was a creation of the ninth-century settlement of the valley of the Duero. Ciudad Rodrigo, established as an episcopal see by Fernando II between 1161 and 1168, has been identified with the Visigothic see of *Caliabria* and its twelfth-century bishops sometimes styled themselves *Caliabriensis*, but the identification is far from certain. Four new dioceses had therefore to be fitted into an area previously parcelled out among only eight. This was one of the causes of the diocesan boundary disputes which troubled the Leonese church in the course of the twelfth century.

It was a more serious matter that the provincial organization of the Romano-Visigothic church was unsuited to twelfth-century conditions.[2] The five Galician sees of Iria-Compostela, Lugo, Mondoñedo, Orense and Tuy, together with the see of Astorga, had been in the metropolitan province of Bracara Augusta, the modern Braga. Salamanca, Coria and *Caliabria* had been in the province of Emerita, the modern Mérida. Braga had been in Christian hands from the ninth

---

[1] Rivera Recio, *La Iglesia de Toledo en el siglo XII*, p. 247 (my translation).
[2] For the background, see D. Mansilla, 'Orígenes de la organización metropolitana en la iglesia española', *Hispania Sacra* xii (1959), 255–91.

century, while Mérida was not reconquered until 1234. There were several problems here. In the first place it was difficult to fit 'new' sees like Oviedo and León into the provincial structure. Second, an entirely new province was created in 1120, when Calixtus II raised the bishopric of Santiago de Compostela to archiepiscopal status—suffragans had to be provided for this new metropolitanate. Third, the provincial geography of the Visigothic period ran counter to the political facts of the twelfth century.

The Spanish metropolitanates were re-established at much the same time; Toledo in 1086, Tarragona in 1089, Braga in 1099 or 1100.[1] When Compostela was added to them in 1120 the pople allotted to it the metropolitan rights of Mérida until such time as that city should be reconquered and its see restored. The Leonese suffragans of Mérida—Salamanca, Coria and Ciudad Rodrigo—were situated a long distance from Santiago de Compostela; a further one, Avila, was in Castile; in addition there were several ancient suffragans of Emerita which were within the frontiers of the new kingdom of Portugal and were restored during the late eleventh and twelfth centuries—Lamego, Viseu, Guarda, Ihanha, Coimbra and Lisbon. Conversely, the Galician suffragans of Braga were in the kingdom of León. It was natural for the archbishops of Compostela to want suffragans close at hand (the Galician satellites of Braga), for those of Braga to desire to incorporate in their province the Portuguese suffragans of Mérida-Compostela, and for the archbishops of Toledo to cast covetous eyes on the cluster of Extremaduran sees which owed loyalty to distant Compostela. This awkward situation gave rise to prolonged dispute between the three archbishoprics in the course of the twelfth century, and exacerbated the political uneasiness which existed between the rulers of León and their contumacious vassal, the count and later king of Portugal. Matters were made worse by the anomalous position of the 'new' sees. Whose suffragans were León and Oviedo? This thorny problem was tactfully resolved—or sidestepped—by exempting them in 1105, so that they came

---

[1] Bishop Pedro of Braga sought the metropolitan dignity uncanonically, from the antipope Clement III, in 1091, for which he was deposed in 1093. His successor Geraldo applied more prudently to Paschal II, and was successful.

under the direct authority of the pope.[1] But whose suffragan
was Zamora? In this case no such ingenious solution was proposed, with consequences that we shall have to examine later
on.

That these issues of ecclesiastical organization were debated
so urgently, so passionately, in the course of the twelfth century sprang from the fact that the Spanish churches, especially
those of the western half of the Peninsula, had undergone a
revolutionary assault from without in the latter part of the
eleventh. The attack had been initiated by popes Alexander
II and Gregory VII, their servants and their allies. The aim of
the reformers had been to bring the Spanish churches into
line with their conception of right ecclesiastical order, especially in matters of discipline and ritual. The series of
events which has chiefly caught and held the attention of
historians was the destruction of the so-called Mozarabic
liturgy. But concentration on this alone, important though it
was, has tended to obscure the fact that what took place was
a radical assault upon a whole ecclesiastical way of life: that
what was destroyed was a branch of the Christian church
which was peculiar, perhaps, in its observances; errant, sluggish
in the eyes of brisker men; certainly not conspicuously loyal
among the children of Rome; but intimately bound up with
the society it served, answering the aspirations of those over
whose spiritual life it kept watch, self-regulating according to
its own notions of what was seemly and expedient. The reformers brought with them a form of ecclesiastical organization which was Romano-Gallic—the pattern of primate,
metropolitan, territorial diocese, archdeaconry, archipresbyterate, and parish; of uniformly-organized cathedral chapter;
of provincial council and diocesan synod. They brought with
them a canon law which overrode local ecclesiastical custom:
so that a seventh was added to the six degrees of relationship
which constituted an impediment to marriage; so that the
rank of Psalmist was dropped from the Minor Orders, redu-
cing the eight orders of the Spanish church to the standard
seven. They altered penitential customs, did away with a
liturgy, and introduced a new script. They made Spanish

---

[1] But this was not the end of the story: see below, pp. 69, 71, 72–3, 75.

churchmen look towards the Roman curia, something they had not done before. In the monastic church they changed the form of tonsure, gave impetus to the process by which St. Benedict's Rule superseded the rules of earlier, local monastic founders, and introduced new monastic orders, especially the Augustinians and Cistercians. In human terms, reform brought an influx of French clergy—and the foreigners got most of the jobs worth having.

These churches, then, became in some sense new recruits to the reformers' conception of Christian order. They were given a new uniform to wear and taught a new drill. They did not always like it. Our concern here is to see how the bishops variously faced up to the challenges, opportunities and humiliations of being reformed.

Unfortunately, we can know very little about these men. The historical literature produced in western Spain and Portugal during this period and surviving to our own day is extremely meagre.[1] Two chronicles only which were composed in the kingdom of León during the first half of the century have come down to us. One of these, the work of bishop Pelayo of Oviedo, contains no material later in date than the year 1109; the other, the *Chronica Adefonsi Imperatoris* already referred to, is an account of the first two-thirds of the reign of Alfonso VII. By comparison with the work of, say, Ordericus Vitalis or William of Malmesbury these works are bald and jejune; and their authors were not concerned with ecclesiastical affairs. Not a single chronicle seems to have been composed in the second half of the century, nor indeed until well on into the thirteenth century, when the tradition of historical writing was taken up again by Lucas of Tuy, Rodrigo Ximénez de Rada of Toledo, and the authors of the *Primera Crónica General*. For the ecclesiastical historian this is especially disappointing. We have no episcopal biographies and no cathedral annals. We have only a very little hagiographical material, only a single monastic chronicle.

One exception, however, must be made. For the history of the see of Santiago de Compostela during the pontificate of Diego Gelmírez (1100–40) the historian is fortunate indeed

[1] It is briefly surveyed by B. Sánchez Alonso, *Historia de la historiografía española* (Madrid, 1941), vol. I.

in the survival of the so-called *Historia Compostellana*.[1] This work was undertaken on the orders of Diego Gelmírez. The canons of Compostela who were its authors several times described it as a *registrum*, a collection of documents. But it was also an account of the achievements, the *gesta* of Diego. Because it was put together at his instance, by his devoted followers and presumably under his supervision, it has also a persuasive purpose; it is Diego's account of himself as he wanted others to see him. No other such work survives. The *Historia* is very long and it is crammed with information. We can know more (in a crude sense) about the public life of Diego Gelmírez than about that of any other of his contemporary bishops in any part of Christendom. It is an oasis in the historiographical desert of twelfth-century León, and we shall have to have recourse to it time after time in the pages which follow. But this procedure is not without its dangers. The authors were not innocent of guile. More especially to our purposes, it is necessary to resist the temptation to generalize on the basis of the wealth of information it provides. What is true of Santiago de Compostela may not be true of León or Orense or Salamanca, still less of the Leonese church as a whole.

With the exception of Diego Gelmírez, these bishops are almost inarticulate. They do not tell us what ideals they held, nor how they tried to put them into practice. We have no collections of their letters. We have no treatises on the office of a bishop, no penitentials, no codes of ecclesiastical custom. We have no secular law-codes which might have told us something of the way in which kings and their advisers saw the place of the church in society at large. The *acta* of a very few church councils survive, but (as we shall see) they are generally uninformative about episcopal attitudes.

What we can perceive about episcopal thoughts and aspirations must be apprehended by the flickering light cast by the evidence of official documents. It is a hazardous busi-

[1] Ed. E. Flórez, *España Sagrada* (*ES*) vol. xx (Madrid, 1765; reptd. 1965). The *Historia* will hereafter be referred to as *HC*. The best discussion of authorship is contained in A. G. Biggs, *Diego Gelmírez, First Archbishop of Compostela* (Washington, 1949), pp. xiii–xxvi: see also B. F. Reilly, 'The *Historia Composelana*: the genesis and composition of a twelfth-century Spanish *gesta*', *Speculum* xliv (1969), 78–85.

ness. Yet if narrative and what might be called technical sources are in short supply, documents are abundant. For the century between 1126 and 1230 a large proportion of the royal charters of the kings of León is available in print (either the full texts or summaries in *regesta* form). Other documents have fared less well. Many monastic cartularies have never been printed; among those that have, the standards of editorial scholarship often leave much to be desired. Some 250 episcopal *acta* have survived; they have never been systematically studied. About 100 unprinted papal bulls have come to light.[1] Hundred upon hundred original private charters await publication and study. The pages that follow depend heavily upon the evidence of these classes of documents. That it has been possible to use them extensively is owing to one important peculiarity of Spanish documents of this period, namely the fact that they are dated. It is rare to find charters which bear no indication of date at all, and most of them—perhaps, in rough terms, nine-tenths—are dated by day, month and Spanish Era. Were it not for this diplomatic convention, the present study could not have been attempted. On the whole the documents present few pitfalls beyond the usual ones attaching to this kind of evidence. Two considerations, however, both palaeographical, should be mentioned here. The first is the 'x with tittle' or as Spanish palaeographers term it the 'x *aspado*' or 'x *con rasguillo*'. Spanish scribes of the twelfth century inherited a custom—traceable in Spanish manuscripts from as early as *c*.800—of abbreviating the numerals XL or XXXX into the form χ^e. This usage seems to have gone out of use in the thirteenth century and it puzzled the compilers of cartularies in the later middle ages, who often rendered χ^e simply as X. It has sometimes misled modern historians as well. The second concerns the disappearance of Visigothic script. This ancient script was on the way out in the twelfth century, though in some areas—notably Galicia and the Asturias, the strongholds of conservatism—it was an unconscionable time a-dying. Visigothic script can be devilishly trying to read. One especially fertile source of error has been the open-ended Visigothic *a*, which looks to our

[1] Dr. Odilo Engels, of Munich, is preparing a collection of *Papsturkunden* in continuation of the work of Paul Kehr. Publication is expected shortly.

eyes uncommonly like a *u*: it is easy to read *Iun.* for *Ian.*, for
example, in dating-clauses. A good many mistakes of chronology can be traced to these sources.

Although the documentary evidence is abundant it yet remains true that there are far fewer sources available to the
ecclesiastical historian of Spain during this period than to his
counterpart in England, France or Germany. Charters are intractable and in many ways dreary materials. Those who use
them depend necessarily upon dating-clauses and witness-
lists, upon diplomatic and palaeographical analysis, upon the
occasional scrap of information concealed in common form.
Reliance upon them is not conducive to easy or pleasant
reading. What is more, they are an uncertain foundation upon
which to base the sort of enquiry we should like to make.
Historians of a dark age—such as, in terms of evidence, this is
—have to deal in the coin of speculation. Our evidence is
tantalizingly ambiguous, inconclusive, when most we wish it
plain and clear. Some will find this study too prone to guess-
work; others will be maddened by the repeated expressions
of doubt with which it is littered. But the very outlines of
our territory are uncharted. Spain was largely untouched by
the German revolution in historical scholarship of the last
century. Ecclesiastical history has been curiously little cultivated in modern Spain. Many Spanish scholars of the last two
centuries have been (one regrets to say) slipshod and credulous. The medieval copyists of cartularies in the kingdom of
León can be shown, time and again, to have been wantonly
ignorant and careless. Many ecclesiastical archives are un-
sorted; to some it is hard to gain entry; in many it is possible
to work for only short periods of the day. The groundwork
of the subject does not exist: even for Santiago de Compostela,
the most important see in the kingdom, possessed of rich
archives, exceptionally fortunate in its local historian Antonio
López Ferreiro, even for Compostela the very succession of
the archbishops during the twelfth century, their names and
their dates, is still not yet certain. We do not even know the
exact date of the death of the great Diego Gelmírez!

Given the present state of scholarship, our course is plain.
The scene must first be surveyed. This laborious task is
attempted in chapter 2, where information relating to the

different bishoprics and those who held them during the century is brought together, and some general remarks are hazarded. It is a clumsy but a necessary introduction to these Leonese churchmen. The bishops speak for themselves only through their *acta*. These documents are studied in chapter 3—the episcopal households and 'chanceries' which produced them, their external appearance and their diplomatic form. The contents of these and other documents are used in chapter 4 to shed light on the activities of bishops within their dioceses. In chapter 5 the relations between bishops and the papacy are subjected to analysis. The chronological scope of the enquiry is bounded by the approximate dates 1100 and 1215. Several of the bishoprics, as it happened, changed hands in about the year 1100, notably Compostela with the advent of Diego Gelmírez, and a new generation of bishops after the years of Gregorian upheaval emerged in the last decade of the reign of Alfonso VI. The year 1215 was marked by the Fourth Lateran Council, which was a landmark in the life of the western church.[1] But these terminal dates are approximate only, and they will sometimes be treated cavalierly.

[1] Dr. P. A. Linehan's study of *The Spanish Church and the Papacy in the Thirteenth Century* (Cambridge, 1971) opens with the years immediately after Lateran IV, so it is the more appropriate that I should bring my essay to a close at that point.

2

THE BISHOPRICS AND THEIR BISHOPS

The lists giving the succession of bishops in each see, which are prefixed to every section of this chapter, will be found to differ from those in previously published works of reference such as P.B. Gams's *Series Episcoporum Ecclesiae Catolicae*. To have cited the evidence upon which the lists are based would have been to weigh the chapter down with a heavy freight of chronological minutiae. The curious will find it set out in the thesis upon which this book is based, a copy of which is deposited in the Bodleian Library. The bishoprics are in roughly the natural order working from south to north. Given the nature of the evidence, this also means working from the hardly knowable to the quite well-known.

CORIA

Navarro	1142	1151
Suero	1155	1168
Pedro	1169	1174 × 1177
Arnaldo I	1181	1197–8
Arnaldo II	1198–9	1211–12
Giraldo	1212	1227

Coria was probably the poorest see in the kingdom of León, and is certainly that about which we know least. The town of Coria was re-conquered by Alfonso VI, lost to the Almoravides after his death, and then again reconquered by Alfonso VII in June 1142. Thenceforward it remained in Christian hands. Alfonso VI, it would seem, had made no attempt to restore at Coria the bishopric which had existed there under the Visigoths; but among Alfonso VII's first actions after the reconquest of 1142 was the reintroduction of a Christian establishment and the appointment of a bishop.[1]

---

[1] *CAI* paras. 159–61. The bishop was referred to as 'novo ordinato' in a royal charter of 30 August 1142: *ES* XIV, pp. 60–1.

All our evidence about the earlier career of the first bishop of Coria, Navarro, comes from a Segovia document of 1148.[1] We learn from this that he had the title of *magister*; that he had been a canon of Segovia; and that, *arctiorem vitam ducere volens*, he had founded a religious house at Párraces— probably for Augustinian canons—to which he had himself retired. Navarro's name suggests that he was a native not of León-Castile but of Navarre, as were, it seems, a good many of the *repobladores* of the dioceses of Segovia and its neighbouring Avila. His experience at Segovia, a church which was busily facing up to the problems of re-establishing ecclesiastical life in a newly-won frontier area, must have commended him to the king as a suitable candidate for the new see of Coria.[2] Unfortunately we know virtually nothing of his episcopate. He was an infrequent witness of royal charters[3], so perhaps he spent most of his time in his diocese. His translation to the more important see of Salamanca in 1151 presumably indicates that the king thought well of him. At one moment only is the veil lifted slightly. Navarro was one of the few bishops of León-Castile to attend the council of Rheims in 1148. After it was over he stayed on at the papal curia for reasons which Eugenius III explained to Alfonso VII:

. . .notum fieri volumus quod Cauriensem episcopum nobiscum duximus retinendum, tum quia in ecclesia que sibi commissa est gravi inopia sicut accepimus premebatur et officium suum ibi exercere utiliter non poterat, tum quia confidimus quod munificentia tua suis debeat necessitatibus honestius providere.[4]

But we do not know whether or not the king responded to the hint.

We have no record of any bishop of Coria between 1151 and 1155; and since no bishop attended the councils of Salamanca (1154) or Valladolid (1155) we may be tolerably certain that the diocese was kept vacant. It is indeed possible that the next appointment was made at the prompting of the

---

[1] D. de Colmenares, *Historia de Segovia* (Segovia, 1637), pp. 134-5.
[2] On Segovia at this period, see M. de la Soterraña Martín Postigo, *Alfonso el Batallador y Segovia* (Segovia, 1967).
[3] He witnesses only five among those known to me between 1142 and 1151.
[4] *MHV* I no. 78 (= JL 9255).

legate cardinal Hyacinth, who visited Spain in 1154-5. The new bishop, Suero, was a religious like his predecessor, having been abbot of Nogales in the diocese of Astorga.[1] Little record of his episcopate has survived. The diocese of Coria seems to have remained poor, exposed and struggling. It may have been difficult to attract settlers to the region, for its situation rendered it vulnerable to attack from south, east and west, while the Sierra de Gata and the broken country known as Las Hurdes made communication with the friendly north difficult. Fernando II in 1183 described the diocese as *deserta adhuc;*[2] clearly *repoblación* was slow and ineffectual. But it was also very necessary, for defence rested upon re-settlement, and the Coria area was of great military importance. The town itself lay between the important Roman roads from Mérida to Astorga and from Salamanca to Coimbra. It was at the southernmost tip of the kingdom of León, marching with the potential enemies Portugal, the Moslem principalities and, after 1157, Castile. It was thrust, in the expressive phrase of the royal charter of 1183, *in faucibus Sarracenorum.*

Bishop Suero may, in his straitened circumstances, have found it impossible to carry out the duties expected of him. The lordship of the town of Coria had been divided equally between the king, the bishop, and the archbishop of Compostela (in whose province the diocese lay) in 1142. In 1163 Fernando II gave exclusive lordship to the church of Compostela, and in 1168 transferred this to the Knights Templar.[3] It is not easy to understand exactly what was being done, but it would seem likely that considerations of military defence were uppermost in the king's mind. At the same time, some steps were taken to increase the modest endowments of the see. Bishop Suero obtained a solemn privilege from Pope Alexander III in 1168 confirming the possessions of his church, and this reveals that Alcántara and Cáceres, conquered by Fernando II in 1166, had been added to them.[4]

---

[1] His career has been studied by A. Andrés, 'Suero, obispo de Coria, (1156–1168)', *Hispania Sacra* xiii (1960), 397–400.
[2] *LFH* IV, ap. lxii, p. 171.
[3] *GRF* pp. 373, 401.
[4] E. Escobar Prieto, 'Antigüedad y límites del obispado de Coria', *BRAH* lxi (1912), at 331–3.

Suero's successor Pedro is no more than a name, and after his death, the date of which cannot be exactly determined, there was another episcopal vacancy, this time of about four years. Arnaldo I, the next bishop, has left some traces of his activity. He introduced the Augustinian Rule for his cathedral chapter before 1185.[1] He acquired two papal privileges, in 1185 and 1186, to buttress the endowments and privileges of his see.[2] One royal charter, from early in his episcopate, shows him as a vigorous defender of his episcopal rights, and hints at the kinds of problem which a bishop had to face in the turbulent society of the frontier.[3]

External enemies remained threatening. Cáceres and Alcántara, lost for a short time to the Portuguese in 1168-9, were taken by the Almohades in 1174. Fernando II failed to recover Cáceres in 1184. The truce with the Almohades in 1191 ensured peace from one quarter. But uneasy hostilities between Portugal and León smouldered on, while in Castile the creation of the diocese of Plasencia in 1189-90 was a warning of the direction in which the ambitions of Alfonso VIII were moving.[4] Neither is there any evidence that the poverty of the diocese of Coria was effectually remedied. Arnaldo I's two successors are no more than names in the witness-lists to royal charters. All we are entitled to say about them is that they hung on. A change came in the thirteenth century. Alcántara fell to the Christian forces in 1212, Cáceres in 1227, and the great prize of Mérida in 1234. The safety of Coria was at last ensured. But for the first seventy years of its existence, after 1142, the history of the diocese is barely more than an uncertain record of a struggle for survival.

CIUDAD RODRIGO

Domingo	1161 × 1168	1172-3
Pedro de Ponte	1174	1190
Martín	1190	1211
Lombardo	1214	1227

[1] This is referred to in a papal privilege of Lucius III dated 19 March 1185: Escobar Prieto, ibid., p. 335.
[2] Printed and discussed by Escobar Prieto, ibid., pp. 335-41.
[3] GRF p. 483.
[4] The creation of the diocese of Plasencia may be followed in GRC nos. 454, 464, 494, 562 and AHN 18/4.

The sources for the twelfth-century history of Ciudad Rodrigo are as meagre as those relating to Coria, but we have the advantage that they have already been carefully studied by Fidel Fita.[1] Reconquered early in the century, we do not know exactly when, the town with its *término* was acquired by purchase by the citizens of Salamanca in about 1135.[2] It is to be presumed that they controlled it until 1161, when Fernando II, eager to strengthen the south-western frontier of his kingdom, took it into his own hands. He introduced settlers there, built a castle, created a bishopric and founded at least two religious houses.

This royal action provoked hostility both from the people of Salamanca who resented the loss of a lordship which they had enjoyed for twenty-five years, and from the king of Portugal who felt himself threatened by the foundation of a fortress so close to his eastern frontier. With the ensuing troubles—the revolt of Salamanca in 1162, the Portuguese invasion of 1163, and in addition an Almohade attack on 'Alsibdat' in 1174—we are not here concerned. But there were also repercussions of an ecclesiastical nature—a quarrel between the churches of Ciudad Rodrigo and Salamanca over their common frontier, and a brush with Pope Alexander III.

The boundary dispute will be touched on later. Here it is enough to say that it was settled, though probably not finally settled, in 1174. The eastern boundary of the diocese was fixed between the little rivers Huebra and Yeltes. The northern frontier was presumably formed by the Huebra and the Duero, the western by the political frontier between León and Portugal, and the southern by the desolate country between Ciudad Rodrigo and Coria.

It was the constitution of the new bishopric which roused the anger of the pope. Fernando II may well have appeared to be creating an entirely new see in 1161. He claimed, however, only to be restoring the Visigothic see of *Caliabria*. Since

[1] F. Fita 'La Diócesis y Fuero Eclesiástico de Ciudad Rodrigo', *BRAH* lxi (1912), 437–48 and 'El Papa Alejandro III y la Diócesis de Ciudad Rodrigo' *BRAH* lxii (1913), 142–57.
[2] BN, MS. 712, fol. 227. The document has recently been edited by H. Grassotti 'Sobre una concesión de Alfonso VII a la iglesia salmantina' *CHE* xlix–l (1969), at 347–8.

no-one knew where Caliabria had been, the claim could not be tested. But the king had certainly acted without any reference to the pope, not only in setting up the diocese, but also in issuing what has been called the *fuero eclesiástico* of Ciudad Rodrigo on 13 February 1161.[1] In this document the king made the remarkable provision that the archbishop of Santiago de Compostela, in whose province the new diocese lay, was to nominate its bishop without any reference to its chapter. The pope's apprehension, known only, unfortunately, from a brief reference in a bull of 1175, was understandable. Since the provision was omitted from a further royal charter of 20 September 1168, it may be suggested that the king had withdrawn it in obedience to papal protests.[2]

How the first bishop reacted to it is as obscure as everything else concerning him. Domingo, presumably appointed in or soon after 1161, is not mentioned by name until 1168, and died in 1172 or 1173 having left no trace at all of any activity in our records. His successor is a little less obscure. Pedro de Ponte was perhaps a native of Galicia,[3] and an important royal servant: a king's clerk from at least 1163, he had been rewarded with prebends at the rich sees of Oviedo and Compostela, and in the years 1170 to 1172 he was the royal chancellor.[4] Among his first actions as bishop was a tactful visit to the papal curia in 1175, from which he returned with a privilege confirming the establishment of the new diocese and condoning, with a mild rebuke, Fernando's initiative.[5] Pedro visited the curia again, in 1179, when he attended the Third Lateran council.[6] Nothing more is known of him, and virtually nothing at all of his two successors, Martín and Lombardo. Their names appear in the witness-lists of royal charters, and Martín once acted as a papal

---

[1] *LFH* IV, ap. xxx, pp. 78–80.
[2] *GRF* p. 402.
[3] This is suggested by a grant he made to the distant Galician monastery of Sobrado in 1189: AHN cód. 976B, fol. 29ʳ.
[4] *GRF* pp. 169–70, 376, 384, 417–18, etc.
[5] JL 12486.
[6] Mansi, *Concilia,* XXII, col. 216.

judge-delegate;[1] but of their actions as bishops nothing can be said and speculation is fruitless.

SALAMANCA

Jerónimo	1102	1120
Giraldo	1120	1123
Nuño	1123	1130
Alfonso Pérez	1130	1131
[Schism	1131	1135]
Berengar	1135	1150
Navarro	1151	1158-9
Ordoño	1159	1164-5
Pedro Suárez de Deza	1166	1173
Vidal	1174	1194-5
Gonzalo	1195	1226

Unlike Ciudad Rodrigo, Salamanca had been the seat of a bishop during the Visogothic period: The see was revived in the ninth century and the succession of its bishops may be traced, if hazardously, until towards the end of the tenth. There they cease, presumably in the wake of Almanzor's campaigns, and we do not know what, if any ecclesiastical establishment existed in the town when it passed again into Christian hands during the reign of Alfonso VI. The resettlement of the vast area between the Duero and the Sierra de Guadarrama was entrusted by Alfonso to his son-in-law Raymond of Burgundy, who was also given, it would seem, wide responsibilities for the restoration of ecclesiastical life.[2] Raymond found a man who must have seemed the ideal pastor for his frontier honour—Jerónimo of Périgord, companion of the Cid, and bishop of Valencia from 1098 until its abandonment by the Cid's widow in May 1102.

Jerónimo, a native of Périgord, where he had been a monk, perhaps at Moissac, had been brought to Spain by Bernardo, archbishop of Toledo, in 1096 or 1097, together with several

[1] León, Archivo de San Isidoro, no. 358. Lombardo may perhaps have been previously archdeacon of Medina and Alba in the diocese of Salamanca: AC Salamanca no. 117. This is the only other occurrence of the name in the documents I have inspected.
[2] Some of his legislation is embedded in the later *fuero* of Salamanca: *Fueros Leoneses*, ed. F. de Onis (Madrid, 1920), Fuero de Salamanca, § 295.

other promising young men, of whom at least six later became archbishops or bishops. After a short spell as a canon of Toledo, he entered the service of the Cid, from whom he received the see of Valencia, being consecrated in Rome by Urban II in 1098. After the withdrawal from Valencia Jerónimo moved directly to the circle of Raymond of Burgundy and his wife Urraca; on 26 June 1102 they were granting endowments to Jerónimo as bishop of Salamanca.[1] In addition, he held the sees of Avila and Zamora in plurality with Salamanca. *Jheronimus episcopus Abelensis* features in an Avila document of 1103.[2] At Zamora he displaced one of Raymond's clerks, Roscelin,[3] and may be traced as bishop of Zamora in three documents, of 1104, 1107, and 1111.[4]

His episcopate at Salamanca has left no trace in our records beyond the occasional appearance of his name in the witness-lists of royal charters.[5] We do however know that he was instructed by Calixtus II to make a profession of obedience to Diego Gelmírez when his see of Compostela was raised to metropolitan status in 1120 and given the rights of Mérida, in whose province the Visigothic bishopric of Salamanca had lain. Eighty years later it was believed that Jerónimo had actually made such a profession.[6] This matter of the metropolitan allegiance of Salamanca was to trouble the diocese during the fifteen years after Jerónimo's death. His successor, Giraldo, may have been another Frenchman (judging only by his name) and seems to have had connections with the church of Compostela. He was expelled from his diocese during the Aragonese invasion in the winter of 1121–2 and seems never to have returned there. The state of confusion into which the diocese had been thrown gave

---

[1] AC Salamanca no. 3. See also R. Menéndez Pidal, *La España del Cid* (7th ed., Madrid, 1969), pp. 547–52.

[2] *Cartulario de San Millán de la Cogolla,* ed. L. Serrano (Madrid, 1930), no. 291.

[3] AC Zamora, Libro Negro, fol. 22^r.

[4] AHD León, Fondo de Sta. María de Otero de las Dueñas, no. 216; Zamora, Archivo de la Delegación de la Hacienda, Pergaminos de Moreruela, unnumbered; AHN 893/7.

[5] One of these was a charter of Teresa of Portugal of 1 August 1112: *DMP* no. 35. This is particularly interesting in view of the fact that Salamanca, Avila and Zamora may have formed part of the county of Portugal for a short period at about this time: cf. *DMP* no. 31.

[6] JL 6827; *MHV* I, no. 199.

archbishop Bernardo of Toledo a chance to challenge the claims of Compostela by consecrating Nuño, the successor of Giraldo. This provoked a storm of protest from Diego Gelmírez, at whose prompting Calixtus II ordered Nuño to make a profession of obedience to Compostela.[1] But the arrangement was unsatisfactory; in addition to which, Nuño does not seem to have been without his shortcomings as a diocesan:[2] and his deposition by a papal legate at the council of Carrion in 1130 very probably took place at the instance of Diego Gelmírez.[3] His successor was clearly Diego's choice. Alfonso Pérez had been a canon of Compostela and is probably to be identified with the *A.Perez* who had been employed by Diego on at least two previous occasions as an emissary to the papal curia.[4] But his tenure of the see was short, for he died at Cluny in November 1131 while returning to Spain after attending the council of Rheims.[5] The ensuing three and a half years were a time of schism in the diocese and of the breakdown of regular episcopal succession. There were at least three candidates: the deposed Nuño, who returned from exile in Portugal, hung on at Salamanca for about three years, was summoned to the papal curia and degraded, enlisted the support of St. Bernard and is last heard of at Cluny; Pedro, the nominee of a prominent loyal layman, Count Pedro López; and a third whose name we do not know, who was put forward by the citizens of Salamanca, and who was described by the archbishop of Toledo as *quidam homo absolute simplex*. The confusion was ended, it would appear, through the intervention of Alfonso VII, who nominated a new bishop, Berengar.

Berengar was a king's man. It has recently been claimed that he was a French relative of Archbishop Raimundo of Toledo.[6] This is possible, though there is no evidence for it. It is more likely, in view of his eastern Spanish name, that he

---

[1] *HC* pp. 404–5, 407–10.
[2] JL 7208.
[3] *HC* pp. 498–9.
[4] *HC* pp. 281, 290, 400–1.
[5] His attendance at Rheims is mentioned in his epitaph, quoted by B. Dorado, *Historia de Salamanca* (Salamanca, 1776), p. 114.
[6] H. Grassotti 'Dos problemas de historia castellano-leonesa (siglo XII)' *CHE* xlix–l (1969), at 149, n. 56.

was a Catalan who had come to the Leonese-Castilian court in the wake of Berengaria, the daughter of the count of Barcelona, whom Alfonso VII had married in 1127 or 1128. But this too is a guess. What is certain is that Berengar acquired the archdeaconry of Toledo and that he was in charge of the royal chancery by June 1134, though we do not find him with the title of chancellor until February 1135.[1] In the summer of 1135 he was promoted to the bishopric of Salamanca. As bishop, he restored stability to the troubled diocese. During his episcopate, the building of the cathedral was begun, and at least three religious houses were founded, one of them by Berengar himself.[2] He remained closely associated with the king, who lavished upon the diocese a series of important privileges.[3] Alfonso VII, indeed destined Berengar for higher things. In 1140–2 he tried to effect Berengar's translation to the archbishopric of Compostela, an attempt that was defeated by Pope Innocent II and the canons of Compostela, despite the king's adroit—and costly—enlistment of Peter the Venerable, abbot of Cluny, on his side.[4] What has not hitherto been noticed is that a second attempt, ten years later, was successful. In 1150 Berengar was elected to the archbishopric, though he did not live long to enjoy it. After his election, he went to Rome for his pallium, and on the way back to his new see, late in 1150 or early in 1151, he fell ill at Burgos and died at Torquemada.[5]

We have already seen that Navarro was translated from Coria to fill Berengar's place at Salamanca. He and his successor Ordoño have left little trace of their activities as bishops of Salamanca. But we know that the period from c. 1140 onwards was an important one in Salamanca's history. The work of colonization was more successful than in any of the areas we have surveyed so far: the tempo of economic life in the diocese quickened and the town of Salamance itself grew

---

[1] León, Archivo de San Isidore, no. 143 (1 June 1134); Rassow, p. 423 (February 1135).
[2] AC Salamanca, no. 17; *MHV* I no. 69.
[3] AC Salamanca, nos. 8–15.
[4] See *LFH* IV pp. 221–6, and the excellent account by C. J. Bishko 'Peter the Venerable's journey to Spain' *Studia Anselmiana* xl (1956), 163–75.
[5] AD Braga, Gaveta dos Arcebispos, no. 4.

rapidly.[1] Bishop Navarro was an active participant in the work of *repoblación*, for which he earned the gratitude of Alfonso VII.[2] Significantly, too, it is during the episcopate of Ordoño that we first hear of the coming of clerks from France to study in the schools of Salamanca, schools which were to blossom into a university half a century later.[3]

The episcopate of Ordoño's successor was also short, but it was an important one. Pedro Suárez de Deza was a native of Galicia who had studied, allegedly, in Paris before returning to the diocese of Compostela with the title of *magister* before August 1162 when he was very probably a canon there. Later, certainly by 1166, he was an archdeacon and it is likely that he was in the household of archbishop Martín. He was royal chancellor in 1165, and in the following year he was promoted to the see of Salamanca to which he was consecrated at the curia by Alexander III. He held the see until 1173, when he was translated to Santiago de Compostela.[4] Pedro Suárez was an active administrator. He carried through certain capitular reforms. He engineered an agreement of confraternity between the chapters of Salamanca and the Castilian see of Avila. He sought lasting settlements in boundary disputes with neighbouring dioceses. He brought his see into a closer relationship with the papacy. He was active in fostering the military orders.[5] He contrived to remain on good terms with the kings both of León and of Castile when it was not easy to do this. And though we cannot prove it, it is reasonable to surmise that he did something to encourage the budding intellectual life of Salamanca.

[1] J. González, 'Repoblación de la Extremadura leonesa' *Hispania* iii (1943), 195-273.
[2] AC Salamanca no. 18.
[3] AC Salamanca no. 27.
[4] For Pedro Suárez's early life, see *LFH* IV, ap. xxxiii; *GRF* pp. 168, 392; J.F. Rivera Recio, *La Iglesia de Toledo en el siglo XII* (Rome-Madrid, 1966), pp. 374-5, n. 54 (the correct date of which is 1166); AC Salamanca nos. 34, 44, 47, 48. There is no good evidence that he had studied in Paris; but Innocent III addressed him in such a way as to make it certain that he had studied and taught theology at some stage of his life: *MHV* I, no. 237, at p. 264.
[5] AC Salamanca no. 77 (capitular reforms); AC Avila no. 5 (confraternity agreement); AC Salamanca nos. 59, 61, 62 (boundary dispute with Ciudad Rodrigo); *ibid.*, nos. 34-58 (relations with papacy); D.W. Lomax, *La Orden de Santiago* (Madrid, 1965), p.6; J.F. O'Callaghan, 'The foundation of the Order of Alcántara', *Catholic Historical Review* xlvii (1961-2), 471-86 (Military orders).

Of his two successors we know disappointingly little, though they occupied the see for over fifty years between them. Vidal was probably promoted from the chapter of Salamanca.[1] The profusion of royal grants made to him suggests, even when we make allowance for the reckless improvidence of Fernando II, that he may have been a royal servant, which would be a plausible background for one who was perhaps a protégé of Pedro Suárez.[2] Gonzalo can be connected more directly with the royal administration. A royal notary in the years 1188-94, he may have held a canonry at Salamanca from as early as 1181. His brother, Martín, was also a royal notary. His nephew Pedro Pérez was a notary from 1203, and royal chancellor from 1213 to 1221 and 1224 to 1230, with prebends at Compostela, Salamanca and Orense. Other members of the family seem to have been lay *tenentes* of Salamanca c.1182 and c.1219.[3] Not surprisingly, Gonzalo was a prominent supporter of Alfonso IX against the pope when the king ran into trouble over his marriages.[4]

ZAMORA

Jerónimo	1102	1120
Bernardo	1121	1149
Esteban	1150	1175
Guillermo	1175	1193
Martín	1193	1217

The history of the diocese of Zamora has much in common with that of her southern neighbour Salamanca. The natural features of the two dioceses are similar, and the societies which inhabited them in the twelfth century were of much the same kind. They were resettled at the same time, and at first under common direction. Both were economically poor and politically vulnerable for most of the first half of the century; with the extension of the political frontier of the kingdom to the south, both experienced economic growth and a more mature social life in its second half. But Zamora, unlike

[1] AC Salamanca nos. 26, 58.
[2] AC Salamanca nos. 63, 64, 65, 85, 86.
[3] *GAL* pp. 358, 481-92; AC Salamanca, nos. 80, 90.
[4] *MHV* I nos. 138 (where 'Vitalem' should read 'Gundisalvem'), 196.

Salamanca, had not been a Visigothic see; it was a creation of the *Reconquista*, founded in the ninth century. The town was sacked by Almanzor, and no bishop can be traced for a century after 1009. In view of this chequered history, it is surprising that the territorial extent of the diocese was never seriously in dispute during the twelfth century. By contrast, the metropolitan loyalties of Zamora were a matter of prolonged and bitter dispute in the course of the century between the archbishops of Toledo, Braga and Santiago de Compostela.[1]

We do not know when the decision to restore the diocese of Zamora was taken. Raymond of Burgundy entrusted the two churches which then existed in the town to a clerk of his own, Roscelin, but this man seems never to have been a bishop. They were transferred to Jerónimo of Salamanca in 1102, who acted, as we have seen, as bishop of Zamora until his death.[2] It was, however, his successor Bernardo who was known as the *primus episcopus Zamorensis de modernis*.[3] Bernardo was another of the young men brought from France by his namesake of Toledo, and before his promotion to Zamora he had been an archdeacon of Toledo.[4] He took active steps towards the restoration of ecclesiastical life in his diocese. He began the building of a new cathedral, organized the chapter and established the rudiments of a diocesan administration. He was active in resettling his diocese; all his surviving *acta* are *fueros de población*.[5] During his episcopate at least two religious houses were founded in the diocese, one of them—Valparaiso—being among the earliest Cistercian foundations in the Peninsula. Throughout his tenure of the see, so far as we can judge, Bernardo remained on the best of terms with Alfonso VII and his influential sister Doña Sancha.

---

[1] See below, ch. 5.
[2] See above p. 38.
[3] So he is described in his epitaph in the cathedral.
[4] F. Fita, 'Bernardo de Périgord, arcediano de Toledo y obispo de Zamora', *BRAH* xiv (1889), 456-61.
[5] AC Zamora, leg. 8, no. 5 (cathedral building, 1135); *ibid*., Libro Negro, fol. 20[V] (cathedral chapter, 1124); *ibid*., Libro Negro fol. 17[V] (archdeacon and two archpriests, 1133); *ibid*., Libro Negro fol. 15[V], leg. 13, no. 25, Libro Blanco, fol. 121[V] (*fueros*).

There are indications, as we shall see later on, that he in his turn made himself useful to the crown.

The bishops of the second half of the century have left fewer traces of their activities. For over forty years after Bernardo's death, the church of Zamora was in the hands of one family, whose members all had French names. Esteban was succeeded after a tenure of twenty-five years by his nephew Guillermo, who held the see for a further eighteen.[1] Guillermo had started as his uncle's chaplain in 1161 and rose to be dean of Zamora in 1170.[2] His brother Helias also did well for himself, he witnesses an episcopal act of 1167 and had acquired an archdeaconry by 1168.[3] It is unfortunate that we know no more about this family.

Martín Arias was a native of Galicia, and a protégé of Archbishop Pedro Suárez of Compostela. He had the title of *magister*, perhaps by dint of study as a canonist.[4] A recent assessment has characterized Martín's episcopate as 'twenty-three years of misrule'.[5] This is not warranted by such evidence as we have. Martín asked leave of Innocent III to resign his see, and it is true that when he was slow to do so he was asked to stand down by Honorius III in 1217. But we know nothing of the circumstances. The large corpus of *acta* which survives from his episcopate[6] shows him as an active administrator; and he was certainly much sought-after as a judge-delegate.[7] He was a considerable builder. And he obtained what was virtually a permanent solution of the problem of Zamora's metropolitan allegiance from Innocent III.[8] This

[1] The relationship is established by ANTT, Colecção Especial, Corporações Diversas, Mitra de Braga, caixa 1, no. 2.
[2] AC Zamora, Libro Negro, fol. 56ᵛ (1161), 27ᵛ-28ʳ (1170).
[3] AC Zamora, leg. 13, nos. 6, 8, 26.
[4] The study of canon law was certainly encouraged at Compostela. Martín Arias is to be distinguished from his successor Martín Rodriguez, bishop of Zamora 1217–38, bishop of León 1238–47, known to the canonists as Martinus Zamorensis, who wrote glosses on Gratian and *Compilatio I*.
[5] P.A. Linehan, *The Spanish Church and the Papacy in the Thirteenth Century* (Cambridge, 1971), p. 292 and n. 7.
[6] I know of thirty-one such documents, which is a large number by Leonese standards.
[7] *MHV* I, nos. 172, 173, 176, 177, 254, 282, 293, 326, 333, 354, 366, 425 *et passim*.
[8] See below, ch. 5.

is no mean record. There is no good reason for supposing that during his retirement in Galicia[1] he was under a cloud.

ASTORGA

Pelayo	1097?	1121
Alo	1123	1131
Roberto	1131	1138
Jimeno Eriz	1138	1141
Amadeo	1141	1143
Arnaldo I	1144	1152-3
Pedro Cristiano	1153	1156
Fernando I	1156	1172
Arnaldo II	1173	1177
Fernando II	1177	1190
Lope	1190	1205
Pedro Andrés	1205	1226

The diocese of Astorga was close to Zamora geographically, but far removed from it in spirit. We have now moved away from the uneasy frontier to the heartlands of the kingdom of León. The diocese comprised the area of the plains surrounding the city; a strip of mountainous country running from the head waters of the river Orbigo down to Sanabria; and beyond this chain of hills the fertile depression known as El Bierzo in which the town of Ponferrada is set. The see was an old one, having been restored about 840. It had a monastic complexion, for some of the monasteries in the monastic 'connection' of St. Fructuosus were revived in the tenth century, notably by Bishop Gennadius (c. 899–920). Astorga was situated at an important point in the road-system of medieval Spain: beside the least difficult of the passes from the Leonese plain into Galicia, at the point where the Roman road from Lugo swung south towards Mérida, and on the pilgrimage road to Santiago de Compostela. Not surprisingly, the see was rich, and we shall find later on that it could afford to support a very large chapter. Constitutionally, Astorga was in the province of Braga. This seems never to have been questioned during the twelfth century. Successive

[1] For which see *LFH* V pp. 117–20.

popes confirmed it, and we possess the texts of several professions of obedience from the bishops of Astorga to their metropolitan.[1]

Nearly all the archives of Astorga were destroyed in the course of the last century. An eighteenth-century index to them survives[2] and this has to be the principal source for the history of the diocese. Information filtered to us in this way is, necessarily, tantalizingly incomplete, and the history of the see cannot fail to be bald.

The diocese suffered during the civil wars between Urraca and Alfonso *el Batallador* after the death of Alfonso VI. What little we know of Bishops Pelayo and Alo shows them attempting to restore ordered ecclesiastical life after the ravages of war.[3] Pelayo may have been an archdeacon of Astorga before his promotion:[4] Alo seems to have been an important officer in the royal writing office.[5] Roberto, Alo's successor, had a French name, and is presumably to be identified with the archdeacon Roberto who subscribed episcopal *acta* of 1117 and 1129-30.[6] Two short-lived bishops succeeded him. Jimeno Eriz, previously an archdeacon, was a member of a prominent local family.[7] Amadeo is only a name.

Arnaldo I was closely associated with the royal court. It has been suggested that he was the author of the *Chronica Adefonsi Imperatoris*.[8] All we know of him for certain is that he was sent on embassies to the counts of Barcelona and Montpellier late in 1146 or early in 1147 and that he served

---

[1] *PUP* nos. 30, 47, 50, 57, 63; AD Braga, Liber Fidei, fol. 153^r (Alo, 1122), 152^v (Arnaldo, 1144), 138^v (Fernando I, 1156).
[2] BN MS. 4357.
[3] E.g., BN MS. 4357, Tumbo Negro nos. 249, 341, 575; AHN cód. 1197B fols. 253^r-255^r.
[4] *ES* XVI, ap. xx, pp. 467-70.
[5] *Recueil de chartes de l'Abbaye de Cluny*, ed. A. Bruel, vol. V (Paris, 1894) no. 3884; cf. also *Docs. Oviedo* no. 121.
[6] *ES* XVI, ap. xxiii, pp. 474-6; AHN cód. 1197B fols. 253^r-255^r.
[7] The family connections may be established from BN MS. 4357, Reales no. 147, Particulares no. 488, and Tumbo Negro nos. 383, 440; BN MS. 712, fols. 85, 88^v-89^v, 90^v-91^r; *ES* XVI, app. xx, xxiii, xxvi pp. 467-70, 474-6, 481-3; *DMP* no. 28; and 'El Tumbo del Monasterio de San Martín de Castañeda', ed. A. Rodríguez González, *Archivos Leoneses* xxxix-xl (1966), no. 14.
[8] By its editor, L. Sánchez Belda: *CAI* pp. ix-xxi. It has been conjectured that he was a Frenchman or a Catalan.
[9] *CAI* para. 203; *Poema de Almería* vv. 361-71.

in the Almería campaign of 1147.[9] Alfonso VII rewarded him well for his loyal services.[1] His successor Pedro Cristiano was a religious; he had been abbot of the Cistercian monastery of San Martín de Castañeda. He was a nobleman by birth, possibly connected with the great count Ponce de Cabrera, who stood high in the counsels of Alfonso VII and later of his son Fernando II.[2] Hardly anything is known of his two successors, Fernando I and Arnaldo II.

Fernando II was praised in the warmest terms by his king, and it would not be unreasonable to guess that he was a royal nominee.[3] His was not a happy episcopate. His desire to reward his relations led to an unseemly dispute with his chapter, in the course of which the bishop was detected in a rash attempt to forge papal letters.[4] Early in the reign of the new king, Alfonso IX, he fell out with the royal court and was expelled from his diocese, after which we lose sight of him.[5] As usual, we know nothing of the circumstances. The new bishop, Lope, probably identical with the archdeacon of that name who appears in documents of 1172 and 1174[6], and presumably—in view of his predecessor's fate—acceptable to the king,[7] found himself saddled with the dispute with the cathedral chapter. Towards the end of his episcopate one of his canons accused him before the pope of perjury, simony and murder (by poisoning); and though the bishop and his supporters rallied, it is clear that the church of Astorga was in a poor way by the time that Lope died in 1205.[8]

Pedro Andrés, a member of the combative chapter[9] and son of a prominent local nobleman, succeeded him. All that

[1] E.g., AHN cód 1197B, fols. 203^V-205^V.
[2] The relationship is a tradition reported by Flórez, ES XVI, p. 214. It is not implausible, for Pedro clearly came of an extremely wealthy family (cf. P. Rodríguez López, Episcopologio Asturicense II (Astorga, 1907), p. 209), and Count Ponce and his family had close connections with the monastery of Castañeda.
[3] GRF p. 481.
[4] A. Quintana Prieto. 'Registro de Documentos Pontificios de la diócesis de Astorga (1139-1413)', Anthologica Annua xl (1963), nos. 19, 21, 22.
[5] Tumbo Viejo de San Pedro de Montes, ed. A. Quintana Prieto (León, 1971), nos. 239, 240; AC León no. 1282; MHV I, no. 278.
[6] AHD Astorga, Cartulario de Carracedo, fol. 109^r; AHN 3536/1.
[7] He supported the king against the papal prohibition of both his marriages.
[8] MHV I nos. 278, 284, 293.
[9] He was dean of Astorga by 1200: AHD Astorga, Cámara Episcopal, I/32.

we know of him is connected with military and political activities, and though he attended the Lateran Council of 1215
we may hazard the guess that he was not the sort of bishop
to whom Innocent III would have committed, from choice,
the reanimation of the life of the church.[1] The legate John of
Abbeville, a churchman whose standards were admittedly
exacting, remarked sourly in 1228 that the diocese was one
in qua nulla erat ordinatio.[2] The records of the late twelfth
and early thirteenth centuries are very meagre; yet it does
look as though he was not exaggerating.

ORENSE

Diego	1097 × 1100	1132
Martín	1133	1156-7
Pedro Seguin	1157	1169
Adán	1169	1173-4
Alfonso	1174	1213
Fernando Méndez	1213	1218

The diocese of Orense, roughly co-extensive with the
modern province of the same name, lay close to the northern
frontier of what in the first half of the twelfth century was
fast becoming the independent kingdom of Portugal. Within
the diocese, the principal manifestation of the strained relations between León and Portugal lay in the complex quarrel
between the bishops of Orense and their metropolitan, the
archbishops of Braga, over diocesan boundaries.[3] It would
appear that the bishops of Orense never wavered in their political allegiance to the kings of León. This was partly because
they were for the most part chosen from among the loyal
servants of the crown; partly because they needed royal protection—to relieve the poverty of their see, and to guard them
against their great ecclesiastical rival in the diocese, the abbey
of Celanova. Founded in 936 by St. Rosendo, it had acquired
a pre-eminence among Galician monasteries owing to its association with the movement of monastic 'reform' which he led
and the great wealth with which the piety of noble families

[1] *GAL* nos. 204, 210, 319; *GRC* nos. 782, 845, 1005-6; *MHV* I, nos. 458, 566.
[2] *ES* XVI, p. 503.
[3] This dispute is discussed below, ch. 4.

had endowed it. This position was enhanced in the century from *c*.970 to *c*.1070, when the bishopric of Orense was abandoned, while the monastery continued to flourish. A prolonged dispute over Celanova's claim to exemption took place in the twelfth century.

The see of Orense was restored in 1071. Diego was its third bishop. Previously a canon of Compostela, he remained an associate of Diego Gelmírez after his promotion, being employed by him, for example, as an envoy to the papal curia in 1118-19.[1] He was a staunch supporter of Queen Urraca in the civil war of her reign.[2] His successor Martín had been one of the royal *capellani*,[3] and that he remained closely connected with the king is shown by the very large number of royal charters which he subscribed during his episcopate. He was, further, employed by Alfonso VII on a mission to the papal curia late in 1135 or early in 1136.[4]

The same close connection with the kings of León seems to have been maintained during the episcopates of Martín's two successors, Pedro Seguin and Adán. Alfonso VII 'rejoiced' in Pedro's appointment, and Fernando II addressed him in terms which suggest that he may have been that king's confessor.[5] Pedro seems previously to have been connected in some way with the church of Compostela.[6] A not implausible tradition has it that he was a Frenchman, from Poitou.[7] We are fortunate in possessing the letter which the chapter of Orense wrote to the archbishop of Braga to announce its election of Adán as Pedro's successor in 1169.[8] We learn that he had been prior of the cathedral, that he was noted for his

---

[1] *HC* pp. 56-7, 265.

[2] *HC* pp. 141, 163, 172-4, 182-4.

[3] AC Orense, Privilegios I/21, 22, 26; D. de Colmenares, *Historia de Segovia* (Segovia, 1937), p. 117.

[4] T. Minguella y Arnedo, *Historia de la Diócesis de Sigüenza y de sus Obispos* (Madrid, 1910), I, 359-60.

[5] *ES* XVII, pp. 253-8.

[6] Assuming his identity with the 'magister P. Seguini' of AHN 556/3; cf. also AHN 512/14.

[7] *ES* XVII, pp. 89-90, for the tradition. There was a Poitevin colony in El Bierzo in the second half of the century, some of whose members shared Bishop Pedro's surname or patronymic: they may be traced in, e.g., AHN cód. 976B, fols. 113^r-119^v.

[8] AD Braga, Liber Fidei, no. 504, fol. 137.

honestas morum, and that he even *non deest in peritia litter-arum.* From other sources we learn that he he been the royal chancellor in 1166-7.[1] Flórez drew attention to a document which referred to an interdict upon the diocese of Orense in April 1173 and surmised that its bishop had defended the marriage of Fernando II to Urraca of Portugal which had recently been dissolved by the legate Cardinal Hyacinth.[2] The guess is reasonable; it is what we should expect from an ex-chancellor whose see lay on the frontier of León and Portugal.

Our last two bishops of Orense are barely more than names, though the first of them occupied the see for nearly forty years. Alfonso may have been dean of Orense before his promotion.[3] Most of what we know of him concerns his somewhat stormy relations with the monasteries of his diocese.[4] His successor Fernando Méndez held the see for only a short time, most of it outside our period. He too was probably dean of Orense before succeeding to the bishopric.[5]

TUY

Alfonso	1097	1131
Pelayo Menéndez	1131	1155-6
Isidoro	1156	1166-7
Juan	1168	1172
Beltrán	1173	1187
Pedro	1188	1205
Suero	1206	1215

Orense was not a rich bishopric; Tuy was certainly poorer. Situated on the north bank of the Miño some ten miles from the Atlantic, it was remote as well, not easily reached from the hinterland of the Spanish peninsula. Its good communications by sea had been its undoing at an earlier date: Viking and Saracen raids had extinguished the bishopric for much of the tenth and eleventh centuries. Restored in 1070, the see

---

[1] *GRF* pp. 168-9.
[2] *ES* XVII, p. 94; the document is now AC Orense, Escrituras XIV/44.
[3] AC Orense, Escrituras XIV/44; AHN 1481/16.
[4] For his relationship with Celanova, see *MHV* I nos. 132, 203, 234, 264, 475. There were quarrels with Osera and Montederramo as well.
[5] AC Orense, Escrituras XIV/72.

had not had time to recover from this unhappy history before the political disputes which led to the secession of Portugal from León broke out early in the twelfth century, and these ran imperceptibly into a time of sporadic warfare and uneasy truces which lasted into the thirteenth. The town of Tuy changed hands several times. Parts of the diocese lay to the south of the Miño, in what became Portugal. Tuy lay in the metropolitan province of Braga. The political allegiance of the bishops, judged on the evidence of their subscriptions to royal charters, wavered uncertainly between the house of León and that of Portugal. No bishopric could have prospered under such handicaps.

Alfonso, third bishop of Tuy after the restoration of the see, has left few traces for the historian. He may have been one of the archdeacons of that name who witnessed a royal charter of 1095.[1] We can trace, with the aid of charter-subscriptions, the way in which he shifted his political loyalties to adapt to changing circumstances during his long episcopate. But this is all that may be said about him. We can form a slightly clearer picture of Pelayo Menéndez who succeeded him in 1131. He was a member of the local nobility, though not of its highest ranks. He was a patron of monasteries: with his brother Suero he tried to restore the monastery of Barrantes in 1151;[2] he was a benefactor of the monastery of Oya, and may indeed have been instrumental in founding this house.[3] At Tuy itself he introduced the Augustinian Rule for his cathedral chapter in 1138.[4]

The first half of Pelayo's episcopate was a time of political disturbance, but its second half, after the treaty between León and Portugal in 1143, was more tranquil. This was not to last. After the death of Alfonso VII in 1157 the tenuous peace broke down, and further warfare occurred in the years 1159-65. Bishop Isidoro, who held the see during these years,

---

[1] P. Galindo Romeo, *Tuy en la Baja Edad Media* (2nd ed., Madrid, 1950), doc. IA.
[2] AD Braga, Liber Fidei, no. 741, fol. 198r; AC Tuy 1/3, 1/4 and 3/7 (the last of which is printed in *ES* XXII, ap. xii, pp. 270-3).
[3] *ES* XXII, pp. 22-4, 267-70; the early history of the house is obscured by a number of forged charters.
[4] AC Tuy 14/10, printed in *ES* XXII, ap. iv, pp. 260-1.

is an obscure figure. Allegedly Portuguese by birth,[1] he seems to have remained loyal to the king of León until the summer of 1163, after which we next find him acting in a plea with the king of Portugal in April 1165.[2] He may have seen which way the wind was blowing, for it was very probably in 1165 that Tuy and the area round it, known as Toroño, was ceded by Fernando II of León to Afonso Henriques of Portugal.

The arrangement did not last for long. In 1169, by a lucky chance, the king of Portugal fell into Leonese hands at Badajoz, and Fernando II was able to exact Tuy and Toroño from him as the price of his release. Having recovered the lost province, Fernando revenged himself upon it for what one suspects was treachery in 1165, and took steps to ensure that the loss should not occur again. The king's actions are bafflingly hard to understand, mainly because the quarrel between the bishop and the *concejo* of Tuy in the mid-thirteenth century led to forgery—or at least liberal interpolation—of the royal charters issued in 1170 which form our sole evidence for them. For Tuy the only permanent result was the bodily removal of the town, on the king's orders, to a new and stronger site, where it has since remained. For Bishop Juan (of whose antecedents nothing is known) the consequences were serious. He had to buy the royal goodwill with a large money payment, he was stripped of some of his property, and (at least for a time) was deprived of some, possibly all, the powers which he had exercised as lord of the town of Tuy.[3] One is tempted to wonder whether it is entirely coincidental that Bishop Juan disappears from our records at a time when a papal legate, Cardinal Hyacinth, was in Spain with full power to depose bishops.

The bishopric had little time to recover from the violent events of 1170. Hostilities between León and Portugal occurred again in 1179 and perhaps in 1188. The general

---

[1] So Flórez, *ES* XXII, p. 90. The tradition cannot be verified, but it is worth noting that an Isidoro (the name was curiously rare in twelfth-century Spain) subscribes a Portuguese royal charter in 1139: *DMP* no. 174.

[2] AHN 1438/1.

[3] For the charters of 1170, see *ES* XXII, app. xiv, xv, pp. 280–4; Galindo, *Tuy en la Baja Edad Media*, docs. VII, IX, and XII; M. Fernández Rodríguez, 'La Entrada de los representantes de la burguesía en la curia regia Leonesa', *AHDE* xxvi (1956) 757–66. For the thirteenth-century quarrel, see *ES* XXII, pp. 290–303.

warfare which engulfed all the Christian kingdoms of the Peninsula broke out in 1196 and dragged on until 1208. The bishops of this period are hardly more than names. Beltrán's obit was recorded in the book of anniversaries of Sta. Cruz de Coimbra; perhaps he retired there after his resignation of the see in 1187.[1] He had received grants from both the king of Portugal and the king of León.[2] Virtually nothing is known of his successor Pedro. The last of our bishops, Suero, had previously been dean of Tuy, and is probably to be identified with the Archdeacon Suero Menéndez, *dilectus* of Fernando II, who had received a grant from that king in 1180.[3] In 1204 the archbishop of Compostela remitted the payment of *votos de Santiago* due from the church of Tuy—an indication of the financial plight of the diocese.[4] It would not be unreasonable to suppose that the see was as poverty-striken at the end of the twelfth century as at its beginning.

SANTIAGO DE COMPOSTELA

Diego Gelmírez	1100	1140
Berengar (elected)	1141–2	
Pedro Helias	1143	1149
Berengar	1150	1151
Bernardo	1151	1152
Pelayo	1153	1155
Martín	1156	1167
Pedro Gudestéiz	1167	1173
Pedro Suárez de Deza	1173	1206
Pedro Múñoz	1206	1224

Some fifty miles to the north of Tuy lies the town of Santiago de Compostela, the seat of what was in the twelfth century incomparably the richest and most renowned of the bishoprics of the kingdom of León. As the shrine of St. James, Compostela attracted pilgrims from all parts of Latin Christendom. Much of the history of the diocese in the twelfth century turns upon the resentments aroused by the prestige

---

[1] *ES* XXII, pp. 100–1.
[2] Galindo, *Tuy en la Baja Edad Media,* doc. XV; *GRF* pp. 464, 470.
[3] Galindo, op. cit., doc. XIV; *GRF* p. 470; AC Tuy 14/42.
[4] AC Tuy 10/21.

and wealth which the pilgrims brought to the guardians of the apostle's resting-place. We are specially well-informed about that history for reasons already discussed.[1] Santiago de Compostela is the only church in twelfth-century León to have left us a considerable piece of native historical writing in the *Historia Compostellana*; its archives have survived in abundance: and it has been fortunate in its local historian, Antonio López Ferreiro.

Yet the survival of the *Historia Compostellana* is not an unmixed blessing. In the first place, its authors were devoted and uncritical admirers of Diego Gelmírez, and they did less than justice to two among his immediate predecessors, Diego Peláez (*c.*1070–88) and the Cluniac monk Dalmatius (1094–5). These bishops anticipated some of the work of Diego Gelmírez. He continued an established tradition, he did not initiate a new one. In the second place, we have no comparable sources for the period after 1140. The archbishops of the years 1140 to 1173 are shadowy figures, and even the second great archbishop of the century, Pedro Suárez de Deza, is a man about whom we know very little. We must beware of looking at the church of Compostela through the glass of the *Historia* alone, and of unduly neglecting that part of the see's history which falls outside its scope.

Yet even when we have taken these considerations into account, Diego Gelmírez remains a commanding figure.[2] A member of the local Galician nobility, he was educated at the cathedral school of Compostela and spent some time in the household of Bishop Diego Peláez, before choosing the high road to ecclesiastical preferment—service to the crown. He spent a little time at the court of Alfonso VI, and then moved to the household of Raymond of Burgundy, count of Galicia, whose *cancellarius et secretarius* he became.[3] At Raymond's instance he became administrator of the vacant diocese during the years 1093–4 and 1095–1100 before becoming its bishop in the summer of 1100.

---

[1] See above, ch. 1, p. 27.
[2] Since I hope to deal with Diego's career in much greater detail elsewhere I have kept this sketch of it as short as possible and reduced references to a minimum.
[3] *HC* p. 20.

Diego devoted his episcopate to the increase of the wealth, fame and power of St. James and his church of Compostela. In fulfilling this aim he was signally successful. His character was not a complex one: ambitious, unscrupulous, tirelessly energetic, he had many of the qualities which make for success in a bishop. To contemporaries, the material prosperity of the see must have been the most obvious indication of Diego's good stewardship. It was based partly on grants of land from the rulers of León-Castile, partly on the offerings of pilgrims, the stream of whom he encouraged until it became a flood, and it enabled him to give outward expression of it by building (among much else) his magnificent cathedral and the imposing palace next to it. Diego himself perhaps measured his success by a different yardstick—the enhanced dignity of his position. Here his most notable triumphs were the elevation of his see to metropolitan status in 1120; his interventions in the confused politics of the reign of Urraca; and the control of the royal chancery conceded to him by Alfonso VII in 1127. These were only the highest peaks in a whole mountain range, but they were those which occasioned him most trouble and afforded him most satisfaction. We today might use a different measure again—the position he built for his church in Galician society. For example, he defended the coasts of Galicia from pirates by building a fleet, he protected merchants from molestation inland, he tackled the problem of disorder by proclaiming the Truce of God, he legislated on prices and measures.

These successes were won only at a price, and the enmities aroused during the archiepiscopate of Diego Gelmírez were extensive, bitter and lasting. They sprang from four roots. First, there was a good deal of friction between Diego and certain of the local nobility—the sort of trouble that was a hazard in the experience of any twelfth-century bishopric, rather than a problem peculiar to the see of Compostela. Second, there was opposition to Diego from certain members of his own chapter and from the townspeople of Compostela. These strands of opposition had different origins, but could come together into something formidable. The citizens resented the archiepiscopal *señorío* over the town, and their grievances erupted into violence on two occasions, in 1116–17

and 1136.[1] What made these revolts specially alarming was
the participation in them of some of the canons. The government of the see under Diego was something of a family affair;
his two brothers, and a nephew, held important charges.
Again he had favourites, *familiares*, upon whose counsel he
greatly relied—the men, indeed, whose views are expressed
in the *Historia*. These men were singled out by the rebels in
1116–17, and some of them suffered.[2] Two in particular
among the canons were mentioned by its authors as the ring-
leaders of this domestic opposition, Bernardo and his relative
Pedro Helias. These were able and powerful men. Both were
originally creatures of Diego and both later quarrelled with
him. Bernardo, engineer, archivist and royal chancellor, he
contrived to ruin in 1133–4. Pedro Helias, dean of Compostela from 1122–4, remained to command the opposition, and
in 1143 he succeeded Diego as archbishop.

The other movements of opposition came from other pre-
lates and from the king. The archbishops of Toledo resented
the concession of the archbishopric to Compostela, were bent
on establishing their own primacy throughout the ecclesiastical provinces of the Spains, and contested certain of Compostela's claims to suffragans. Generally, they were jealous of
Compostela's fame and huge wealth; whatever it became later,
Toledo was not a rich see in the twelfth century.[3] Braga and
Compostela squabbled over suffragans and lands, with a
bitterness which increased as the political separation of
Portugal from León became an accepted fact.

The quarrels with the king were rooted in certain harsh
facts of twelfth-century royal finance. We have already seen
that the sudden cutting-off of the revenue drawn from *parias*
as a result of the Almoravide invasion had presented the
crown with a prolonged and severe financial crisis which
handicapped its operations throughout the century.[4] Among

[1] *HC* pp. 215–49, 567–78. L. Vázquez de Parga, 'La revolución comunal de Compostela en los años 1116 y 1117,' *AHDE* xvi (1945), 685–703, adds nothing to
HC and *LFH* and does not to my mind satisfactorily establish the communal
quality of the revolt.
[2] Diego's brother Gundesindo, for instance, was murdered: *HC* pp. 232–3.
[3] A point emphasized by J.F. Rivera Recio, *La Iglesia de Toledo en el siglo XII*
(Rome–Madrid, 1966), p. 43.
[4] See above, ch. 1, p. 5.

remedial expedients, that which has left the most obvious traces in our records was the spoliation of the secular church, resorted to with varying degrees of success by Urraca, Alfonso VII and Fernando II. The richest see in the kingdom was Santiago de Compostela, and it is not surprising to find that rulers made repeated efforts to tap its resources. Sometimes, as Diego found in his relations with Alfonso VII, a mutually acceptable bargain could be struck; he received the privilege *de bonis non occupandis* in 1128 by giving the king *immensam pecuniam. . .incomputabilem pecuniam.*[1] At other times he was less fortunate.

The stresses set up by these enmities weakened the archbishopric during the years 1140 to 1173. This is an obscure period in its history, but an important one. The sources are so poor that even the chronology of the archbishops who succeeded Diego Gelmírez in these years is in doubt.[2] Berengar, who failed to secure the see in 1141-2 but succeeded in 1150-1, had previously been bishop of Salamanca.[3] At Compostela he was the royal candidate in 1141-2, and was strongly opposed by the local candidate, Pedro Helias, dean of Compostela, the erstwhile opponent of Diego Gelmírez. Pedro was an old man, he had been a canon in 1102,[4] and his tenure of the see was uneventful.

Berengar succeeded him in 1150-1, but for so short a time that he eluded the vigilance even of López Ferreiro, and was in turn followed by Bernardo, previously bishop of the Castilian see of Sigüenza from 1121 to 1151. Bernardo was a Frenchman, a native of Agen, who had been brought to Spain by Archbishop Bernardo of Toledo. He had become a canon, and then precentor, of Toledo, and then bishop of Sigüenza. His uncle was bishop of Segovia, and his brother bishop of Palencia. Both these men were closely associated with Alfonso

---

[1] *HC* p. 465.
[2] In 'The Archbishops of Santiago de Compostela between 1140 and 1173: a new chronology' (forthcoming in the periodical *Compostellanum*) I have set out what seems to be the most likely succession.
[3] See above, pp. 39-40.
[4] *HC* p. 57. The reading in *HC* p. 56, 'Anno M.C.XX.Kal.Maii' should be corrected to 'Era. MCXℯ. X Kal.Maii', which is found in the earliest extant MS. of the *HC*, Salamanca, Biblioteca de la Universidad, MS. 2658, fol. 24ʳ.

VII, and so was Bernardo—he had served in the royal chancery, for he subscribes two royal diplomas as *imperatoris capellanus*.[1] The bishopric of Sigüenza was a difficult assignment. Not only was it a newly-restored diocese, Bernardo being its first bishop, but it was also close to the no-man's-land where Castile and Aragon marched together. Bernardo tackled the business of restoring ecclesiastical life and resettling the land with energy. Such success as he had was mainly owing to the consistent support of Alfonso VII, with whom he perforce remained closely linked. As a candidate for the see of Compostela Bernardo looks like a king's man. Whether he was equally acceptable to Galician opinion we do not know. In any event, he held the archbishopric for a very short time.

His successor Pelayo was a local man, previously an archdeacon in the diocese.[2] His relations with the ageing Alfonso VII seem to have been good. It was during the archiepiscopate of his successor Martín that relations with the crown deteriorated into open conflict. Martín had been bishop of Oviedo from 1143 to 1156, but it seems probable that he too was a native of Compostela or its neighbourhood.[3] In 1160 he and Fernando II quarrelled bitterly.[4] The sources of the dispute are obscure. What is clear is that the quarrel lasted seven years, in the course of which Martín was twice expelled from and twice restored to his see, royal nominees being substituted during each period of exile (1160–4, 1165–7). He died soon after his final restoration in 1167. His successor was definitely a king's man; formerly tutor to Fernando II and royal chancellor in 1159–60, he had been bishop of Mondoñedo since 1155.[5] At Compostela he may have done some-

[1] On Bernardo's family and career, see Rodrigo, *De Rebus Hispaniae*, VI, 26; T. Minguella y Arnedo, *Historia de la Diócesis de Sigüenza y de sus Obispos* (Madrid, 1910), I, 56–65 and appendix, docs. I–XXXIV; D. de Colmenares *Historia de Segovia* (Segovia, 1637), pp. 118–19; AHN 18/2, 3.
[2] *LFH* IV p. 254 and ap. xxiii, pp. 64–6.
[3] He is called 'iacobita' in three private charters of 1150–4: *Colección Diplomática del Monasterio de San Vicente de Oviedo*, ed. P. Floriano Llorente (Oviedo, 1968), nos. CCXLI, CCXLIV, CCXLVII. For his episcopate at Oviedo, see below, pp. 74.
[4] R.A. Fletcher 'Regalian right in twelfth-century Spain: the case of archbishop Martín of Santiago de Compostela', *Journal of Ecclesiastical History* xxvii (1977) pp. 337–360.
[5] For his episcopate at Mondoñedo, see below, p. 63–4.

thing to remedy the ills which had been caused in the life of the archbishopric during the upheavals of the years 1140–67. He carried out some reforms in the chapter and was quick to establish friendly relations with the nascent Order of Santiago.[1] But his tenure of the see was not long. The primacy dispute re-opened; he may have fallen foul of Cardinal Hyacinth during his legatine visit of 1172–3; his past may have proved embarrassing; he may have lost the support of Fernando II. For whatever reason, he resigned his see in 1173 and was succeeded in it by Pedro Suárez de Deza, another ex-royal chancellor and previously bishop of Salamanca.[2]

The effects of the confused events between 1140 and 1173 were serious. Owing to the short archiepiscopates, there had been a break in the continuity of archiepiscopal action and guidance which must have weakened the archbishopric both morally and financially. The temporalities of the see had been despoiled by Fernando II and encroached upon by some of the local nobility, notably some of the members of the Traba family. The chapter had been internally divided: this was most evident during the time of Archbishop Martín, when the opposition to him was headed by one of his canons, the archdeacon Fernando Curialis, who was nominated by the king to the archbishopric in 1160–1. Relations with Braga and Toledo had been poor: the loyalty of Compostelan suffragans in Portugal and Extremadura was severely strained. In the various tribulations of the see the popes, when not hostile like Adrian IV, were too fearful, like Alexander III, of alienating royal support to venture to do much for a persecuted archbishop. We hear nothing of disaffection in the town of Santiago de Compostela: but, this apart, every element of opposition roused by the policies of Diego Gelmírez had become menacing after his death.

Pedro Suárez's tenure of the see was long, but we are oddly ill-informed about it. No biography has survived (if one were ever written) and documents from Compostela are rather scarce. The best guide to his work was given long ago by

---

[1] *LFH* IV app. xl, xlii, xlv, pp. 99–101, 105–6, 111–14.
[2] See above, p. 41.

López Ferreiro.[1] In brief, he restored the position of the see of Compostela and based its new security upon friendships rather than upon enmities. The stages by which this was achieved are lost to us, but something of Pedro's methods may be gleaned from the surviving sources. He settled any outstanding disputes with the lay nobility and maintained good relations with them thenceforward. With both Fernando II and Alfonso IX he succeeded in keeping on good terms, even at the period of the interdict imposed on the kingdom of León in punishment of the incestuous marriages of the latter. He effected certain reforms: a reorganization of the machinery of diocesan administration; the promulgation of capitular statutes; a sustained attempt to secure a revenue, with royal assistance, from the *votos de Santiago*. He completed the building operations at Santiago de Compostela, which had probably been suspended between 1140 and 1173, and it is to his archiepiscopate that the *pórtico de la gloria* belongs. Himself a theologian and perhaps a canon-lawyer, he patronized other canon-lawyers like Bernardus Compostellanus Antiquus and possibly Martín Arias of Zamora. His relations with the papacy were close: he attended the Third Lateran Council in 1179, secured papal support for the reforms he wished to introduce and, above all, received favourable rulings from Innocent III on the question on his suffragans; Coimbra and Viseu were given up, but Lisbon, Evora, Lamego and Idanha were definitively placed in the province of Santiago de Compostela, while Zamora, on which there was no ruling, fell in to Compostela in the course of the thirteenth century.

The stability thus achieved was needful; but the vaulting ambitions of the days of Diego Gelmírez had been discarded. Pedro Suárez's successor Pedro Múñoz was another Galician who had been associated with the see of León, as dean and then, very briefly in 1205–6, as bishop.[2] His archiepiscopate has left little trace in our records. He seems to have continued the modest labours of his predecessor, conscientiously and successfully enough. But the heroic days of the see of Santiago

---

[1] *LFH* IV, pp. 311–50; V, pp. 7–44.
[2] For his episcopate at León, see below, p. 72.

de Compostela, one cannot help but feel, had passed, never
to return.

MONDOÑEDO

Gonzalo	c.1071	1108?
Pedro	1109?	1110
Nuño Alfonso	1112	1136
Pelayo	1136	1155
Pedro Gudestéiz	1155	1167
Juan	1169	1172
Rabinato	1172	1199
Pelayo	1199	1218

Mondoñedo was a miserable little diocese. Its land was
economically unremunerative and exposed to attack from the
sea; the endowments of the bishopric were meagre; and the
bishops were overshadowed in wealth and influence by the
great monastery of Lorenzana. The see entered the twelfth
century inauspiciously, under Bishop Gonzalo, a member of
the great Galician house of Traba.[1] Gonzalo struggled to hold
on to what he had and to get more, but to no avail. He failed
to defend the territorial integrity of his diocese against the
acquisitiveness of Diego Gelmírez;[2] he failed to retain control
of outlying enclaves of his territory in the diocese of Braga;[3]
and he failed to pull off a rather dubious deal with Alfonso
VI which would have given him a large tract of the lands of
the monastery of Lorenzana.[4]

Gonzalo's successor was one Pedro, whose episcopate has
hitherto gone unnoticed. He is no more than a name to us,
but there are faint hints in the surviving sources of difficulties,
perhaps even of schism in the diocese.[5] He appears to have

[1] I take on trust López Ferreiro's assertion (*LFH* III, pp. 265, 322) that Gonzalo
was the brother of Pedro Froílaz de Traba, though I have not been able to corro-
borate it from the sources which I have inspected.
[2] *HC* pp. 74-84, 374-8.
[3] *PUP* no. 4; cf. also P. David, *Études historiques sur la Galice et le Portugal*
(Lisbon-Paris, 1947), pp. 160-5.
[4] This very complicated story may be followed in the Lorenzana cartulary, AHN
cód. 1044B, fols. 14v-16v, 30r-34v, 48r-v, 78r-79r, 80r-81r, 112r, 128v-130r,
and in AHN 1067/1, 2.
[5] R.A. Fletcher, 'Obispos olvidados del siglo XII de las diócesis de Mondoñedo
y Lugo', *Cuadernos de Estudios Gallegos* xxviii (1973), 318-25.

resigned his see. His successor Nuño Alfonso is better known to us. He had received his early training at the hands of Diego Gelmírez and had been a canon, and later treasurer, of Compostela. He was employed by his patron on three missions to the papal curia between 1100 and 1104, and was one of the authors of Book I of the *Historia Compostellana*.[1] He was evidently regarded as a close and trusted intimate, and it is reasonable to suppose that it was at least partly at the instance of Diego that he became bishop of Mondoñedo in 1112.[2]

The most important event of his episcopate was the movement of the seat of his bishopric from San Martín de Mondoñedo to Villamayor de Brea (the present town of Mondoñedo), some ten miles inland to the south. The decision to move it was taken at the council of Palencia in 1113.[3] We are not told why it was taken, and it has been assumed that the old site on the coast was dangerously exposed to the attacks of Moorish, 'Norman' and 'English' pirates, such as we know occurred sporadically throughout this period.[4] But piracy was no new phenomenon, and no historian who accepts this explanation has been able to show convincingly why the translation took place in 1113 and not at any other time. On the other hand we do hear of a serious dispute between Bishop Nuño and the monastery of Lorenzana in 1112.[5] This was a recurrence of one of the troubles which had vexed Bishop Gonzalo, and since the monks had now found a protector in Count Rodrigo Vélaz—a powerful Galician nobleman who was probably descended from the tenth-century founder of the monastery—the bishop's discomfiture may have been acute. It is at least possible that the translation of the see in 1113 was an attempt to move its centre away from an area close to Lorenzana and in the heart of Count Rodrigo's lands between the rivers Eo and Sor, where it seemed bound to cause trouble.

Later on in life, Nuño Alfonso became an important royal

[1] *HC* pp. 26, 30–1, 44, 56, 144–6, 148, 252.
[2] This is certainly hinted at in *HC* pp. 144–5.
[3] For the date, see JL 6396, 6460; *ES* XVIII, ap. xix, pp. 342–4.
[4] E.g., *HC* pp. 133–5 (English pirates); 197–9 (Saracen raids), See the editor's introduction to *De Expugnatione Lyxbonensi* ed. C.W. David (New York, 1936) for a general survey of this maritime activity. The subject needs further research.
[5] AHN cód. 1044B, fols. 14v–15r, 128v–129v.

servant. The wording of a royal charter of 1 June 1125 suggests that already by that date he was in the service of the young Alfonso VII.[1] In 1126 he appears among a number of *regales nuntii*, and he subscribes five royal charters of the same year as *capellanus regis*.[2] The fact that in 1133 he was given the custody of the luckless ex-chancellor Bernardo suggests that he had remained closely attached to the crown.[3]

On his resignation in 1136—he retired to Compostela where he founded a house of Augustinian canons[4] —he was succeeded by Pelayo, previously abbot of Lorenzana. This is a tantalizing scrap of knowledge. Had the monks managed to slip their own candidate into the vacant see? If so, was this in opposition to the royal will? Pelayo received not a single royal grant during his nineteen-year episcopate, and subscribed remarkably few royal charters.[5] Moreover, his tenure of the see came to an abrupt end when he was deposed at the council of Valladolid in 1155—a council in which the king played an active part.[6]

Pedro Gudestéiz was elected at once to fill the vacant see, which he held until his promotion to the archbishopric of Compostela in 1167. There is every reason to suppose that he was a royal appointment. Previously a canon and then prior of Sar—the house of Augustinian canons founded by Nuño Alfonso—he had been tutor to the young Fernando II.[7] During that king's reign he reaped the fullness of his reward. Virtually all the royal charters of the years 1159–63 were witnessed by him, which testifies to his position as a close

---

[1] *ES* XVIII, ap. xx, pp. 344–5, 'pro servitio fideli'.
[2] *HC* pp. 432–4. The royal charters are AC Salamanca, no. 6; *Recueil des chartes de l'Abbaye de Silos*, ed. M. Férotin (Paris, 1897), no. 39; AC León, nos. 1015, 1368; *Colección de Fuentes para la Historia de Asturias*, vol. I, *Monasterio de Cornellana*, ed. A.C. Floriano (Oviedo, 1949), no. v.
[3] *HC* p. 557.
[4] *LFH* IV, ap. viii, pp. 21–5.
[5] Only eleven among those known to me: five between 1136 and 1148, six between 1152 and 1154.
[6] AHN 899/1 (printed in Escalona, *Sahagún*, pp. 537–8). For Alfonso VII's demeanour at the council, see C. Erdmann, *O Papado e Portugal no primeiro século da História Portuguesa* (Coimbra, 1935), ap. vi, pp. 92–3.
[7] *LFH* IV, pp. 248, 284, 299. In *LFH* IV, ap. xxi, p. 59, the subscription 'Petrus ecclesie beati Iacobi cardinalis' should continue 'Sarensisque prior conf.'; see the original, AHN 524/3. A charter of 9 May 1150, printed in *BCM Orense* vii (1923–(1923–6), 209–14, sheds some light on his activities as prior of Sar.

royal counsellor. He was the king's chancellor in 1159-60, and in 1167 his *mayordomo;*[1] he accompanied the king into Castile, and was present at Agreda when Fernando II and Alfonso II entered into alliance;[2] and he received generous grants from the king. Above all, when the great dispute between Fernando II and Archbishop Martín of Compostela broke out in the 1160s, Pedro Gudestéiz was one of the nominees whom the king tried to foist upon the 'vacant' diocese.

On his translation to Compostela he was succeeded at Mondoñedo by a certain Juan, who is only a name to us. After a short episcopate, Juan was followed by another bishop, Rabinato, who had been closely connected with the royal government. He had served in the chancery of Alfonso VII, probably also in that of Fernando II.[3] Before his promotion he had held in addition an archdeaconry in the diocese.[4] During his episcopate the seat of the bishopric was moved yet again: in 1182 it was shifted from Villamayor de Brea to Ribadeo, at the mouth of the Eo, where it was to stay for about the next fifty years.[5] The king's words, in the royal charter which is our only record of the decision, are vageu—*pro ipsius ecclesie statu meliori*—but there are hints of conflict with the local nobility, and we may sense that the period at Villamayor, from 1113 to 1182, had been no more happy than the period before that at San Martín de Mondoñedo.

Very little is known of Rabinato's successor Pelayo. His family may have come from the diocese of Astorga, where his mother (*sic*) had held the patronage of a canonry.[6] The few

---

[1] *GRF* pp. 167, 397; J. González, 'El Fuero de Benavente de 1167', *Hispania* ii (1942), 619-26. I know of no other instance of an ecclesiastic's holding the office of royal *mayordomo*.
[2] J. Villanueva, *Viage Literario a las iglesias de España* xviii (Madrid 1851), ap. liii, pp. 326-8. He may also have been sent on an embassy to Ramón Berenguer IV, count of Barcelona, between 1158 and 1162: *Colección de Documentos Inéditos del Archivo de la Corona de Aragón* (Barcelona, 1849), IV, no. cxliii, pp. 336-7.
[3] AHN 1616/21; AC León, no. 337; *GRF* p. 479.
[4] AHN cód. 1439B, fol. 90.
[5] *ES* XVIII, ap. xxvi, pp. 360-2.
[6] *ES* XVIII, p. 148.

documents we have concerning his episcopate show him acquiring land near Ribadeo and raising funds for the building of a cathedral there.[1]

LUGO

Pedro II	c.1098	1113
Pedro III	1113	1133?
Guido	1135?	1152
Juan	1152	1181
Rodrigo I	1181	1182
Rodrigo II	1182	1218

Lugo, to the south of Mondoñedo, was the seat of a bishopric next in importance, among Galician sees, to the metropolitan at Compostela. Like Astorga, Lugo owed its standing to its position on the Roman road from Mérida to the northwest and on the pilgrimage route from France to the shrine of St. James. Already before 1100 it was a busy town, the site of a royal mint and of a monthly market to which merchants came under royal protection.[2] Not long before the beginning of our period, in 1085-6, the hold of Alfonso VI over Galicia had been challenged by a serious revolt, whose centre lay in Lugo, led by Count Rodrigo Ovéquiz. The re-establishment of royal power in the area had been effected largely by a close association of king and bishop; and this, together with the privileges already held by the bishops—notably the *señorío* of the town of Lugo—contributed to make them both rich and powerful when our period opens.

Little is known of Bishop Pedro II, beyond the fact that he resigned his see at the council of Palencia in 1113.[3] The guarded words of our authority suggest that he had been a somewhat ineffective diocesan, unable adequately to care for his see during the troubled years of the war which followed the death of Alfonso VI. His namesake and successor seems to have been more forceful. Like many another bishop he

---

[1] *GAL* nos. 132, 168, 242; AC Mondoñedo, carpeta del siglo xiii (unnumbered documents), a papal bull of 23 January 1208.

[2] *Docs. Galicia* nos. 178, 184.

[3] *HC* pp. 182-3. He is described as *religiosus* in an act of his successor, which might mean that he retired into a monastery: *ES* XLI, ap. ii, pp. 296-301.

was promoted from the royal service; he had been a *capellanus regine* before his appointment, and there are indications that he remained closely attached to the queen.[1] He reorganized the chapter of Lugo, was active in acquiring endowments for his see, started to build a new cathedral and maintained close relations with the papacy.[2] To some of these activities we shall have to return later on.

His successor Guido was French by birth,[3] and had previously been prior of the chapter of Lugo.[4] Having said this, however, we have said all that we can of him. He in his turn was succeeded by Juan, a Benedictine monk who had been abbot since at least 1145 of the important monastery of Samos. That he was acceptable to the king is shown by the letter which Alfonso VII wrote to the archbishop of Braga requesting his consecration.[5] He seems to have been extensively employed in the royal service during his episcopate. He went on probably two royal embassies to the papal curia. He acted as a *pesquisador*.[6] Yet another side of his secular activities is illustrated by a record of his having preached a campaign against the Moors of Mérida.[7] Fernando II spoke approvingly of him,[8] and Bishop Juan in return received royal assistance in his own troubles—for example, in enforcing episcopal authority over the town of Lugo when the citizens were in revolt in 1159-61 and 1178.[9] At the same time he contrived to remain a loyal suffragan of the archbishop of Braga, who was the closest adviser of Fernando II's enemy

---

[1] *HC* pp. 183-4, 359.
[2] *ES* XLI, ap. ii, pp. 296-301 (capitular reorganization); AHN 1325C/7, 19, 22 (endowments); AHN 1325C/21 bis, AHN cód. 1043B, fol. 59^r, marginal annotation (cathedral building); AC Lugo, leg.3, no. 2, Libro de Bulas Apostólicas, no. 1 (papal privileges of 1123, 1131).
[3] P. Arias, 'Don Juan I, abad de Samos y obispo de Lugo' *BCM Lugo* iii (1949), 256-63, quotes a Samos document of 1149 which comments 'Lucensem sedem francigena Guido regebat'.
[4] AHN 1325C/19, 21 bis, 22.
[5] *ES* XLI, ap. ix, p. 311.
[6] *Documentos para la Historia de las Instituciones de León y de Castilla (siglos X-XIII)*, ed. E. de Hinojosa (Madrid, 1919), no. xliv, pp. 71-2.
[7] AHN 1082/11, of 6 April 1164, 'et hoc fuit in tempore quando predicavit episcopus domnus Iohannes quod fuissent in fossado ad Meridam'. The campaign —perhaps we should say, the proposed campaign—seems to be otherwise unknown.
[8] *ES* XLI, ap. xix, p. 331.
[9] *GRF* pp. 47-8, 248-50; *Docs. Galicia,* nos. 379, 382.

the king of Portugal: it was on orders from Braga that Juan consecrated Guillermo bishop of Zamora in 1175, in defiance of the wishes of the archbishop of Compostela and his suffragans.[1] Though he acted as an intermediary between king and pope in the dispute over archbishop Martín of Compostela in the 1160s, he was in other respects a devoted servant of the papacy. He sought decretal letters from Alexander III, probably attended the Lateran council of 1179, and reformed his cathedral chapter at the bidding of the legate Cardinal Hyacinth.[2]

Juan's successor has almost entirely escaped the notice of historians, who have been content to follow Risco, the eighteenth-century editor of *España Sagrada*, in assuming that one bishop named Rodrigo presided over the see of Lugo from 1181 to 1218. In fact there were two Rodrigos, Rodrigo Menéndez and Rodrigo Fernández.[3] Rodrigo Menéndez had been a royal clerk; he had been in the service of Fernando II even before the latter's accession to the throne in 1157.[4] He had been dean of Lugo from at least 1168, and may have been an archdeacon from as early as 1155.[5] His short episcopate was troubled by strained relations with the citizens of Lugo, as was also the much longer episcopate of his namesake and successor. Rodrigo II, despite the length of his tenure, has left us few traces of his activity beyond a good collection of *acta* which will claim attention in a later chapter. The indications are that he too was promoted from the royal service.[6] He held his own against the rebellious citizens; he defended the boundaries of his diocese against the encroachments of León and Orense; he may have added to the cathedral of Lugo.[7] But, like so many of his contemporaries in the second half of the century, he remains obscure.

---

[1] ANTT, Colecção Especial, Corporações Diversas, Mitra de Braga, caixa 1, no. 2.
[2] JL 13796, 14005 (for the address of the former to the bishop of Lugo see Mansi, *Concilia,* XXII, col. 411); AC Lugo, Libro de Bulas Apostólicas, no. 4; AHN 1325F/9 (printed inaccurately in *ES* XLI, ap. xvii, pp. 326–8).
[3] R.A. Fletcher, 'Obispos olvidados del siglo XII de las diócesis de Mondoñedo y Lugo', *Cuadernos de Estudios Gallegos* xxviii (1973), 318–25.
[4] *GRF* p. 345.
[5] AHN 1325D/9, 18, 20; 1325E/4, 5, 12, 17, 18.
[6] *GRF* p. 485.
[7] AHN 1326A/15; 1326B/9, 13 ter; 1326D/20.

LEÓN

Pedro	1087?	1111?
Diego	1112–13	1130
Arias	1130	1135
Pedro Anáyaz	1135	1139
Juan	1139	1181
Manrique de Lara	1181	1205
Pedro Múñoz	1205	1206
Pelayo Pérez	1207	1208
Rodrigo Álvarez	1208	1232

León and Oviedo, our last two bishoprics, had certain features in common. Neither had been a bishopric during the Visigothic period, they were products of the *Reconquista*. Both had enjoyed a time of wealth and renown which was fading in the twelfth century. The see of León had but recently passed its prime. Under the kings of the tenth and eleventh centuries León had been the *urbs regia*: the most frequent residence of the kings of León, the heart of their 'empire' whose nature has been so hotly disputed by historians, its church the favoured recipient of their most splendid acts of piety and, at the end, their mausoleum. A change came during the reign of Alfonso VI. His conquest of Toledo, the gradual absorption of Galicia under his sway and the preservation of the union of Castile with León all tended to make the monarchy less exclusively 'Leonese' than it had been. The town was prosperous—it had an important Jewish community—and the last of the king-emperors, Alfonso VII, was crowned there in 1135. Yet one has a sense that the bishops of the twelfth century were gradually, and sometimes painfully, adjusting themselves to changed and straightened circumstances.[1]

One of the thorns in the bishops' sides, at least during the first half of the century, was the claim of the church of Toledo that León should be numbered among her suffragans, a claim which was given effect by papal recognition in 1099.

---

[1] A comparison with León's neighbouring see of Palencia, in Castile, is not inapt: see A.D. Deyermond, *Epic Poetry and the Clergy: Studies on the 'Mocedades de Rodrigo'* (London, 1968), especially chs. 4 and 5.

The most notable achievement of our first bishop, Pedro, was to secure a privilege of exemption from Paschal II in 1104.[1] Little is otherwise known of him, and the end of his episcopate is blanketed in obscurity. He was expelled from his see by the king of Aragon in the war that followed the death of Alfonso VI, probably after the battle of Candespina in 1111, and died in exile. The vacant see was usurped for a short time by Archbishop Maurice of Braga, before the accession of Bishop Diego.[2]

The new bishop was a nephew of his predecessor.[3] Within his diocese, much of his work was devoted to repairing the damage wrought in the years of war. We find him exploiting new sources of revenue, restoring the property of the chapter and the ecclesiastical routine of the cathedral, settling a dispute with his chapter.[4] He had also to continue the struggle with Toledo. At first he lost the ground gained by his uncle, for in 1121 León and Oviedo were declared suffragans of Toledo by Calixtus II, a ruling which was confirmed by Honorius II in 1125.[5] But at some point between then and 1130 Diego contrived to have the decision reversed and to regain his lost exemption.[6] It is possible that the conflict with Toledo may help to explain the most puzzling feature of Diego's episcopate—its end. He was deposed at the council of Carrión in 1130. We do not know why this happened, but

---

[1] AC León, no. 6328, is the original of the bull of exemption, and lies behind the misleading summary of JL 6058. León's claims to exemption were based in part on the celebrated forgery of the so-called 'División de Wamba': see L. Vázquez de Parga, *La División de Wamba* (Madrid, 1943), pp. 112–14. It is significant of the common interests of León and Oviedo that the Leonese claim features only in those MSS. emanating from the Oviedo *scriptorium*.

[2] P. David, 'L'Enigme de Maurice Bourdin', in his *Etudes historiques sur la Galice et le Portugal* (Lisbon-Paris, 1947), pp. 441–501, especially pp. 459–62. David's conclusions must stand, but there are minor corrections to be made to his chronology, e.g. Pedro did not die 'vers la fin de llll': he was still alive, in exile in Galicia, on 13 June 1112; AHN cód. 1044B, fols. 14^v–15^r.

[3] This is stated in a royal charter of 27 March 1122: AC León, no. 1009, printed in *ES* XXXVI, ap. 1, pp. cvi–cviii.

[4] See two *acta* of 1120 and a royal charter of 4 November 1123: AC León, nos. 1383, 1384 (inaccurately printed in *ES* XXXV, ap. iv, pp. 417–21 and XXXVI, ap. xlviii, pp. civ–cvi); *ES* XXXVI, ap. lii, p. cx.

[5] JL 6934, 7231. For the correct date of the latter, see *MHV* I, no. 64.

[6] All direct evidence of this is lost, but it may be inferred from Innocent II's reactions in 1130.

we may suspect the machinations of the Toledan party. Our suspicions are strengthened by what we know of Diego's successor Arias. He was consecrated by the archbishop of Toledo, who thereby earned a rebuke from Innocent II.[1] We sense a Toledan connection, but unfortunately know too little of Arias to be able to substantiate it. His successor Pedro may well have been a protégé of Archbishop Diego of Compostela. His connections seem to have been with Galicia. He witnessed one of Diego's *acta* in 1136.[2] Still more significantly, Innocent II wrote to Diego warning him not to consecrate him.[3] Now Pedro's patronymic was Anáyaz, and it is at least possible that he is to be identified with Pedro Anáyaz, canon and then dean of Compostela, the trusted clerk of Diego Gelmírez, whom he had sent on an important mission to the papal curia in 1118.[4] It would not be unreasonable to suppose that Diego, fearing Toledan pretensions over the see of León, took steps—precisely how we do not know—to insert his own candidate there.

His successor Juan had a different background. His father Albertino[5] was a native of León or its neighbourhood, and very probably of French extraction.[6] He was a man of considerable standing in the royal government during the first two-thirds of the reign of Alfonso VII.[7] There is some reason to suppose that his son Juan was below the canonical age at the time of his appointment to the see in 1139. We may feel confident that as a young man on his promotion, the son of a powerful local man who was also a prominent royal servant, he owed his position to royal favour. That he was certainly a king's man after his promotion is put beyond any doubt by references to him in royal charters.[8] We know little,

---

[1] JL 7735.   [2] *LFH* IV, ap. viii, pp. 21–5.   [3] JL 7735.

[4] For Pedro's patronymic, AC León, no. 1396: for the career of Pedro Anáyaz, *HC* pp. 44, 56, 64, 101, 108–111, 196, 258, 276 (274), 278 (276), 370, 378, 504.

[5] The relationship is established by AHN 896/15 and AC León, no. 1396.

[6] There was a French colony in León sufficiently numerous to warrant a reference to the *vicus Francorum* as early as 1092. The name Albertinus is of course a French, not a Spanish name.

[7] He held local office as *merino* in León, witnessed a number of royal charters, acted on confidential missions for Alfonso VII and is found as some sort of royal justice in a Segovia land-suit. I hope to study his career in more detail elsewhere.

[8] See especially the words of Fernando II in a charter of 1183, quoted in *ES* XXXV, p. 221.

unfortunately, of the secular activities which such a man must have undertaken in the royal service. We can trace him on one occasion as a secular *tenente*.[1] He subscribed a large number of royal charters. But this is as much as we can say. We are rather better informed about his activities as a churchman. He preserved León's privilege of exemption, not without difficulty, against renewed attack from Toledo.[2] His surviving *acta* suggest an energetic administrator. He was a terror to his opponents. When he tried to take over the monastery church of San Isidoro and turn it into his own cathedral the saint had to intervene to prevent his doing so.[3] When a band of eager spirits in the cathedral chapter wanted to introduce the Augustinian Rule he hustled them off to found their own house elsewhere.[4]

On his resignation, presumably owing to age, in 1181, Juan was succeeded by Manrique de Lara. He was a member of the greatest noble family of Castile—not León—and is therefore one of the very few of our bishops of whom we can say with certainty that he came from the very highest rank in society. His father Pedro Manrique was not one of the most distinguished members of the family, but he had made a splendid marriage to Sancha, *infanta* of Navarre.[5] The son of this union, the future bishop, had held certain offices in the church of León before 1181; the office of *cantor* from at least 1165, and that of archdeacon from at least 1168.[6] It is difficult to believe that his promotion to the episcopate did not owe something to royal influence. Certainly, as a bishop, he was spoken of warmly by Fernando II and Alfonso IX, and it is no surprise to learn that he took the royal side against the pope in the disputes over the marriages of Alfonso IX.[7]

---

[1] *Cartulario del Monasterio de Eslonza*, ed. V. Vignau (Madrid, 1885), no. cxv, of March, 1173.

[2] AC León, no. 6327.

[3] León, Archivo de San Isidoro, códice no. LXI ('Liber de Miraculis Sancti Isidori'), cap. 43, fols. 65ᵛ–66ᵛ.

[4] León, Archivo de San Isidoro, no. 98 (inaccurately printed in *ES* XXXVI, ap. liv. pp. cxv–cxviii).

[5] AC León, no. 1437, establishes Manrique's membership of the family, on which see *GRC* I, pp. 259–93 abd above all L. Salazar y Castro, *Historia Genealógica de la Casa de Lara* (Madrid, 1694–7).

[6] AC León, nos. 1413, 1416.

[7] *GRF* p. 514; *GAL* nos. 116, 119, 150; *MHV* I no. 138.

He pursued his predecessor's feud with the canons of San Isidoro, for which the saint blinded him in return, and started to build a new cathedral, but otherwise he has left little record of his long episcopate.[1]

Manrique's successors were very short-lived. Pedro Múñoz, a Galician by birth, and dean of León from at least April 1201,[2] was translated to Compostela after an episcopate of less than a year. Pelayo Pérez died before his consecration. Rodrigo Alvarez was bishop for twenty-four years, but the major part of his episcopate falls outside our period. Consequently he has left little trace upon those records of his first few years which have come down to us.

OVIEDO

Pelayo	1101?	1130
Alfonso	1130	1142
Pelayo (again)	1142	1143
Martín	1143	1156
Pedro	1156	1161
Gonzalo	1161	1175
Rodrigo	1175	1188
Menendo	1188	1189
Juan	1189	1243

The see of Oviedo, squeezed between the Cantabrian mountains and the Bay of Biscay, had become progressively more isolated from the main currents of Leonese life ever since the Asturian kings had moved the principal seat of their government from Oviedo down to León early in the tenth century. During the twelfth, the virtual independence of the Asturias was being whittled away. Two serious rebellions, in 1132 and 1164, challenged the encroachments of royal authority, but could not hold up its advances altogether. The bishops of Oviedo had also to face a challenge—a determined attempt by the archbishops of Toledo to incorporate Oviedo in their ecclesiastical province. Like León, Oviedo was declared a suffragan of Toledo in 1099, acquired exemption in

[1] 'Liber de Miraculis Sancti Isidori' c. 50; Lucas of Tuy, *Chronicon Mundi*, in *Hispania Illustrata* (Frankfort, 1608), IV, p. 110.
[2] *ES* XXXVI, ap. lx, pp. cxxix–cxxx; *MHV* I no. 286.

1105, lost it again in 1121, and then had to wait nearly forty years before regaining it.[1] It is from this context that the works of Bishop Pelayo *el Fabulador* have come down to us. Pelayo is the only one among our bishops who has left a body of writings behind him. Some of his work was original, as for instance the chronicle which deals with the years 982 to 1109,[2] but a large part of the *corpus* consists of interpolations into earlier works and especially into earlier documents, and it is to this activity that Pelayo owes the nickname which scholars have given him. His work cannot be called an impressive intellectual achievement, but it is of considerable interest to the student of Spanish history, and deserves more critical attention than it has yet received.[3] It was designed to serve a purpose. Pelayo wished to exalt the see of Oviedo, partly through its relics, partly through its glorious past which he had so artfully touched up, the better to be able to establish its independence of any metropolitan. Indeed, he went to far as to claim that the see of Oviedo had itself been a metropolitan see in the ninth and tenth centuries.[4]

We would gladly know more of Pelayo than we do. Nothing is known of his background, and the manner in which his episcopate came to an end raises questions which cannot be answered. Like Diego of León, Pelayo was deposed by the legate Cardinal Humbert at the council of Carrión in February 1130.[5] As usual when we search for the reasons behind this we are left groping in darkness. Clearly it must have been in the interests of the church of Toledo to have Pelayo out of the way. What we cannot do is to connect his successor Alfonso with the Toledan interest. Alfonso's career, indeed, is bafflingly hard to make out. We may presume that he was a local man, for he had relatives holding land in the Asturias.[6] A royal grant to him dated 18 August 1132 indicates loyalty

[1] JL 6039, 6931, 6934, 7231.
[2] *Crónica del Obispo D. Pelayo,* ed. B. Sánchez Alonso (Madrid, 1924).
[3] Parts of it have been studied: see, for example, L. Vázquez de Parga, *La División de Wamba* (Madrid, 1943) and F.J. Fernández Conde, *El Libro de los Testamentos de la Catedral de Oviedo* (Rome, 1971).
[4] D. Mansilla, 'La supuesta metrópoli de Oviedo' *Hispania Sacra* viii (1955), 259-74.
[5] *HC* pp. 498-9.
[6] *El Libro Registro de Corias,* ed. A.C. Floriano (Oviedo, 1950), II, 14-17.

to Alfonso VII during the revolt of Count Gonzalo Peláez,[1] and he was certainly present at the imperial coronation in 1135. Our most surprising record of him comes from two papal bulls of 1133.[2] We learn from these that the legate—presumably Humbert—had forbidden him to receive consecration, that he had defied this order, and that now, at the request of the archbishop of Santiago de Compostela and the bishops of Lugo and León, he was excommunicate. What was going on? We simply do not know. Whatever it was, the king paid no attention to it; he subscribed one of the bishop's *acta* dated August 1133, shortly after the arrival of the papal bulls.[3] This might be construed as a faint hint that Bishop Alfonso's connections were with royal circles.

He died early in 1142 and was succeeded by—Pelayo. After his deposition he had presumably continued to live in Oviedo: in 1136 he had granted some lands near León to the canons of Oviedo, describing himself as *quondam Ovetensis ecclesie episcopus*.[4] He returned to the see in 1142 and occupied it until the early summer of 1143.[5] His successor Martín was elected at the council of Valladolid in September. He was a native of Galicia, and had previously been connected, though we do not know exactly how, with the church of Compostela, for he is referred to as *Iacobita* and as *Compostellanus* in several documents during his episcopate at Oviedo.[6] He may be identical with the Martín Martínez who subscribed an act of Diego Gelmírez in 1136.[7] This, and the fact that on the evidence of his subscriptions to royal charters we may judge him to have been an assiduous attender at the royal court, especially in the years 1152-6, perhaps help to explain why he was an acceptable choice for the archbishopric of Compostela in 1156. He attended the council of Rheims in 1148,[8] and saw to the settlement of two longstanding boundary

---

[1] *Docs. Oviedo,* no. 149.
[2] JL 7610, 7611.
[3] *Docs. Oviedo* no. 150.
[4] *Docs. Oviedo* no. 151.
[5] Ibid., nos. 154, 155; *ES* XXXVIII, p. 109.
[6] *Colección Diplomática del Monasterio de Belmonte,* ed. A.C. Floriano (Oviedo, 1960), nos. 20, 21; and see the references cited above, p. 58.
[7] *LFH* IV, p. 263 and ap. viii, pp. 21-5.
[8] *PUP* no. 46.

disputes with the sees of Lugo and Orense, but we know no more of his episcopate at Oviedo. His successor Pedro was a black monk who had been abbot of San Vicente de Oviedo for over twenty-five years.[1] He must therefore have been an elderly man in 1156, and his episcopate was a short one. But it was important, for in 1157 Pedro visited the papal curia and brought back two bulls from Adrian IV by which the exemption of the see was renewed.[2]

This time it was not to be reversed. Alexander III confirmed it in 1162,[3] and we do not hear that it was ever afterwards called in question. This confirmation was given, we may assume, when Pedro's successor visited the curia for consecration. This man, Gonzalo Menéndez, is probably to be identified with the archdeacon of the same name whom we can trace in Oviedo documents from 1136 onwards.[4] During his episcopate the second great Asturian rebellion occurred. Very little is known of this, in the absence of any contemporary narrative source for the reign of Fernando II, but one thing is clear: Bishop Gonzalo was a strong supporter of the king and helped him to put down the rebels.[5] He had his reward. Royal donations, which had been a trickle under Alfonso VII, became a torrent under his son. We know Fernando II to have been recklessly extravagant yet even so the largesse poured out on Bishop Gonzalo and his see was altogether exceptional. Yet in this respect Gonzalo's episcopate compares ill with that of his successor Rodrigo. Like Gonzalo, he had previously been an archdeacon of Oviedo;[6] more significantly, he had been the king's chancellor in 1167–8.[7] Lands and privileges rained down upon him from the king, who spoke of him in extravagantly fulsome terms.[8] Rodrigo repaid

---

[1] He became abbot in 1129–30; *Colección Diplomática del Monasterio de San Vicente de Oviedo*, ed. P. Floriano Llorente (Oviedo, 1968), no. CCLVI.

[2] *ES* XXXVIII, p. 158; *Docs. Oviedo*, nos. 165, 166. That Pedro sought a double safeguard is some measure of his anxiety.

[3] *Docs. Oviedo*, no. 175 (incorrectly dated by the editor).

[4] Ibid., no. 152, for the first occurrence of the name.

[5] Ibid., no. 179 (= *GRF* p. 384); cf. also AHD León, Fondo de Sta.María de Otero de las Dueñas, no. 243.

[6] *Docs. Oviedo*, no. 181; *Colección Diplomática del Monasterio de San Vicente de Oviedo*, ed. P.Floriano Llorente (Oviedo, 1968), no. CCCXII.

[7] *GRF* p. 169.

[8] *Docs. Oviedo*, nos. 188, 190, 193, 204.

the debt. He lent his king money; he served in the royal army at the siege of Cáceres in 1184.[1] There is also some evidence that Fernando II used him as something like a viceroy over the difficult province of the Asturias.[2] After Fernando's death his son Alfonso IX accepted and confirmed the special position of the bishop of Oviedo.[3]

Did it persist? We do not know. Rodrigo's successor Menendo Menéndez held the see for a very short time and has left correspondingly few records of his episcopate. Our last bishop, Juan González, had a very long episcopate. Most of the first ten years of it was spent in a bitter quarrel with Alfonso IX. Juan was the only bishop in the kingdom of León who opposed Alfonso's two marriages which were condemned by Celestine III on the grounds of consanguinity. The king's answer was simple and rapid; the bishop was exiled and his property confiscated.[4] He was restored only at the express command of Innocent III.[5] We know little more about his long episcopate, but it would be misleading to cast him as a stern upholder of the canon law of the church simply because he stood up to Alfonso IX. Much later on, in the 1220s, his doings were being investigated, and some ugly facts were coming to light.[6] Whatever the state of the church of Oviedo in the last decade of the twelfth century, it was in a very bad way thirty years later, and it would seem that Bishop Juan was largely to blame for this. But these murky transactions lie beyond our period, and thus outside our scope.

The foregoing survey, if it has achieved no other end, will have shown conclusively how little we really know about these bishops. Any general remarks about them must be so hedged about by words of caution as to render their force

---

[1] Ibid., nos. 200, 201.
[2] Ibid., no. 202; *Colección Diplomática del Monasterio de San Vicente de Oviedo*, ed. P.Floriano Llorente (Oviedo, 1968), no. CCCXIV.
[3] *GRF* p. 473; *GAL* no. 16; *ES* XXXVIII, p. 170.
[4] *Colección Diplomática del Monasterio de San Vicente de Oviedo*, ed. P.Floriano Llorente (Oviedo, 1968), no. CCCLXVI.
[5] *MHV* I, no. 144.
[6] *MHV* II, nos. 477, 494.

almost null. Yet there are questions to be asked and answers, however hesitant, to be given.

Who chose bishops? We are desperately ill-informed about the conduct of episcopal elections, but what little we do know of them suggests that the wishes of the king were powerful, perhaps decisive elements in the process of choice. Evidence survives to shed some light on four elections only— those of Iñigo to the (Castilian) see of Avila in 1133, of Berengar to that of Salamanca in 1135, of Juan to that of Lugo in 1152, and of Adán to the see of Orense in 1169.[1] We hear of electors submitting their choice to the king (Avila and Lugo), of elections taking place in the presence of the king (Salamanca and Lugo), of a cathedral chapter (Orense) seeking royal permission to make a free election (in which a man who had recently been the royal chancellor was chosen). These consultative processes—which were regarded as standard practice in thirteenth-century Spain[2]—were a familiar stage in the business of bishop-making in twelfth-century Europe, and most historians are agreed that they were usually rather less innocent than they appear. Clearly it would be improper to generalize upon so slender a factual basis as four episcopal elections; nevertheless the evidence that we have is suggestive. There is, as we shall see, further and less direct evidence which points in the same direction.

How many of the bishops of the kingdom of León were not of Spanish birth? Four were certainly Frenchmen—Jerónimo of Avila-Salamanca-Zamora, Bernardo of Zamora, Guido of Lugo and Bernardo of Sigüenza-Compostela; the appointments of the first three fell in 1102, 1121 and c.1135 respectively, while Bernardo was appointed to Sigüenza in 1121 or 1122 and translated to Compostela in 1151. We have seen that there is a not implausible tradition that Pedro Seguin of Orense, appointed in 1157, was a Frenchman. Arnaldo I of Astorga, appointed in 1144, may have been

---

[1] *HC* pp. 536-40, 562-5; AD Braga, Liber Fidei, fols. 99^v, 106^r, 151^v-152^r (ptd. inaccurately *ES* XLI ap. ix, p. 311); ibid., fol. 137.
[2] *Las Siete Partidas del Rey D.Alfonso el Sabio*, ed. Real Academia de la Historia (Madrid, 1807), Part I, tit.5, ley xvii; London, British Library, Add. MS. 20787, fols. 20^v-21^r (the earlier version of the *Primera Partida:* I am grateful to Miss E.S. Procter for directing my attention to this important manuscript).

French; his name is French, and he was employed on an embassy to the count of Montpellier. Several other bishops have French names, and though this is not necessarily an indication of French birth it is worth listing them: Giraldo of Salamanca (appointed 1120), Roberto of Astorga (1131), Esteban (*Stephanus*) of Zamora (1150) and his nephew and successor Guillermo (*Guillelmus*, 1175), Arnaldo I and Arnaldo II of Coria (1181, 1198–9), Giraldo of Coria (1212). Bernardo of Sigüenza-Compostela belonged to what may be called a French episcopal dynasty, for his uncle was bishop of Segovia and his brother bishop of Palencia, while his nephew succeeded him at Sigüenza. It is worth remarking again, in this context, that the see of Zamora was in the hands of a single family whose traceable members all had French names for most of the second half of the century (1150–93). It is but rarely that we hear from what part of France these men came. Jerónimo and the two Bernardos brought to Spain by Bernardo of Toledo, came from the Périgord-Agenais area of south-western France, which was his own homeland. Pedro Seguin of Orense may have come from Poitou. Of the origins of the others we know nothing.

These facts—and speculations—should be considered against the background of an influx of Frenchmen into Spain in the eleventh and twelfth centuries, already alluded to in chapter 1. We note first that all the appointments of 'certain' Frenchmen occurred during the first half of the century, and most of the appointments of 'probable' Frenchmen too. Alfonso VII, in particular, seems to have been a great promoter of Frenchmen to bishoprics, in the Leonese half of his dominions as in the Castilian. In Castile the sees of Burgos, Osma, Palencia and Tarazona each received at least one French bishop during his reign, Segovia and Toledo at least two, and Sigüenza three. This is broadly speaking in accordance with the findings of Défourneaux, who argued that French participation in Spanish affairs slackened after the middle of the century. We cannot, indeed, be absolutely certain that a single Frenchmen was appointed under Fernando II or Alfonso IX. Second, these appointments were all—with the single exception of Pedro Seguin of Orense—to bishoprics which included lands where French *repobladores* had settled (e.g. Salamanca, Zamora, Coria) or which lay on the pilgrimage road to Santiago de Compostela (e.g. Astorga, Lugo), along which so many Frenchmen travelled and in whose towns so many of them made their homes. In contrast no Frenchman seems ever to have been appointed to the remoter, and poorer, sees like Tuy or Mondoñedo.

Frenchmen were not the only foreigners to try their luck in León. Lombardo of Ciudad Rodrigo may have been an Italian. It is just possible that he got a foothold in Spain as the result of a papal provision.[1] Navarro of Coria-Salamanca looks like a native of Navarre. Berengar of Salamanca-Compostela may have been a Catalan. Manrique of León was a Castilian. Isidoro and Beltrán, both of Tuy, were possibly natives of Portugal. The small numbers of these other foreigners serves mainly to give greater prominence to the French. But the total numbers should remind us that Spain in general and León-Castile and Portugal[2] in particular, was seen as a land of opportunity in the twelfth century—and that not only for secular churchmen; French monks were flocking to Spain in large numbers and rising to positions of importance in Spanish monasteries. One wonders how many ambitious Spanish clerics found their hopes of preferment dashed by the promotion over their heads of a foreigner. Our sources do not tell us, of course, but one would not be surprised to learn that there was some resentment.

Eight of the bishops of the kingdom of León during the century were regular religious.[3] Four were black monks: Jerónimo again (appointed 1102), Pelayo I of Mondoñedo (1136), Juan of Lugo (1152) and Pedro of Oviedo (1156). Two were Cistercians: Pedro Cristiano of Astorga (1153) and Suero of Coria (1156). Two were Augustinian canons: Navarro of Coria and later of Salamanca (1142) and Pedro Gudestéiz of Mondoñedo-Compostela (1155). One of these

---

[1] We have seen that he might have held an archdeaconry in the diocese of Salamanca (above, p. 37), and we know of provisions to Salamanca in the late twelfth and early thirteenth centuries (below, p. 216). But this is a long shot.
[2] Where there were several French bishops and where the first bishop of Lisbon was an Englishman, Gilbert of Hastings.
[3] Of course, bishops might retire into religion, (e.g. Nuño Alfonso of Mondoñedo) but I am here concerned only with their lives before they reached the episcopate.

appointments fell under Alfonso VI, none under Urraca, seven under Alfonso VII, none under Fernando II (though he did promote his old tutor from Mondoñedo to Compostela) and none under Alfonso IX. Five of Alfonso VII's appointments of regulars fell in the last few years of his reign, when he was an old and ailing man[1] perhaps specially concerned to appoint those as bishops who were best placed to provide intercession for his soul. The high number of appointments of regulars in his reign generally may go some way to explain his good posthumous reputation with monastic chroniclers like Lucas of Tuy. It is interesting to note that within thirteen years of the arrival of the Cistercians in the kingdom of León two of their number had been promoted to the episcopate. It is interesting too, and in keeping with the trend elsewhere in Europe that the last forty years of the century should have seen no promotions of regulars to the episcopate.

Royal servants or associates, curial bishops, formed at all periods of the century a far higher proportion of the episcopate than either of the groups hitherto considered. Those who worked in the royal household and chancery are most easily identified as royal servants; and we may extend the group by including those who performed special tasks for a ruler (e.g. going on diplomatic missions) or who were spoken of by him in terms of warm approbation such as to suggest a close relationship of service and trust. Thus, for instance, Berengar of Salamanca and later of Compostela was Alfonso VII's chancellor in 1134–5; Arnaldo I of Astorga served on diplomatic missions in 1146; Fernando II of Astorga was fulsomely praised by King Fernando II. Bishops who fall into one of these three categories number twenty-three out of seventy-seven appointments to bishoprics made in the course of the century.

This figure, of nearly one-third of all appointments, is a remarkably high one—and we should do well in this context to bear in mind both the generally meagre nature of the sources

---

[1] Towards the end of his life his state of health was on at least one occasion sufficiently alarming to be recorded in the dating-clause of a royal charter: 'in illa serra de Secobia quando ibi imperator infirmitate detemptus (*sic*) iacuit. . .mense iunio post festum beati Iohannis', AHD León, Fondo de Gradefes, no. 80, a charter of 1156.

at our disposal, and the scraps of more tenuous evidence for connecting some other bishops with royal circles. Of eight episcopal appointments in Urraca's reign, three went to curialists; eight out of thirty-three under Alfonso VII; nine or perhaps ten out of twenty-four under Fernando II; and one or perhaps two out of seventeen in Alfonso IX's reign down to 1215. These figures have to be treated with caution: all too frequently we do not know exactly when appointments were made, nor can we be certain which ruler (if any) was promoting a candidate at any particular moment—Alfonso VII might have had a hand in some of Urraca's later appointments, the young Fernando II in some of his father's later Galician appointments. Nevertheless it does seem to be broadly true to say that Urraca and Fernando II were more ready to reward their servants with bishoprics than either Alfonso VII or Alfonso IX. No fewer than five ex-chancellors and at least two royal notaries received bishoprics under Fernando II, and it was another ex-chancellor, Fernando Curialis, whom the king tried to substitute for Archbishop Martín of Compostela in the 1160s. It is sufficiently clear that, as in other areas of Europe at the same date, service to the crown was the high road to ecclesiastical preferment.

Service to the crown did not end with promotion to the episcopate, far from it. There is plentiful evidence that bishops, like other great men, were bound to provide troops for service in the royal army, and indeed to serve in person. That they both were required to, and disliked it, is evidenced by the fact that they condemned the practice at the council of Palencia in 1129:[1] but there is no evidence that the kings paid any attention to this condemnation. Diego Gelmírez in 1113 secured from Queen Urraca an exemption from serving personally, though he was still required to send his knights (*milites*) to serve *more solito*; and he did himself serve on at least three later occasions.[2] Bishops served on the Almería campaign of 1147.[3] Bishop Juan of León referred casually to military service, *quando episcopus ibat in fossato*, in an act

---

[1] *HC* pp. 485–6.
[2] *HC* pp. 169, 249–50, 446, 586.
[3] *CAI, Poema de Almería*, lines 361–3.

of 1165.[1] Charter evidence reveals that Archbishop Pedro Suárez served on the Jérez campaign of 1176 and that Rodrigo of Oviedo served at the siege of Cáceres in 1184.[2] Likewise it strongly suggests that other bishops served at least from time to time; we might instance Bernardo of Zamora, Pelayo Menéndez of Tuy, Pelayo of Mondoñedo and Ordoño of Salamanca.[3] Unhappily we have no evidence about how the performance of service was organized—how quotas were fixed (let alone what they were), how long the annual period of service was, whether the custom of taking a money payment (*fonsadera*) by way of commutation was commonly adopted.

We find bishops performing other services which may be called in a general sense administrative and political. It is clear that the king looked to his bishops to perform certain functions which were a necessary part of the business of government, and it must be supposed that this consideration was not lost sight of when episcopal appointments were being made. They acted as royal judges; we find four bishops hearing a land-plea between the monasteries of Antealtares and Melón in 1161 on the orders of Fernando II.[4] As *pesquisadores* they conducted royal inquisitions, as did Bernardo of Zamora in 1149.[5] They assisted in royal schemes of resettlement (*repoblación*) of reconquered territories.[6] Episcopal lordship of towns, which could be troublesome as well as profitable, relieved the crown of onerous administrative responsibilities—for the towns of Santiago de Compostela, Tuy, Orense, Lugo and (for varying periods of time) Oviedo, Ciudad Rodrigo and Coria. If many bishops-to-be served in the royal chancery before their promotion, some did so afterwards; Nuño Alfonso of Mondoñedo is an example.[7] We have already seen them going on embassies—to the papal curia, to the king of Aragon, to the princes of southern France—and

[1] AC León, no. 1413.
[2] *GRF* pp. 453, 495, 498.
[3] AC Zamora, leg. 8, nos. 6, 8; leg. 14, no. 24: AC Tuy 1/7: *GRF* p. 370.
[4] AHN cód. 324B, fol. 239.
[5] *LFH* IV, p. 238, n.2 and ap. xviii, pp. 49–50.
[6] AC Salamanca, no. 18 (Navarro of Salamanca).
[7] Above, p. 63.

preaching recruiting sermons for royal military campaigns. They tended to support their king against the pope; and if they didn't, they suffered, like Juan of Oviedo.

Leonese government finance during the twelfth century is wrapped in almost impenetrable obscurity. It seems reasonably clear, however, that rulers exacted a proportion of their revenues from the episcopal sees of their kingdom, at least in a sporadic way, by fair means or foul. The foul were, predictably, straightforward spoliations: in times of war when pressed for money, or simply as a punitive measure; Urraca was several times guilty of the first, while the second is instanced in Fernando II's treatment of the see of Tuy in 1170 or Alfonso IX's of that of Astorga in 1189–90. The fair consisted of the invocation of certain rights which gave a veneer of legality to the business of royal exactions; regalian rights during vacancies and the right to receive hospitality or dues in lieu thereof from the bishoprics. The exercise of regalian right at the see of Compostela is well-attested.[1] That it was widely invoked at least towards the latter end of the century, presumably by the impecunious Fernando II, is suggested by the general renunciation of it which Alfonso IX was compelled to make in 1194, and compelled to make again in 1208.[2] Hospitality is a darker matter: yet, once more in the reign of Alfonso IX, we find bishops trying to escape from it or to reduce its burden; Bishop Manrique of León, significantly enough, twice thought it worth his while to seek exemption from rendering hospitality to his king.[3]

The signs are that the king found his bishops useful. They may have found him indispensable. His power protected their endowments; his authority gave effect to their decisions. As the drafter of one of Alfonso VII's charters observed, rule over the churches had been entrusted to the king by God.[4] As far as we can see, the Leonese bishops acquiesced. There was ònly one serious battle between 'church' and 'state' during the century, the quarrel between Fernando II and

---

[1] *HC* pp. 464–5, and the article referred to above, p. 58, n. 4.
[2] *GAL* nos. 84, 221.
[3] *GAL* nos. 33, 190, and cf. also no. 237.
[4] T.Minguella y Arnedo, *Historia de la diócesis de Sigüenza y de sus obispos* (Madrid, 1910), I, ap. xxxi, p. 386.

Archbishop Martín of Compostela in the years 1160–7;[1] Martín's episcopal colleagues seem to have shown precious little support for him. When kings got into trouble for marrying within the prohibited degrees they could usually rely upon their bishops to back them up.

Willingness to acquiesce may have been caused by self-interest; to it may also have contributed the strands that went into a bishop's social, moral, and intellectual constitution. It is not easy to discover much about the social origins of the bishops, for the simple reason that it is curiously rare to learn their patronymics. Since in the absence of local chronicles the historian relies heavily on the evidence of patronymics in tracing family connections, it is very difficult indeed to discover anything about the relatives of the bishops and thus to make any reliable inferences about the social background of the episcopate. We might have made a guess about Bishop Manrique of León's distinguished family connections on the basis of his name, for it was common in the Lara family, rare elsewhere. But we learn of them solely through the survival of a document which records a loan he made to his sister, the wife of Count Armengol VIII of Urgel, in 1182;[2] in this document the sister's full name is mentioned, Elvira Pérez de Lara. So slender are the threads by which our knowledge hangs.

When we are in a position to learn anything, we usually find that the bishops were men of some standing in society. Occasionally they were of the highest social rank, like Gonzalo of Mondoñedo or Manrique of León. Sometimes they were of distinguished but less exalted birth, like Jimeno Eriz of Astorga or Pelayo Menéndez of Tuy. Sometimes they were not much more than well-to-do and well-connected, like Diego Gelmírez or Juan Albertino of León. We never hear of men who were raised up from nothing to the episcopate.

It is a little surprising to find so few of the members of the higher nobility of León occupying bishoprics. The Traba family was big; its members basked in the sun of royal favour throughout the century; yet its only venture into the

---

[1] Cf. above, p. 58.
[2] AC León, no. 1437.

episcopate came with Gonzalo's long tenure of the see of Mondoñedo. The fact that Manrique of León became blind should alert us to the possibility, it can be no more, that a career was found for him in the church because a physical defect, failing eyesight, rendered him unfit for the life of a secular nobleman. Certainly his family showed as little interest in acquiring bishoprics in Castile as did the Traba in León. Was the aristocracy uninterested because the bishoprics were on the whole (as we shall see later) rather poor? Or was the royal hold so strong that aristocrats were excluded, passed over in favour of the incoming Frenchmen or the ubiquitous chancery servants? Arguments could be marshalled to support either of these possibilities, but they would be rather a display of ingenuity than any real advancement of our understanding. We may be nearer an answer when historians address themselves to that most urgent of *desiderata*, a study of the Spanish nobility in the early Middle Ages.

None of the bishops seems to have been remarkable for intellectual attainments. The schools of western Spain were undistinguished until the rise of Salamanca in the second half of the century. The French bishops seem to have come mainly from the south-west of France, not from the intellectually precocious north and east. Pelayo of Oviedo was a man of antiquarian interests who put his learning—and his invention—at the service of his see. (Would he have bothered if that see's position had not been threatened?). Diego Gelmírez knew some canon law. He could quote the phrase, a little later to be so notorious, *Non iudicabitur bis in idipsum*, and there were some canon law texts at Compostela in his day.[1] The canonical collection known as *Polycarpus* was dedicated to him.[2] But he cannot be called a scholar; nor can those who came after him, of whom we may be reasonably certain that they were not unacquainted with the canon law, like Pedro Suárez de Deza or Martín I of Zamora. (The two latter, along with Navarro of Coria-Salamanca and perhaps Pedro Seguin of Orense, were *magistri*.) Apart from Pedro Suárez there was not a single theologian among the bishops, nor a

---

[1] *HC* pp. 361, 380.
[2] *LFH* III, ap. xxix, pp. 83–4.

single patron of theological studies. In the sources at our disposal there are strikingly few references to learning among Leonese churchmen. This serves to confirm the impression of general mediocrity which is forced upon us by the records of the Leonese episcopate in the twelfth century. These records, we must reiterate, are singularly meagre. Yet even when every allowance is made for this, it has to be said that there is never a moment between 1100 and 1215 when we may say of the Leonese episcopate, taken as a whole, that it formed a distinguished body of men—as Dom David Knowles could justly say of Becket's episcopal colleagues in England. But this is to anticipate. We must let the bishops speak for themselves. In so far as they speak to us at all, they do so through their *acta*.

3

EPISCOPAL ACTA

The *acta* which have come down to us from the sees of León are few, and the incidence of survival is uneven. The lesser bishoprics have left us very few indeed: we have only one from Coria, two from Ciudad Rodrigo, seven from Orense, twelve from Tuy, thirteen from Mondoñedo. Some of the more important bishoprics have produced almost as few: there are only nine from Salamanca, ten from Astorga, and sixteen from Oviedo. The greatest see has left us, appropriately, the largest number of *acta*; we have fifty from Santiago de Compostela. Zamora and Lugo are close behind, with forty-eight and forty-five respectively, while from León there are thirty-six.[1] This paucity of documents is thrown into relief by comparison with the state of affairs in England. The *acta* of the bishops of Chichester between 1075 and 1207 run to over 150.[2] Archbishop Theobald of Canterbury has left us over 300.[3] Gilbert Foliot's *acta*, as bishop of Hereford and London, number 187,[4] Stephen Langton's as archbishop of Canterbury 143.[5] This shortage of *acta* from the Leonese sees is in itself interesting. Of course much material may have perished accidentally. Thus, for instance, the archives of the cathedral of Astorga were almost completely destroyed by fire in 1810. Again, Spanish care for records has been, and unfortunately too often still is, extraordinarily slovenly. Yet even when every allowance has been made it remains true that Leonese bishops, and indeed Spanish bishops generally,

---

[1] In the thesis upon which this book is based, Appendix II, pp. 385–426, there may be found a complete catalogue of the *acta* whose characteristics will be discussed in this chapter. It is too long to be included in the present work.

[2] *The Acta of the Bishops of Chichester, 1075–1207,* ed. H. Mayr-Harting (Canterbury and York Society, vol. cxxx, 1962).

[3] A. Saltman, *Theobald, Archbishop of Canterbury* (London, 1956).

[4] *The Letters and Charters of Gilbert Foliot,* ed. C.N.L. Brooke and A. Morey (Cambridge, 1967).

[5] *Acta Stephani Langton,* ed. K. Major (Canterbury and York Society, vol. l, 1950).

did not produce the sheer volume of documents that marks the work of their contemporaries in twelfth-century England.[1]

A good many of the surviving *acta* have come down to us in cartulary or other copies. Only thirteen of the fifty *acta* from Compostela are originals. We have only three originals from Mondoñedo, only four from Orense, five from Tuy and six from Astorga. On the other hand, at least twenty-nine of León's thirty-six are originals; the same number of originals comes from Zamora; and at least thirty-four of Lugo's forty-five are originals. This shortage of original documents seriously diminishes the value of the lessons which can be learnt from a diplomatic and palaeographical study of the *acta*.

Where documents, especially original documents, are scarce, and where the basic task of studying their diplomatic has never before been attempted, it is notoriously hard to detect any but the most impudent forgeries. It may be that as an explorer in uncharted territory I have been too credulous of what I found there: further study alone will tell. We have no formularies to guide us from this period, and the reader who has made his way through the preceding chapter will know how pathetically little we know of these bishops and their doings. But we have to take the evidence as we find it. And we must try first of all to discover something about the human context in which these documents are produced.

THE BISHOP'S HOUSEHOLD

It is in the episcopal household that we must start. The *Historia Compostellana* at one point speaks of Diego Gelmírez as being accompanied on one of his journeys by his *clerici, milites et famuli*,[2] and this rough and ready classification, implied in many other passages of the *Historia*, provides us with a starting-point. His *famuli* and *milites* need not detain us. We hear enough about them to be sure that Leonese bishops, like their contemporaries elsewhere, had large lay contingents in their households. Our principal concern is with

---

[1] I am greatly indebted, in this chapter, to those who have worked on English *acta*, in particular to F.M. Stenton, 'Acta Episcoporum', *Cambridge Historical Journal* iii (1929), 1-14; to C.R. Cheney, *English Bishops' Chanceries 1100–1250* (Manchester, 1950); and to the works mentioned in the four preceding notes.
[2] *HC* p. 329.

the *clerici*. On the analogy with the experience of twelfth-century bishops in England we should expect to find that in the earlier part of the century the clerks of a bishop's 'household' were the archdeacons of his diocese, the canons and dignitaries of his cathedral, and any other clerks or chaplains of his own choice. The bishop, in short, transacted business in and with his cathedral chapter. Later on, we should expect to see the emergence of a compact group of trained clerks, professionals equipped to deal with a larger volume and a greater complexity of business, who formed a household distinct from the cathedral clergy; while the men who made up the latter body gradually disappeared from the witness-lists of the bishop's charters. It has been claimed that such an evolution may be detected in the Castilian bishopric of Palencia during the episcopate of Ramón, who occupied the see from 1148 to 1184.[1] Can we trace a similar process in León?

An account of an early episcopal *familia* is to be found in what Rodrigo Ximénez de Rada has to tell us about the young men whom Bernardo of Toledo brought to Spain in 1096-7.[2] It falls a little outside the geographical scope of this book, though several of these men succeeded to positions of importance in the Leonese church—Jerónimo of Salamanca-Avila-Zamora, Bernardo of Zamora, Bernardo bishop of Sigüenza and archbishop of Compostela. To them we may add Geraldo archbishop of Braga; Maurice Bourdin, bishop of Coimbra, archbishop of Braga, and finally the Emperor Henry V's antipope Gregory VIII; Raimundo, bishop of Osma and archbishop of Toledo; and the three Pedros, bishops of Osma, Palencia and Segovia. All of these men became canons, dignitaries or archdeacons of the cathedral church of Toledo before their promotion to the episcopate. In no sense did they form a separate episcopal household.

Of far greater importance for our purposes is the material contained in the *Historia Compostellana*. When Diego Gelmírez acquired the see of Compostela in 1100 he at once took up the task of reorganizing the chapter which had been started by bishop Diego Peláez (1070–88). He established the

[1] D.W. Lomax, 'Don Ramón, bishop of Palencia (1148–84)', in *Homenaje a Jaime Vicens Vives,* ed. J. Maluquer de Motes I (Barcelona, 1965), 279–91.
[2] Rodrigo, *De Rebus Hispaniae,* VI, 26–7.

number of canons at seventy-two, and on 22 April 1102 he
took their oaths of obedience to him. Their names are recorded in the *Historia Compostellana*, thus giving us a complete list of the canons of Compostela in the early years of
the century.[1] Some of these men were inherited by Diego
from his predecessors. The archdeacon Juan, for example, is
presumably to be identified with Archdeacon Juan Rodríguez,
traceable from 1087 onwards. He subscribed an episcopal act
of 1101: we also find him, in the company of his bishop, at
the royal court at Burgos in 1107. We hear no more of him
after about 1108.[2] But several of these canons were men
chosen by Diego himself, whose help he wanted in his schemes
for the betterment of his church, and upon whose loyalty he
hoped he could rely.[3] Some of them we have already met,
like Nuño Alfonso who acquired the see of Mondoñedo in
1112, or Pedro Helias, who succeeded Diego at Compostela
in 1143. We can discover something of several others, and it
will be instructive to examine the careers of some of them.

Another who later acquired a bishopric was Hugo, bishop
of Porto from 1113 to 1136. Perhaps a native of the town of
Compostela, and certainly brought up with (*secum*) Diego
Gelmírez, he was by 1102 a canon and *capellanus* of Compostela. Diego Gelmírez employed him on at least four occasions as an envoy to the papal curia, twice before he became
bishop of Porto and twice afterwards. He was one of the authors of the *Historia Compostellana*. We know too that he
accompanied Diego on his celebrated 'visitation' of the properties of the see of Compostela at Braga, when the relics of
St. Fructuosus were removed to Santiago de Compostela.[4]
Another among the canons who served Diego as an emissary
to the popes was Pedro Fulco, who acted in this capacity on
at least five and probably six occasions between 1119 and

---

[1] *HC* pp. 56-7.
[2] For Juan Rodríguez, see *LFH* III, ap. iv, pp. 28-30; ap. xvi, pp. 52-3; ap. xxiii,
pp. 70-3: *HC* p. 73. He had visited the papal curia in 1099, presumably at the
bidding of Diego Gelmírez, who was then in charge of the vacant see of Compostela: *Docs. Oviedo* no. 121.
[3] For his misgivings about their loyalty—some of which were later proved all too
correct—see *HC* p. 55.
[4] For Hugo, see *HC* pp. 28, 34, 39, 42, 56, 145, 202, 252, 280-1.

1135.[1] He evidently did his work well, for Diego granted him lands and a church 'in pheodum. . .quia ipse cardinalis in eius servitio et in itinere Romano multum et fideliter laboraverat', and Innocent II twice singled him out for praise.[2] Pedro Fulco evidently made a speciality of negotiating with the popes. But his master's relations with the curia were close, and several other canons of the original creation were used in the same task.[3] Both Hugo and Pedro Fulco appear in the subscription lists to Diego's *acta*, Hugo in 1115 and Pedro Fulco in 1122.[4]

Nuño Gelmírez, the bishop's brother, was a canon in 1102 and later became treasurer of the cathedral. He is also described as the bishop's *clericus*. He went on a mission to Paschal II in 1101, but his true bent seems to have been for secular business, for he appears frequently in the *Historia* in a military context. He subscribed an episcopal act of 1115.[5] Pedro Astruárez, a canon in 1102, subscribed *acta* of 1113, 1115 and 1122. Diego employed him on a fund-raising mission to Apulia and Sicily in 1124.[6] Pedro *iudex* of the 1102 list is probably identical with Pedro Daniéliz, who held that office between 1090 and at least 1122.[7] He subscribed *acta* of 1113, 1115 and 1122, and is probably to be identified with the Pedro *iudex* who was sent on a mission to Queen Urraca in 1119.[8]

This, however, is to speak only of those who were canons of Santiago de Compostela in 1102. There were others of Diego's closest *familiares* who entered the cathedral chapter later on. Geraldo, for example, does not appear as a member of the chapter until 1118, though it is probable that he had become a canon a few years earlier. He was a Frenchman,

---

[1] *HC* pp. 290, 394, 441–2, 490, 509.
[2] *HC* pp. 441, 511, 567.
[3] E.g. Archdeacon Geoffrey, four times between 1101 and 1110 (*HC* pp. 31, 44, 79, 84–5); Pelayo Díaz, sent in 1125–6 (*HC* p. 441).
[4] *LFH* III, ap. xxxiii, pp. 97–104; *HC* p. 378.
[5] For Nuño Gelmírez, see *HC* pp, 30, 56, 66, 100–1, 105, 110, 111, 133, 169, 329, 330; *LFH* III, ap. xxxiii, pp. 97–104.
[6] For Pedro Astruárez, see *HC* 56, 378, 401; *LFH* III, ap. xxxiii, pp. 97–104; AHRG, Documentos Particulares, San Payo de Antealtares, no. 27.
[7] *LFH* III, ap. v. p. 33; AHN 512/9. His office carried responsibility for the administration of the town of Santiago de Compostela.
[8] *HC* p. 279 (277).

very probably a native of Beauvais, and the most prolific of
the authors of the *Historia Compostellana*. Diego employed
him twice on missions to the papal curia, in 1118 and 1119,
and he subscribed one of Diego's *acta* in 1122. The frankly
and sometimes fanatically partisan attitude he adopted towards Diego in the *Historia* shows us, if proof were needed,
that he was a trusted intimate of his master.[1]

It would be easy, though tedious, to multiply examples.
These were the men who formed the 'household' of Diego
Gelmírez. They subscribed his *acta*. They served on missions
to popes and kings. They recorded his *gesta* for posterity.
They led troops and garrisoned castles for him. Time and
time again, as the *Historia* tells us, they provided him with
counsel. And all the more important of them were canons,
dignitaries or archdeacons of his cathedral church. There was
no sharp distinction between household and cathedral chapter.

We know far more about the see of Compostela than we
do about any other in the kingdom of León. But what evidence we do have suggests that similar arrangements prevailed
elsewhere. In the *Libro Gótico*, the cathedral cartulary of
Oviedo whose preparation was sponsored by Bishop Pelayo,
Pope Paschal II is figured in one of the illustrations as
handing the solemn privilege of exemption granted in 1105
to one Ivo *magister*.[2] (The name, which is extremely rare in
Spanish documents, must indicate a Frenchman.) It can
hardly be doubted that this man is identical with the archdeacon Ivo who appears in Oviedo documents of about the
same date, and who subscribed an episcopal act of 1117.[3]
Here we have the same combination as we found at Compostela—an archdeacon who witnesses *acta* and is employed by
his bishop on important missions to the papal curia. We find
exactly the same combination at a rather later date. Archdeacon Tomás of León subscribed five of Bishop Juan's *acta*
and one of Bishop Manrique's.[4] Manrique employed him on

---

[1] For Geraldo, see *HC* 214, 265, 274 (272), 297, 373, 378, 456, 462.
[2] AC Oviedo, Libro Gótico, fol. 83^r.
[3] *Docs. Oviedo*, no. 138.
[4] AC León nos. 1413, 1416, 1420, 1422, 1426, 1434. The first of these has been
printed by C. Sánchez Albornoz, *Estudios sobre las Instituciones Medievales
Españolas* (Mexico City, 1965), pp. 313-4; the last in *AHDE* xxv (1955), 92-3.

a mission to the papal curia in 1181.[1]

It is only occasionally that we can discover how bishops communicated with distant popes and kings, whom they sent to conduct their negotiations for them. How did Pedro of Lugo get his papal privileges of 1123 and 1131?[2] He may have sent *familiares*. He may have gone in person—though he can hardly have gone unaccompanied; and we have no record of his attendance at the councils, Lateran II and Rheims, which were being held when the bulls were issued. What we can say, however, is that the men who are likely to have performed this sort of task are also those whose names appear in the witness-lists to episcopal *acta*. A few examples will suffice. A charter of this same Bishop Pedro of Lugo, dated 19 March 1132,[3] is subscribed by four cathedral dignitaries, a *capellanus* (of the bishop?), *omnes canonici*, three prominent local laymen, and *omnes burgenses*. An act of Bishop Pelayo of Mondoñedo, dated 1143, is subscribed by two dignitaries, three archdeacons, and a *presbiter*.[4] An act of Bishop Alo of Astorga of 10 April 1129 is witnessed by a cathedral dignitary and four archpriests.[5] The magnificent charter of Bishop Diego of León dated 8 January 1116 is subscribed by, among many others, the prior of the chapter, three archdeacons, and *ceteri archidiaconi et canonici*.[6] When Bishop Diego of Orense granted a *fuero* to the townsmen of Orense in about 1122, his charter was subscribed by five archdeacons, two priests and two other witnesses who were probably members of the chapter.[7] A grant made by Bishop Pelayo Menéndez of Tuy to the monastery of Oya in 1145 was witnessed by a cathedral dignitary, three archdeacons, three named canons and *omnis conventus canonicorum*, and seven important local laymen.[8]

[1] Referred to in AC León 1434 (see preceding note): 'pro expensis quas magister Thomas fecerat Rome'. Tomás is also called *magister* in private charters: AHN 1690/14, AC León 1419.
[2] AC Lugo, leg.3, no. 2; Libro de Bulas Apostólicas, no. 1.
[3] Printed below, pp. 118-9.
[4] AC Mondoñedo, carpeta del siglo XII, unnumbered.
[5] AHN cód. 1197B, fols. 253r-255r.
[6] AC León no. 1362, indifferently edited *ES* XXXVI, ap. xlvi, pp. c–ciii.
[7] AC Orense, Privilegios I/1, ptd. *Colección de Fueros Municipales y Cartas Pueblas*, ed. T. Múñoz y Romero (Madrid, 1847), I, 499-500.
[8] AHN cód. 60 B, fols. 2r, 136r, ptd. *ES* XXII, ap. xi, pp. 269-70.

Enough has by now been said to show that throughout the kingdom of León during the first half of the century the bishop's household in the strict sense of the term did not exist. This is exactly what we should expect to find. Did a household in the stricter sense emerge in the second half of the century? Such evidence as there is suggests that such an evolution did not occur. Let us look first of all at the bishopric of Lugo. From two documents drawn up late in 1194 and early in 1195 we can piece together a list which is probably complete of the names of those who made up the cathedral chapter at that time.[1] An unusually informative private charter of 1213 furnishes us with the names of some at least of those who had been canons in 1194-5 and who were still living eighteen years later.[2] We have twenty-two *acta* from the diocese of Lugo for the period 1195-1216, for seventeen of which we have witness-lists. Study of these lists shows conclusively that members of the cathedral chapter were still witnessing the bishop's *acta*. Lope, precentor of the cathedral, who spanned the period, subscribed no less than twelve of them. Juan, a *iudex*, who may have died in 1214, subscribed eight. Juan the dean, who died between 1213 and 1216, subscribed six: one of the archdeacons, yet another Juan, four. Among the canons who were still alive in 1213 or later, Pelayo Baldouini witnessed five, Fernando Ovéquiz four, Juan Rolán three and Pelayo Sebastiani also three. Reginald, a canon who cannot be traced later than 1204, subscribed four. Of those who appear for the first time in the Lugo records after 1194-5, two archdeacons witnessed four *acta* each, and another witnessed three.

The same state of affairs is revealed by the records of the diocese of Zamora. In a document relating to the dispute over the metropolitan loyalties of Zamora we have a list of some of the canons of the cathedral towards the end of the century:[3]

---

[1] AHN 1334/7, ptd. *ES* XLI, ap. xxiii, pp. 341-3; AHN 1241/4 and 1326A/14, ptd. ibid., ap. xxiv, pp. 344-8.
[2] AHN 1326G/1.
[3] AD Braga, Liber Fidei, no. 732, fol. 196^V.

Isti sunt qui sciunt quando Zamorensis episcopus bone memorie Guilel-
mus fuit consecratus a Lucensi et cum Legionensi et Ovetensi episcopis,
de mandato domni Iohannis Bracarensis archiepiscopi. Domnus Mames.
Iohannes Didaci. Monio Longus. Martinus Constancius. Raimundus.
archidiaconus domnus Stephanus. et Aldouinus. et magister Rodericus.
. . .'

Now most of these men were frequent witnesses of episcopal
acta in the period *c*.1180–*c*.1210. Mames, canon and later
magister scolarum subscribed six; Juan Díaz, four; Munio
Longus, five; Martín Constancius, three; Raimundo, only one;
Archdeacon Esteban, at least eight; Aldouinus, three; Mr.
Rodrigo, three. Another canon, Pedro García, not in the
above list, subscribed six. Several more canons subscribed one
or two *acta*.

From León, Bishop Juan (1139–81) has left us sixteen
acta, all but one of which have witness-lists. Archdeacons
were frequent witnesses. Archdeacon Arias subscribed nine
out of the fifteen, Fernando and Hugo eight each, Tomás five
(as we have already seen) and Gozelmo three, Martín and
Albertino only one each. Equally frequent were the cathedral
dignitaries and the ordinary canons. Mr. Enrique, the dean,
subscribed nine. Pedro Gutiérrez, the precentor, subscribed
three; his successor Albertino, five. Bermudo, who held the
office of *magister scolarum* or cathedral chancellor, subscribed three. Mere canons are not easy to distinguish from
laymen but there does seem, nearly always, to be a sprinkling
of them in most of the witness-lists. What is true of Bishop
Juan's *acta* is also true of those of his successor Manrique
(1181–1205). Exactly the same sort of witness-lists are
found, a mixture of archdeacons, dignitaries, canons, laymen
and episcopal *clerici*, right up to, and beyond, the end of
Manrique's episcopate. The point needs no demonstration in
detail here, but may be readily appreciated by study of *acta*
of July 1203 and January 1206.[1]

The abundant *acta* from the Compostela of Archbishop
Pedro Suárez (1173–1206) tell the same tale. In one of 1194
we find the dean, the precentor, three archdeacons, five

---

[1] AC León no. 1428, ptd. below, Appendix no. XXX: AC León no. 1474, ptd. *ES*
XXXVI, ap. lxi, pp. cxxxi–cxxxii.

cardinals, and no fewer than twenty-three of the canons.[1] In one of 1204, there appear the names of the dean, the precentor, an archdeacon, a cardinal and a canon.[2] In another of 1204 we find the dean, four archdeacons, the *magister scolarum*, a cardinal, a *iudex*, and four canons.[3]

It may be objected that the evidence cited hitherto does not adequately prove the argument being advanced, namely that there are no signs of any distinction between episcopal household and resident cathedral chapter. Why should a bishop having the right to collate to dignities and prebends not have regularly rewarded his own special servants with these offices and perquisites? After all, it was the cheapest means of payment available to a needy bishop. Even supposing, however, that we had far fuller resources of information available, it would still be difficult to show that what we are witnessing in these documents is the practice by which bishops rewarded servants with prebends, rather than the practice by which bishops availed themselves of the services of the chapter as a whole. With so little evidence to go on it is clearly out of the question to hope that the argument can be conclusive. A strong impression remains, however, that a distinct household organization, in the sense in which that phrase is used by students of contemporary English ecclesiastical institutions, is not something that one may confidently add to one's mental picture of a Leonese bishop of the later twelfth century.

Of course, bishops did have some advisers and servants who were distinct from their chapters. These men can sometimes be distinguished by their titles, especially when that is *clericus* or *capellanus*. The title *magister* is not necessarily indicative of a close connection with the bishop, though *magistri* were evidently sought after by bishops. We have already met Mr. Ivo at Oviedo and Mr. Tomás at León—both of them archdeacons—while just across the Castilian frontier Bishop Jaime of Avila commanded the services of *magister*

---

[1] AHN 1334/7, ptd. *ES* XLI, ap. xxiii, pp. 341–3.
[2] AC Zamora, leg. 13, no. 9.
[3] AC Tuy 10/21, ptd. below, Appendix, no. XXXII.

Iohannes capellanus episcopi at the end of the century.[1] At Lugo, Bishop Pedro III referred to *capellanus noster* as early as 1120,[2] though without naming him, and a list may be drawn up of those who bore the title in that diocese during the century—Fernando Bermúdez in the 1160s, Fernando González in 1170, Pedro Yáñez in 1196, Sancho Bermúdez in 1211-12 and García Eriz in 1211-16.[3] There were others also who were entitled merely *capellanus*, without the decisively proprietary word *episcopi*; Anaya in the 1120s, Juan Menéndez in the 1150s, and Pelayo in the 1190s.[4] At León, an act of 1133 was subscribed by Nuño, *capellanus episcopalis curie*, and the same document mentions Pedro *levita episcopi*.[5] At Salamanca, one Juan, *capellanus episcopi Salamantini*, subscribes a private charter of 1171.[6] It may be significant for our enquiry that on the whole it is rather rare for such men to subscribe episcopal *acta*. Bishops had their domestic chaplains, but when business was to be transacted it would seem that they turned to their archdeacons, dignitaries and canons. They did so throughout the century.

THE CHANCERY

There is little evidence of elaborately organized episcopal chanceries in the kingdom of León. This should not surprise us, for the royal chancery was itself a rudimentary affair until well on into the reign of Alfonso VII. Alfonso VI had had *notarii* who wrote or dictated his charters. Under his daughter Urraca an official with the title of *cancellarius* makes an occasional appearance at their head. Alfonso VII continued his mother's practice from his accession in 1126 until 1135. In the latter year the chancellorship was given to Master Hugo, and it was he who was responsible for the standardization and fixing of diplomatic forms, for the introduction of new chancery practices such as the use of the seal, and for

---

[1] AHN 19/7.
[2] AHN cód. 1043B, fols. 49^r-50^r and 50^v, ptd. *ES* XLI, ap. ii, pp. 296-301.
[3] AHN 1325 E/15, 19 bis; 1326A/23; 1326F/2, 12; 1326 G/11, 24; AHN cód. 417B, no. 80.
[4] AHN 1325C/10; 1325D/8, 18, 20; 1325 H/16 bis; 1334/7.
[5] AC León no. 1390, ptd. *ES* XXXVI, ap. liii, pp. cxi-cxiv.
[6] AC Salamanca no. 71.

the training of a team of clerks who perpetuated his influence after his own tenure of the office came to an end in 1151. Developments during the reigns of Fernando II and Alfonso IX grew naturally out of the reforms of Master Hugo, and it was not until the reign of Alfonso X that radical new departures in chancery practice occurred.

Little by little, the higher nobility of León-Castile followed the lead set by their rulers. The Galician count Suero Bermúdez had a *notarius* called Juan who drew up a document for him in 1119.[1] The Castilian count Manrique de Lara had a document written by his *capellanus*, Sebastian, in 1153; by 1156 he was employing one Sancho, who styled himself the count's *cancellarius*.[2] Were the bishops following suit?

Very occasionally, episcopal officials with the title of chancellor appear in our documents.[3] An act from the diocese of Oviedo, dated 19 January 1154, was subscribed by Pedro, chancellor of the bishop of Lugo.[4] The document does not survive in the original, and the possibility of scribal error should not be ruled out (e.g., *cancellarius* for *capell--anus*). The title does not occur again among the Lugo *acta*. These considerations should put us on our guard. It is however quite possible that Pedro the chancellor is to be identified with the otherwise unknown Pedro who wrote four charters for the bishop between 1155 and 1171.[5] From the diocese of Astorga we have a reference in a very late copy. A royal charter dated 19 April 1157, surviving only in a cartulary copy of the eighteenth century, was subscribed by *Facundus canonicus Astoricensis et chancellarius episcopi.*[6] This man is surely to be identified with Facundus, canon of Astorga, the scribe of an episcopal act of 1154.[7] Once more,

---

[1] AHN 1325C/7.

[2] AC Sigüenza, Particulares, no. 9, ptd. T. Minguella, *Historia de la diócesis de Sigüenza y de sus obispos,* (Madrid, 1910), I, ap. xxxvi; L. Sánchez Belda, 'En torno de Tres Diplomas de Alfonso VII', *Hispania* xi (1951), 47–61.

[3] It is worth labouring the point that these men really are episcopal chancellors, and not cathedral chancellors in disguise: the latter title did not exist in the kingdom of León. Cf. below, ch. 4, p. 147.

[4] *Docs. Oviedo* no. 163.

[5] AHN 1325D/11 (ptd. *ES* XLI, ap. xi, pp. 316–318), 1325D/14, 1325E/18, 25.

[6] AHN cód. 1197B, fols. 60^r–62^r.

[7] AHD Astorga (at present displayed in the Museo de la Catedral), ptd. *ES* XVI, ap. xxviii, pp. 484–6.

this is the only occurrence of the title among the Astorgan *acta*.

The evidence from the diocese of Santiago de Compostela is a little fuller. An act of Archbishop Martín of 27 July 1158 carries the scribal subscription *Pelagius de Vizu clericus iussu magistri Petri domni archiepiscopi cancellarii notuit et confirmavit*.[1] A later act of Archbishop Martín, dated 19 December 1164, was subscribed by *Magister Petrus diaconus domni archiepiscopi cancellarius*.[2] An act of his successor Pedro Gudestéiz, of 12 February 1171, bears the subscription of *Ego Petrus prepositus ecclesie beati Iacobi canonicus et domni archiepiscopi cancellarius*.[3] The first two references seem to be to the same man; the third may be to another Pedro. Once more, none of these documents is original. Again, too, these three occurrences of the title are the only ones among the *acta* from Santiago de Compostela.

It is interesting to note that these were the three dioceses in which the episcopal seal first appears as a form of authentication for *acta*, and that it is from precisely this period, in the third quarter of the century, that the earliest seals survive. As we shall see, bishops adopted the use of the seal shortly after the royal chancery had done so, and possibly in imitation of it. Were they copying royal practice as well by giving a title to the man who had the custody of their seal? It is reasonable to assume that they were. What is surprising is that the title is not found again until well on into the thirteenth century.[4] It was a flash in the pan. Were the bishops in question simply experimenting with fancy titles? It may have been so.

The existence of an officer bearing the title of chancellor does not necessarily tell us anything about the drafting and writing of episcopal *acta*. We should look rather to men who can be associated with the production of a given text. There are various ways in which this may be done. Where we have a good crop of *acta* for any period of a few years, issued by

[1] AHN cód. 976B, fols. 14ᵛ–15ʳ.
[2] Ibid., fol. 15.
[3] *LFH* IV, ap. xlv, pp. 111–14.
[4] Cf. the diocese of Pamplona, where an episcopal chancellor makes a similar isolated appearance in an act of 1135: AC Pamplona, no. 180.

the same bishop, to different beneficiaries, but written by the same scribe, we may be confident that this is an episcopal scribe, working for an episcopal 'chancery'. One Pelayo wrote four charters for Bishop Juan of León in the period 1144-68: but his case is easy, for in one of them he describes himself as *episcopi scriba*.[1] Another Leonese scribe was Bermudo, who wrote four, possibly five, documents for the same bishop between 1153 and 1157.[2] Bermudo gives us no indication of any position he may have held in Bishop Juan's household; he may be identical with the Bermudo who was *magister scolarum* of the cathedral in 1165 and 1168,[3] so he was then certainly a member of the chapter, and may already have been a canon in the 1150s. A scribe named Juan wrote both for Bishop Juan and for his successor Manrique.[4] In the diocese of Lugo we have already come across the Pedro who wrote four charters for Bishop Juan between 1155 and 1171.[5] Our earliest two surviving *acta* from Zamora, dated 1133 and 1146 were written by one Pelayo.[6] Two later Zamoran *acta*, of 1182 and 1186, were written by Juan Facundi.[7] A scribe named Hilario wrote an act of Bishop Adán of Orense of 1173, and another of Bishop Alfonso in 1194.[8]

All too often, of course, the scribe's name occurs but once, and we can know nothing about him at all. Such for instance are the Julián who wrote once for Pelayo of Oviedo, the Pedro who wrote for Pelayo of Mondoñedo, the Nuño who wrote for Beltrán of Tuy.[9] And there are many others.

---

[1] León, Archivo de San Isidoro, no. 98 (ptd. *ES* XXXVI, ap. liv, pp. cxv–cxviii); AC León nos. 1400, 1406, 1416.
[2] AC León nos. 1405, 1408, 1415, 1387 (ptd. C. Sánchez Albornoz, *Estudios sobre las Instituciones Medievales Españolas* (Mexico City, 1965), pp. 308-12); AC León no. 1402, (ptd. *Bulletin of the Institute of Historical Research* xlv (1972), 127-8).
[3] AC León nos. 1413, 1416.
[4] AC León nos. 1413, 1434.
[5] See above, p. 98.
[6] AC Zamora, Libro Negro, fol. 15^V (ptd. below, Appendix, no. VII). leg. 13, no. 25 (ptd. *AHDE* vi (1929), 430-32).
[7] AHN 3576/13; AC Zamora leg. 13, no. 41.
[8] AC Orense, Escrituras, XIV/44, 72.
[9] *Docs. Oviedo* no. 146; AC Mondoñedo, carpeta del S.XII, unnumbered; AC Tuy 10/11.

Sometimes, however, the scribes gave themselves some distinctive title which points to their association with the bishop's secretariat, as the Leonese scribe Pelayo, to whom we have just referred, called himself *episcopi scriba.* Thus for example we have Pedro *notarius* and Juan *notarius* in two *acta* from Astorga; Geraldo *notarius* in a Salamancan act; Felix *notarius* in one from Compostela.[1] But even these instances have to be treated with caution for, as we shall see, bishops sometimes employed notaries who were in the service of the urban *concejo*, whom we can but uncertainly, if at all, regard as episcopal servants, and we have no guarantee that the men just enumerated do not fall into that category.

We are on sure ground only when a connection specifically with the bishop is expressed. Arias Martínez, *levita et notarius episcopi* drew up one of the acts of Bishop Diego of León.[2] Pelayo Sebastiánez identifies himself as *canonicus et diaconus, episcopi notarius* at the foot of one of the acts of Rodrigo II of Lugo.[3] Without this unambiguous title, he drafted four other *acta.*[4] Ordoño Michaelez appears a little later as holder of the same office: he wrote eleven charters for Rodrigo II, in four of which he styles himself *episcopi notarius.*[5] Three Zamoran *acta* were drawn up for Bishop Martín by Miguel Rodriguez, *notarius domni M. Zemorensis episcopi.*[6] Our earliest surviving act from Compostela was written by Pedro *abbas Termarum Contines et canonicus sancti Jacobi etiam et notarius domni Didaci presulis.*[7] We find the same elsewhere. In the Castilian diocese of Palencia, to give but one example, Juan *pontificis notarius* wrote for Bishop Pedro in 1127.[8]

Occasionally, we have other evidence apart from the documents themselves to assist us. Diego Bodán, canon of

---

[1] AHN cód. 1197B, fols. 253ʳ-255ʳ; ibid. fols. 335ʳ-338ᵛ; AC Salamanca no. 88; AHN 524/3.
[2] AC León no. 1362 (ptd. *ES* XXXVI, ap. xlvi, pp. c-ciii).
[3] AHN 1241/4 and 1326A/14 (ptd. *ES* XLI, ap. xxiv, pp. 344-8).
[4] AHN 1325H/17; 1326A/1; 1326A/21 and 1506/5; 1326A/22.
[5] AHN 1326D/5, 12, 13, 15, 17, 22; 1326E/16; 1326F/12, 16; AHN cód. 417B, no. 80; AHN 1326G/11. These documents fall between 1202 and 1214.
[6] AC Zamora leg. 13, nos. 10, 14; AC Zamora, Libro Blanco, fol. 166ʳ.
[7] Ptd. *LFH* III, ap. xvi, pp. 52-3; cf. also *HC* pp. 57, 108-9.
[8] Salamanca, Biblioteca de la Universidad, MS. 1964, fol. 11ʳ.

Compostela in 1102 and described as a *clericus* of Diego Gelmírez, was employed by the latter to draw up a chirograph
in 1107-8.[1] Pedro Marcio wrote an act of Archbishop Pelayo
of Compostela. He was one of the canons, and we know of
him as the 'copyist'—by which we should probably understand 'forger'—of the notorious diploma of Ramiro I upon
which rested the claims of Compostela to the *votos de Santiago*.[2]

What is striking about the material which has been quoted
is that in several instances the bishops' scribes and notaries
were members of the cathedral chapters. It may be suspected
that this was so in many of the instances where the scribe is
no more than a name. This is quite consistent with the arguments which have been advanced concerning the bishops'
households. It may be worth pointing out that in the only
source which has something to tell us about episcopal
archives—namely, the *Historia Compostellana*—it is clear that
there was no distinction between the records and valuables of
the bishop and those of the chapter; all alike were kept together in the cathedral treasury.[3] It is difficult to believe that
bishops had 'chanceries', in the sense of distinct establish-
ments staffed by trained and professional officials, who
worked in accordance with their own routines and habits and
traditions.

We have, finally, some evidence for 'external' writing of
episcopal *acta*, by the beneficiary or some other outside
party. It was not unknown for the royal chancery to use the
services of external scribes, even after the reforms of Master
Hugo the chancellor. A grant by Queen Urraca to the monastery of Sahagún in 1116 was written by a monk of that house
iussu abbatis; a charter of Alfonso VII for the church of
Salamanca, dated 3 January 1136, was written by Arsenius,
sancte Marie canonicus et episcopi B. capellanus; when Fernando II granted land to San Vicente de Oviedo in 1159 the

---

[1] *HC* pp. 57, 66. See also M. Suárez and J. Campelo, *La Compostelana* (Santiago
de Compostela, 1950), p. 73, n. 3.
[2] *LFH* II, p. 137. On the forgery and its probable date see T.D. Kendrick, *St.
James in Spain* (London, 1960), especially pp. 196–9.
[3] E.g., *HC* pp. 187, 420, 488, 495.

charter was drawn up by García, a monk of that house.[1] Two
of our episcopal *acta* were certainly drafted by royal scribes
and a third may have been. When Pelayo of Oviedo exchanged
some land with Count Suero Bermúdez in 1117 the charter
recording this was drawn up by Juan, a royal notary.[2] A
grant by Archbishop Martín of Compostela to the monastery
of Sobrado, dated 10 May 1165, was also drawn up by a
royal notary.[3] Palaeographical considerations, and the character of the witness-lists, strongly suggest that a grant by
Bishop Pelayo Menéndez of Tuy, of 1152, was also written
by a royal scribe.[4] It is probable that these were drafted by
royal scribes on the occasion of visits by bishops to the royal
court—yet another suggestion (it cannot be more than this)
that bishops were not accompanied by a trained secretarial
staff of their own.

Another practice is illuminated for us by an act from Tuy.
Bishop Suero of Tuy came to an agreement with the monastery of Osera over disputed churches and tithes, the terms of
which were committed to writing in a document dated 29
January 1213.[5] Now this was drawn up in Ribadabia—*apud
burgum Ripe Avie in ecclesia sancti Genesii*—which is a good
twenty-five miles from Tuy where the resident cathedral
chapter, with its scribal resources, was of course situated.
The scribe of the document, Nuño Menéndez, described himself as *notarius burgi*—the (or a) town notary. The most
probable explanation is that the bishop, lacking his own
secretariat, called on the services of a professional scribe from
Ribadabia hired for the occasion.

Of course any bishop (we might think) could be caught
napping, without his clerks. But this is no isolated example.
In the diocese of Compostela, four of the eight surviving *acta*
of Pedro Suárez for which we know the name of the scribe

---

[1] AHN 893/16; AC Salamanca, no. 8; *GRF* p. 355. The Salamanca charter is not
altogether trustworthy.
[2] *Docs. Oviedo,* no. 137.
[3] AHN 528/13. The foot of the parchments is now very ragged, but the words
notarius regis can just be detected. The script and format are certainly those of
the royal chancery.
[4] AC Tuy 10/10 (ptd. below, Appendix, no. IX).
[5] AHN 1512/13.

were drafted by Lope Arias, who described himself usually as
notarius Compostellanus, once as *notarius Compostellani
concilii*—notary of the *concejo* of Compostela, i.e., of the
town council—and once as *publicus notarius*.[1] He also wrote,
as we should expect, several private charters conveying land
in the town of Santiago de Compostela.[2] He had a pupil,
Pelayo Martínez, who copied an act drafted by his master,
and also wrote private deeds.[3] Now the archbishop of Compostela was also lord of the town, so that the public notaries
there were, in a sense, 'his' clerks. But clearly they were not
members of an archiepiscopal 'chancery'. This may be an
appropriate place to note that at least one of the other four
acta which have scribal subscriptions was written by an
external scribe.[4]

In the diocese of Lugo we have an even more remarkable
illustration of the activities of a municipal scribe. Lugo was
another town over which its bishop had the *señorío*. Fortu-
nately for us, a considerable number of private deeds relating
to sales, exchanges and leases of real property in and just outside the town has been preserved, and the vast majority of
these, during the period *c*. 1170–1215, were drafted by one
Román, *Lucensis notarius*.[5] He was also working for the
chapter: he wrote a charter for Rodrigo I Menéndez while
the latter was still dean of Lugo.[6] More to our purpose, he
wrote six *acta* for the bishops during the period 1175–1210.[7]
This was a period, as we have seen, when the bishops sometimes used notaries of their own. There seems to be no intelligible reason why some of their acts were drafted by their

---

[1] Santiago de Compostela, Biblioteca del Seminario, MS. 72. (This 'manuscript'
is a bundle of original charters; the separate parchments are not numbered. This
act is fragmentary, but the scribal subscription is clear.); AHN 1334/7 (ptd. *ES*
XLI, ap. xxiii, pp. 341–3); ptd. *LFH* V, ap. v, pp. 15–17; AC Tuy 10/21 (ptd.
below, Appendix, no. XXXII).
[2] E.g., AHN 512/16, 17; 524/1.
[3] AC Tuy 10/21 (ptd. below, Appendix, no. XXXII); AHN 512/19.
[4] Santiago de Compostela, Archivo de la Universidad, Fondo de San Martín
Pinario, Pergaminos Sueltos, no. 15.
[5] They are scattered throughout AHN 1325E–1326G.
[6] AHN 1325F/19 bis.
[7] AHN 1325F/19; 1082/19 and 1326C/28; 1326D/17; 1326E/11; 498/11;
1326E/21.

own staff, some of them by the public notary of the town. It is at least clear that if they can be said to have had a 'chancery' of their own, they used its services only intermittently. But its very life may have been intermittent.

To sum up, we have little evidence that bishops had 'chanceries' in twelfth-century León. Such writing-offices as they may have had were not sophisticated organizations; they may have been extremely rudimentary. Bishops probably did not have occasion to do much writing. When they did have to produce *acta*, and had to cast about for scribes, they sometimes turned to 'external' scribes of one sort of another; frequently (and I am tempted to say 'usually') they looked to their cathedral chapters; sometimes they did have trained men of their own. Very occasionally these scribes gave themselves exotic titles, probably modelled on those used in the royal chancery. To those who are accustomed to the neat instruments produced in the chanceries of English bishops it will all sound rather primitive. We should be prepared for some of the documents that were produced to look a little odd.

THE DOCUMENTS : EXTERNAL FEATURES

The diplomatic of these documents shows considerable variety. If they have anything in common, it is a certain archaism. The documents are characterized by solemn and cumbrous wording; by frequent use of the preliminary chrismon and arenga; by rambling sanctions, elaborate dating-clauses and lengthy witness-lists. Their script is usually a formal rather than a business-hand: the autograph subscription, the *signum* and the chirograph are more common forms of authentication than the seal. In all respects they rather resemble the 'diploma' than the 'writ' (to use these terms in a loose and general sense). Leonese bishops did not develop those terser instruments for making known their wishes which are so prominent a mark of government, whether secular or ecclesiastical, in other parts of Europe during the twelfth century.

The *acta* also show extensive borrowing by episcopal 'chanceries' of the forms and practices of the royal chancery of León-Castile. Nearly all the royal documents that survive from the twelfth-century are diplomas, elaborate in form and beneficial in purpose. Kings were slow to adopt new diplomatic forms such as the written order (called by students of Spanish diplomatic the *mandato*) or the letter patent (*carta abierta*); as also to adopt new techniques like the use of the seal. Bishops followed kings pretty faithfully. This is a little surprising, seeing that it occurred at a time when episcopal chanceries in other parts of Europe were tending towards imitation of the forms and even the verbal rhythms of the papal chancery.

Signs of Authentication

It will be appropriate to begin with a brief consideration of the ways in which royal documents were authenticated. During the first half of the century the seal was almost certainly not used in the royal chancery of León-Castile, instruments being authenticated by *signa*, sometimes also by chirograph.[1] The earliest employment of the seal in the chancery of Alfonso VII which I have been able to trace occurs in 1146.[2] It was used sporadically during the remainder of his reign,[3] but did not displace the *signum*. Instead, *signum* and seal co-existed until the end of the period with which we are concerned, and indeed for some chancery products such as the *privilegio rodado* until the end of the Middle Ages. The *signum* adopted in the Leonese royal chancery from early in the reign of Fernando II was the *rueda*, a form derived at one remove (as we shall see) from the *rota* of the papal chancery.

Among the *acta* we have to reckon with four forms of authentication—the autograph subscription, the *signum*, the

---

[1] For royal chirographs, see for example AC León no. 1019 (of 1148) and AHN 898/13 (1152). Photographs of the *signa* used by Queen Urraca may be found in A. Eitel, 'Rota und Rueda', *Archiv für Urkundenforschung* v (1914), 299–366; of those used by Alfonso VII in Rassow's standard work on the diplomatic of his documents, ibid., x–xi (1928–30).

[2] R.A. Fletcher, 'Diplomatic and the Cid revisited: the seals and mandates of Alfonso VII', *Journal of Medieval History* ii (1976), 305–37.

[3] E.g., British Library, Add. Ch. 71357 (4 June 1147); AHD Astorga, Cámara Episcopal, I/7 (19 April 1150); AHN 1030/19, ptd. Rassow pp. 113–14 (4 December 1152); Madrid, Instituto de Valencia de Don Juan, B.A.2/3 (19 December 1153). The earliest use of the seal by a lay nobleman which is known to me occurs in a charter of Count Manrique de Lara dated 5 December 1153: AC Sigüenza, Particulares no. 9.

chirograph and the seal.[1] The first of these methods, though not common, occurs sporadically throughout the period under review, not only in the episcopal *acta* themselves but also in the private charters which bishops confirmed or witnessed. We have two excellent examples of the autograph subscription of Diego Gelmírez, in the *privilegio del agua* which he granted to the monastery of San Martín Pinario in 1122, and in a charter granted by Bermudo Pérez de Traba to the monastery of Sobrado in 1138.[2] More than eighty years later the archbishops of Santiago de Compostela were still on occasion employing the autograph subscription; Pedro Suárez de Deza used it in two *acta* of 1204.[3] We also find it used now and then by the bishops of León, Orense, Salamanca, Tuy and Zamora.[4] This was not a Leonese peculiarity. The archbishops of Toledo, for instance, sometimes used it.[5]

The *signum* is so common that we may well call it the standard form of authentication in Leonese *acta* of the twelfth century, as it certainly was in royal documents. The antecedent of the *signum* was probably the sign of the cross drawn beside the name of the witnesses who subscribed documents. This, the simplest form of *signum*, was occasionally employed by the bishops of the twelfth century.[6] But *signa* of the period are commonly so elaborate and distinctive that it is more plausible to believe that they were thought of not as copies of or developments from some remote exemplar but simply as a guarantee against fraud and as a means of enhancing the solemnity of the instruments which they

---

[1] By 'autograph' subscription I mean the writing of his own name and title with his own hand by the bishop who passed the act in question; by *signum*, a written device which either replaces or accompanies the subscription of the bishop. A good many *signa* may be autograph, but certainty on this question is naturally elusive.

[2] AHN 512/9 (ptd. below, Appendix, no. V); 526/7. The latter document bears also the autograph subscription of Guy, bishop of Lescar in south-western France.

[3] AC Zamora, leg. 13, no. 9; AC Tuy, 10/21 (ptd. below, Appendix, no. XXXII).

[4] AC León, nos. 1400, 1401; AC Orense, Escrituras XIV/72; AC Salamanca, nos. 88, 112; AC Tuy, 10/21; AC Zamora, leg. 12, no. 2 (ptd. below, Appendix no. XXIV).

[5] The latest example known to me comes from 1214: AHN 3018/17 (= Sección de Sellos, 39/9).

[6] E.g., by Arnaldo II of Astorga in 1174, by Manrique of León in 1182: AHN 3536/I, AC León, no. 1438.

authenticated. While there is immense variety in the forms of surviving *signa*, certain recurrent types can be distinguished. The most famous of these is the *rota*. This circular design had been used by the popes as an additional means of authenticating their solemn privileges from the pontificate of Leo IX, though it attained its final form only in that of Paschal II. It was copied in two areas of western Europe, in the royal chancery of Norman Sicily and in the kingdom of León-Castile. In the latter region it was adopted by Diego Gelmírez at Compostela; two other bishoprics, Mondoñedo and Lugo, followed suit; and it was finally taken up by the royal chancery where, as the *rueda*, it gave its name to the *privilegio rodado*.[1] This is, incidentally, one of the very few certain examples of borrowing by a bishop from the papal chancery and then by kings from an episcopal chancery. It has been argued that Diego Gelmírez adopted the *rota* only after he became an archbishop in 1120, and indeed the earliest original document which bears his *rota* is a private charter of 1125 which he confirmed.[2] But there is reliable evidence that he used it before 1120. His subscription of a royal charter of 31 March 1116 is accompanied by his *rota*: the document survives only in a copy of the late twelfth century, but Diego's title, placed inside the *rota*, is *Didacus II^s episcopus*— not *archiepiscopus*.[3] He may have used it long before that, for it occurs in the same form in a royal charter of 1 April 1101, which survives in a notarial copy of the fifteenth century, and in another of 9 May 1112, surviving only in a cartulary copy of the seventeenth century.[4] It also appears in a private charter of 1105 and an act of 1115.[5] Some of his successors continued to use the *rota* to authenticate their documents. A few examples of its use by Bernardo survive, and several of its use by Martín. The latest surviving example

---

[1] These developments are surveyed by A. Eitel, 'Rota und Rueda', *Archiv für Urkundenforschung* v (1914), 299–336.
[2] Santiago de Compostela, Biblioteca del Seminario, MS. 72.
[3] AHN 1857/13.
[4] AHN 1749/1; cód. 15B, fol. 80^r.
[5] Santiago de Compostela, Archivo de la Universidad, leg. 81, no. 74/19; *LFH* III, ap. xxxiii, at p. 102.

comes from the archiepiscopate of Pedro Suárez de Deza, and is dated 1174.[1]

From Compostela, use of the *rota* spread to Mondoñedo and to Lugo. Bishop Nuño Alfonso of Mondoñedo used it when subscribing an act of Diego Gelmírez in 1122 and a royal document of 1135.[2] In the diocese of Lugo it was used by bishops Guido and Juan, the latest example coming from 1175.[3] In the hands of Lugo scribes it sometimes departed from the papal form which it had retained in the dioceses of Compostela and Mondoñedo. No instance of the use of the *rota* in any diocese has survived from the last quarter of the twelfth century.

The *rota*, then, was not commonly used in episcopal chanceries, and four other recurrent types of *signum* may be distinguished. The most bizarre of these is that which may be called the 'Visigothic' type, for its elaborate convolutions were clearly derived from the *signa* which were used for the authentication of the charters of the ninth, tenth and eleventh centuries, the classic period of Visigothic cursive script. These in their turn would seem to have descended from the *signa* 'embellished with flourishes' which were employed in Spain in the seventh century.[4] The variety of the surviving *signa* of this type defies any attempt at generalization. One can say merely that the Visigothic *signum* was an abstract design which often included the letters of the bishop's name concealed among its wriggling lines or brought together in a clumsy monogram. It was a *signum* of this type which was used by Queen Urraca, and it is therefore no surprise to find it extensively employed by Pedro III, bishop of Lugo, who had been a royal clerk: he used it to authenticate his own *acta* and to confirm private charters.[5] His *signum* was not dissimilar to Urraca's but it may equally well have been derived

---

[1] E.g., AHN 524/3, (Bernardo); AHN 1126/9 (Martín); AC Salamanca, no. 61 (Pedro Suárez: ptd. below, Appendix, no. XV).

[2] AHN 512/9 (ptd. below, Appendix, no. V); 556/1.

[3] Several of the Lugo examples are illustrated by Eitel in the article already cited. The latest one, Eitel's *Abbild.* no. 6 (p. 309) is now AHN 1325F/16 bis.

[4] Cf. P.D. King, *Law and Society in the Visigothic Kingdom* (Cambridge, 1972), p. 104, n. 7.

[5] E.g., AHN 1325C/4, 8, 9, 12, 15, 19, 21 bis. For the former, see below pp. 119, and illustration facing p. 118.

from that used by his predecessor and namesake, Pedro II, an example of which survives in a private charter of 1108.[1] A *signum* of this general type was used also by Archbishop Pedro Helias of Compostela.[2] Did he perhaps eschew the new-fangled *rota* because it had been associated with his opponent Diego Gelmirez?

A further type of *signum* may be called the quatrefoil type. Its design was simple; a rectangle enclosing the name of the bishop, each of whose sides bulged into convexity. The bulges were often pronounced, so that the design resembled four leaves or petals sprouting from the bishop's name. This type of *signum* was used only in the dioceses of León and Lugo, during the episcopates of the two bishops named Juan in the middle years of the century.[3] Yet another type may be called the pictorial type. A not uncommon form of this was the drawing of a hand grasping an episcopal crozier, usually placed after the bishop's subscription.[4] But other forms are also found. Bishop Pedro of Tuy, presumably in allusion to his namesake who was called to become a fisher of men, drew a fish after his subscription when witnessing a document of 1204.[5] Over in Navarre, Sancho de Larrosa, bishop of Pamplona from 1122 to 1142, drew a man's bearded head after some of his subscriptions.[6] Finally, the stylization of a common word would produce a *signum*. Martín I of Zamora elaborated the abbreviation *ss.*, for *subscripsi* or *subscribo*, into the pattern ⊠ which he used very frequently as a *signum.*[7]

Some form of *signum*, then, was extremely common in Leonese *acta* of the twelfth century. Yet the chirograph was about as common as the *signum*. Of six original *acta* from Astorga, four were authenticated by chirograph; twenty-three

[1] AHN 1325C/2.

[2] León, Archivo de San Isidoro, no. 98; AHN 556/3.

[3] E.g., AHN 896/16; AC León, nos. 1400, 1401; AHN 1325D/17, 18.

[4] E.g., AC León, nos. 1381, 1383 (ptd. E. Valiña Sampedro, *El Camino de Santiago* (Salamanca, 1971), ap. 2, pp. 230–2); *Docs. Oviedo,* no. 147.

[5] AC Tuy, 10/21 (ptd. below, Appendix, no. XXXII).

[6] Pamplona, Archivo General de Navarra, Sección de Clero, Irache, Adiciones no. 7 (1136); AC Pamplona, no. 199 (1138).

[7] E.g., AC Zamora, leg. 12, no. 3; leg. 13, no. 1; leg. 33, no. 2.

out of thirty-one from León; three out of six from Salamanca; eight out of thirteen from Santiago de Compostela; and no fewer than twenty-six out of twenty-nine from Zamora. There is much variety, both in the letters employed and in the mode of application. The truncated letters may form the word *chirographum*; they may be the letters of the alphabet; they may compose some pious formula. They may run along the top of the text, or down one side. The chirograph may be polled or it may be indented; if the latter, the indentations may be sharp or they may be undulating.

The seal has been left to the last among the signs of authentication, because it appeared so late and spread so gradually in the episcopal 'chanceries' of the kingdom of León. The earliest episcopal seals from the kingdom of León-Castile come from the Castilian half of the kingdom. When Bishop Bernardo of Sigüenza introduced the Augustinian Rule for his cathedral chapter in 1144 the two copies of the document recording the detailed arrangements were sealed.[1] A later act of the same bishop, dated 1149, not long before his translation to Compostela, was also sealed.[2] In the primatial see of Toledo an act of Archbishop Raimundo of 1145 was authenticated by a seal.[3] Both Bernardo and Raimundo were Frenchmen, and were promoted from the circle round Archbishop Bernardo of Toledo. Bernardo of Sigüenza, as we saw in Chapter 2, had served in the royal chancery of Alfonso VII.

It is not until a date ten years after this first occurrence of sealing that we find, among our surviving documents, any evidence of the practice in the Leonese half of the kingdom. The following list shows the dates at which an episcopal seal first appears among the documents surviving from each diocese:

---

[1] AC Sigüenza, Particulares, nos. 4 and 5 (ptd. Minguella, *Historia de la Diócesis de Sigüenza* (Madrid, 1910), I, ap. xxiii, pp. 375–7. The impression of the seal does not survive.

[2] AC Sigüenza, Particulares, no. 7 (ptd. ibid., ap. xxviii, p. 383). Here again, the impression does not survive.

[3] AC Pamplona, no. 237 (ptd. P. Kehr, *Papsturkunden in Navarra und Aragon,* no. 50). Here once more the impression of the seal is missing. Mr. Robert, who drafted this document, may be identical with the English translator, Mr. Robert of Ketton.

27 January 1154	Astorga (*ES* XVI, ap. xxviii, pp. 484–6)
27 March 1171	Lugo (AHN 1325E/25)
14 January 1174	Santiago de Compostela (AC Salamanca, nos. 61, 62; below, Appendix, nos. XV and XVI).
16 June 1181	Salamanca (AC Salamanca, no. 78; below, Appendix, no. XVII).
6 February 1182	Zamora (AHN 3576/13).
4 July 1184	Orense, Oviedo (AC Burgos, no. 234).
8 March 1190	León (AC León, no. 1448).
13 June 1190	Mondoñedo (AHN cód. 63B, no. 108).
30 June 1200	Tuy (AHN 1796/4; below, Appendix, no. XXVI).

Even when we make due allowance for the scrappy and unsatisfactory nature of our evidence, the spread of the new device seems to have been slow.[1] Furthermore bishops, like kings, used sealing apparently at random after its first introduction; it did not displace other methods of authentication, but co-existed with them.

There is of course a possibility that Leonese bishops had used seals before the date of our first recorded seal, 1154, and that all examples of them have perished. On balance, the evidence is against this. No original episcopal act from the first half of the century bears traces of sealing. No reference is made by the compilers of cartularies to earlier seals, whereas they do on occasion refer to the sealing of later documents.[2] The earliest episcopal seal of which we know was affixed to a document which bears a date soon after the first evidence of sealing in the royal chancery and in two Castilian dioceses; so soon that it is tempting to guess that Leonese bishops were following examples set either by their Castilian

---

[1] And not just in León. In the documents I have consulted (and I should emphasize that I have made no systematic search among Castilian and Navarrese documents) episcopal seals first appear at Palencia in 1163, at Burgos and Pamplona in 1176 and at Avila in 1181.

[2] See below, Appendix, no. XXXI, where the seventeenth-century copyist noted that this document of 1204 had been sealed.

colleagues or by their ruler. As against this, we should set the earlier occurrences of the word *sigillum*. There are several of these in the *Historia Compostellana*. In 1122 Diego Gelmírez and Nuño Alfonso of Mondoñedo ratified the settlement of a dispute between them *propriis sigillis*; letters from the bishops were sent to Pope Calixtus II in 1123 *uniuscuiusque sigillo munitas*; and in 1134 or 1135 Raimundo archbishop of Toledo concluded a letter to Diego Gelmírez with the words, 'Valete. Sigillo Scemorensis signavimus has litteras, quia non habebamus ibi nostrum'. But it would be rash to assume too readily that in the examples quoted[1] the word *sigillum* means what we should call a seal. It is more likely that it meant some sort of device—e.g., a stencil with which to trace the *rota*—to assist the scribe to draw the *signum*, and thus by extension the *signum* itself.[2] This can only have been the meaning of the word in the royal chancery of Queen Urraca. When she observed that her charter of 20 March 1124 to the church of Zamora was *imperiali sigillo decoratam*, she was referring to a *signum*, for she had no seal.[3]

If bishops, however hesitantly, adopted the use of the seal during the second half of the century, whose example were they following in doing so? The mode of application of episcopal seals was always that used in the royal chancery: no bishop's seal in twelfth-century León was applied directly to the face or dorse of the document, nor to parchment *sur simple queue* or *sur double queue*; all were pendent, from leather, silk or hempen cords. This is exactly how royal seals were affixed. (It is also, of course, how papal *bullae* were affixed.) On the other hand, royal and episcopal seals were different shapes. Royal seals were circular, episcopal seals were oval. The earliest traceable episcopal seal, from the diocese of Astorga in 1154, is now missing, but is illustrated in an eighteenth-century sketch by Flórez:[4] the style of the drawing is far removed in spirit from the twelfth century, but there can be no mistake about the oval shape of the seal. All

[1] *HC* pp. 377, 383, 565.
[2] Dr. P. Chaplais first directed my attention to this possibility. See also P. Galindo Romeo, *La Diplomática en la Historia Compostelana* (Madrid, 1945), p. 21.
[3] AC Zamora, Libro Negro, fols. 20ᵛ–21ʳ.
[4] *ES* XVI, p. 486.

other episcopal seals which have been inspected are oval. The
impressions of the seals of Raimundo of Toledo and Bernardo of Sigüenza are also missing, so we do not know what
shape they were, but it may be presumed that they were oval.
Certainly the seals were pendent, Bernardo's from tags of
leather, Raimundo's from tags of red-and-blue-striped silk.
The evidence is not very helpful. Leonese bishops may have
been following royal practice. They may have been fired by
the example of their Castilian colleagues. They may have
adopted the use of the seal directly from beyond the Pyrenees. After all, of the four dioceses where such seals first
appeared, two were on the pilgrim route (Astorga, Lugo),
one was the goal of the pilgrims (Compostela) and the fourth
was attracting foreign students to its schools (Salamanca).

Before we leave the topic of signs of authentication, one
final point should be noticed—the common employment of
multiple authentications, i.e., of two or more of the methods
that have been discussed, in the same document. We may indeed say that it is rather unusual for *acta* to be authenticated
in only one way, as for example two Mondoñedan acts were
by chirograph alone, one of Archbishop Martín of Compostela
by a *rota* alone, two from Tuy only by seals and one from
Orense only by autograph subscriptions.[1] Examples of
double authentications can be found in nearly every diocese,[2] and examples of triple authentications are by no
means rare.[3] What we should make of this curious feature of
Spanish diplomatic—for we find it also in the royal chancery,
and among the Castilian sees[4]—is not clear. One obvious
comment is that this was a specially cumbrous way of producing documents; they could not have been issued with
much despatch; but perhaps the total number of documents

[1] AC Mondoñedo, carpeta del siglo XII, unnumbered (1128, 1143); AHN 528/13
(1165); AHN 1796/4, AC Orense, Privilegios II/20 (both of 1200); AC Orense,
Escrituras XIV/72 (1194).
[2] E.g., Bishop Vidal of Salamanca's act of 1181 (ptd. below, Appendix, no XVII)
was authenticated by chirograph and by seal.
[3] E.g., Bishop Martín of Zamora's act of 1208 (ptd. below, Appendix, no.
XXXIII) was authenticated by autograph subscriptions, chirograph and seals.
[4] E.g., an act of Rodrigo Ximénez de Rada, archbishop of Toledo, of 1214, was
authenticated by autograph subscriptions, chirograph and seals: AHN 3018/17
(= Sección de Sellos, 39/9).

issued was never large and speed in the transaction of business never a necessity.

Script and Format

Two changes were taking place in the twelfth century in the script of episcopal as of other documents: from Visigothic script to what Spanish palaeographers call *francesa*, i.e., that development from the Carolingian miniscule which had become the most common script written in western Europe by 1100, and which was in Spain particularly associated with the influx of Frenchmen which took place from c.1070; and within the forms of *francesa* from a formal or book-hand to a business or charter-hand. The speed with which these changes occurred has been somewhat over-estimated by historians.

Visigothic script still had a long life before it in the year 1100, especially in the Asturias and Galicia, the most conservative regions of the kingdom of León. Royal documents in Visigothic script cease with the death of Queen Urraca, though some of the early ones of Alfonso VII retain traces of it, and a charter of his sister Doña Sancha dated as late as 1158 was written in Visigothic script.[1] Private charters in this script continue numerous in the second and third quarters of the century, and even in the last two decades documents can be found whose script is more Visigothic than *francesa*.[2] The fortunate survival at León of a private charter dated 1155 seems to show us the approximate date at which men began to experience difficulty in reading the older script.[3] At the foot of the document there is written out, in what seems to be a contemporary hand, the letters of the alphabet in *francesa*, and immediately below that the corresponding characters in Visigothic script. The charter itself is in Visigothic script; the alphabets were written by a different hand. Was a man accustomed to reading the *francesa* script trying to learn the Visigothic script in order to read this, or another,

---

[1] L. García Calles, *Doña Sancha, Hermana del Emperador* (León, 1972), ap. no. 53, pp. 169–70. The scribe was from the Asturias.

[2] E.g., AHN 1566/17 (1170), 529/17 (1172), 1082/16 (1187), 1325H/19 (1191), 1751/5 (1195), 1197/1 (1196).

[3] León, Archivo de San Isidoro, no. 298.

document? So it would seem. At any rate, this dual alphabet
was copied out at least sixty years after the alleged 'abolition'
of the Visigothic script in western Spain.

So it is not at all surprising to find a few episcopal *acta*
written in Visigothic script. We have only one original among
the *acta* of Diego Gelmírez, dated 1122, and that is written
in an unusually pure Visigothic script.[1] An early Lugo act,
of 1119, is in the same script, though elements of *francesa*
are already present.[2] The same is true of two early *acta* from
Oviedo,[3] and of two from Mondoñedo;[4] even in the latest of
these, of 1143, the intrusion of *francesa* has not seriously
marred the fundamentally Visigothic character of the script.
It is significant that these examples come from Galicia and
the Asturias. We have several early originals from the see of
León, and the script of all of them is *francesa*.[5]

About the second change, from a formal to a business
hand, it is difficult to be precise. Far too little work has been
as yet devoted to Spanish palaeography of this period; there
is no settled body of definitions which the historian may use
when he wants to attach a label to a particular script. One
man's hasty or sloppy formal hand is another man's careful
or elaborate business hand. We may, however, be clear on
some points. The scribes of the royal chancery under Alfonso
VII and Fernando II never developed a sophisticated charter
hand such, for example, as is understood by those who use
the term to describe the products of the Plantagenet or
Capetian royal chanceries in the second half of the twelfth
century. This is certainly also true of the 'chanceries' of the
Leonese bishops. Episcopal scribes were however gradually
moving towards the sort of business hand favoured by the
royal scribes, and this movement produced a script betwixt
book-hand and charter-hand which is the most typical hand
among the *acta* from the second half of the century, when
originals become reasonably abundant.[6]

---

[1] AHN 512/9 (ptd. below, Appendix, no. V).
[2] AHN 1325C/9 (ptd. below, Appendix, no. III).
[3] Ptd. *Docs. Oviedo,* nos. 134, 135.
[4] AC Mondoñedo, carpeta del siglo XII, unnumbered.
[5] E.g., AC León, no. 1384 (ptd. below, Appendix, no. IV).
[6] This development may most easily be studied in the *acta* surviving from the dioceses of León, Lugo and Zamora.

Despite this development and the pleasant, easy script to which it gave birth, the handwriting of Leonese *acta* remained far more formal than that of their English counterparts in the twelfth century. This could be demonstrated, short of prolonged study of the originals, only by the provision of photographic facsimiles, for which no place can be found in an essay of this nature. Scribes did not develop those tricks and dodges which would have enabled them to complete their task more quickly and more easily. Their hands were more often upright than sloping. Ligatures were of an elementary kind. They were sparing of abbreviations. These and other features may be seen in the act of Bishop Pedro III of Lugo reproduced below.[1] For its day, 1132, its script was quite advanced. There was not much change during the rest of the century. The *acta* of Bishop Martín of Zamora at the end of our period, business-like instruments though they were, were written in a script which would have been considered antiquated in the England of their day.

The same may be said of the general format of the documents. This tended to be lavish. Some of the early *acta* have an immensely spacious and extravagant format. In Diego Gelmírez's act of 1122, so frequently referred to already, there is a generous margin at the left-hand side and the text itself occupies only half the area of parchment. The opening words of the *arenga* are in spidery Visigothic majuscule. The subscriptions and *signa* are scattered haphazardly beneath the sprawling, leisurely autograph of the archbishop himself. And the document is big; 58 cm in breadth by 49 cm in depth. But it is by no means exceptional. Two early *acta* from León[2] are respectively 73 × 49 cm and 73 × 41 cm; in these two only about half the total area of the parchment is covered with the text, the remainder being reserved for the witnesses, whose names have, however, been disposed into some sort of order in columns. A document of 1159 drawn up for Fernando Curialis[3] is of precisely this large and splendid type. So are

---

[1] Facing p. 118.

[2] AC León, nos. 1362, 1384 (the latter ptd. below, Appendix, no. IV).

[3] AHN 1126/9; not of course strictly speaking an episcopal act, since Fernando did not style himself archbishop of Compostela until a few months later.

some of Pedro Suárez's, from both ends of his long archiepiscopate.[1] The neat chirographs of Juan of León might
seem to mark a new departure, with their narrow margins,
small script and almost standard shape and size; but even
these make generous provision for the witnesses and allow
the scribe enough space to indulge his taste for fancy *signa*.[2]
And the document with which he recorded his foundation of
a house of canons at Carbajal yields little or nothing to those
of his predecessor Diego for sheer extravagance.[3] Similarly
the *acta* of Martín of Zamora, though generally sober and
economical in format, are yet more generous of space than
English *acta*.[4] Thus on the whole the *acta* are showy. This
strengthens the impression that they were occasional rather
than routine productions.

THE DOCUMENTS: INTERNAL FEATURES

Most of the surviving *acta* are cast either in the form of a
diploma or in forms closely related to it. The supremacy of
this form is the most striking diplomatic feature of the
Leonese *acta*. To show what is understood by the term 'diploma' it will be best to set down in full an example of what
we take to be the genre and then to examine its component
parts in the light of other documents like it. In the spring of
1132 Bishop Pedro III of Lugo exchanged some land with
one of the canons of his cathedral named Pedro Díaz. To record this transaction the bishop employed one Diego,[5] who
drew up the document which follows and dated it 19 March
1132. This is what Diego wrote:

XPS. Quod ab ecclesie prelatis perhenniter institutum est atque
canonice sancitum.eorum posteris nos convenit insinuare.scripturarum
titulo inpresso. Eapropter ego Petrus.III.^s dei gratia Lucensis ecclesie
episcopus consilio et auctoritate / meorum canonicorum suffultus
dignum duxi per presentis scripture seriem tibi Petro Didaz clerico et

---

[1] AC Salamanca, no. 61 (ptd. below, Appendix, no. XV); AC Zamora, leg. 13,
no. 9.
[2] E.g., AC León, nos. 1400, 1401.
[3] León, Archivo de San Isidoro, no. 98.
[4] E.g., AHN 3576/16, where a good quarter of the parchment is unused.
[5] Diego wrote at least three other documents for Bishop Pedro; AHN 1325C/18,
20, 22 (the second of these ptd. below, Appendix, no. VI). Nothing is known
about him.

Document drawn up for Bishop Pedro III of Lugo in 1132. Reproduced from the Archivo Histórico Nacional, Madrid. Sección de Clero, Carpeta 1325 C. no. 21 bis

canonico nostro conferre illas casas integras que fuerunt ospicium quondam peregrinorum que eciam sunt prope ecclesias sancte Marie et sancti Petri. / intra muros Lucensis civitatis site.ex una parte terminantur per casas que fuerunt de Garcia Cidiz et de Iohanne Ferrario ex alia vero per illas que fuerunt de Petro Ectaz et de Iohanne Diaz.de inde per viam que ducit ad ecclesiam. / Adicimus eciam tibi unum agellum qui est in suburbio civitatis circa viam et subtus que discurrit de castello prefate civitatis ad villam de Castineiras. et qui est inter ortum palacii et terram Pelagii Gondemariz.ab alia vero parte ubi ortus cano- / nice iacet terminatur per suos marcos subtus fontem positos. Has denique casas predicto modo descriptas et hunc agellum prefatis terminis circumventum.damus vobis ac semini vestro per huius nostre firmitatis scripturam pro aliis vestris / domibus bonis ac spaciosis que ad ecclesie sancte Marie parietes propagandos atque ad atria sunt valde necessarie. De iure igitur nostro et potestate amodo sublata.vestro sint dominio vestreque progeniei per henniter iniuncta et confirmata.et sit licitum vobis vendere / et donare pro velle vestro. Siquis autem huius nostre promulgacionis conscius eam temerariis vexacionibus conturbare voluerit.omnipotentis Dei ma勾勿malediccionem incurrat et nostre excommunicationi sub iaceat. atque insuper calumpniate rei duplo composito. Perpetue stabi / litatis rigorem obtineat scriptura hec. Facta est namque die sabbati X⁰IIII.⁰ Kalendas. Aprilis. Era.M.CaL^{a}XX^a Ego Petrus episcopus iam dictus quod fieri iussi manibus propriis roboro et confirmo signo mei roboris inpresso. (*Signum of Pedro III*).

(*1st column*)
Qui presto fuerunt
Iohannes testis
Pelagius testis
Froila testis

(*2nd column*)
Iudex Pelagius conf.
Prior Guido conf.
Archidiaconus Rodrigus conf.
Primicerius Petrus conf.

(*3rd column*)
Pelagius Iohannis conf.
Martinus tesorarius conf.
Anagia capellanus conf.
Omnes canonici conf.

(*4th column*)
Munio Pelaiz conf.
Veremudus Pelaiz conf.
Pelagius Petriz conf.
Omnes burgenses conf.

(*5th column*) Didacus notuit.

This instrument[1] shows in its form certain general but striking similarities to the products of the royal chancery of León-Castile during the first half of the twelfth century. Pedro III had been a clerk in the chancery of Queen Urraca,

[1] AHN 1325C/21 bis. Perhaps original, perhaps a closely contemporary copy. Written in a neat *francesa* on a parchment 52 cm × 20 cm. Authenticated by an episcopal *signum* of the 'Visigothic' type. See the photograph of this document facing p. 118.

but this in itself is not sufficient to explain the similarities found, not only in this and other Lugo *acta*, but also in the *acta* of those bishops who had no close connections—that we know of—with the royal court and writing office. Nearly all documents emanating from the chanceries of Urraca and Alfonso VII were in diploma form. Little is known at present about the origins of this form, but it seems to have grown out of the forms of previous types of royal document in the course of the tenth and eleventh centuries.[1] Certainly by the end of the reign of Fernando I in 1065 the diploma was the accepted and normal form for all royal documents, so far as we can judge from surviving originals and copies. The form comprehended a number of variations, and continued to do so until well into the twelfth century; it was not until the advent of Master Hugo the chancellor in 1135 that forms became relatively more fixed.[2] Kings did not issue diplomas alone. Mandates of Alfonso VII survive in small numbers, none of them unfortunately in its original form.[3] Naturally, as being closely tied to the circumstances of the moment at which they were issued, they were not preserved with that care which was lavished on royal diplomas; many, therefore, may have perished. Yet one has the impression that government was not yet, to any great extent, a matter for writing; and that chancery practice, and not simply the ravages of time, mice, damp and neglect, is responsible for the fact that royal mandates do not become frequent before the reign of Alfonso IX.[4] Throughout the century the most characteristic royal instrument remained the diploma.

---

[1] This is my tentative conclusion from a comparison of the charters studied by L. Barrau-Dihigo in his 'Étude sur les actes des rois Asturiens (718-910)', *Revue Hispanique* xlvi (1919), 1-192 with those later documents which he had edited at an earlier date under the title 'Chartes royales léonaises 912-1037', *Revue Hispanique* x (1903), 350-454. The diplomatic of royal documents during the reigns of Fernando I and Alfonso VI needs expert study.

[2] On the royal chancery in the reigns of Urraca and Alfonso VII see L. Sánchez Belda, 'La Cancillería Castellana durante el reinado de Doña Urraca', *Estudios dedicados a R. Menéndez Pidal* IV (1953), pp. 587-99, and above all P. Rassow, 'Die Urkunden Kaiser Alfons' VII von Spanien', *Archiv für Urkundenforschung* x (1928), 328-467.

[3] I have discussed them in 'Diplomatic and the Cid revisited: the seals and mandates of Alfonso VII', *Journal of Medieval History* ii (1976), 305-37.

[4] Alfonso IX's mandates are discussed in *GAL* vol. I, pp. 500-502.

While the Lugo act of 1132 is very like the royal charters of the early twelfth century, there are no similarities between it and contemporary papal documents—no borrowings of phrase or rhythm such as Professor Cheney noted among English episcopal *acta* (though admittedly *acta* of a slightly later date).[1] Yet Lugo was a bishopric which enjoyed specially close relations with the papacy in the late eleventh and early twelfth centuries. Bishop Amor may have attended the council of Clermont in 1095; certainly he was appealing to Urban II at that time for the restitution of lands and rights allegedly filched from his see by the bishops of Oviedo, Mondoñedo and León. His successor Pedro II continued the suit during the pontificate of Paschal II. Pedro III himself acquired two solemn privileges, from Calixtus II and Innocent II, and continued to press the claims of his see during the legatine visit of cardinal Humbert in 1130.

The exchange which the act records seems to have been necessitated by Pedro III's building operations. (It provides, incidentally, important evidence for dating the construction of the cathedral of Lugo and makes necessary some revision of accepted ideas about its architectural history.) Our first reaction to a casual reading of the text might be that this is a curiously elaborate way of recording a property transaction which was not of the first importance. It is now time to turn to a consideration of the component parts of the instrument, and to compare them to similar parts of other *acta* produced in the twelfth century in the other dioceses of the kingdom of León. Among the lessons we shall learn from this analysis is that the Lugo document is not nearly so elaborate as some of the other surviving *acta*.[2]

The Invocation

The act opens with a pictorial invocation, the chrismon or

---

[1] C.R. Cheney, *English Bishops' Chanceries 1100–1250* (Manchester, 1950), pp. 69–81.

[2] In order to avoid unwieldy footnotes, I have in the pages which immediately follow cited only a small number of documents, limiting myself where possible to those which have been printed in reliable editions. Readers who will be satisfied only with fuller citations may refer to pp. 184–94 of the thesis on which this book is based: the mode of reference adopted there is explained in a footnote on p. 128, and the *acta* are catalogued in Appendix 2, pp. 385–426.

XP monogram. This form is not uncommon among the *acta* of the first half of the century,[1] but it gradually becomes less common, though here and there we find examples of its use almost up to the end of our period.[2] Far more common, though absent from the Lugo act, is the verbal invocation. Here as elsewhere we find great variety and within this variety a gradual movement from elaboration to simplicity. Invocations such as this are not unusual during the first half of the century:[3] *'In honore et nomine sancte Trinitatis, Patris et Filii et Spiritus Sancti amen, quem catholica fides personaliter unum Deum colit et trium essentialiter'*. But throughout the century we find simpler ones, and these finally come to predominate. The most popular were, 'In nomine Patris et Filii et Spiritus Sancti amen'[4] or 'In nomine domini nostri Iesu Christi amen'[5] or simply 'In Dei nomine'.[6]

The 'Arenga'

In the Lugo act the chrismon is followed by a brief *arenga*. This form, again, is by no means unusual among the *acta*, though often it is a great deal more elaborate than it is in this instance. Here it takes the form of a short reflection upon the necessity of committing transactions to writing. This is parallelled in other episcopal *acta*,[7] but other forms are to be found. There occur, for example, pious sentiments of this sort:[8] 'Fundamentum aliud, ut ait apostolus, nemo potest ponere preter id quod positum est, quod est Christus Iesus'; or other sentiments less pious in tone:[9] 'Quicquid episcopus ad utilitatem ecclesie cum canonicorum consilio et bonorum hominum providencia disposuerit, huiusmodi dispositio firma

---

[1] E.g., AC León, no. 1384; AHN 512/9; AC Zamora, Libro Negro, fol. 15^V (all three ptd. below, Appendix, nos. IV, V, VII).

[2] E.g., AC Orense, Escrituras XIV/72 (1194); AC Oviedo, carpeta 5, no. 4 (1203).

[3] Ptd. *Galicia Histórica, Colección Diplomática* (Santiago de Compostela 1901), pp. 140–1. I have been unable to trace the MS.

[4] E.g., AHN 3536/1 (1174); AC Zamora, Libro Negro, fol. 54 (1176); AHN 1481/18 (1205); AHN 1512/13 (1213).

[5] E.g., AC Tuy 10/21 (ptd. below, Appendix, no. XXXII).

[6] E.g., AC León, no. 1428 (ptd. below, Appendix, no. XXX).

[7] E.g., AC Tuy, 10/10 (ptd. below, Appendix no. IX).

[8] AC Tuy, 14/10 (ptd. *ES* XXII, ap. vi, pp. 260–61).

[9] AHN 1325E/25.

in posterum permanebit'. We also find exhortations on the
desirability of almsgiving,[1] and observations on the duties
of a bishop.[2] On several occasions we find an opening preamble which is not an *arenga* properly so-called, but a *narratio* explaining which course of events gave rise to the
drawing-up of the document. This normally occurs in documents recording agreements between contending parties, a
special class of document about which I shall have something
to say shortly.[3]

The Title

Pedro III's title in the act of 1132—*ego Petrus III^s Dei
gratia Lucensis ecclesia episcopus*—is couched in the form
most common among the Leonese *acta* of the twelfth century. Bishops nearly always spoke of themselves in the first
person singular and, though a little less frequently, qualified
their names with the words *Dei gratia*. Use of the first person
plural occurs, of course, where the bishop is speaking for
others as well as for himself, but when this is not so its use
is extremely rare; it is to be found only four times among the
surviving *acta*, and in certainly one of these instances, and
probably two others, the bishops were using formulae that
had reached them from abroad.[4] There are some variants
upon the customary *Dei gratia. . .episcopus*. Pelayo referred
to himself as *presul* of Oviedo, Nuño of Mondoñedo called
himself the *indignus vicarius* of his see, Juan of Lugo styled
himself *qualiscumque Lucensium minister*, and Lope of
Astorga in 1201 adopted the title, not uncommon in France,
of *minister humilis*.[5] Diego Gelmírez once called himself

---

[1] E.g., AHD Astorga, Cartulario de Carracedo, fols. 58^V–59^V (ptd. below, Appen-
dix no. XXXI).
[2] E.g., AHN 512/9 (ptd. below, Appendix no. V).
[3] See below, pp. 129–30.
[4] Juan of León's *epistola formata* of 1153 was certainly a foreign form; see R.A.
Fletcher, 'An *Epistola Formata* from León', *Bulletin of the Institute of Historical
Research* xlv (1972), 122–8. The indulgences issued by Lope of Astorga and
Rabinato of Mondoñedo were probably foreign forms, the first is ptd. below,
Appendix no. XXXI, and the second in 'La Colección Diplomática de Jubia', ed.
S. Montero Díaz, *Boletín de la Universidad de Santiago de Compostela* vii (1935),
no. CVI, p. 108. The fourth instance is AHN 1796/4 (ptd. below, Appendix no.
XXVI), a document whose formulae show clear traces of papal diplomatic.
[5] Ptd. *Docs. Oviedo* no. 134; AC Mondoñedo, carpeta del siglo XII, unnumbered;
AHN 1325D/9; AC Orense, Privilegios II/21.

bishop *divina disponente clementia.*[1] We also find *Dei nutu* and *Dei permissione.*[2] But *Dei gratia. . .episcopus* remained the favourite form. When Diego Gelmírez exercised legatine powers he commonly added et *S.R.E.legatus.*

The Sanction

After invocation, *arenga* and title came the matter of the document, the *dispositio.* This in its turn is followed in our Lugo act by the final protocol—sanction, corroboration, date, confirmation and witnesses. This is in no sense a standard order; confirmation may precede date, sanction may follow corroboration. But when all these elements are present they frequently come in this order.

In Pedro III's charter, the sanction is a double one. Those who infringe the terms of the act are to incur penalties both spiritual and temporal; the whole is expressed in reasonably moderate language. We can point to far more elaborate sanctions than this. Here, for example, is Bishop Esteban of Zamora in an act of 1164:[3]

Siquis autem hoc factum nostrum irrumpere temptaverit, tam de nostris quam de extraneis quisque ille fuerit sit maledictus et excommunicatus et a fide Christi separatus et cum Iuda proditore dampnatur et non videat que bona sunt in Ierusalem celeste neque pacem in Israel et pariat ipsa hereditate duplata vel triplata in tali vel meliori loco. . . .

But most sanctions are a good deal simpler. Nearly all mention spiritual penalties; several combine spiritual with temporal;[4] a few have only the latter.[5]

The Corroboration

The form of words used shows some variety. The wording in bishop Pedro's act—*perpetua stabilitatis rigorem obtineat scriptura hec*—occurs not infrequently. In a grant by Suero of

---

[1] *HC* p. 176.
[2] AC León, no. 1390 (ptd. *ES* XXXVI, ap. liii, pp. cxi–cxiv); AC Orense, Privilegios I/13.
[3] AC Zamora, leg. 13, no. 27. For another elaborate sanction, see AHN 512/9 (ptd. below, Appendix no. V).
[4] E.g., AHD Astorga, Cámara Episcopal, I/11; AC Salamanca, no. 78 (both ptd. below, Appendix nos. X, XVII).
[5] E.g., AHN 1325H/8 (ptd. below, Appendix no. XXI).

Coria dated 1156 we find *et hoc meum factum semper maneat firmum*.[1] Diego Gelmírez's *privilegio del agua* of 1122 reads:[2] 'et hoc nostrum voluntarium beneficium incon (cussum) permaneat in secula seculorum (amen)'. Bishop Juan of León rounded off the *fuero* he granted to the settlers of Buenaventura in 1169 with the words *et hec carta semper sit firma in omni tempore*.[3] Bishop Alo of Astorga employed the formula *et hoc testamentum plenum et firmum habeat roborem* in an act of 1129.[4] Other variations could be listed. If any general tendency during the course of the century may be discerned it is for corroborations, like sanctions, to become a little shorter and simpler.

The Date

This is one of the most characteristic features of the Leonese *acta*, as it is of all Spanish documents produced during the twelfth century. Episcopal professions of obedience and the letters which bishops sent did not normally bear dates; but these apart, *acta* which are not dated are very scarce. Of the nine such which have survived, five are copies whose originals may have been dated, and a further one may be a copy.[5]

Elements used in the dating-clauses of Leonese *acta* may be classified into five types: dating by day, month and Spanish Era; by the name of the monarch; by the name of the bishop; by the name of dignitaries at the royal court; and by the names of local *tenentes*. The first of these methods is by far the most common, and Bishop Pedro's act of 1132 provides an example of it. There are minor variations upon it: sometimes only the year is found;[6] sometimes only the year and the month;[7] very occasionally, reckoning *anno*

---

[1] Ptd. *Hispania Sacra* xiii (1960), 399–400.

[2] AHN 512/9 (ptd. below, Appendix no. V).

[3] AC León no. 1320.

[4] AHN cód. 1197B, fols. 253^r–255^r.

[5] E.g., AHN 18/4 (6) is a copy and the text is truncated; AC León no. 1410 may be a copy. Both are ptd. below, Appendix nos. VIII, XX. AC Zamora, leg. 33, no. 1 (ptd. D.W. Lomax, *La Orden de Santiago* (Madrid, 1965), ap. 5, p. 235) is an original bearing no date.

[6] E.g., AC Zamora leg. 14, no. 26 (ptd. below, Appendix no. XXXIV).

[7] E.g., *Docs. Oviedo*, nos. 146, 150, 151.

domini is used, sometimes in conjunction with the Era,[1] and sometimes by itself.[2]

It was not at all uncommon for more than one of these elements to be used together. We have only one example of the employment of all five at once, in the extraordinarily complex dating-clause of Bishop Pedro of Astorga's general confirmation to the monastery of San Martín de Castañeda.[3] Several examples of the use of four elements have survived. Thus, for instance:[4]

Facta carta boni moris sub Era MᵃCᵃLXᵉᵃIᵃ et quodum VIII Kalendas Maii. Regnante imperatore Adefonso in Legione et in Toleto cum coniuge sua domna Rica. Poncio de Minerva turres Legionis tenente. Martino Nepzani in Legione villicante. Petro Christiano in Astoricensi sede episcopo. Petro Drago in eadem villa villicante.

As an instance of the use of three elements we have,[5] 'Facta carta Era MᵃCCᵃXXXIIᵃ VIII Kalendas Augusti. Regnante rege Alfonso in Legione, Gallecia, Asturiis, Extrematura. Iohanne Fernandi tenente Limiam'. And there are many examples of the use of only two, as,[6] 'Facta scripti pagina in ERA MᵃCᵃLXᵉᵃ.VIᵃ et quot II Nonas Iulii. Regnante rege Fernando in Legione et Galletia et rege Sancio in Toleto et Castella'. A few other dating elements appear, but infrequently. An act of bishop Vidal of Salamanca of 1187 refers to the pope of the time, *presidente in sancta Romana ecclesia Urbano papa III.*[7] Recent events of local importance were sometimes used to fix a date; a *fuero* granted by Bishop Esteban of Zamora was dated 1161, *ipso anno quo populata est Ledesma et Civitas Rodrigo.*[8] The indiction is very occasionally found,[9] the year of a bishop's episcopate a little more frequently.[10]

[1] E.g., AC León, no. 1362 (ptd. *ES* XXXVI, ap. xlvi, pp. c–ciii).
[2] E.g., *LFH* IV, ap. 1, pp. 122–4.
[3] Ptd. *ES* XVI, ap. xxviii, pp. 484–6.
[4] AC León, no. 1401; cf. AC Zamora, Libro Negro, fol. 15ᵛ (ptd. below, Appendix no. VII).
[5] AC Orense, Escrituras XIV/72; cf. AHD Astorga, Cámara Episcopal I/11 (ptd. below, Appendix no. X).
[6] AHN cód. 976B, fols. 14ᵛ–15ʳ; cf. ibid., fol. 29ʳ (ptd. below, Appendix no. XXII).
[7] AC Salamanca, no. 94.
[8] AC Zamora, Libro Negro, fol. 7ʳ.
[9] E.g., AC León, no. 1362 (ptd. *ES* XXXVI, ap. xlvi, pp. c–ciii).
[10] E.g., AC Salamanca, nos. 61, 62 (ptd. below, Appendix nos. XV, XVI).

More common than these later specialities, but even so by no means frequent, was the addition of the place of issue to the dating-clause. When this is found, it occurs usually with a preposition—*in Legione, apud Fradexas*[1]—or with the use of the locative—*Medine, Tude*[2]—though these usages are sometimes expanded; a judgement by Bishop Lope of Astorga was dated *apud Astoricam in palacio epsicopi* and one by Pedro Suárez of Compostela *in sancta Cruce de Castrelo ubi erant multi congregati*.[3] In adding the place of issue bishops may have been following the practice of the royal chancery whose scribes added it with fair regularity after the advent of Master Hugo in 1135.

The Confirmation

This form does not call for much comment. Bishop Pedro's confirmation in the act of 1132 is of a not unusual and fairly simple type. We may compare Bernardo of Zamora in a *fuero* granted in the following year, *Ego Bernardus Zamorensis episcopus in hanc kartam que fieri iussi manus meas (sic) roboravi*,[4] or Pelayo Menéndez of Tuy in 1152,[5] 'Ego Pelagius episcopus hoc scriptum quod cum canonicorum conventu tibi L.et fratri tuo Petro fieri iussi in curia domini Adefonsi imperatoris proprio robore confirmo'. This is rather more elaborate. But some bishops went even further. Here is Diego of León in 1116;[6]

Ego Didacus Legionensis ecclesie gratia Dei episcopus hanc cartam testamenti quam fieri iussi et legi, hilari animo in ecclesia sancte Marie multis nobilibus Legionis adstantibus et videntibus manibus meis roboravi.

During the century the forms employed tended to become simpler, sometimes to disappear altogether. *Ego Martinus*

---

[1] AHN 963/20; AC Zamora, leg. 14, no. 26 (both ptd. below, Appendix nos. XII, XXXIV).

[2] AC Salamanca, no. 78; AHN 1796/4 (both ptd. below, Appendix, nos. XVII, XXVI).

[3] AC Orense, Privilegios II/21; AHN 1750/20.

[4] AC Zamora, Libro Nego, fol. 15^V (ptd. below, Appendix no. VII).

[5] AC Tuy 10/10 (ptd. below, Appendix no. IX).

[6] AC León, no. 1362 (ptd. *ES* XXVI, ap. xlvi, pp. c-ciii).

Zamorensis confirmo is how Martín of Zamora confirmed a
number of his *acta*,[1] and this brevity was not unusual by his
time.

The Witness-lists

Witness-lists were usual at the foot of beneficial documents. Sometimes they are introduced by the phrase *Qui
presentes fuerunt,* but this is not common. The phrase used
in Pedro of Lugo's charter of 1132, *Qui presto fuerunt,* is
unique among the surviving *acta*. Witnesses sometimes pre-
face their name with the word *Ego*, though this is not the
case in the 1132 act. Their names are always in the nomina-
tive case, and are always followed by the word *testis* or *confirmo* or *subscribo*; of these, *testis* is the least common. The
witnesses are normally listed in columns, but sometimes their
names run straight across the parchment, sometimes they are
scattered apparently at random. They vary greatly in number.
There is a tendency for the number of witnesses to decline in
the course of the century, though *acta* with long witness-lists
were still being produced into the thirteenth century. Where
there are scribal subscriptions it is more common for these
to follow than to precede the witness-lists.

Acta which exhibit the diploma form in its fullness, like
the document of 1132 which was the starting point of this
discussion, never predominate at any period of the twelfth
century. But we find a great many *acta* which have several,
but not all, the characteristics of the diploma; thus for
example there are diplomas without an *arenga*, without a
corroboration, without a confirmation, with terse sanctions
or dating-clauses, with short witness-lists. Their general
similarity to the fully-developed diploma is such that, in
order to avoid lengthy discussion and perplexing categori-
sation, they have been counted among the diplomas and
some of the examples cited above have been picked from
among them. The diploma, either in its developed form or in
a modified form, was by far the most common instrument
employed by Leonese bishops during the twelfth century.
Now this form is usually associated by students of

---

[1] E.g., AC Zamora leg. 12, no. 2 (ptd. below, Appendix no. XXIV).

diplomatic with transactions of some solemnity. But what is striking about the Leonese *acta* is that the form was so often used for recording transactions which were far from solemn. We find it used, as we should expect, for general confirmations to religious houses and for *fueros*.[1] But we also find it employed for recording contracts of vassalage between a bishop and one of his men,[2] for recording sales of land,[3] for the recognizance of private debts,[4] and for the granting of licences to build churches.[5] The Leonese bishops were not adventurous. They did not try to devise new forms to meet new needs, but were content to trim what they had to say to the Procrustes' bed of the diploma. It is for this reason above all that the diplomatic of these instruments may be called archaic.

Is there, indeed, any evidence at all for experiment with new forms? Bishops certainly had other forms at their disposal, which they were prepared to use now and again, as occasion demanded. One of these was the *notitia*, or record of a lawsuit. This was introduced, usually without any of the customary opening protocol, by a preamble cast in the form of a *narratio* explaining why the dispute had arisen, and what course it had taken. The *narratio* moves insensibly into a *dispositio* setting out the steps which had been taken to effect a reconciliation between the contending parties, and the terms of that reconciliation. The final protocol is usually brief, but it is normal to find both date and witness-lists. This type of document was inherited by bishops from the past; a good many such survive from the tenth and eleventh centuries, and some of the twelfth-century examples have archaic features.[6] When Pelayo of Oviedo came to an agreement in 1104 with Count Fernando over two *monasteria* in the town

[1] E.g., Pedro Cristiano's general confirmation to Castañeda (ptd. *ES* XVI, ap. xxviii, pp. 484–6); Bernardo of Zamora's *fuero* to the settlers of Fuentesauco (ptd. below, Appendix no. VII).
[2] E.g., AHN 1326A/1 (Rodrigo II of Lugo, 1193).
[3] AC Orense, Escrituras XIV/72 (Alfonso of Orense, 1194).
[4] AC Zamora, leg. 13, no. 40 (Martin of Zamora, 1197).
[5] AC Zamora, leg. 13, no. 26 (ptd. below, Appendix no. XIII).
[6] One of these is the use of the word *intentio*, (where one might expect to find *contentio*) to mean 'a dispute', as in the phrase *Orta fuit intentio*; for an example, see below, Appendix no. VIII. The usage is quite common in documents of the eleventh century.

of Oviedo possession of which had been disputed between them, it was in a document of this sort that the terms were recorded.[1] Another instance can be found in the document recording the settlement between Nuño Alfonso of Mondoñedo and Count Rodrigo Vélaz in 1128.[2] Yet another is that ending the dispute between Bishop Arias of León and Count Rodrigo Martínez over lands that had belonged to Pedro Peláez.[3]

Professions of obedience constitute another class of documents which had a stereotyped form. Several are preserved in the *Historia Compostellana*, and many more in the Liber Fidei, the cathedral cartulary of Braga. A comparison between the oath sworn by the mysterious Pedro of Mondoñedo to Archbishop Maurice of Braga (*c*.1109) and that sworn by Giraldo of Salamanca to Archbishop Diego Gelmírez of Compostela (1121) reveals identical forms.[4] Clearly, bishops and their metropolitans had access to a standard form of instrument, designed for a specific purpose, which they adopted and used. It had probably been introduced to western Spain by the French clergy who arrived towards the end of the eleventh century.

Much the same may be said of indulgences. There is sufficient general similarity between the two indulgences we have and those which survive from other parts of Latin Christendom to make us reasonably sure that bishops had access to a standard form, or a range of possible standard forms from which they might choose one that seemed fitting. Again, Juan of León's *epistola formata* of 1153 was just such a stereotyped form, though a highly unusual one for its date.[5] Canons of councils and the 'private' correspondence of the bishops naturally had their own forms too.

But to show that bishops knew of other types of document and that they sometimes used them does not take us much further. Of course they did. What we should really

[1] Ptd. C.M. Vigil, *Asturias Monumental* (Oviedo, 1887), pp. 85–6.
[2] AC Mondoñedo, carpeta del siglo XII, unnumbered.
[3] AC León, no. 1410 (ptd. below, Appendix no. VIII). The document is unusual in bearing no date.
[4] AD Braga, Liber Fidei, fol. 151ʳ, (ptd. below, Appendix no. I), *HC* p. 341.
[5] For the documents referred to here, see above p. 123, n. 4.

like to know is whether they themselves experimented with
new forms, whether they themselves made any attempt to
escape from the heavy hand of the diploma. Some signs of
experimentation there are, towards the end of the century.
Let us take first of all the document in which Pedro Suárez
of Compostela recorded his ruling in a dispute over diocesan
boundaries between the sees of Salamanca and Ciudad Rodrigo in 1174.[1] Some of the features of the diploma are still
there—the multiple authentication (autograph subscription,
chirograph, *rota* and seal) and the long witness-lists; this was,
after all, an important ruling and the archbishop was acting
as a papal judge-delegate. But others are conspicuous by their
absence: there is no invocation, no sanction. Further features
are there too, which are new and unusual. In the first place,
the act is cast in epistolary form; the archbishop addresses
himself to the dean and chapter of Salamanca and the prior
and chapter of Ciudad Rodrigo, and greets them. Second,
there are clear signs of the influence of the papal chancery.
After the *salutatio* the *arenga* beginning *Ex iniuncto parvitati*
is closely modelled on a form of *arenga* commonly used by
the popes. The next sentence begins with an introductory
Eapropter, which is another curial feature. The dating-clause,
both in its form and in its position after the subscriptions,
recalls the dating-clauses of papal solemn privileges. And an
attempt is made, if not consistently maintained, to reproduce
the rhythmic *cursus* of the papal chancery. Third, the language is simple and direct; there is none of the bombast or
verbiage we so often find in the diploma.

This document does not stand alone. Some of its features
are to be met with in other of Pedro Suárez's *acta*, for example, in the mandate of about 1188 by which he ordered
the archdeacon, clergy and people of Plasencia to obey the
bishop of Avila.[2] We find them also in an award by Bishop
Pedro of Tuy of 1200:[3] there is the same epistolary form,
the same reminiscences of curial phraseology (*Quoniam in*

---

[1] AC Salamanca, no. 61 (ptd. below Appendix no. XV).
[2] AHN 18/4 (6) (ptd. below, Appendix no. XX). The latter part of this document
is missing.
[3] AHN 1796/4 (ptd. below, Appendix no. XXVI).

presencia nostra, auctoritate qua fungimur), the same simplicity. A judgement by Manrique of León, dated 1182, shows
some traces of papal influence; and he too used an epistolary
form of address in some of his *acta*.[1] A Lugo act of 1202 be-
trays the same features.[2] The impetus behind these developments came, it may be suggested, from the Compostela of
Pedro Suárez. I say this not merely because it is in one of his
acts that the new tendencies appear for the first time. It is
rather because it is likely that he had studied abroad and had
thereby had opportunities to learn how bishops conducted
their business elsewhere; because he enjoyed close relations
with the papacy; and because he was an efficient administrator.

But Pedro Suárez had also been Fernando II's chancellor
before he reached the episcopate as bishop of Salamanca, and
this should remind us that bishops were still learning from
kings as well as starting to learn from popes. (Since so many
of them became bishops after service in the royal chancery,
perhaps it would be more accurate to say that bishops continued to draw on their own previous experience as royal
servants to assist them in their work as diocesans.) Towards
the end of the reign of Fernando II the so-called *carta
abierta*, or letter-patent, was developed by the royal chancery, and came to be widely used during the reign of his son
Alfonso IX.[3] This form of document, normally beneficial in
purpose, was characterized by the terseness of its phraseology
and above all by the general notification with which (usually
after a short invocation) its text opened—*Notum sit omnibus*,
or some variant upon this.[4] Bishops were not slow to follow
suit. Pedro Suárez himself used it, for example in a grant to
the church of Tuy in 1200.[5] It was employed very extensively by Bishop Martín of Zamora, who was a protégé of
Pedro Suárez and enjoyed close relations with the royal court,

---

[1] AC León, nos. 1397, 1444.
[2] AHN 1326D/3, (ptd. below Appendix no. XXVIII).
[3] For discussion, see *GRF* pp. 236-7; *GAL* vol. I, pp. 498-500.
[4] For examples, see *GRF* pp. 329-30 (no. 53); *GAL* nos. 21, 28, 29, 36, 44, 78,
90, 96, etc. It will be seen that the forms were as yet far from fixed.
[5] AC Tuy 10/21, (ptd. below, Appendix no. XXXII).

though there is no evidence that he had been employed in the Leonese chancery.[1] The new form can also be traced in the dioceses of León, Salamanca, Lugo and Oviedo.[2]

These examples come from the early years of the thirteenth century. It is clear that by this date bishops were beginning to experiment with new diplomatic instruments. But the contrast in forms should not be exaggerated. Bishops seem to have handled the new ones cautiously, sometimes clumsily, at first. And if these developments have been glanced at only cursorily, this is justified by the consideration that over the period as a whole the diploma reigned supreme, that its use persisted to the end of our period and beyond it.

A treatise could be written about the episcopal *acta* from the twelfth-century kingdom of León. The remarks in this chapter constitute only a sketch. They will have succeeded in their purpose if they have shown how deeply conservative the bishops were in these matters: how slow they were to develop their household organization; how sluggish and primitive were their secretarial arrangements; how tenacious were their scribes of old forms and old appearances. Administrative innovation is not everything. Historians commonly pay it more attention than it deserves. Perhaps this antique machinery sufficed to answer the bishops' administrative needs. But we have yet to examine what it was that bishops were trying to do.

[1] E.g., AC Zamora leg. 13, no. 13; leg. 14. no. 26 (both ptd. below, Appendix nos. XXXIII, XXXIV).
[2] E.g., AC León, no. 1474; AC Salamanca, no. 112; AHN 1326G/11, 24; AC Oviedo, carpeta 5, no. 4.

4

CHURCH GOVERNMENT

In the early summer of the year 1169 the king of Portugal, Afonso Henriques, led an army to the extreme south of his dominions, into the no-man's-land where Christian and Moslem met. An adventurer named Geraldo Sempavor— Gerald the Fearless, dubbed by modern historians the Cid of Portugal—had succeeded in capturing the city of Badajoz. He was being hard-pressed by its erstwhile Almohade rulers, and the king went to his relief. The king of León, Fernando II, judging that Badajoz lay within his own sphere of influence and that the Portuguese had no business to be there, hastened south to oppose them. In the confused fighting in the town the Portuguese were routed by the Leonese troops and their king, fleeing on horseback, struck the projecting hinge of one of the gates and was flung to the ground with a broken leg, where he was found and taken prisoner by the Leonese. For Fernando II the event could not have been more fortunate; he was able to extract certain disputed territories in the north as the price of the king's release. One of these was Toroño, the land round Tuy; another was the upper valley of the river Limia, some forty miles to the east; still another was the wild and desolate country which stretches beyond the Limia towards Verín (now in Spain) and Chaves (now in Portugal). The latter territory was divided in the twelfth century into two districts known at the time as *Capraria* and *Lobarzana*.

These two areas had for some time been the subject of dispute between León and Portungal; they had also been disputed between the two dioceses of Orense and Braga. For about a generation before 1169 they had formed part of the diocese of Braga. When the king of Portugal abandoned political control of them, so too did his archbishop of Braga abandon ecclesiastical control, and *Capraria* and *Lobarzana* became part of the diocese of Orense. What this meant quickly became clear. Fernando II's lieutenant in the region expelled the archdeacon and archpriests of the church of Braga on the orders of the king and handed ecclesiastical control over to two canons who were acting on behalf of the church of Orense. Shortly afterwards an archdeacon was appointed, and under him an archpriest. The archpriest, accompanied by a layman appointed by the king's lieutenant, went to the region to extract as much as he possibly could, as our source frankly tells us, from the parish clergy there because they were still inclined to Braga and unwilling voluntarily to make their due payments to the church of Orense. Intimidation had to be used; the resulting spoils were divided between the archpriest and his lay assistant. This story, instructive in more ways than one, may fittingly serve to introduce the subject of church government.[1]

The administrative framework within which Leonese bishops had to operate was similar to that known throughout western Christendom. But for several reasons their task was made complicated. New ways of organizing a church had been introduced, under Franco-papal influence, in the latter part of the eleventh century. A series of popes, legates and immigrant French bishops attempted to impose a pattern of metropolitan and territorial diocesan organization upon a Leonese-Castilan church which had only haltingly known these things before. The process of setting them up and making them work was not easy. Simultaneously, churchmen were faced by the task of extending their ecclesiastical organization into the areas of territory reconquered from the Moslems, and reconstructing a Christian church there upon new foundations. This again was never easy. Bishops could usually count upon the help of kings, but they were to run up against the interests of other groups, notably the Military Orders, and they were to be inhibited for much of the time by sheer lack of resources. Confusion was worse confounded by the fact that there had taken place neither in the old Christian areas of the north nor in the new Christian areas of the south that clean sweep of ancient institutions and customs which would have rendered the work of the innovators incomparably easier. Features of an older order stuck up through rifts in the new like ancient geological features in a

---

[1] The tale has to be pieced together from a series of depositions taken in 1193–4: AC Orense, Obispo y Dignidades, no. 17.

younger landscape. Bishops were faced by old territorial divisions, old conciliar practices, old intellectual interests, old loyalties, old attitudes on the part of churchman and layman alike. There were, finally, random complicating factors. Some of these were political, like the gradual drawing apart of the county of Portugal from the kingdom of León; some were personal, like the ambitions of Diego Gelmírez for his church at Compostela; some were social, like the burgeoning of towns along the pilgrimage route, or the violent tenor of like along the southern frontier.

METROPOLITAN ORGANIZATION

'A la fin du XIe siècle ou au début du XIIe, Rome impose à l'Espagne des archevêques.'[1] It is true that late Roman and Visigothic Spain had known metropolitans;[2] but the organization over which they presided had crumbled after the Islamic conquest. When it was revived by the reforming popes of the Hildebrandine period it had two new features: archbishops were tied to the papacy by the necessity of seeking their pallia from Rome; and as metropolitans set over ecclesiastical provinces, they were given defined powers over their suffragan bishops. It may be as well to run over once more the structure that resulted. Toledo became a metropolitan see in 1086, Tarragona in 1089, Braga in 1099 or 1100, Santiago de Compostela in 1120. As far as the kingdom of León was concerned, the sees of Astorga, Lugo, Mondoñedo, Orense and Tuy were suffragans of Braga. Salamanca, Ciudad Rodrigo and Coria were suffragans of Compostela; so too were Avila in Castile, and—though Braga disputed this—Lamego and Lisbon in Portugal. The sees of Oviedo and León were exempted from any metropolitan supervision and placed under the direct protection of the papacy, a state of affairs that was disputed by the archbishops of Toledo for at least part of the century, as we have seen. Toledo had no certain suffragans in León, but had

[1] M. Cocheril, *Études sur le monachisme en Espagne et au Portugal* (Paris-Lisbon, 1966), p. 23.
[2] D. Mansilla, 'Orígenes de la organización metropolitana en la iglesia española' *Hispania Sacra* xii (1959), 255–91.

designs over two further sees. One of these was Salamanca; the other was Zamora, a 'problem' see, over which the three metropolitans of Toledo, Braga and Compostela wrangled for the better part of eighty years.[1]

Was the ecclesiastical province a functioning unit of church government? It looks as though metropolitans wanted it to be. We have seen already that they tried to extend their provinces. León and Oviedo, exempted in 1104–5, were declared suffragans of Toledo by Calixtus II in 1121. León escaped the Toledan grasp between 1125 and 1130, Oviedo in 1157. The appointment of Bernardo, the protégé of the archbishop of Toledo, to the see of Zamora in 1120, is an indication of Toledo's desire to scoop Zamora into her province. The consecration of Nuño of Salamanca by Archbishop Bernardo of Toledo in 1124 was certainly seen at Compostela as an attempt by the Toledan interest to extend metropolitan power over a new see. Metropolitans tried too to ensure that their local sympathizers were placed in control of their suffragan sees, and to exact professions of obedience from them when they consecrated them. That these attempts appear sporadic may be owing only to the patchy nature of our evidence. Giraldo of Salamanca may have had Compostelan connections; Alfonso Pérez certainly did; so too, later on, did Pedro Suárez. Pedro de Ponte of Ciudad Rodrigo was another who was closely connected with the church of Compostela. The professions of obedience sworn to Diego Gelmírez by Sancho of Avila (in 1121) and Iñigo of Avila (1133) are preserved in the *Historia Compostellana*.[2] The richest surviving collections of professions of obedience is preserved in the *Liber Fidei* of Braga. Thus we have from the see of Mondoñedo professions preserved from Pedro (1110?), Nuño (1112), Pedro Gudestéiz (1155), Juan (1169) and Rabinato (1173);[3] from the see of Astorga the professions of Alo (1122), Arnaldo I (1144) and Fernando I (1156);[4] from Tuy, those of Alfonso (c.1100), Pelayo Menéndez (1131),

---

[1] The case of Zamora is discussed at length below, ch. 5 pp. 195–203.
[2] *HC* pp. 323, 537.
[3] AD Braga, Liber Fidei, fols. 138^V, 146^V, 150^r, 151^r, 153^r.
[4] Ibid., fols. 138^V, 152^V, 153^r.

Isidoro (1156), Juan (1168) and Beltrán (1173).[1] The archbishop of Braga was quick to exact professions from the first
two bishops of the see of Lamego, restored early in 1147,
and from the first bishop of Lisbon, the Englishman Gilbert
of Hastings.[2]

These facts in themselves, however, tell us little or nothing
about the working of the province as a unit of government.
Did the metropolitans hold provincial councils? Did they
conduct visitations of their suffragan sees? There is little
evidence that provincial councils were held, and we can be
certain that they were not held regularly. Let us look at the
evidence from Braga. In 1148 Archbishop João of Braga
held a *colloquium* in his cathedral church attended by his
suffragans the bishops of Porto, Lamego, Viseu and Coimbra
and *quidam archidiaconus civitatis Ulixbone nomine Elde-
bredus* (though, surprisingly, not the recently appointed
bishop of Lisbon).[3] We learn from another source that the
king of Portugal also attended.[4] Was this intimate little
gathering a 'provincial council'? Not one of the Galician
suffragans of Braga attended it; and it is clear that the main
purpose of the meeting was to hear a summons to the council
of Rheims delivered by a papal messenger, the clerk Boso. It
sounds rather like the larger gathering assembled at Palencia
by Alfonso VII at about the same time, *quando prefatus
imperator habuit ibi colloquium cum episcopis et baronibus
sui regni de vocatione domni pape ad concilium.*[5] We hear of
three other assemblies at Braga, one between 1148 and 1166,
and two between 1175 and 1188, which may have had the
character of provincial councils: but we have little information about who attended, and none at all about the business
they met to transact.[6] The evidence for the holding of these
last three assemblies comes from sworn depositions taken
towards the end of the century in the prolonged suit between
Braga and Compostela over the suffragan sees disputed
between them. One of the best ways of demonstrating the

---

[1] Ibid., fols. 70^V-71^r, 138^V, 151^r.   [2] Ibid., fols. 71^r, 118^V, 138^V.
[3] Ibid., fols. 117^V-118^r.
[4] AD Braga, Gaveta dos Arcebispos, no. 4.
[5] León, Archivo de San Isidoro, no. 146.
[6] AD Braga, Gaveta dos Arcebispos, nos. 4, 39.

subjection of a suffragan was to show that its bishops attended councils convened by the metropolitan. We can be sure that if the Braga party could have mustered more councils to buttress their case at Rome they would have done so. The fact that they referred, and only vaguely at that, to a mere three such meetings in the whole of the second half of the century is a sure sign that provincial councils (or whatever we choose to call them) were few and far between.

The evidence from the province of Santiago de Compostela is consistent with that from Braga. It all comes from the epis-copate of Diego Gelmírez, that is to say, from the *Historia Compostellana*. We have no hint that any councils were held by any later archbishop until the middle of the thirteenth century. Diego Gelmírez held six councils at Compostela, in 1114, 1121, 1122, 1124, 1125 and 1130.[1] But it is very doubtful whether we can call any one of these a provincial council in the true sense of the term. Three of them—those of 1121, 1122 and 1124—were legatine councils, held by Diego during the period while he exercised the prerogatives of a legate of the Roman church; he held them for the bishops of those churches over which his powers extended, not as a metropolitan for his suffragans. Thus the council of 1121 was held *ex praecepto domini papae*; that of 1124 was attended by the bishops of Astorga, Lugo, Mondoñedo, Tuy, Porto, Zamora, Salamanca and the bishop-elect of Burgos, together with twenty-seven abbots and other *religiosis personis et bonis clericis*. The character of the council of 1125 must hav have been rather different, for by that date Diego's legation had lapsed. We do not know exactly who attended, but it cer-tainly included, alongside the churchmen, *comites et principes*, the magnates of Galician lay society. Though they did confer *primum de ecclesiasticis negotiis*, most of the busi-ness of the council seems to have been secular—for it is well to remember that Diego was playing an important part in the political affairs of Galicia at this time. The earliest council, of 1114, seems to have been different in character again. At that time Diego was not an archbishop. The council was attended by the bishops of Tuy, Mondoñedo, Lugo, Orense

---

[1] *HC* pp. 191–2, 308, 359, 417–19, 427–30, 500–1.

and Porto, all of them suffragans of Braga,[1] a number of abbots, and *comites et ceteros terrae optimates*. Diego seems to have reached back to an earlier tradition of what has usefully been called an 'interdiocesan synod'; for the council was called to report and publish the canons of the council of León, held a month earlier under the presidency of the archbishop of Toledo, for the benefit of those in Galicia who had been unable to attend it; just as the council of Compostela of 1056 was held in order to disseminate the decrees of the council of Coyanza (1055) in Galicia.[2] The 1130 council looks rather like it. It was attended by the bishops of Mondoñedo, Lugo, Porto, Tuy and Avila, together with the abbots *totius provinciae*, whatever this phrase may mean. Apart from the consecration of a new bishop for Salamanca, the main purpose of the council was to publish the decrees passed at the council of Carrión, held two months earlier by the legate cardinal Humbert.

As for visitations, there is practically no evidence for them at all. Two archbishops of Braga were said to have visited Zamora and to have been received as metropolitans, Paio Mendes (1118-37) and João Peculiar (1138-75).[3] But Zamora, as we shall see, was a rather special case. When João Peculiar passed through Coimbra on his way back from Rome (whence he was returning with his pallium), Bishop Bernardo *recepit eum in processione. . .et dimisit ei domum suam et ivit ad aliam et procuravit eum.*[4] So a lord would expect to be received by one of his men. Other reports to the same effect could be cited, but they hardly add up to a systematic scheme of visitation. From Compostela, we have no evidence at all. If Diego Gelmírez wished to see his far-flung Extremaduran suffragans, they came to him, he did not go to them. He was always far readier to visit the royal court than the distant and struggling bishoprics of Avila or Salamanca.

Our evidence, such as it is, suggests that the province was

---

[1] At that time the archbishop of Braga, suspended from office, was prosecuting an appeal in Rome.
[2] Cf. G. Martínez Díez, 'El Concilio Compostelano del reinado de Fernando I', *AEM* i (1964), 121-38.
[3] ANTT, Coleccão Especial, Corporacões Diversas, Mitra de Braga, caixa 1, no. 2.
[4] AD Braga, Gaveta dos Arcebispos, no. 4.

not an important unit in ecclesiastical governments. Metropolitans wanted a following of loyal and obedient suffragans, but the rights they claimed to exercise over them were few, being limited in practice to consecration and the taking of a profession of obedience. There is no evidence for the regular holding of provincial councils properly so-called, nor for regular visitations; though if an archbishop found himself at the seat of one of his suffragans, he expected to be fittingly received. One's impression is that metropolitans desired to exercise no systematic supervision of their suffragans' diocesan work. It is true that they were not required to do so until after 1215. Yet metropolitans in some parts of Europe had taken steps in the period between the Third and Fourth Lateran councils to give their office practical force, by holding councils, by conducting visitations, and by so doing to provide occasions for the exercise of metropolitan jurisdiction. There is no sign that these tendencies were present in León.

DIOCESAN BOUNDARIES

An enormous amount of energy was expended in the course of the twelfth century in disputes over diocesan boundaries. Such disputes were not peculiar to Spain, but they were more common there than in other countries of western Europe. In England, for example, diocesan boundaries had in general become fixed at an earlier date, and were normally coterminous with the secular boundaries of the shire. In Spain, as we saw in chapter 1, the circumstances of the *Reconquista* gave rise to a desire to restore the ecclesiastical arrangements of the Visigoths: but partly because these arrangements were imperfectly known, partly because new sees had been created since the Visigothic period, the attempt to give effect to this desire gave rise to quarrelling over diocesan boundaries. A further cause of dispute was political. Hostilities over boundaries were exacerbated where a dispute over political frontiers in the same territory also existed. Finally, we should note the coincidence in time between the age of diocesan boundary disputes in western Spain and the period of strong foreign, Franco-papal, influence upon the church there. Little emphasis had been placed on the territorial diocese during the tenth and eleventh centuries. Behind the disputes of the twelfth one can detect the pressure of orderly minds. The haphazard arrangements of an earlier day were not good enough for them; they wanted instead to see the land neatly parcelled out in territorial dioceses of roughly equal size, with frontiers that were fixed and known.

There were many such disputes during the century. For example, between Compostela and Mondoñedo; between León and Lugo, León and Astorga; between Astorga and Orense, and Braga, and Zamora; between Salamanca and Zamora, and Avila, and Ciudad Rodrigo; and so on. Accounts of them make tedious reading. It will be enough to refer here to three examples. A boundary dispute between the dioceses of Salamanca and Ciudad Rodrigo was settled by the archbishop of Compostela in 1174.[1] This was a fairly simple case. Ciudad Rodrigo was a new see, founded in 1161, with no Visigothic precursor on that site, and carved out of the diocese of Salamanca. No wonder there was friction. But there were no ancient claims, nor documents to justify them, which might have delayed a settlement. And there was the imperious will of Fernando II to hasten one, together, apparently, with the desire of both parties to reach a compromise. The settlement reached, though possibly shaken from time to time,[2] seems to have endured, so one may assume that the arrangements made by Archbishop Pedro Suárez in 1174 worked satisfactorily.

The dispute between Lugo and León was a very different affair. It lasted the better part of a century and gave rise to a great deal of litigation. The course of the dispute has recently been carefully surveyed,[3] and only a few comments need be made on it here. First of all, it brings out well the way in which these disputes aroused feelings of intense local loyalty among bishops and cathedral chapters. They put the interests of their own church before any others and were prepared to go to extraordinary lengths to protect or exploit

[1] AC Salamanca, nos. 61, 62 (ptd. below Appendix nos. XV, XVI).
[2] Papal bulls of 1196 and 1210 hint at some bickering: AC Salamanca, nos. 105, 126.
[3] E. Valiña Sampedro, *El Camino de Santiago, Estudio Histórico-Jurídico* (Salamanca, 1971), ch. 5.

them. Second, it demonstrates how difficult it was for men to reach a decision on the basis of the available evidence. The Lugo party resorted to forgery to assist their case; but the effect of forgery was rather to postpone than to hasten a decision. Third, it shows how hard it was to find a tribunal whose decisions the parties to the suit would accept. At various times the kings of León, the archbishops of Toledo and Compostela, several popes and two papal legates, all heard the case; but at various times the decisions of each and all were flouted or disregarded by one or other of the parties.

The dispute between the churches of Orense and Braga, mentioned at the beginning of the present chapter, was of a different kind again. The area in dispute lay between the upper valley of the river Limia to the west and the town of Bragança to the east, which was then, as it is still, the frontier district between León and Portugal. Political tensions added fuel to the flames of ecclesiastical rivalry: significantly, one of the minor actors in the conflict stated that he held his archdeaconry *nomine Bracarensis ecclesie et regni Portugalliae*,[1] and we have already seen that an important turning-point in the dispute came about as the result of a political event, the capture of the king of Portugal in 1169 and his cession to Fernando II of León of some of his northern territories as the price of his release.

Wearisome though these disputes are (and the reader has been let off very lightly), they do have significance in the ecclesiastical history of twelfth-century Spain. By and large, they were resolved. In many instances of dispute (though not quite all), frontiers were fixed and the territorial diocese established. This was an important administrative achievement, and it brought Spain into conformity with the practice of most of the rest of Latin Christendom. In the course of their progress towards settlement, the quarrels gave rise to ever-increasing resort to the papal curia. It is a commonplace that papal jurisdiction enlarged its scope during the twelfth century through the demands of litigants; and this was as frequent in Spain as anywhere else. The fact that boundary disputes were more common in Spain than elsewhere meant

[1] AC Orense, Obispo y Dignidades, no. 17 bis.

that curial intervention in them was one of the more important levers used by the popes to extend their judicial authority
over western Spain. At the same time, it should be borne in
mind that papal decisions could be flouted and that churches
usually needed the assistance of the lay power to enforce
ecclesiastical rulings.

Other questions remain, to which no answers can be given.
Did the energies which bishops and chapters and local clergy
expended in these often unseemly quarrels cause them to be
slack in attending to urgent pastoral needs? It may have been
so. Certainly it is hard to think of the servants of the bishop
of Orense who bullied the wretched populace of *Lobarzana*
and *Capraria* into producing *vota* as worthy pastors of their
flocks.[1] Was the state of endemic hostility between neighbouring sees an important factor in inhibiting the Leonese
church from presenting a united front in the face of aggression
on the part of kings? We may guess that it was, but we have
no means of measuring its strength. The emotions generated
and sustained within the diocesan community in the course
of these disputes seem to have been powerful. This community found the focus of its activities and loyalties in the
cathedral chapter.

THE CATHEDRAL CHAPTER

The bishops cannot be considered in isolation from their
cathedral chapters. We have seen already that there is good
reason for supposing that they transacted diocesan business
in and with their chapters; and it will be suggested that
throughout the century in the kingdom of León the diocese
was a living and working, a coherent unit, of ecclesiastical
government—something which it was ceasing to be in some
other areas, for instance northern France. At the heart of the
diocese was the cathedral chapter. Something, however cur-
sory, must be said about its organization.

Of the twelve Leonese cathedrals all but two had secular
chapters during the twelfth century. The chapters of the remaining two adopted the Augustinian rule, Tuy in 1138 and

[1] Take this, for example: the archpriest of the archdeacon of Orense 'coegit
ipsum testem extrahere vota de ipsa ecclesia quia si non fecisset aufferebant ei
domum et quicquid habebat. . .', AC Orense, Obispo y Dignidades, no. 17.

Coria between 1181 and 1185.[1] Why did they do this? There is no reason to suppose that the men concerned were ascetically-minded, that they preferred the austerities of a regular life to the ease of a secular. The answer may be that the Augustinian Rule offered solid economic advantages which poorly-endowed cathedrals could ill afford to forego. Common control of property was less likely to lead to waste than the prebendal system, and throughout Europe it tended to be the poorer type of see that went Augustinian; for example Sigüenza in Castile, or Carlisle in England.

Though the ten remaining cathedral chapters were secular, nearly all had certain elements of a common life. We hear of common refectories,[2] and sometimes of a common dormitory,[3] for the canons. It is to be presumed that in the old-established cathedrals these arrangements were survivals of the observance of an earlier day. One of the canons of the council of Compostela of 1056 had required cathedral chapters to have *unum refectorium* and *unum dormitorium*.[4] The author of that part of the *Codex Calixtinus* known as the 'Pilgrim's Guide', who was writing towards the middle of the twelfth century, observed that the Rule of St. Isidore was observed by the canons of Compostela.[5] It is not clear what he meant by this, for Isidore composed no Rule for canons, and as a statement of customs obtaining in the twelfth century it is incorrect; but his remark may represent a memory, perhaps confused, of an earlier order of things. We do, however, find these same elements of a common life in some of the newly restored sees, at Zamora and Salamanca, for

---

[1] See above, ch. 2, pp. 34, 51.
[2] E.g., for Astorga, BN MS. 4357, Tumbo Negro, nos. 633–5, 639; for León, AC León, nos. 1362, 1390 (ptd. *ES* XXVI, app. xlvi, liii, pp. c–ciii, cxi–cxiv); for Lugo, AHN 1325D/11 (ptd. *ES* XLI, ap. xi, pp. 316–18); for Oviedo, *Docs. Oviedo* no. 151; for Compostela, *HC* p. 55; for Zamora, AC Zamora, leg. 8, no. 5.
[3] E.g., *HC* p. 243.
[4] C.I, section 2; for the acts of the council, see G. Martínez Díez, 'El Concilio Compostelano del reinado de Fernando I', *AEM* i (1964), 121–38.
[5] *Le Guide du Pèlerin de St.-Jacques de Compostelle*, ed. J. Vielliard (4th ed. Mâcon, 1969), p. 120; cf. *LFH* III, p. 253. For discussion of the appearance of regular cathedral chapters in western Spain during the eleventh century, see C.J. Bishko, 'Fernando I y los orígenes de la alianza castellano-leonesa con Cluny', *CHE* xlvii–xlviii (1968), 64, 83. Professor Bishko would see here the influence of the Cluniacs.

example, and across the Castilian frontier at Avila.[1] So it would seem that the newly-constituted dioceses adhered to the traditional Leonese way—if Professor Bishko is correct, perhaps we should say 'Franco-Leonese' way—of organizing cathedral chapters.

We know a little about the organization of these chapters in the twelfth century, considerably more about their organization in the thirteenth. But we must beware of using this thirteenth-century material as a guide to twelfth-century conditions. Some of the changes that took place after 1215 were far-reaching, and even though thirteenth-century capitular statutes may often have done no more than formalize existing customs, we can never be sure of this; and so we must eschew them here.[2]

The size of chapters varied from cathedral to cathedral, just as it did in England or in France, depending on the resources of the see. We have no evidence about numbers from several sees, and it is unfortunate that these are the smaller or poorer ones—Ciudad Rodrigo, Coria, Mondoñedo and Tuy. Orense had thirty-six canons in 1198, but we do not know whether this figure included the twelve *portionarii* who were mentioned at about the same time.[3] Lugo was bidden by Cardinal Hyacinth in 1173 to have thirty canons and twenty *prebendarii*, and this was a reduction in size.[4] Bishop Diego established forty canons, *tam maiores quam minores*, at León in 1120; by 1224 the establishment had grown to fifty canons, twenty-five *portionarii* and twelve choir-boys.[5] Oviedo might have had as many as sixty canons in 1117[6] and Astorga was allowed seventy by Celestine III in 1191.[7] At

---

[1] AC Zamora, leg. 8, no. 5; AC Salamanca, no. 19; AHN 18/10, 19/1-3.

[2] For thirteentn-century capitular reforms, see D. Mansilla, *Igelsia castellano-leonesa y curia romana en los tiempos del rey San Fernando* (Madrid, 1945), pp. 193–222.

[3] *MHV* I, nos. 158, 163.

[4] AHN 1325F/9 (ptd. inaccurately *ES* XLI, ap. xvii, pp. 326–8).

[5] AC León no. 1384 (ptd. below Appendix no. IV).

[6] *Docs. Oviedo* no. 138.

[7] What is known about this lost papal bull is to be found in A. Quintana Prieto, 'Registro de documentos pontificios de Astorga (1139–1413)', *Anthologica Annua* xi (1963), 189–226.

Compostela, Diego Peláez instituted twenty-four canons; Diego Gelmírez increased this to seventy-two; Pedro Suárez later tried to restrict a growth in numbers which dangerously encroached upon the see's resources; yet by 1245 the chapter was eighty-six strong.[1]

The members of these chapters were of various ranks. At the summit were the dignitaries, among whom were the archdeacons. After them came the canons properly so-called; then *portionarii*; finally *duplarii* and *pueri*. The dignitaries held capitular offices or dignities. The canons and *portionarii* held prebends, but the *portionarii* were required to be resident and had no power to deliberate in meetings of the chapter; they look like minor canons. A *duplarius* is first mentioned in a Compostela document of 1170 where he is recorded as a substitute for one of the dignitaries, saying his *officium divinum* for him while he is engaged in his non-choral duties;[2] presumably therefore the four *duplarii* found by 1245 were substitutes for the four principal dignitaries. The *duplarius* was a humble member of the chapter of Compostela, ranking beneath the *portionarii minores*. *Pueri*, of course, were choir-boys.

The organization of the cathedral dignitaries which we find in the kingdom of León is, broadly-speaking, similar to the 'four-square' organization familiar in northern France and England, built upon the four offices of dean, precentor, chancellor and treasurer. But Spain had a different nomenclature, which she shared with certain other cathedrals in the south of France, and which might have been introduced thence in the latter part of the eleventh century. The dean was normally called the *prior*, the precentor was sometimes called the *primicerius*, the treasurer customarily the *sacrista*, and the chancellor always the *magister scholarum*. In the course of the century the nomenclature of northern Europe was gradually adopted, with the exception of the title of chancellor. (Those who hold the office in Spanish cathedrals today are still called *maestrescuela*.) The stages by which the new titles appeared, and the occasional co-existence for a

---

[1] *HC* pp. 55, 544; *LFH* IV, ap. liii, pp. 135-8; Mansilla, op.cit., p. 200.
[2] *LFH* IV, ap. xlii, pp. 105-6.

time of the new with the old, need not concern us here. Certain cathedrals had other dignitaries: at Compostela there were seven cardinals.[1]

A very few instances of statute-making by bishops and their chapters have come down to us from the twelfth century, most of them from Compostela. Pedro Gudestéiz issued a constitution in 1169 concerning prebendaries who were absent for study, and another in 1170 defining the duties of the *magister scolarum*.[2] Pedro Suárez made certain arrangements relating to the offices and revenues of the dean and the four archdeacons in 1177, which was confirmed by Alexander III in 1179, together with various other capitular reforms of which no texts survive.[3] A little later the statute concerning absence for study was confirmed and amplified.[4] Pedro Suárez had previously, while bishop of Salamanca, made statutes there requiring stricter observance of the rule of residence; we know of these from the papal confirmation, dated 9 June 1170.[5] The only other possible evidence we have of capitular statute-making by a bishop comes from the diocese of Astorga, where Bishop Lope is said to have made some statutes in 1204, but we do not know what they were about.[6] This exhausts our evidence for the practice. The following century, by contrast, was to see a flood of capitular legislation, especially in the years 1228-50.

Temporalities were normally divided between bishops and their chapters. It has been said that this process occurred gradually between the years 1100, by which date such a division had been made at Palencia, and 1234, when Gregory IX assumed that it was standard in Spain.[7] It seems likely that it tended to take place during the first half of this period of about 130 years, and that it may even have taken place before 1100 in some cathedrals. At Lugo, for example, such a

---

[1] See A.G. Biggs, *Diego Gelmírez* (Washington, 1949), pp. 242-4, and references there given.

[2] *LFH* IV, ap. xl, pp. 99-101; ap. xlii, pp. 105-6.

[3] *LFH* IV, ap. l, pp. 122-4; ap. liii, pp. 135-8 (where incorrectly dated to 1178).

[4] *LFH* V, ap. vii, pp. 21-3.

[5] AC Salamanca, no. 77.

[6] BN MS. 4357, Particulares no. 71; the bald eighteenth-century summary gives very little information.

[7] Mansilla, *Iglesia castellano-leonesa*, pp. 193-4.

division was formally made in 1120, but Bishop Pedro's act
speaks of some earlier and similar division effected by Bishop
Amor, who had died by 1096.[1] At León and Oviedo, *acta*
from 1116 and 1117 respectively refer to division of temporalities before the death of Alfonso VI in 1109,[2] while at
Compostela the measure seems to have been carried out by
Diego Gelmírez as part of his capitular reforms of 1100-02,
though it may go back to the episcopate of Diego Peláez.[3]
The step seems to have been taken by the new sees soon after
their restoration. So, at any rate, at Avila, where a division
had certainly been made by the time of Bishop Iñigo (1133-*c.*
1158), possibly before him by Sancho I (1121-33).[4] At
Salamanca the chapter was handling all its own affairs by the
1170s,[5] an indication that a division had been made by then.
We have no information from Zamora, Ciudad Rodrigo or
Coria. Where documents survive which recorded the details
of these divisions we sometimes have hints of conflict over
revenues between bishops and chapters which had occasioned their making. They did not necessarily obviate such
conflict for the future. At Astorga, where such a division had
been made before 1122,[6] conflict over revenues was one of
the issues in the sordid quarrels towards the end of the century. At Tuy, where a division was made when the chapter
adopted the Augustinian Rule in 1138, Alfonso VII had to
act *ad removendam dissensionem* between the bishop and
his canons eighteen years later, in 1156.[7]

Until a great deal more work shall have been done, we can
make only more or less ill-informed guesses about the sort of
men who made up the cathedral chapters, and about the
means by which they were chosen. One's impression is that it
was with the bishops that choice lay in the last resort. It

[1] *ES* XLI, ap. ii, pp. 296-301.
[2] *ES* XXXVI, ap. xlvi, pp. c-ciii; *Docs. Oviedo* no. 138.
[3] *HC* p. 256.
[4] AHN 19/1-3.
[5] AC Avila, no. 5; AC Salamanca, nos. 57, 60, 78.
[6] AHN cód. 1197B, fols. 253^r-255^r.
[7] AC Tuy 14/10, 1/7 (ptd. *ES* XXII, app. vi, xiii, pp. 260-61, 273-7). The two
vicarii who appear in a Tuy act of 1152 (ptd. below, Appendix no. IX) were presumably appointed one by the bishop, the other by the chapter, for the separate
administration of their divided temporalities.

cannot reasonably be doubted that kings were able to reward their servants with capitular office, with the acquiescence of their bishops. Was this acquiescence willing, or not? We do not know. There are a very few examples of papal provision to cathedral prebends during this period, which are discussed elsewhere.[1] We do not hear much of conflicts between bishops and their cathedral chapters. Disputes over temporalities sometimes occurred, as we have seen, and Diego Gelmírez found himself at loggerheads with his chapter from time to time. But the evidence for unanimity—for instance, in the litigation over diocesan boundaries—is far more plentiful than that for disunion. Bishop and chapter seem to have formed a close-knit community; more so, one may suspect, than was commonly the case over the larger part of twelfth-century Latin Christendom.

ARCHDEACONS AND ARCHPRIESTS

The local administration of the diocese was in the hands of archdeacons and archpriests. Archdeacons were the deputies of the bishops, chosen by them to be their closest administrative assistants: there is no sign of the bishop's Official in Spain at this period. In those dioceses which already existed in the year 1100 there were several archdeacons. The number of them in any one diocese varied in the course of the century, though there was a tendency for them to become fixed in the latter part of it. In the newly-restored dioceses the practice seems to have been for the early bishops to have been assisted by but a single archdeacon, more being created at a later date when episcopal administration became busier. Thus in the diocese of Santiago de Compostela there were at least five archdeacons in the period 1100–08. It seems to have been a favourite number, for we find five at Tuy in 1112, at Lugo in 1119, at Mondoñedo and Orense in 1122.[2] At León there were six in 1133, and at Oviedo the amazing figure of eleven in 1117.[3] At Compostela Pedro Suárez

---

[1] See below, ch. 5, pp. 216-7.
[2] AC Tuy 3/22; AHN 1325C/9 (ptd. below, Appendix no. III); *HC* pp. 376-8; AC Orense, Privilegios I/1.
[3] *ES* XXXVI, ap. liii, pp. cxi–cxiv; *Docs. Oviedo* no. 138.

stabilized the number of archdeacons at four in 1177.[1] At Lugo, too, the number seems to have stood at four in the early thirteenth century.[2] In the 'new' diocese of Zamora there seems to have been only one archdeacon for about half a century after the establishment of the see; two appear for the first time in 1176,[3] and the number remained at two for the rest of our period. At Avila likewise, the bishop was assisted by only one archdeacon from the restoration of the see down to the 1170s, when the numbers were multiplied and territorial designations appeared—a senior archdeacon of Avila, and archdeacons of Olmedo, Arévalo and (for a short time) Plasencia.[4] The bishops of Salamanca had two archdeacons from at least 1133; by 1174 there were three, an archdeacon of Salamanca, and archdeacons of Alba de Tomes and Ledesma.[5]

Archdeacons were appointed by bishops, as far as we know. Of course, some archdeacons may have owed their position to noble or royal patronage. Among the former should perhaps be numbered Manrique de Lara, archdeacon of León before his promotion to the episcopate in 1181. There are several examples of royal chancery servants who held archdeaconries: to give but two examples, Fernando Curialis and Pelayo de Lauro, who both served as chancellor to Fernando II, held archdeaconries in the church of Compostela. Yet the interest which worked in favour of such men must have been channelled through the bishops. We have already seen[6] that archdeacons tended to be closely associated with bishops in the transaction of diocesan business; and have observed as well that bishops did not seek new servants, the Official and his staff, to replace or outflank archdeacons. There is, indeed, a good deal of evidence to suggest that relations between bishops and their archdeacons were generally

[1] *LFH* IV, ap. 1, pp. 122-4.
[2] This may be inferred from AHN 1326C/9, 10, 20; 1326D/3, 17, 24; 1326E/19, 20.
[3] AC Zamora, Libro Negro, fol. 29.
[4] AHN 18/5, 8, 10, 12; 19/1-3, 9.
[5] AC Salamanca nos. 7, 17, 20, 25, 61 (the latter document ptd. below, Appendix no. XV).
[6] See above, ch. 3, pp. 88-97.

harmonious. Besides their prominence among the witnesses of episcopal *acta*, we find archdeacons in charge of *sede vacante* administration, for instance at Astorga in 1122 and Oviedo in 1143. In León there is not a trace of jurisdictional disputes between bishops and archdeacons, in marked contrast to the situation in twelfth-century France. The archidiaconate was a well-established rung on the ladder which led to the episcopate.[1] Throughout the century, archdeacons seem to have been closely associated with their bishops. It is another sign of the coherence of the diocesan establishment.

We have observed that territorial archdeaconries appear in the southern dioceses in the second half of the century. In the northern part of the kingdom they are traceable from a much earlier date. In the diocese of Oviedo, Bishop Pelayo in 1117 granted to his cathedral chapter the *archidiaconatus Ovetensis*, an area with territorial limits which were laid down in the act, limits which were said to have existed *prisco tempore*. Strong hints of similar territorialization are given in an act of the same date from Astorga. Two documents from the diocese of León, of 1116 and 1120 speak to us quite clearly of territorial archdeaconries. They are implied in the diocese of Mondoñedo in a document of 1122.[2] In the diocese of Lugo, four territorial archdeaconries—of Neira, Sarria, Aviancos and Deza—are mentioned in late twelfth-century documents; but these areas were referred to as administrative divisions of the diocese in several much earlier papal bulls, in 1123, 1130 and 1131; while an episcopal act of 1120 strongly suggests territorialized archdeaconries. It would seem reasonable to take the process of territorialization in the diocese back to at least the time of Bishop Pedro III (1113-33).[3] In the boundary dispute between Orense and Braga all the witnesses who made depositions in 1193-4 assumed that the archdeaconries of Baroncelle and Vinhais were fixed territorial areas, and had been such since at least

---

[1] As may be appreciated from the material contained in ch. 2.
[2] *Docs. Oviedo* no. 138; *ES* XVI, ap. xxiii, pp. 474-6; *ES* XXVI, ap. xlvi, pp. c-ciii; E. Valiña Sampedro, *El Camino de Santiago, Estudio Histórico-Jurídico* (Salamanca, 1971), ap. 2, pp. 230-2; *HC* pp. 376-8.
[3] AHN 1325G/24, 1325H/5; 1326B/24; AC Lugo, leg. 3, no. 2; Libro de Bulas Apostólicas, no. 1; *ES* XLI, ap. ii, pp. 296-301.

the episcopate of Bishop Martín of Orense (1132–57).[1] In the diocese of Tuy there is a possible reference to such territorial boundaries in a document of 1112.[2]

The evidence from the diocese of Compostela is fuller. When Pedro Suárez fixed the number of archdeaconries at four in 1177, he at the same time assigned to each one seven archipresbyterates. The names of these archdeaconries and archipresbyterates may be traced back to an earlier period; and in our sources they are always spoken of as fixed territorial areas. Let us take but one instance. One of the four archdeaconries of 1177 was that of Nendos, the area of which lay between the towns of Corunna and Betanzos. The references to it in the *Historia Compostellana* make it clear that this was a territorial archdeaconry in the early part of the century.[3] Juan Rodríguez appears to have been archdeacon of Nendos in about 1108, Paschal II named it as a division of the diocese of Compostela in 1110. Diego Gelmírez acquired several churches *in Nendos*. Another of its archdeacons, Pedro Crescóniz, was imprisoned by Count Fernando Pérez de Traba in 1134. We have independent confirmation of this Pedro's tenure in a charter of 1118 which refers to his activity in *nostra terra ligandi et solvendi* and *nostra terra* is revealed as *territorio Nemitus* (= Nendos) *inter duos fluvios Menendi et Barrosa subtus Monte Castro*.

The territories which were attached to archdeaconries—and archipresbyterates—in Galicia in the twelfth century may have been the survivals of a very much earlier administrative order. In a remarkable article published some thirty years ago the late Pierre David investigated the structure of the Galician church in the last days of the Suevic kingdom, in the third quarter of the sixth century.[4] The names of some of the churches which then constituted the 'administrative divisions' of the several dioceses re-emerge as the names of certain territorial divisions of the twelfth century. Thus, for

---

[1] AC Orense, Escrituras, XII/III; Obispo y Dignidades, nos. 17, 17 bis.
[2] AC Tuy, 3/22.
[3] For what follows, see *HC* pp. 70, 73, 85, 174–5, 188, 547; AHN cód. 977B, fols. 54ᵛ–55ᵛ.
[4] 'L'Organisation ecclésiastique du royaume suève au temps de St. Martin de Braga' in his *Études historiques sur la Galice et le Portugal*, pp. 1–82.

example, the church of *Turonio* in the diocese of Tuy re-
appears as the district of Toroño, an archdeaconry by the late
twelfth century; in the diocese of Compostela, the Suevic
churches of *Salinense* and *Pestemarcos* are met with again in
Pedro Suárez's archdeaconry of Salnes and archipresbyterate
of Postmarchos; in the diocese of Orense we meet the church
of *Bibalos* again in the archdeaconry of Búbal. Of course, it is
a long jump from the sixth century to the twelfth and most
of the stepping-stones in between have been shown—after
Barrau-Dihigo's savagely destructive criticism of the early
royal charters—to be treacherous. We do not, mercifully, have
to make it here. But ancient administrative arrangements are
notoriously hard to change and the possibility should certainly be borne in mind that the pattern of local diocesan
administration which meets us in the twelfth century was in
part at least only a palimpsest written over the arrangements
of an earlier day, whose lineaments we can only dimly, very
dimly, discern.

On the other hand, the officers who were charged with
administrative tasks seem to have been new. The diocesan
administration of the tenth and eleventh centuries, and the
very term itself may be inappropriate, is as yet an impene-
trably dark business. The title of archdeacon is exceedingly
rare in any genuine document earlier than c.1090–1100; the
mid-century councils of Coyanza (1055) and Compostela
(1056) know nothing of them. In northern France, western
Germany and south-eastern England the appearance, multi-
plication and territorialization of archdeaconries was taking
place from the late ninth and early tenth centuries; in south-
western France the same process started later, and was continuing—so far as we can see, but already we are in very
murky territory—throughout the eleventh century. Did the
southern French clergy who acquired bishoprics in Spain
from about 1080 onwards bring with the the organization to
which they were becoming accustomed—as they seem to have
brought the notion of the territorial diocese, and as the
legates who accompanied them brought a scheme of metropolitan organization? Further study alone will enable us to
answer this question. All we can say at the moment is that we
might expect the answer to be affirmative.

Archpriests stood in the same relation to archdeacons as archdeacons did to bishops. We have been told that 'the general equivalence of the terms rural dean and archpriest is well-established',[1] and this judgement, founded in the main upon study of conditions in England and France, is applicable also to the kingdom of León. Archpriests do not bulk large in our sources, though we do find them in every diocese. They seem to have been people of fairly humble status: it is noteworthy that several of the archpriests cited in the Orense depositions do not have patronymics, and it is very rare indeed to find an archpriest subscribing an episcopal act. There is a good deal of evidence for territorial archipresbyterates. It is of the same kind as that for the territorial archdeaconry, and we need not bother with it here.[2]

Who appointed archpriests? The Orense depositions are our best source of information about archpriests in Galicia. The witnesses were not being asked to declare the principles of ecclesiastical government and they do not tell us in so many words. Sometimes they said vaguely that archpriests held their offices *ab Auriensi ecclesia*. Sometimes, though rarely, they brought the bishop into it and could say of archpriests that they *tenebant ipsam terram, ab Auriensi episcopo*. But nearly always they associated archpriests closely with archdeacons. Thus we can hear of an archdeacon *cum archipresbitero suo*, or of an archpriest *tenentem ipsam terram ab N. archidiacono*, and similar phrases.[3] The actual subordination of archdeacons to archpriests is brought out well in some of the tales the witnesses had to tell. The following testimony was offered by Pedro Sánchez, who had himself been an archpriest in part of the territory disputed between the churches of Braga and Orense:

et vidit sub eo (*sc.* bishop Martín of Orense) M. Auriensem archidiaconum qui diu tenuit totam ipsam terram ab eo et post ipsum vidit N.

---

[1] A. Hamilton Thompson, 'Diocesan organisation in the Middle Ages: archdeacons and rural deans', *Proceedings of the British Academy* xxix (1943), 153–94, at p. 175.
[2] E.g., Mondoñedo: *HC* pp. 74–84, 374–8; Salamanca: AC Salamanca, no. 95; Zamora: AC Zamora leg. 16, 1ª parte, no. 18.
[3] The phrases are taken from AC Orense, Escrituras XII/III and Obispo y Dignidades no. 17 bis. The secular terminology is worth noticing.

Auriensem archidiaconum similiter tenentem totam ipsam terram et quia ipse non audebat ire ad ipsam terram commisit eam V. Danielis a quo iste testis tenuit eam per biennium donec recepit eam Al. archidiaconus Bracarensis. Interrogatus quomodo recepisset eam respondit quod vidit eum venientem ad se et dicentem sibi 'Respondete mihi de ista terra quia mihi data est' et ipse non fuit ausus contradicere et dedit ei redditus sicut solebat dare Auriensi ecclesie. Et cum ipse diceret 'Non dabo vobis redditus quia de Auriensi ecclesia teneo ego terram istam' dixit idem archidiaconus 'Mihi data est terra quia non placet regi. . . quod Aurienses veniant ad terram istam. . . .

Archpriests, then, were probably appointed by archdeacons, perhaps after consultation with the bishop, and were certainly at their beck and call. This was not always so. A bull of Clement III of 1188 reveals a rather different state of affairs in the diocese of Salamanca.[1] The bishop had appointed an archpriest for Alba de Tormes. The clergy of Alba refused to accept him, and the bishop put in his place a different nominee. He proved no more acceptable, and was roughly handled by the populace, at the bidding of the clergy, which led to interdicts and excommunications until eventually the case came before the curia. The clergy of Alba claimed that they had the right, which they had exercised for over forty years, to choose their own archpriest. No reference is made to the archdeacon of Alba. It would be rash to read any general lessons from an isolated case of this sort, but it may be that in the new sees bishops tried to play a more directly supervisory role in the local affairs of the diocese than they did elsewhere.

What did the administrative activities of archdeacons and archpriests consist of? The scanty evidence at our disposal offers us hardly any information. Archdeacons were meant to examine the fitness of ordinands, to make annual visitations of their archdeaconries, to hold meetings of their parish clergy. On one occasion on which we hear of the first of these functions it seems to have been in the hands of the archpriest rather than the archdeacon: we are told—again by one of the witnesses in the Orense-Braga suit—that Bishop Pedro of Orense (1157–69) refused to ordain some clerks from Vinhais *quia non erat cum eis archipresbiter suus per*

[1] AC Salamanca, no. 95: *Inter venerabilem,* 7 October 1188.

quem testificaretur utrum essent digni.[1] On another occasion, however, the task was in the hands of the archdeacon: Bishop Manrique of León laid down that the Hospitallers' priests were to be presented, before institution, to the archdeacon, *qui de sciencia eius et moribus diligenter inquirat.*[2] Of meetings of the clergy of an archdeaconry we have some hints: thus for example,[3]

et audivit quod Al. archidiaconus dum teneret terram de Capraria fecit letanias cum clericis et laicis ipsius terre in sancta Martha qui locus est in termino de Capraria, et vidit hominem eiusdem archidiaconi venientem ad patruum suum et precipientem ei ex parte archidiaconi quod iret ad ipsas letanias, et propter infirmitatem non potuit ire et misit illuc nuntium suum cum oblatione. . . .

These *letaniae* seem to have been gatherings—perhaps we should call them archidiaconal synods or rural chapters—of local clergy and sometimes, as in the instance quoted, of laity too. The evidence suggests that they were held principally for the purpose of extracting a lenten 'offering' from the local clergy; significantly, the interest of the story just quoted centres upon the despatch of an *oblatio*. Nearly all our information about visitation is concerned with what archdeacons could, or could not, get out of it. We hear much of rights, practically nothing of duties. Archdeacons have *vocem ecclesiasticam* over their churches;[4] they have full right, *tota directura.*[5] The principal component of this right is hospitality. The monks of Eslonza were to receive the *archidiaconum terre preter hospites cum X hominibus et VI equitaturis* at their church of Villafáfila, once a year as it would seem.[6] The archdeacon of Toro and the clergy of Toro quarrelled *super quibusdam procurationibus ratione visitationis quas idem archidiaconus ab eisdem clericis exigebat.*[7]

---

[1] AC Orense, Escrituras XII/III.
[2] AC León, no. 1438.
[3] AC Orense, Obispo y Dignidades, no. 17.
[4] AHN cód. 1044B, fol. 11ʳ.
[5] AC Orense, Obispo y Dignidades, no. 17.
[6] AHN 963/20 (ptd. below, Appendix, no. XII).
[7] AC Zamora leg. 36, no. 6.

When an archdeacon conducted a visitation he was 'procured' with a meal, (*prandium*). Things did not always go smoothly. Alvito, archdeacon of Braga, visited the church of *Osori*, prudently coming well protected, *cum militibus armatis*; there he ate the meal *quod solebat inde dari archidiacono*, but the meal was served grudgingly and unwillingly by the priest of the church, the archdeacon in fact was received *male*; so he excommunicated the priest.[1] Twelfth-century archdeacons do not have a good name, and the nature of the surviving sources from the kingdom of León is such that they are unlikely to appear in a good light in them. In Normandy, Ordericus Vitalis assumed that the local clergy were oppressed by *iniustis circumventionibus archidiaconorum*.[2] The parish clergy of León cannot speak to us at all; but could they do so we should not be surprised to learn that they agreed with Ordericus.

THE ACTION OF THE BISHOPS

We have been led insensibly from consideration of the structure of ecclesiastical administration to consideration of its workings, at the local level where archdeacons and archpriests operated. It is high time that we turned to the actions of the bishops. What were they trying to do? Can we indeed discover anything at all about the manner in which they interpreted their task? It is certainly not easy to do so. We could look to bishops' own statements or to statements made by their partisans; we could examine the legislation enacted by them in church councils; we could consider whether the recorded motives of laymen, in their dealings with the church, suggest that bishops were putting pressure upon them to make them act in certain ways; or we could attempt to draw conclusions from the surviving episcopal *acta*.

The first of these methods is not open to us. We have no treatise from the pen of any one of these bishops outlining what he conceived to be the duties and ideals of himself or his colleagues in twelfth-century León; and to speculate about

---

[1] AC Orense, Obispo y Dignidades, no. 17 bis.
[2] *The Ecclesiastical History of Orderic Vitalis*, ed. M. Chibnall, II (Oxford, 1969), p. 26.

what he might have written is useless. Statements by partisans
of one prelate are to be found in abundance in the *Historia
Compostellana*, but they are not always unambiguously helpful. For example, we are told that Diego Gelmírez, in about
the year 1106, *ecclesiam S.Michaelis de Bojone de quorun-
dam militum potestate, qui eam quasi pro sua tenebant, justa
liberatione liberavit.*[1] The writer clearly considered Diego's
action a worthy one; it was a *justa liberatio*. But why? Because the knights were in possession of a church, which a
layman might not be? Or because they had seized a piece of
property belonging to Santiago? Today we should make a
distinction between the pastoral action of a bishop and the
watchfulness of a lord over his properties. But this may be
anachronistic. Did the writer so distinguish? Did Diego? We
shall see later on that there is evident a mingling of lordship
and pastoral care in the actions of the Leonese episcopate,
a mingling which recalls earlier centuries than the twelfth.
At the moment it is enough to point out that the statements
of episcopal partisans about their masters' intentions are
pitted with snares for the unwary beyond the obvious ones
of bias and *parti pris*.

The evidence of conciliar legislation is also hard to use,
but for different reasons. Most of the legislation that we have
is simple restatement of that enacted in councils presided
over by the pope. It would be unwise to assume (as is sometimes done) that such reiteration empowers the historian to
treat these decrees as mere formality. Yet it is difficult to see
anything distinctive about the attitudes of the Leonese episcopate when these are cloaked in the words devised by other
men, elsewhere. Perhaps we should not be searching for the
distinctive. It is significant, after all, that papal decrees were
received and respected in León, and the fact will be given its
due weight in a later chapter. And sometimes a distinctive
note is struck. The canons of the council of Valladolid, held
in September 1143 under the presidency of the legate Cardinal Guido, restated the decrees passed at the second Lateran
council of 1139.[2] One of the canons however, c.22, was not

---

[1] *HC* p. 59.
[2] The Valladolid decrees are to be found in *PUP* no. 40.

drawn from the Lateran II decrees, and it is reasonable to suppose that it was devised specially to meet a Spanish need. Its concern was that *ignotos clericos* or clergy *de alienis episcopatibus* should not be received by bishops *sine commendatitiis litteris*. It may not be entirely coincidental that the only example of such letters which has come down to us from the period we are concerned with was issued by a bishop who had attended the council and at a date only ten years later—the curious *epistola formata* issued by Juan of León in 1153.[1] Here we seem to have evidence for episcopal observance of a conciliar decree framed by bishops in concert with a papal legate to meet a need experienced by the Leonese authorities, namely the need for the control of vagrant clergy.

When laymen surrendered proprietary churches into ecclesiastical hands, why did they do so? The only honest answer is that we can never really tell. The motives imputed to them were recorded by clerical scribes, who may have accurately recorded them, may have put their own construction upon them, may simply have snatched at an appropriate formula from the common stock lying ready in the formularies which are lost to us. But let us assume—a large assumption—that the recorded motives do tell us something of the actual motives of donors. If these express the sentiment that lay tenure of churches is wrong, we may fairly suppose that someone has been working on lay proprietors, persuading them that they are guilty of a breach of ecclesiastical law. This 'someone' will not necessarily have been a bishop, but, given the concern with this matter displayed in conciliar legislation enacted by bishops, the impulse, if it was there, probably came in large measure from episcopal circles. But was the impulse there? The most common of all recorded motives were such desires as *pro remedio anime mee et parentum meorum, pro anniversariis faciendis, pro fratrum orationibus*, and the like. Some grants were made in composition for wrongs done. In 1133 Sancho Sánchez gave the church of *Ruix* to the monastery of San Martín Pinario, 'pro multa mala que feci in ipso monasterio, fregi suum cautum. . .et raubavi vestras greges cum vestris equabus cum suo kaballo et raubavi vestras vacas

[1] Ptd. *Bulletin of the Institute of Historical Research*, xlv (1972), pp. 127–8.

et prendidi vestros homines. . .'.[1] Again, in 1170, Count Rodrigo gave the church of Sarria to the see of Lugo, *pro sacrilegii compositione*, because 'olim diabolico furore arreptus, armata manu. . .ecclesiam sancte Marie de Mal in territorio de Ventosa que est in Lucensi episcopatu, partim demolitus, partim ignis combustione in cinerem redigens destruxi'.[2] Yet only one document among all those that have been inspected contains a categorical statement of what we are searching for. In 1190 Juan Suárez gave his share (*integram porcionem*) in the church of Ceruela, which *jure hereditario habere debeo*, to Bishop Rodrigo II and the church of Lugo.[3] He or the scribe tells us why, and the reasons are interesting. Inside the church he had struck and wounded its priest, Martín Pérez. Juan, dean of Lugo, sent him to Arnaldo, bishop of Coria, *pro absolutionis beneficio, cui a domno papa concessa erat tunc temporis haec potestas*. Arnaldo heard his confession, and returned him to his own bishop for absolution, recommending that he make compensation in due form by surrendering his share of the church. When he did so, he acted not only *pro peccato illo*, but also because his tenure of a share of the church had been against canon law, *quam contra sacros canones detinebam*. This looks like a clear case of episcopal persuasion acting upon a lay parcener to bring about a proper conformity with the law of the church. It is a unique case; and we should remember too how late in date it is.[4]

The bishops' *acta* will prove to be our best guide. We find in them no general statements, no enunciation of ideals, no articulate 'programme'. But some notions can be ferreted out of them about what bishops were actually doing, perhaps even, more hazardously, about what bishops thought they were up to.

But before we turn to them, we must look a little more

---

[1] AHN 512/10. [2] AHN 1325E/23.
[3] AHN 1325H/12.
[4] J.F. Lemarignier, in F. Lot and R. Fawtier (eds.), *Histoire des institutions françaises au Moyen Age,* vol. III 'Institutions ecclésiastiques' (Paris, 1962), pp. 108-9, cites examples of the motive of 'consciousness of wrong-doing' in holding churches from the late eleventh century in France.

closely at the setting in which bishops worked, the legal and customary environment, the social context. So little work has been devoted to Spanish social history that the following remarks can be offered only with the greatest trepidation. They are necessarily based on impressions, which one day, it is to be hoped, will be corrected. So much by way of apology.

Our concern is with an institution with which we have already made some play, the proprietary church, for it is with the parish churches which serve the spiritual needs of the people that a bishop's work is in the last resort concerned—who provides them, who has charge of them, what goes on in them. There can be no doubt that there were very many proprietary churches in the kingdom of León in the late eleventh and early twelfth centuries. Let us look at a few examples. In the diocese of Oviedo, the monastery of Cornellana had been founded in 1024 by Cristina, daughter of Bermudo II of León (984–99) and her husband Ordoño, son of Ramiro III (966–84).[1] Cristina herself entered the house to spend the latter part of her life there. After her death, and whether what occurred was in accordance with her wishes or not we cannot tell, the lands of the monastery, which had been among the lands of the family, were divided among her three children, two sons and a daughter. A further subdivision among heirs took place in the next generation. Of this generation, one of the ladies, Enderquina, married Count Suero Bermúdez. Count Suero was a nobleman of the highest rank and of great wealth; traceable in close association with the Leonese monarchs from c.1098 to c.1133, he was for the author of the *Chronica Adefonsi Imperatoris* a *vir in consilio strenuus, veritatisque inquisitor*. By a series of deals with his relatives he managed to reunite the lands of the monastery into his own hands, after which he made Cornellana and its properties over to Cluny, in 1122. The remainder of the story does not concern us here; what is significant for our purposes is the number of churches which the family had owned. They are enumerated in the charter of donation of 1122.

[1] For what follows, see *Colleción de Fuentes para la Historia de Asturias*: vol. I, *Monasterio de Cornellana,* ed. A.C. Floriano (Oviedo, 1949), nos. i–v; *CAI* para. 2; *Docs. Oviedo* no. 143; *Recueil des chartes de l'Abbaye de Cluny,* ed. A. Bruel (Paris, 1894), vol. V, no. 3958.

Queen Urraca had given Count Suero one church (*ecclesiam*) and three or perhaps four *monasteria*.[1] He had acquired by inheritance or by his own efforts (*de parentibus nostris vel de nostris ganantiis*) three churches, half of a fourth and a share (*portionem*) in a fifth. These were certainly his 'own' churches. Those given by the queen had been granted by charter, *per incartationes*, the normal mode of alienating property in perpetuity to be held *iure hereditario*, as countless royal diplomas testify. The others he referred to as his *hereditates*, along with estates (*villas*), a fortress (*castellum*) and male and female slaves (*servos et ancillas*).

We move westwards into the diocese of Mondoñedo, and a little backwards in time, where we are confronted by the tangled history of the lands of Ermesenda Núñez.[2] The lady Ermesenda belonged to a family quite as exalted as that associated with the monastery of Cornellana, for she was descended from Count Osorio Gutiérrez, founder of the monastery of Lorenzana in 969 and cousin of the great monastic founder, St. Rosendo of Celanova; one of their aunts was married to Ordoño II of León (914–24); and their grandfather Hermenegildo Gutiérrez, count of Tuy and Porto, had been Alfonso III's *mayordomo* and conquerer of Coimbra in 878. Ermesenda was the last of her line. She found herself in the quite unusual position of having no kin at all, as she herself explains—*Ego vero non habeo filio quia nunquam habui virum, nec frater, nec soprino, nec ulla gens*. Consequently, she had a completely free hand in the disposal of her property. Or so she thought. Others did not so think, and the conflicting claims that arose after her death in about 1084 were not resolved for at least a generation. These lawsuits, though of the utmost interest, are not our concern here, which is rather with an earlier grant she made to the monastery of Chantada in 1073. Here, along with estates, silver plate, books, silken clothing, and the horses, coats-of-mail and swords which she had inherited from her brother, we find casually mentioned *una ecclesia media de sancto*

---

[1] It is a measure of our general ignorance of Spanish ecclesiastical history that we do not know how to translate this word. Certainly, in the present context, 'monasteries' would be misleading.

[2] For what follows, see especially AHN 1067/1, 2.

Christoforo que comparamus de Leovegildo Fataliz. Here again a church is being treated like any other bit of property; it, or a share in it, can be bought or sold; it can be left by will.

We move yet further to the west, into the lands where the great family of Traba held sway. It was a new family, rising from obscurity in the middle years of the eleventh century to surpass all other Galician families by the early twelfth. Bermudo Pérez de Traba founded a monastery for his daughter Urraca, to which he gave the church of *Genrozo* in 1138.[1] Half of the church he had inherited from his *avis et parentibus*, and it had come to him *in particione inter fratres meos et sorores*. The other half had passed at an earlier date from his family into royal hands, but had returned to Bermudo in the form of a grant from Alfonso VII as a reward *pro servicio et fidelitate*.

Suero Bermúdez, Ermesenda Núñez, and Bermudo Pérez were people who stood very high upon the social ladder. But such people were not alone in owning and trading in churches. Nuño Crescóniz and his wife, with Diego the priest and Suero the priest, and all their relatives, were humbler people, who gave their church (*nostra ecclesia*) at *Aurivizes* to the monastery of Carboeiro in 1131, explaining that they had inherited it from their ancestors who had built it and left it to them. So was Suero Froílaz, who gave *ecclesia mea propria* which he had inherited from his grandfather to the same house in 1142.[2] Diego Múñoz was another man of middling rank, though he had splendid connections for his uncle was the great Archbishop Diego Gelmírez. When in 1151 he was about to leave *in hostem contra Cordobam* he prudently made a will, which has survived. His bequests included a ninth-part share in the church of *Brion*; an eleventh part of the church of *Lauro*, and in addition a further third of that church which he held as a fief (*prestimonium*) of the monastery of San Martín Pinario; a share in another church, whose place-name is now illegible; a fifth part of the church

---

[1] For what follows, see AHN 526/7, 13.
[2] 'La Colección Diplomática del Monasterio de San Lorenzo de Carboeiro', ed. M. Lucas Alvarez, *Compostellanum* ii–iii (1958–9), nos. XLII, XLVII.

of *Transmonte* (in which church he and his sister held jointly a full half and two-ninths of the other half); and a share in the church of *Ermedelo*.[1] A few years earlier the *heredes* of the church of Barrantes, in the diocese of Tuy, had met to constitute the place a Benedictine monastery. These were not big men; they consisted of the bishop of Tuy, his brother Suero and Juan *Tirans*, and their other relations, and they had to buy the favour of the *dominus terre*, Count Gómez Núñez, with cash before they could set up the monastery.[2] It is worth noting, incidentally, that the heirs acted because the church *non erat tractata sicut decebat, quia parochiani erant in ea*. They were taking their responsibilities as proprietors seriously. Back in the diocese of Oviedo, the two brothers Pedro and Fernando Núñez, who gave the church of Selgas to the see of Oviedo in 1114, were not important noblemen.[3] They had built the church themselves, and the gift was to take effect only after their death; what was more, *si ex nostra progenie aliquis sacerdos fuerit qui eam tenere voluerit*, he was to hold the church for life.

Galicia and the Asturias were the areas of large estates and big lords. Though we hear much of churches which had been divided into shares, these shares seem to have been distributed among the members of a single kin. The founders of the churches, who had acquired a founder's rights over them, seem usually to have been individuals, or a man and wife, or two brothers. The same phenomenon is found further to the south, in the lands round Astorga and León.[4] But here we find something else as well. For this was not the land of big lordships but of smaller holdings, not of large proprietors but of those humbler people whom medieval historians, vaguely and perhaps in desperation, call 'free peasants'. The phenomenon we meet here seems to be that of common ownership of churches by village communities. In 1126 the inhabitants of Corporales, fifty of whom are named, *et cuncto concilio de Corporales a minimo ejus usque ad maximo*

---

[1] *Galicia Histórica, Colección Diplomática* (Santiago de Compostela, 1901), no. XXIX.
[2] *ES* XXII, ap. xii, pp. 270–73.   [3] *Docs. Oviedo* no. 136.
[4] For example, AC León, no. 1382 (ptd. below, Appendix no. II).

tam viris quam feminis, gave their church of San Juan to the monastery of San Pedro de Montes.[1] In 1104, fifteen householders, with their wives and children, did the same with the church of Quintanilla. So, later in the same year, did sixteen laymen, some in explicit association with brothers, sisters or children, with the church of Paradela.[2] It is hard to believe that those who made up these groups were related to one another by ties of blood.

But the underlying notions are the same. However many they be, and whether they be related or not, these are still proprietors of proprietary churches. We are witnessing once more in short 'the persistent tendency to treat the organization of religion as a branch of secular life, and consequently to bring the property on which this organization was based under the same rules as secular property'.[3]

Further to the south, in the lands most recently reconquered, it is harder to find evidence of the existence of proprietary churches. Few documents have survived which relate to this area, in comparison with the great wealth of documentary evidence from Galicia. Yet even when allowance is made for this, one is left with an impression that the institution was rare in the southern dioceses. Of course, examples can be found. The church of Sta. María de la Vega, just outside the town of Salamanca, which was given to San Isidoro de León in 1166 by Velasco Iñigo, his wife Amadonna Domínguez, and his sister Justa, looks like one; it had probably, though not certainly, been built by Velasco.[4] In 1159 Count Osorio and his wife Teresa granted to the see of Zamora the *tercias* in five churches *quas hereditario iure obtinemus*.[5] But examples are few and far between, while in Galicia they are abundant. Moreover, there is some negative evidence suggesting the general rarity of proprietary churches (though the problem of deciding how much weight should be given to it is a delicate one): for instance, it is noteworthy

---

[1] *Tumbo Viejo de San Pedro de Montes* ed. A. Quintana Prieto (León, 1971), no. 135.
[2] Ibid., nos. 116, 117.
[3] R.W. Southern, *The Making of the Middle Ages* (London, 1953), p. 128.
[4] AC Salamanca, nos. 16, 43; León, Archivo de San Isidoro, nos. 308, 324.
[5] AC Zamora, leg. 14, no. 27.

that there is not a single reference to a proprietary church among the twelfth-century charters relating to the abbey of Moreruela, between Salamanca and Zamora, even though it attracted numerous grants from lay donors.[1] A charter of Alfonso VII, dated 30 April 1154, shows us that when Castronuño was resettled by Count Núño Pérez de Lara (who gave his name to the place) he was given help (*adiutorium*) by Bishop Navarro of Salamanca and his archdeacon Ciprián, who built churches in and near the new settlement and equipped them with liturgical books and vestments; the king gave the bishop rights over these churches.[2] So responsibilities were divided; the count had his sphere of action and the bishop his; the bishop's responsibilities and rights were respected and enforced by the king. Was it easier for bishops to protect what they conceived to be their rights in the frontier dioceses than it was in the dioceses of the north? Perhaps it was.

Much remains unclear about these churches. We do not know exactly what the rights of proprietors were. We rarely know what was involved when they surrendered these churches to a bishopric or a monastery. Although a rough pattern in the distribution of proprietary churches within the kingdom of León has been suggested, it remains to test this pattern in the light of further research. And we shall never know what was the absolute number of proprietary churches.

It is time to turn once more to the bishops. We know that proprietary churches were transferred from lay to ecclesiastical hands in large numbers during the century, in León as in other parts of Europe. Most of our evidence for the existence of these churches comes indeed from the documents recording such transfers. Nothing can be said that is not a guess about the rate at which transfer took place. Very little seems to have occurred before the last quarter of the eleventh century; the process was far from complete by the date at which

[1] AHN 3548–3550, *passim*.
[2] AC Salamanca, no. 18. The churches in the *termino* of Castronuño numbered no fewer than twenty-two by the year 1177, as we learn from a bull of Alexander III: AC Salamanca, no. 49.

our survey ends, in 1215.[1] The bishops may, as we have seen, have actively encouraged the process. There is further evidence for this among their *acta*, which we must now consider.

Let us take first an early act from the see of León, dated 26 April 1117. It concerned the *monasterium* of San Tirso, situated near the town of León, which was held by a number of lay proprietors.[2] Bishop Diego had a claim upon it because, as the proprietors were brought to admit, half of it belonged to the cathedral church of St. María of León. A settlement was reached between the contending parties. The proprietors were to surrender the lands of San Tirso and the bishop was to build and settle (*construat et populet*) the *monasterium*. The proprietors were to have a hand in the election of its abbot; they were to increase its endowments and to 'defend' it; any of them seeking hospitality was to be received *sicut hereditarius*, and they were to have the right to enter it *si forte aliquis illorum ad inopiam devenerit*. The two parties bound themselves under threat of severe monetary penalties to observe the agreement. What was happening here? The bishop was concerned about the rights of himself and his church as proprietors; he was anxious to recover rights and properties which had slipped from his church's grasp. He defined, recognized and confirmed the rights of the lay proprietors who were his partners. He accepted that laymen had such rights, either because he was content to do so, or because he had no other choice.

Two years later, Pedro III, bishop of Lugo, gave the church Sta. Eulalia to one Miguel Peláez.[3] We do not know whether the beneficiary was a layman or a clerk. The grant, duly witnessed by the chapter of Lugo, was framed in entirely secular terms. The only stipulation that the bishop made was that the church should revert to the see of Lugo on Miguel's death. No other controls were imposed; or, to be strictly

---

[1] Cf. P. Galindo Romeo, *Tuy en la Baja Edad Media* (2nd ed., Madrid, 1950), pp. 77-8.

[2] AC León, no. 1382 (ptd. below, Appendix, no. II). The precise status of the house is not clear. It was a *monasterium* and it was to have an *abbas*. But we have no evidence that there were ever monks there in the twelfth century, and later it formed the endowment for one of the prebends of León cathedral.

[3] AHN 1325C/9 (ptd. below, Appendix, no. III).

accurate, none was stated in the bishop's charter. We may think it likely that Miguel Peláez had to swear an oath to the bishop such as that sworn by Pedro Daniéliz in 1130.[1] Pedro too had received a church from the bishop; he swore that he would be the bishop's *vassallus sine alio domino* for the church *quam vos datis mihi ad tenendam*; that he would care faithfully, *ut prudens agricola*, for its endowments; and that he would render to his lord the traditional third part of all the tithes. Nothing at all is said about his spiritual duties.

These documents take us into a world in which bishops accepted the proprietary church system; in which they talked about the churches under their care, and handed them out to their subordinates, like so many secular estates; and in which they made little or no attempt to exert an episcopal as opposed to a lordly control over what went on in them. But it was a world whose end was approaching. In 1143 Gonzalo Bermúdez and his wife gave a church which they had built to the see of Oviedo.[2] They were to hold it for their lifetime; afterwards it was not to be leased (*detur in prestamine*) to anyone but given to a religious man chosen by the bishop and chapter (*detur religiose (sic) homini episcopi et capituli dispositione*). One would like to know who made this stipulation. The see was vacant at the time, and was being administered by the archdeacon Froilán Garcia. The charter of donation was certainly drawn up by the beneficiaries. Or does the phrase indicate a new attitude among lay donors? Sometimes bishops bought lay proprietors out. In 1158 Bishop Esteban of Zamora came to an agreement with the lay proprietors of the church of Villardondiego.[3] The background to this seems to have been an attempt on the part of the bishop to supplant them by instituting a priest of his own choosing in the church. The contending parties agreed that the priest should be chosen in future after consultation between them; that no other church should be founded in the

[1] AHN 1325C/20 (ptd. below, Appendix, no. VI).
[2] *Docs. Oviedo* no. 155. The terms of the grant should be compared with those of the grant made by Pedro and Fernando Núñez in 1114, referred to above, p. 165. For a church given in *prestamine* by the bishop and chapter of Oviedo as late as 1165, see *Docs. Oviedo* no. 180.
[3] AC Zamora, Libro Negro, fol. 5ᵛ (ptd. below, Appendix, no. XI).

village; and that the bishop should get his *tercias*. For all this the bishop paid, with two plots of land. Yet the most vital provision came last of all: *et ipse episcopus sit heres in ipsa ecclesia.* The church of Villardondiego was to pass from lay to episcopal control. A somewhat similar case may be cited from the diocese of Tuy, the details of which are furnished in an act of Bishop Beltrán dated 30 December 1183.[1] Pelayo Menéndez, bishop of Tuy from 1130 to 1156, had acquired from one Pedro Pérez his share in the *monasterium* of Pesegueiro in return for a grant to him for life only of the church of Santiago in Vigo. On his death his son, Pedro Pérez II, held onto the church of Vigo *iniuste*. After a lengthy dispute it was agreed that he too was to be allowed to retain the church for his own lifetime, on payment of a steep annual render in cash and under certain other conditions, after which it was to revert to the cathedral church of Tuy.

We also find bishops intervening when laymen granted parish churches to monasteries. In 1163 Archbishop Martín of Compostela confirmed the monastery of Tojos Outos in possession of the church of San Felix at *Syaria* which had been given to it by one García on the occasion of his departure for Jerusalem: the archbishop noted that the grant had been made *per nostram licenciam*, and he stipulated that the monastery was to defend the church *ab omni heredum voce vel requisicione.*[2]

Again, bishops seem to have been anxious to retain control of churches in newly-founded settlements. In 1161 Bishop Esteban of Zamora granted a *fuero* to the settlement of Las Morarelias.[3] He laid down that he would build the church there and *mittam clericum meum quemcumque voluero.* What was more, if the priest were accused of any misdemeanour, he was to be arraigned before the bishop's court, not before the *concejo* of the village; though the *concejo* was to be allowed to share any fines which the bishop might impose upon him. One may recall here the emphasis laid by his

---

[1] AC Tuy 10/11. [2] AHN cód. 1002B, fols. 187^V-188^r.
[3] AC Zamora, Libro Negro, fol. 7^r.

predecessor Bernardo upon the bishop's church, *ecclesia episcopi*, in the *fuero* granted to Fuentesauco in 1133.[1] A later example from further north concerns Benavente in the diocese of Astorga, a new town to which Fernando II had granted a *fuero* in 1167. A document of 1199 (surviving only in an eighteenth-century abstract) reveals Bishop Lope of Astorga anxious to retain control of all newly-founded churches.[2] In the diocese of Salamanca, we have already seen Bishop Navarro controlling the founding of churches round Castronuño, while Count Nuño Pérez de Lara was responsible for the secular *repoblación*. They seem to have worked harmoniously together, which is only to say that we hear of no squabbles in the documents that have come down to us. Relations were sometimes strained. Fernando II decided to settle Ledesma, in the same diocese, in 1161, and put the arrangements into the hands of Count Ponce de Cabrera.[3] The bishop of Salamanca was to have charge of the church of Ledesma. But we learn from a papal bull of 15 July 1166 that Count Ponce had seized the church and given it to the Hospitallers; they had then granted it to a knight who had taken up residence within the church with his mistress. This story bears all the marks of a tale told by the complainants, the bishop and chapter of Salamanca, and the reality proved to be rather less scandalous than this. One suspects that the usurpation occurred in 1163 at the time of the Portuguese invasion of the exposed frontier region on which Ledesma lay, when the needs of defence were pressing and the Hospitallers could make what terms they chose. What is significant is that they were extraordinarily hard to get out. They were still there in 1177, if not later; and they were still being eyed with suspicion—together with another menacing body, the knights of the Order of Santiago—in 1192.[4]

Occasionally, lay proprietors might be expropriated. The abbot of Oya, on the Atlantic coast near Tuy, had been

---

[1] AC Zamora, Libro Negro, fol. 15[V] (ptd. below, Appendix, no. VII).

[2] *GRF* p. 397; BN MS. 4357, Tumbo Negro no. 607.

[3] For what follows, see *GRF* pp. 44-6; AC Salamanca nos. 46 (1166), 38 (1170), 45 and 50 (1177), 52 and 53 (1178?). The last two of these papal bulls are hard to date, and may well be earlier than 1178.

[4] AC Salamanca, no. 100.

complaining for a long time about the *heredes* of the church
of Sta. Marina at *Rosal* who refused to surrender a quarter
share of the church. In 1200 Bishop Beltrán of Tuy took the
opportunity presented by their failure to obey three summonses to attend his court to hear the matter to dispossess
them.[1] He did this for their contumacy, not because they
were holding a church contrary to canon law; but it is significant that the engine of punishment he chose was dis-
possession, rather than (say) the monetary fine which had
been stipulated by bishop Diego of León in 1117.

The evidence so far cited is necessarily scattered both in
time and place but it does suggest some tentative conclusions.
Proprietary churches were certainly passing from lay into
ecclesiastical hands. Bishops were encouraging the movement, with more energy (it would seem) as the century wore
on. Their activity had to take on different forms in the
different parts of the kingdom. In the north, faced with an
entrenched system of *Eigenkirchen*, they bought out lay
proprietors, insinuated themselves as their heirs by bending
to their own purposes the well-established legal device of the
donatio post obitum, or seized pretexts to get rid of them.
It must have been a slow process, and we should guard against
too ready an assumption that effort was consistent or progress steady. In the south, where the proprietary church was
barely established, their task was the different one of trying
to prevent its taking root.

As a corollary of the slow erosion of the proprietary
church, we should expect to find the emergence of the
notion of the *ius patronatus*. We do find the terms, and presumably the ideas, but they were late to appear and not
widely diffused. The *patronus* of a church is first mentioned
in a Salamanca act of 1181, and appears again in a Zamora
act of 1212.[2] *Ius patronatus* is referred to in an act of Archbishop Pedro Suárez of 1185—which might have been drafted
by the archbishop of Toledo's writing-office—and in one of
Bishop Martín Arias of Zamora dated 1214.[3] And that is the

---

[1] AHN 1796/4 (ptd. below, Appendix, no. XXVI).
[2] AC Salamanca, no. 78 (ptd. below, Appendix, no. XVII); AC Zamora, Libro
Blanco, fol. 32^r.
[3] AHN 18/17; AC Zamora, Libro Negro, fols. 67^v–69^r.

extent of our evidence. It may be significant that from a
decretal letter of 1209 despatched to the bishop of Orense
we may learn that the bishop's query which had elicited the
letter showed familiarity with the idea but unfamiliarity with
the details of canonical practice.[1]

What else were bishops trying to do in and with the parish
churches of their dioceses? We might expect to find them
trying to supervise appointments to cures; displaying concern for clerical education, celibacy, income and security of
tenure; instituting perpetual vicarages; attempting to supervise the building of new churches. Some of these matters
have left their mark in our texts, not all. We hear of church-
building undertaken by the bishops,[2] and we can see that at
least in the second half of the century they were trying so far
as possible to control the building of churches. Esteban,
bishop of Zamora, gave Pedro Díaz and other merchants of
Zamora permission to build a church to serve the hospital
which they had founded below the town by the new bridge
over the Duero.[3] We learn from an act of Bishop Vidal of
Salamanca that his predecessor Pedro Suárez had while
bishop of Salamanca given one Berengar and his two sons
permission to build a church.[4] One of the quarrels between
the bishops of Astorga and the Hospitallers was that they had
built churches without episcopal licence in the diocese.[5]
When Rodrigo II of Lugo granted the church of *Monseti* to
Urraca Adefonsi as a benefice for life in 1182, he required
her to build the church there, and laid down exactly how she
was to do it and when; the apse and the portal were to be of
ashlar and the remaining walls of rubble, and the whole church
was to be finished by 1 March 1186.[6] Guillermo, bishop of
Zamora, licensed the knights of the Order of Santiago to

---

[1] *MHV* I no. 397.
[2] E.g., *HC* pp. 186–7, 372, 472.
[3] AC Zamora leg. 13, no. 26 (ptd. below, Appendix, no. XIII). This was of course
not a parish church.
[4] AC Salamanca, no. 78 (ptd. below, Appendix, no. XVII).
[5] Papal bulls of 4 August 1182 and 27 March 1198 in A. Quintana Prieto, 'Registro de documentos pontificios de la diócesis de Astorga (1139–1413)', *Anthologica Annua* xi (1963), 189–226.
[6] AHN 1325G/13 (ptd. below, Appendix, no. XIX).

build a church at *Campluma*, near Zamora; his successor Martín allowed one Ramiro to build a church at Lacuna Toral in 1199.[1] And there are further examples of episcopal control from the same diocese.[2]

In documents of this sort, we hear a good deal about episcopal rights, rather less about the endowments of local churches, and practically nothing at all about the clergy who were to serve them. For example, in the act of Bishop Vidal of Salamanca referred to above[3] the bishop stressed the money payment that was due from the patron every year and ordered that episcopal interdicts and excommunications were to be observed. Nothing was said about the endowments of the church—though it was implied that they were adequate, and likely to grow—nor about the clery who were to have charge of it. Again, when Martín of Zamora granted a church at Toro to the monastery of *Arvas* in 1194 he stipulated that *tercias* were to be rendered to the bishop and laid down that

omnem reverentie subjectionem, et omnia plenaria iura que predicte Zemorensi ecclesie in aliis sue diocesis ecclesiis debentur et observantur ei semper exhibeatis et fideliter observetis.[4]

Sometimes bishops were more positive over the question of endowments. It is again from the Zamora *acta* that our most revealing instances come.[5] Here is one from the year 1203. Martín of Zamora had had a church built on some land of his own near Toro. He granted it for life to one Domingo Menéndez, presumably the priest who was to serve it. The profits from tithe were to be divided in the usual way, two-thirds to the priest and church, one third to the bishop. Another man, Menendo, who called himself a *nutritus* of the cathedral church of Zamora and the bishop's *vasallus*—might he have been Domingo's father?—gave four *aranzadas* of vineyard and a share in a watermill, which Domingo Menéndez

[1] D.W. Lomax, *La Orden de Santiago 1170–1275* (Madrid, 1965), Ap. no. 5, p. 235 (probably of 1185–6); AC Zamora leg. 33, no. 2 (ptd. below, Appendix, no. XXV).

[2] AC Zamora leg. 13, nos. 1, 37; Libro Negro, fol. VI[r] of preliminary quire with unnumbered folios.

[3] Cf. above, p. 173, n. 4.

[4] AC Zamora, Libro Negro, fol. 65.

[5] E.g., AC Zamora, leg. 13, nos. 26, 39 (ptd. below, Appendix, nos. XIII, XXIX).

was to hold for life, after which they were to 'remain to' the church (*remaneant ecclesie*). Furthermore, Menendo undertook to leave the houses (*domos*) in which he and his wife lived to the church after his death. It is pretty clear, though it is not stated explicitly, that these arrangements had been made at the instance of the bishop. Should we call this the institution of a perpetual vicarage? Perhaps we should. The arrangements made certainly bear a resemblance to those which were being made elsewhere in contemporary Christendom. What is really noticeable is the absence of technical terms. The word *vicaria* never occurs in the documents which have been consulted, and the instance just quoted is the only example of something like a perpetual vicarage which has come to light.

Some concern was shown for the character of the parish clergy. Successive ecclesiastical councils forbade clerical marriage and unchastity—Compostela in 1114, Burgos in 1117, Sahagún in 1121, Palencia in 1129, Valladolid in 1143 and 1155. How widespread such shortcomings were we have no means of telling. There is some evidence that throughout the following century they were indeed widespread. Attempts were certainly made to examine the fitness of priests before their institution: we have evidence of this from the dioceses of Tuy and Zamora, and, over the Castilian frontier, Avila.[1] But whether such attempts were regular or sporadic we have no means of ascertaining. Neither do we know anything at all about the steps taken (if any) by bishops to ensure that the lower clergy had a modicum of education.

Bishops would be successful in their aims only if they had at their disposal a machinery of diocesan administration, in working order, to enforce their wishes. The essential elements of such a machinery were visitations, synods and the holding of courts. Visitation is referred to in a matter of fact way in our sources, which is some justification for supposing that it took place frequently, perhaps regularly. Thus the authors of the *Historia Compostellana* introduced an anecdote about Diego Gelmírez with the words, 'Cum honores et ecclesias, veluti bonus pastor, in sua diocesi sancta visitatione

---

[1] AHN 1512/3; AC Zamora, Libro Negro, fols. 66^V–67^r; AHN 18/12.

pervisitaret. . .', and a little later they observed that disorder was so rife in Spain that, 'pontifices. . .nec etiam suas proprias dioceses secure visitare audebant'.[1] A bishop of Lugo could refer at about the same time to the 'prandiis, que mihi reserventur cum ipsam terram visitavero annuatim pontificali more'.[2] When the countess Teresa of Portugal gave the *monasterium* of Azere to the bishop of Tuy in 1125 it is plain that she expected him to visit it at least once a year, for he was to conduct ordinations there *per singulos annos*.[3] So too in the dioceses of the central part of the kingdom:[4] and in the southern parts where we find the bishop of Zamora stipulating in 1208 that *si ei placuerit singulis annis visitet ecclesias* in the valley of the Guareña.[5] Monasteries too were to be visited. *Receptio* was one of the rights going to make up *ius pontificale* which Nuño of Mondoñedo claimed over the monastery of Lorenzana in 1128; it was part of the *ius pontificale* which Bishop Martín of Oviedo renounced in favour of the exempt abbey of Samos in 1150.[6]

What actually happened on these visitations? Some clues have already been given. Diego Gelmírez visited not only his churches but also his *honores*, i.e., his lands. Pedro of Lugo spoke of visitation in his act of 1120 simply because he wished to ensure that he retained for himself the right of procuration. In this connection, the following instances may be noted. The bishops of León insisted upon the hospitality due to them from the *monasteria* of their diocese in the same sort of terms in which they spoke of that due from the settlements of *repobladores* upon their own estates. They could lay down both this, 'recipiatur vero episcopus. . .in ipsis villis et monasteriis descriptis, et detur ei impensa dum in ipsis hospitari voluerit. . .' and this, 'Procurabunt etiam episcopum splendide et eos qui cum eo erunt, una die in unoquoque anno, idem populatores, si advenerit in ipsa villa, et recipient

---

[1] *HC* pp. 59, 147.
[2] *ES* XLI, ap. ii, pp. 296–301 (1120); cf. ibid., ap. v, p. 306 (1138).
[3] *DMP* no. 70.
[4] BN MS. 4357, Particulares no. 385 (Astorga, 1213).
[5] AC Zamora, leg. 13, no. 13 (ptd. below, Appendix, no. XXXIII).
[6] AHN cód. 1044B, fol. 12[r]; *BCM* Lugo III (1949) pp. 256–63.

in domibus suis bestias suas cum hominibus suis et canonicorum ibidem quandocumque advenerint'.[1] These documents do not specify the size of the episcopal retinue. But some bishops clearly had to bargain. The monks of San Román de la Hornija kept the bishop of Zamora down to an entourage of fifteen horsemen.[2] Yet bishops expected to be well received. Rodrigo II of Lugo stated that he was to be entertained *splendide. . .tamquam ipsius ecclesie dominum* by Teresa Peláez, to whom he had granted a church *in prestimonium* in 1189.[3] The priest of *Requeixu* was to receive him whenever he came *sicut fidelis vasallus et amicus suum recipit dominum.*[4] One recipient of a church was required to construct a special building (*domum*) near the church in which the bishop might be suitably (*honeste*) received in the course of visitations.[5] The church of Compostela certainly had houses or palaces of this kind in which the bishops or archbishops might be lodged during visitations: Diego Gelmírez spent his own money on repairs to those in the Tierra de Campos early in his episcopate.[6]

It is plain that visitation was a good deal more than a matter of pastoral care. The hospitality that bishops sought may have formed an important part of their revenue. Bishops expected to do well out of it, and sometimes they did very well indeed; the theft of the relics of St. Fructuosus from Braga was referred to by the authors of the *Historia Compostellana* as a visitation.[7] The *prandia* to which they were entitled seems usually to have been exacted in kind, though there is some evidence for commutation towards the end of the century; Guillermo of Zamora exacted one gold piece (*aureum*) annually from the church of Villafranca de Duero, and Rodrigo II of Lugo ten *solidi* from the church of Barrantes.[8] It was presumably on the occasion of visitation that

---

[1] AC León nos. 1362, 1466 (ptd. *ES* XXXVI, ap. xlvi, pp. c–ciii; ap. lx, pp. cxxix–cxxx).
[2] AC Zamora, leg. 13, no. 1.
[3] AHN 1325H/8 (ptd. below, Appendix, no. XXI).
[4] AHN 1326A/1.
[5] AHN 1325G/13 (ptd. below, Appendix, no. XIX).
[6] *HC* p. 69.   [7] *HC* p. 36.
[8] AC Zamora, leg. 14, no. 28; AHN 1325H/17 (ptd. below, Appendix, no. XXIII).

bishops collected the other dues which came to them from the parish churches of their dioceses, namely the third part of the tithes and a ram,[1] though we do hear of officials, *terciarii*, whom the bishop might send to carry out apportionment and collection.[2] Sometimes these dues were commuted too.[3]

But it would be perverse to suggest that episcopal visitation was no more than the occasional descent of a rapacious lord, though it must often have looked like that to the visited. Not all visitations need have been as stirring as the occasion when Diego Gelmírez visited the monastery of Anteoltares in about 1129-30; the abbot, convicted of having kept seventy (*sic*) concubines, was deposed, and the monks were told to get their hair cut.[4] We may guess that some of the matters discussed earlier—church-fabrics, clerical celibacy, etc.—were investigated during visitations; but we do not really know what went on.

The other occasion for the collection of revenue and for the exercise of pastoral responsibilities was the meeting of the bishop's synod. Here too we have a number of fragments of evidence whose cumulative force is impressive. The abbot of Samos was required to attend the bishop of Lugo's *concilium* in 1145; in 1154 the abbot of Castañeda was exempted from attending the bishop of Astorga's *synodum sive concilium*.[5] Manrique of León seems to have held synods twice a year; Martín of Zamora once a year.[6] Archbishop Pelayo of Compostela's requirement that the heads of the religious houses of his diocese should attend the celebration of Santiago's day at Compostela every year would have provided the occasion for holding a synod, though nothing was said of one.[7] One of the counts against the abbot of Celanova in 1198 was that he had refused to attend the bishop of Orense's synod and had prevented others from doing so.[8] In

---

[1] *Docs. Oviedo* no. 199, where the three renders are lumped together.
[2] E.g., AHN 18/17; AC Zamora leg. 14, no. 28.
[3] E.g., AHN 963/20 (ptd. below, Appendix, no. XII).   [4] *HC* p. 508.
[5] *ES* XLI, ap. vii, pp. 308-9; *ES* XVI, ap. xxviii, pp. 484-6.
[6] AC León no. 1438; AC Zamora, leg. 13, no. 1.
[7] *LFH* IV, ap. xxiv, pp. 67-8.   [8] *MHV* I, no. 132.

Castile, we hear of annual synods in the diocese of Burgos in 1205, and of what seem to be regular synods in the diocese of Avila in 1181.[1] But as with visitations, so with synods; we do not really know what went on when they met.

The council of Burgos in 1117 laid down that clerks were not to take disputes with other churchmen to secular tribunals. Presumably the bishops were to hear such cases. But whether the bishops' courts were bodies distinct from the diocesan synod, if so, who sat in them; how far their competence extended; and what sort of business came before them, we simply cannot tell. When the bishop of Tuy expropriated the heirs of the church of Rosal in 1200[2] he summoned them to his 'presence' and he sought the advice of 'prudent men'. When the bishop of Zamora heard a dispute between his cathedral canons and the clergy of the town at about the same date it was heard *coram nobis*.[3] When an earlier bishop of Zamora heard a dispute between the abbot of Moreruela and the people of Junciel in 1168 he delegated the case to four laymen to judge, and their judgement was ratified by the bishop in his cathedral church.[4] But information of this kind is not helpful. The documents are too lean and sparse, and their wording too vague, to allow us to answer the questions we have posed.

Such is the evidence. That it is a pitifully inadequate basis on which to found judgements about the pastoral action of the bishops of León is all too apparent. What concluding observations we may offer have necessarily to be somewhat neutral in tone. It is clear that a pattern of diocesan administration—in large part an imported one—took root in western Spain during the twelfth century. The indications are that the machinery of government was in reasonably good order. The diocese appears as a working unit of church government; bishops show signs, albeit the evidence is fragmentary, of responsible pastoral care. Yet one is left with an impression that there was little development over the century. (If we are

[1] Ibid., no. 313; AHN 18/12.   [2] Cf. above p. 172.
[3] AC Zamora, Libro Negro, fol. 85[r] (ptd. below, Appendix, no. XXVII).
[4] AC Zamora, leg. 13, no. 6.

correct in associating innovation with the immigrant French clergy it may be useful to bear in mind that this influx seems to have ceased after *c*.1150). Leonese church government in the latter part of the century may have been as old-fashioned as the appearance of the documents which are the main source of our information about it. Secular terms survived in the bishops' *acta* long after they had been banished from the ecclesiastical documents of northern Europe. New Romano-canonical terms were slow to appear and seem to have been handled with little assurance at first. Bishops seem to have been unfamiliar with practices which were becoming standard elsewhere; it is significant, for instance, that they did not consistently insert themselves into the process by which proprietary churches were surrendered into ecclesiastical hands by insisting that such surrenders be mediated through them alone, as trustees of all ecclesiastical rights in their dioceses. If Leonese churchmen were ignorant of reforming currents of thought, these facts would be the more intelligible: but, as we shall shortly see, there is evidence that relations between these churchmen and the papal curia became close during the course of the century. Yet the legate John of Abbeville was scandalized in 1228–9 both by what he found in Spain and by the absence of what he had hoped to find. He was probably a man who was easily shockable, certainly one whom shock made vociferous; but his judgements cannot simply be set aside. Perhaps it would be charitable to conclude that the administration of the secular church of the Leonese kingdom under Fernando II and Alfonso IX was not all that it might have been.

5

THE LEONESE EPISCOPATE AND THE PAPACY

Towards the end of the thirteenth century an inmate of the monastery of Villanueva de Lorenzana in the diocese of Mondoñedo put together a cartulary out of the muniments of his house. Certain features of the early documents puzzled him: why for instance had the tenth-century founders not sought papal confirmation of the privileges which they had lavished upon their monastery? In an aside to the reader he tried to explain; in those days people did not go to Rome.[1] About 150 years earlier one of the authors of the *Historia Compostellana* said much the same thing. Writing of the period before the reign of Alfonso VI (1065-1109) he said that no Spanish bishop was accustomed to render duty and obedience to the Roman church.[2]

As far as concerns the kingdom of León there is every likelihood that these observations were correct. We have hardly any flickerings of papal interest in the ecclesiastical affairs of western Spain before the pontificate of Urban II (1088-99). Pelayo of Oviedo concocted two letters of Pope John VIII to Alfonso III (866-911) which he inserted into the tenth-century chronicle of Sampiro.[3] They are easily detected as forgeries on diplomatic grounds; still, it was a cruel mischance which led him to pick on the only ninth-century pope whose register has survived. No genuine documents lay behind these spurious bulls. At some point before the abolition of the Mozarabic rite a cardinal-legate seems to have visited Santiago de Compostela where, so the story went in the twelfth century, he was insulted by the bishop.[4] In 1084 Jarenton, abbot of Dijon, visited Coimbra in the course

---

[1] AHN cód. 1044B, fol. 30r.

[2] *HC* p. 253.

[3] J. Pérez de Urbel, *Sampiro, su Crónica y la monarquía leonesa en el siglo X* (Madrid, 1952), pp. 285-9.

[4] *HC* p. 253. Paul Kehr suggested that the legate may have been Hugh Candidus and the date about 1067.

of a legatine journey undertaken on the orders of Gregory VII.[1] The imposition of the Roman rite did indeed bring the Leonese bishops into sudden and painful contact with the wishes of Rome; but the new liturgy did not conquer the far north-west until the latter part of the 1080s. We have no papal privileges indicating contact between Leonese church-men and the papacy, no record of Leonese attendance at papal councils, no hint of any pilgrimages to Rome. Import-ant decisions about the government of the church were taken locally; for example, the decision to restore the sees of Braga, Tuy and Orense in 1070-1.

By the time of the pontificate of Innocent III the scene had completely changed. Relations between Leonese church-men and the papal curia were frequent and close. The popes were receiving visits from churchmen and despatching legates and fund-raisers. They issued privileges, heard appeals, ap-pointed judges-delegate, answered questions, listened to com-plaints. Their registers are full of letters rebuking, scolding, chiding, warning, informing, advising, and sometimes even praising the men who made up the Leonese episcopate.[2] The change is remarkable, but it can hardly be called surprising. It fits snugly into a pattern which has already been made familiar by those historians who have studied the relations between the popes and the churches of the outlying Euro-pean kingdoms over the same period. In particular, it corres-ponds to what we know of the relations between the popes and the other kingdoms of the Iberian peninsula.[3] Papal 'influence' was not felt outside Catalonia in the first half of the eleventh century. Between about 1050 and 1080 it began

[1] J. Mattoso, Le Monachisme ibérique et Cluny (Louvain, 1968), p. 121; cf. also The 'Epistolae Vagantes' of Gregory VII, ed. H.E.J. Cowdrey (Oxford, 1972), no. 54.
[2] The enregistered material relating to Spain and Portugal from the pontificates of Innocent III and Honorius III is most easily accessible in MHV I and II.
[3] On this topic see, in general, P. Kehr, Das Papsttum und der Katalanische Prin-zipät bis zur Vereinigung mit Aragon (Berlin, 1926), and his 'El Papado y los reinos de Navarra y Argaón hasta mediados del siglo XII' in EEMCA ii (1946), 74-186; A. Durán Gudiol, La Iglesia de Aragón durante los reinados de Sancho Ramírez y Pedro I (Rome, 1962); P. David, Études historiques sur la Galice et le Portugal (Lisbon-Paris, 1947); L. de la Calzada, 'La proyección del pensamiento de Gregorio VII en los reinos de Castilla y de León', Studi Gregoriani iii (1948), 1-87; C. Erdmann, O Papado e Portugal no primeiro século da história portuguesa (Coimbra, 1935).

to be felt in Aragon, Navarre and Castile. After about 1080 it crept slowly westward into León and Portugal. The evidence by which we may plot its course consists in the main of surviving papal bulls directed to Leonese churchmen or concerned with ecclesiastical affairs. In what follows I shall attempt to characterize its nature and impact.

The change may be familiar, but we cannot take it for granted. It will be as well to examine with some care the early manifestations of contact between Leonese churchmen and the popes. They occurred during the pontificate of Urban II.

In 1088 the bishop of Santiago de Compostela, Diego Peláez, was bullied by Alfonso VI into resigning his see at the council of Husillos in the presence of the ex-legate Richard of Marseilles. The king's anger against him had probably been provoked by his complicity in the Galician revolt of Count Rodrigo Ovéquiz in 1087-8. Alfonso flung him into prison and replaced him as bishop of Compostela by a loyal and reliable Castilian monk, Pedro de Cardeña. This occasioned an outburst of rage from the pope, which found expression in three bulls dated 15 October 1088: the diocese was laid under an interdict until Diego should be released, and its clergy and people were rebuked for allowing the intrusion of Pedro; Alfonso VI was ordered to set Diego free, and Pedro was deposed and summoned to Rome.[1] This sudden intervention in the affairs of the most distant of all the Spanish dioceses is the earliest manifestation of direct and forceful papal activity of which we have record in the kingdom of León. Now the bulls of 15 October 1088 were issued at the same time as two others which were, directly or indirectly, in favour of Bernardo, archbishop of Toledo, and which, above all, designated him as primate of all Spain.[2] It is not unlikely that those which concerned the recent struggle over the church of Compostela were sought at the instance of Bernardo, and should be seen as an earnest of his determination to make his primacy an active force rather than a theoretical distinction. At the same time, it is clear that Urban II

[1] JL. 5367-5369.   [2] JL 5366, 5370.

was angry at the presumption of Richard of Marseilles in exercising legatine powers when in fact his legatine office had already lapsed, and was happy to be able to take advantage of the presence of Archbishop Bernardo at the curia to arrange for issuing a sharp rebuke to Richard.[1]

This early intrusion into Leonese ecclesiastical affairs was soon followed by others. In 1089 Pedro bishop of León appeared at the curia to confess that he was not of legitimate birth and to seek a dispensation.[2] In 1095 the bishop of Santiago de Compostela, Dalmatius, attended the council of Clermont *cum quibusdam comprovincialium episcoporum*: among these was certainly Amor, the bishop of Lugo, in whose favour Urban II issued a bull dated 28 November 1095, by which the bishops of León, Oviedo and Mondoñedo were ordered to restore certain lands which rightfully belonged to the bishopric of Lugo; an order which was repeated a little later, between 1096 and 1099, since the three offending bishops refused to act.[3] Dalmatius himself got a confirmation of the transfer of the seat of his bishopric from Iria to Compostela, and the valuable privilege of exemption.[4] A few years later, at the end of Urban II's pontificate, Bishop Martín of Oviedo sought and received a solemn privilege confirming the property of his church.[5]

This evidence is important not merely as the first indication of the opening-up of relations between the Leonese church and the papal curia, but also as the foreshadowing of the ways in which such relations would become closer as the twelfth century advanced. During Urban II's pontificate we see bishops looking to the pope as the fount from which privileges might flow; as an arbiter in disputes and the defender of the weak in adversity; and as the guardian of what is loosely called 'reform'. These spurs to episcopal initiative in seeking the papal curia did not alter as such during the twelfth century, as will become clear from a more detailed examination of the surviving evidence.

---

[1] J.F. Rivera, *La Iglesia de Toledo en el siglo XII* (Rome-Madrid, 1966), p. 137.
[2] JL 5390.
[3] *HC* p. 20; AHN cód. 1043B, fol. 38ᵛ, 39ʳ.
[4] JL 5601.   [5] JL 5785.

PAPAL PRIVILEGES

Papal privileges were of two kinds, those which confirmed archbishops and bishops in the possession of rights or properties, and those which granted them new rights, distinctions or immunities. We possess forty-six such documents despatched between 1095 and 1215 to the bishoprics of the kingdom of León. As usual, the evidence has survived unevenly; seventeen privileges to the church of Compostela have come down to us; none has come down from the sees of Salamanca and Tuy —which does not mean that their bishops did not acquire any.[1]

Such privileges were always sought by the beneficiary, never granted on papal initiative, and there is reason to suppose that they were expensive. Frequently, we know nothing of the reasons which led bishops to acquire them. Such is the case, for example, with those granted to the churches of Zamora and Astorga in 1151 and 1162 respectively.[2] When we do know something of the background we often find that they were sought in the course of disputes; they were a stage in litigation, so to say, rather than a casual form of insurance. The best example of this is furnished by the series of privileges granted to the see of Lugo in 1123, 1131, 1156, 1161, 1172, 1179 and 1185, which was connected with the dispute over diocesan boundaries between the bishoprics of Lugo and León. In the same way the privileges granted to Compostela in 1103 and 1110 were related to the dispute with the see of Mondoñedo over certain archipresbyterates, while that granted to Orense in 1203 was occasioned by the dispute between the bishops of Orense and the monastery of Celanova.[3]

Bishops also sought distinctions from the papacy, to mark them out, if their ambition or their piety so led them, from

[1] The surviving privileges are proportioned as follows: Santiago de Compostela 17, Lugo 7, Oviedo 6, León 6, Coria 3, Mondoñedo 1, Astorga 1, Zamora 1, Ciudad Rodrigo 1, Salamanca and Tuy 0. I use the word privilege here to refer to their content, not to their form. Not all were cast in the diplomatic form of a 'solemn privilege', e.g., that granted to the bishop of Oviedo on 27 April 1157, a photograph of the original of which may be seen in *Docs. Oviedo*, lam. 8.
[2] AC Zamora, Libro Blanco, first (unnumbered) folio; JL 10802.
[3] JL 5942, 6264; *MHV* I, no. 266.

their fellows. Diego Gelmírez acquired a number of such distinctions—the institution of cardinals at Compostela, the *pallium*, permission for the dignitaries of the chapter to wear mitres adorned with gems for the greater feasts, permission for Diego himself to wear the tunicle and stole.[1] Like his adoption of the use of the *rota*, discussed in a preceding chapter, these distinctions were intended to enhance the dignity of Diego's see and to make it, to outward appearance, similar in certain ways to the papacy. The policy was continued by his successors. Pedro Helias acquired from Eugenius III in 1145 the privilege of carrying his cross raised before him throughout his province, even in the presence of papal legates,[2] and Pedro Suárez may have acquired the privilege of Jubilee from Alexander III in 1181.[3]

More important were the grants of ecclesiastical authority, or status, or immunity. Here the most far-reaching concessions were those of Calixtus II to Diego Gelmírez in 1120 and 1124, when he raised the see of Santiago de Compostela to metropolitan status.[4] Three sees were exempted from the authority of their metropolitans during our period; Compostela in 1095, León in 1104 and Oviedo in 1105.[5] The see of Compostela was also, for a very brief time, exempted from recognizing the primatial authority of the archbishop of Toledo.[6]

We have detailed knowledge on no more than two occasions of how these privileges were acquired. Both concern the church of Compostela. The first is the account of how Diego Gelmírez got his pallium in 1104, and the second is the account of the lengthy series of negotiations which led up to his greatest triumph, Calixtus II's raising of his see to metropolitan status in 1120. The stories are well-known and there is no need to go over them again here.[7] It will be sufficient to make some comments.

[1] JL 5881, 5986, 6042, 6466.
[2] *LFH* IV, ap. xiv, pp. 39–41.
[3] *LFH* IV, ap. liv, pp. 138–42; but this bull may not be genuine.
[4] JL 6823, 7160.
[5] JL 5601; AC León no. 6328; JL 6039.
[6] JL 9808 (not earlier than 16 May 1154) and 10141 (9 February 1156). For the dating of the earlier of these two bulls, see Fita in *BRAH* xiv (1889), 550–1.
[7] *HC* pp. 42–50, 255–94: see also A.G. Biggs, *Diego Gelmírez*, pp. 47–51, 140–56.

The history of these transactions sheds a vivid light upon the ways in which relations between a particular church and the papacy actually worked. Three points call for comment. The first is obvious: such negotiations did make for very frequent contact with the papal curia. There was coming and going on these pieces of business, lovingly chronicled by the authors of the *Historia Compostellana*, almost continually between 1095 and 1120, and indeed beyond, since the transfer of the metropolitanate of Mérida to Santiago de Compostela was not made permanent until 1124. Second, it is clear that it was impossible to get valuable privileges without extensive, and costly, intrigue. This was, notoriously, one of the criticisms levelled at the papacy throughout the twelfth century, so this Spanish evidence shows us nothing new; but it does offer us some choice illustrations of how these things were managed. Gelasius II was offered 100 gold pieces as a *benedictio* in 1118.[1] Calixtus II seems to have received much more.[2] Cardinal Deusdedit was bought with a prebend at Compostela while on a legatine visit in 1118.[3] Not for nothing does the author of the *Historia Compostellana* offer us a long narrative of the quarrel and subsequent reconciliation between Abbot Pons of Cluny and Pope Calixtus; for perhaps Diego would never have secured his prize without the powerful advocacy of Cluny.[4] In the third place, it is clear that these privileges were granted where possible only in return for a *quid pro quo* not necessarily to be reckoned in hard cash—a point to which we shall have to return shortly.

Diego's negotiations are unusually well-chronicled. But similar journeyings and intrigues, pleadings and bribes, hopes and fears, must have lain behind similar privileges about the background to which we know nothing. How did Archbishop Pelayo of Compostela contrive to get for himself in 1154 a privilege exempting him from recognition of Toledan primacy? To what intrigues did this give rise during the legatine visit of Cardinal Hyacinth in 1154 and 1155? How was it

---

[1] *HC* p. 265.   [2] *HC* p. 274 (272).
[3] *HC* p. 268.
[4] *HC* pp. 284–5: and see also C.J. Bishko, 'The Spanish journey of Abbot Ponce of Cluny', *Ricerche di Storia Religiosa* i (1957), 311–19.

that Archbishop Juan of Toledo managed to get it reversed in 1156? We do not know the answers to these questions, but we may be sure that the negotiations which lay behind these bald and silent documents were not a whit less complex than those in which Diego Gelmírez had engaged at an earlier date. The same may be said of the acquisition and defence of their privileges of exemption by the sees of Oviedo and León, of which something has been said in an earlier chapter.

One of the most significant features of Diego's success in acquiring the pallium in 1104 was that Paschal II exacted a solemn undertaking in return. This was embodied in an oath by which Diego swore loyalty to the pope and his successors, promised to attend papal councils and to receive papal legates dutifully, and undertook to journey to Rome once in every three years either in person or by sending representatives.[1] The bishops of Compostela were already bound by the terms of their privilege of exemption of 1095 to go to the pope for consecration. These additional requirements indicate that papal privileges were more than just a simple sale of honours: they were also a means by which the apparatus of papal authority was extended over areas of the catholic church which had not known it before. A little before copying the oath which Diego swore, his biographer wrote,[2] 'quia nullus episcoporum huius ecclesie Rome sponte fuerat, tanto affectu precordialissime dilectionis dominus papa hunc suscepit. . .paucissimos ita suscepisse arbitramur'. But Paschal II was not merely, as his biographer would have us believe, doing honour to Diego; he was also welcoming back a lost sheep into the fold.

RECOURSE TO ROME—THE EARLY STAGES

It is only very mildly surprising to find Leonese bishops seeking privileges from the papacy after about 1100. It is much more so to find them appealing to the pope as to an arbiter in their disputes and their shield against oppression. The course upon which they entered here rapidly 'snow-balled'. Appeals, notoriously, generated more appeals, and

[1] *HC* p. 50.   [2] *HC* p. 47.

they still more. The process once begun quickly gathered a momentum of its own. But why did it start in the first place? This question can easily be overlooked, for the practice of appealing to the pope seems, to the historian with his hindsight, natural and normal. But Leonese and Castilian bishops had never done it before the end of the eleventh century. It was extraordinary, and by no means natural. A number of answers, rather than any single one, may be suggested to the question here posed.

The influx of French clergy towards the end of the eleventh century, and above all the arrival in Spain of Bernardo of Toledo, was perhaps the first important factor.[1] These men, however open they may have been to the charges of ecclesiastical empire-building or of feathering their own nests, were carrying out needful ecclesiastical reorganization, frequently if not invariably in the face of powerful vested interests which were bitterly opposed to them. They needed, therefore, support from outside. This was the more so in that some of their constitutional reforms were such as could be sanctioned only by the pope. In addition, Bernardo had himself been a monk at Cluny with Eudes of Châtillon, later Pope Urban II. Both left Cluny at about the same time (1078–80), both made their mark in different ways during the succeeding few years, and they came together again after their respective promotions, Eudes's to the papacy in March 1088, and Bernardo's to the see of Toledo in December 1086. The first and most important evidence of their renewed contact came in the five bulls of 15 October 1088, to which we have already had occasion to refer; among them was a papal ruling on the vital question of the primacy of the Spains, giving it unequivocally to Toledo and ordering other metropolitans to submit. This was the first instance of a decision on an important and disputed question of ecclesiastical organization which the pope and the pope alone had the right to decide. The enforcement of the decision was a different matter; and in fact it turned out to be the prelude

---

[1] See, in general, M. Défourneaux, *Les Français en Espagne aux XIe et XIIe siècles* (Paris, 1949), ch. i, and J.F. Rivera, *La Iglesia de Toledo en el siglo XII* (Rome-Madrid, 1966), ch. iii.

to over a century of dispute. But that in no wise affects the present argument. Bernardo had turned to the pope in 1088, and he continued to do so during the rest of Urban's pontificate, down to 1099.

A second instance of the way in which it was the French clergy who started to turn towards the papacy may be given from the career of St. Geraldo of Braga. Geraldo, one of Bernardo's young men, brought from France to join his household in Toledo, had been given the church of Braga in 1095 or 1096, and had soon afterwards—it is not known exactly when—restored it with papal sanction to metropolitan rank. His predecessor in the see, Pedro, had been active in the work of restoration, but had fallen under a cloud owing to his dubious negotiations with the imperial antipope, and had been deposed in 1093. There was thus a short vacancy before Geraldo received the see, during which some of Pedro's work was undone. Geraldo was faced with the task of renewed reconstruction, and it was to the pope that he looked for assistance, especially in the work of recovering the lost temporalities of his see. This emerges clearly in the five bulls issued by Paschal II on 1 April 1103:[1] to give but one example, Pelayo bishop of Astorga was ordered by the pope to restore certain territories round Bragança to the church of Braga. Here again we have a newcomer turning to the pope for a ruling on a question of ecclesiastical property and administration which he himself was powerless to settle.

There were certain obvious lessons to be learnt from the course of action pursued by Bernardo of Toledo, Geraldo of Braga, and other French bishops. Within the kingdom of León the bishop who learnt them most thoroughly and practised what he had learnt with the most marked success was of course Diego Gelmírez. The lesson was simple: if he were to survive, as between Toledo and Braga, he would have to have similar recourse to the highest ecclesiastical authority. And this, as we have already seen, he triumphantly did.

It would be otiose to follow him again through the tortuous diplomacy by which he was enabled to elude both the Scylla of Braga and the Charybdis of Toledo. But we may profitably

---

[1] *PUP* nos. 3–7.

turn instead to another dispute in which Diego was engaged, for an illustration of a further important factor impelling Leonese ecclesiastics to look towards Rome. And this was the intractable nature of the disputes which arose. It was virtually impossible to solve them in Spain, partly because passions so quickly became inflamed, partly because clear documentary evidence which would serve to settle them did not exist, partly because the higher ranks of the hierarchy were so riven with jealousies that there was no generally recognized authority within Spain whose decisions would be binding.

There are plenty of illustrations of these points in the history of the dispute between the dioceses of Santiago de Compostela and Mondoñedo over the archipresbyterates of Bezoucos, Trasancos and Seaya which took place between 1102 and 1122.[1] Diego Gelmírez first made the claim that these properly belonged to his diocese in 1102. Gonzalo of Mondoñedo refused to give them up·to him. Diego replied by bringing the matter up at the council of Carrión in 1103. Shortly after the council, on 4 February 1103, Bernardo of Toledo wrote to Gonzalo ordering him to restore the areas to Compostela. But Bernardo was later accused of being lukewarm in the dispute—which is all too likely, seeing that he was being called on to help his enemy Diego Gelmírez—and certainly the letter he wrote to Gonzalo was chiding rather then severe. Gonzalo took no notice of Bernardo's letter. Diego's next step was to turn to Rome. On 1 May 1103 Paschal II ordered Gonzalo to give back the disputed areas.[2] Of course he did not do so: but he did go to the curia, to put his own version of the case. And this in turn led Paschal II to summon representatives from both sides for a hearing in his presence in 1104. We need not follow the case any further on its tortuous path, which ended in a victory for Compostela in circumstances which are somewhat obscure, beyond observing that one of the reasons why the path was so tortuous was the lack of documentary evidence. Paschal clearly wanted this, since some written matter was sent to him at his

[1] *HC* pp. 74–84, 374–8.   [2] JL 5943.

request in 1105. But this seems to have been no more than the testimony of those who were alive at the time, *memoriae suae testimonium.*[1] This was not enough, and each side resorted to forgery or interpolation of early documents.

Such contacts with the papal curia were made closer by the way in which lesser disputes would creep in for consideration when greater matters were under discussion. For whatever reason, recourse was had to Rome by a bishop; we do not know what passed between the pope and the bishop (or his representatives) when they met at the curia; but clearly far more than the single problem which had occasioned their meeting. A good instance of this occurs in the course of the archipresbyterates dispute. It concerned the abbey of Cines.[2] This appears to have been the proprietary monastery of Count Pedro Froílaz de Traba, the greatest nobleman in Galicia and the brother of Bishop Gonzalo of Mondoñedo. It had originally been a house of nuns, but at some time and by some process lost to us had become a house of monks. Count Pedro seems to have wished to turn it once more into a nunnery. At this point, in 1103, when Diego Gelmírez was appealing to the pope in the archipresbyterates dispute, he also sought a ruling in the Cines case. Paschal II told him to restore the abbot and have the nuns moved elsewhere. The upshot was that the abbot was finally reinstated, though perhaps not until 1107 or 1108. He was again expelled, *violenter*, by the count, and the failure of the Galician bishops to do anything about this brought a rebuke from the pope. Soon afterwards, in all probability, Pedro Froílaz himself visited the curia and demonstrated to the pope's satisfaction that Cines had originally been a nunnery. Paschal II therefore changed his tune. Cines was to become a nunnery once more, and only if it should prove impossible to effect this was it to become a house for monks.

A still smaller dispute which was brought before the pope when a greater matter was being discussed concerned a sub-

[1] JL 6043.
[2] JL 5944, 6001, 6027. These bulls cannot be dated accurately; the dates suggested by Jaffé are perhaps a little too early. The house lay in the diocese of Compostela. Its early history is exceedingly obscure; see AHN 494/10, 11, and AHN cód. 259B, fols. 5^V–7^r.

deacon, otherwise unknown to history, named Suero.[1] Not only was Suero of illegitimate birth, but his manner of life was more secular than befitted one of his ecclesiastical rank, and, above all, he had deprived one of Diego Gelmírez's clerks, Pedro *capellanus*, of the third part of the church of San Miguel in Santiago de Compostela. Now this Pedro was one of Diego's envoys to the pope in 1110.[2] Having failed to get redress from Suero at home, he turned to the pope 'ad domini papae celsitudinem confugium fecit, cernendo Suarium iniustitiae nebula esse obductum' before whom he stated his case, in Latin, says the author of the *Historia Compostellana* not without a trace of pride (*querimoniam latine ventilavit*). Paschal II ordered Diego to restore Pedro's rights to him.

Finally, there were special reasons why the popes should have been particularly concerned with the civil war within the kingdom of León-Castile which succeeded the death of Alfonso VI in 1109, and why it should have been the largest question upon which they were called to arbitrate in the early twelfth century. Alfonso VI's plan to marry his daughter Urraca to Alfonso el Batallador, king of Aragon, raised in the most acute form the problem of the relation between practical politics and the still only hazily defined canon law of marriage. It may be doubted indeed whether Alfonso's scheme was ever feasible: the Aragonese were the hereditary enemies of the Leonese and Castilians; no woman had ever reigned over León-Castile before. It was virtually certain that civil war would break out, as indeed it quickly did. War among the Christians gave the Almoravides, recently victorious at the battle of Uclés in 1108, their opportunity to regain lost ground, and the Christians found that they were vulnerable. This also was a matter of deep concern to the popes, impelling them to do all that they could to bring about a settlement of the civil war, so that the Christians might turn together against the Moslems.[3] The civil war, moreover, led to attacks on the property and persons of ecclesiastics. In such instances, again, the popes were swift

---

[1] *HC* pp. 87–8.   [2] *HC* p. 84.
[3] E.g., JL 6397.

to intervene when called upon to do so: Alfonso el Batallador imprisoned the bishop of Orense and expelled the bishop
of León from his see for opposing the marriage, and he may
have encouraged the rebels against abbatial authority at the
monastery of Sahagún;[1] Urraca imprisoned Diego Gelmírez
in 1121;[2] Teresa of Portugal imprisoned the archbishop of
Braga in 1122.[3] Finally, Calixtus II had a personal interest
in the outcome of the civil war, for, as we have seen, Urraca
was his sister-in-law and her son Alfonso Raimúndez was his
nephew.[4]

These, then; the influx of French clergy and their reforming programme; the example they gave to Leonese
ecclesiastics, notably to Diego Gelmírez; the intractable nature of ecclesiastical problems in Spain; the tendency for
lesser disputes to be carried along in the wake of greater; and
direct papal interest in Spanish politics—these are the causes
to which we must look if we would seek to explain why it
was that Leonese bishops began to look towards the papal
curia for a solution of their problems in the crucial early
period from 1088 to 1124. There do not appear to have been
any obstacles to the free flow of papal authority apart from
the hazards of distance or of circumstances. The secular
rulers did not forbid intercourse with the papacy on prin-
ciple, though they tried to impede it now and again for
special reasons—as for example when Alfonso el Batallador
tried to prevent communication between Diego Gelmírez
and popes Paschal II and Calixtus II, or when Urraca stopped
Diego from attending the council of Rheims.[5]

Such contact with the papacy as an arbitrator once established in this early period would, as we have said, increase
with a momentum of its own as time went on, unless some
special series of events were to halt it (which did not happen).
The disputes involving bishops which arose and which were
referred to the papacy during the remainder of our period
were of five different kinds. The most famous of these was

[1] *HC* p. 141; Escalona, *Sahagun*, pp. 308-14.   [2] *HC* pp. 327-35.
[3] JL 6987, 6988.   [4] This comes out strongly in JL 6828.
[5] *HC* p. 279 (277).

the claim of the archbishops of Toledo to ecclesiastical primacy within Spain and their insistence that the other archbishops and bishops of Spain should give formal recognition thereof. Only a little less acrimonious and certainly more complicated were disputes among metropolitans as to their respective suffragans. On a diocesan, as opposed to a provincial level, were boundary disputes between neighbouring bishops. Within the diocese itself, bishops might find themselves at loggerheads with their chapters, with monasteries, with the military Orders, with the lay nobility or with the towns. Finally, bishops might fall out with the king.

The well-charted ground of the primary dispute has recently been mapped again by Father Rivera, and we need not go over it once more here.[1] Let us instead consider a representative example of one of the other two categories of dispute.

THE ZAMORA IMBROGLIO

The thorniest of all disputes over suffragans was that which concerned the metropolitan allegiance of the bishop of Zamora. Was the bishop of Zamora a suffragan of Toledo, or of Braga, or of Compostela? This question, raised soon after the creation of the see early in the twelfth century, gave rise to about a century of controversy before it was finally settled, more by the weariness of the parties than by formal judgement, in favour of Compostela. Though the story has been discussed fairly recently by the bishop of Ciudad Rodrigo,[2] a little more material has since then come to light which makes it worth summarizing again.

Down to the year 1120, as we have seen, Zamora formed part of the bishopric of Salamanca,[3] which when Santiago de Compostela became an archbishopric was included within her province. When the diocese of Zamora was formally established in 1121, it was given rights over lands hitherto in the diocese of Astorga, which was a suffragan of Braga.[4] But

---

[1] *La Iglesia de Toledo,* chs. vii and viii.
[2] D. Mansilla, 'Disputes diocesanas entre Toledo, Braga y Compostela en los siglos XII al XIV', *Anthologica Annua* iii (1955), 89–143. See also Rivera, *La Iglesia de Toledo,* pp. 306–13.
[3] See above, ch. 2, p. 38 and *PUP* no. 99.   [4] *PUP* nos. 12, 25.

the first bishop of Zamora, Bernardo, was a creature of the archbishop of Toledo; besides which, the church of Toledo claimed metropolitan rights over all bishops who, for whatever reason, did not have a metropolitan, and it could be argued that Zamora's bishop was one of these. Thus, early in its history, the church of Zamora was subjected to the claims of three different and rival archbishops.

It was Alo, bishop of Astorga, who first took the dispute to a higher authority, during the second legatine visit of Cardinal Deusdedit. At the council of Valladolid in 1123, Deusdedit ruled that Bernardo should continue to be bishop of Zamora, administering the territories he already held, for the rest of his life or until he should be translated to another see; after which time the territories were to revert to the church of Astorga and the bishopric of Zamora was to be abolished.[1] But this decision was very rapidly reversed:[2]

Cum autem in eodem loco multitudo populi excrevisset, dictus Toletanus et princeps terre nepos bone memorie Calixti pape predecessoris nostri. . .rogaverunt eum, ut sepedictum episcopum in Zemorensem presulem confirmaret; quorum precibus acquievit, dans eidem episcopo in mandatis, ut interim nulli professionem faceret nec ecclesiam sibi commissam permitteret alii subiugari donec instrueretur ab ipso quid eum facere oporteret.

This must have occurred before 13 December 1124, the date of the death of Calixtus II; the *princeps terre* was clearly Alfonso Raimúndez, and the archbishop of Toledo must have been Raimundo, since Bernardo had died on 6 April 1124.

So matters remained for the rest of the episcopate of Bernardo of Zamora. A number of solemn privileges was granted by the popes to the church of Braga during these years, but in none of them was Zamora mentioned as a suffragan of Braga.[3] However, Braga was later to claim that some sort of *de facto* subjection of Zamora to herself did exist: three clerks could be produced at a much later date who remembered the time[4] 'quando Zamorensis episcopus

---

[1] *PUP* no. 25.
[2] *MHV* I no. 199, at p. 221.
[3] *PUP* nos. 30, 41, 47.
[4] AD Braga, Liber Fidei, fol. 196ᵛ.

bone memorie B. erat subditus Bracarensi ecclesie tempore archiepiscopi domni Pelagii'. Yet a fourth recalled that he[1] 'fuit loco Zamore ubi archiepiscopus Bracarensis Pelagius receptus est cum processione in ecclesia Zamorensi ab episcopo et clero illius ecclesie, et tunc audivit quod publice dicebatur quod erat suus dominus et archiepiscopus, et. . . vidit ipsum archiepiscopum consecrantem ecclesiam unam in Zamorensi episcopatu ad Zinellas inter Zamoram et Scemam et ibi predicavit'. The references are of course to Paio Mendes, archbishop of Braga from 1118 to 1137. They cannot be regarded as entirely reliable—the evidence produced by Braga was rejected more or less *in toto* by her opponents—but there is no reason why we should reject them out of hand.

But if Braga was active, so also was Toledo. And her efforts were crowned with success. Lucius II declared Zamora to be among the suffragans of Toledo. The bull containing this decision has been lost, but it was referred to by Eugenius III in 1153;[2] 'papa Lucius Bernardo bone recordationis episcopo Zamorensi fecerat (mandatum) ut Toletano archiepiscopo obediret'. Innocent III was also to refer to it in 1199.[3] Bernardo of Zamora died a few years later, in 1149. His successor, Esteban, was consecrated by Raimundo, archbishop of Toledo. However, Deusdedit's ruling of 1124 had never been rescinded, so in consecrating a new bishop for Zamora Raimundo was flouting it. The Braga party, it seems, did not hesitate to point this out, and lodged an appeal to the pope, which Raimundo imprudently disregarded.[4]

The consecration of Esteban must have occurred late in 1149 or early in 1150. On 16 May 1150 the archbishop of Braga made a sensible move; he did his obedience to the archbishop of Toledo as primate: it must have been intended to mollify the pope, and it probably did so. A little later, on 22 January 1151, the issue of a solemn privilege for the church of Zamora suggests that Bishop Esteban, or his representative, was at the papal curia for a discussion of Zamoran

---

[1] ANTT, Colecção Especial, Corporações Diversas, Mitra de Braga, caixa 1, no. 2, at lines 52–5.
[2] *PUP* no. 51.   [3] *MHV* I, no. 199, at p. 221.
[4] JL 9487.

ecclesiastical affairs.[1] On 6 June of the same year, Eugenius III sent Raimundo of Toledo a sharp rebuke for consecrating the new bishop and summoned him to the curia for an investigation.[2] We do not know whether or not he went, and he died on 20 August 1152.

The ensuing months were a time of frenzied activity. In February 1153 Juan, the archbishop-elect of Toledo, went to the curia for consecration. But João Peculiar, the archbishop of Braga, was also there, and the two disputed the case in the pope's presence. Eugenius III reversed the decision of his predecessor Lucius II, and declared Zamora a suffragan of Braga.[3] This was confirmed by Adrian IV in 1157 and by Alexander III in 1163,[4] and was, effectively, the end of Toledo's serious claims over Zamora.[5]

However, for Braga it was by no means the end of the struggle. In the first place, Bishop Esteban of Zamora would not submit to her. He was later said to have repented of this on his deathbed in 1175.[6] And he was certainly the victim of punitive measures during his lifetime:[7] 'Et omnes isti et alii sciunt quod bone memorie Stephanus fuit suspensus ab episcopalibus officiis longo tempore quia nolebat debitam obedientiam prestare Bracarensi archiepiscopo secundum mandatum curie Romane'. Although, as Innocent III realized, Esteban evidently relished the *de facto* independence which he and his church experienced while metropolitans wrangled distantly over him, he did have some grounds for contumacy towards Braga. Much water had flowed under the bridges since João had done obedience to Raimundo of Toledo in 1150, and João was refusing to do it to Juan, Raimundo's successor as archbishop of Toledo from 1153 to 1166. For this he was suspended from his office and his suffragans were

---

[1] AC Zamora, Libro Blanco, first (unnumbered) folio.   [2] JL 9487.
[3] *PUP* nos. 51, 52. The original letter close announcing the decision to Alfonso VII is in AC Toledo X.2.F.1.1.a., and is edited in part by Rivera, *La Iglesia de Toledo*, p. 311, n. 54.
[4] *PUP* nos. 57, 63.
[5] Rodrigo Ximénez de Rada made a final claim in 1217, but it does not appear to have been taken at all seriously.
[6] ANTT, Colecção Especial, Corporações Diversas, Mitra de Braga, caixa 1, no. 2, at lines 30-35.
[7] AD Braga, Liber Fidei, fol. 196^V.

absolved from their obedience to him by Cardinal Hyacinth in 1155,[1] and again by Alexander III in 1161.[2] Esteban seems to have used these rulings as a pretext for never returning to the Braga fold, and for this he suffered further at the hands of Cardinal Hyacinth, on the latter's second visit to Spain in 1172-3.[3]

The second reason why Braga's hold on Zamora was so insecure was owing to the claims of the church of Santiago de Compostela to be the metropolitan of Zamora. The chronology of this part of the dispute is obscure, but an outline of events can be dimly discerned. At some point Alexander III,[4] 'de consilio fratrum suorum invenit quod Compostellanus archiepiscopus convenire posset episcopum Zamorensem et episcopus deberet ei secundum iuris ordinem respondere'. This must have taken place after 1163, when Alexander III last confirmed the rights of Braga over Zamora. It is unlikely to have happened before 1168, since the see of Compostela under Archbishop Martín was in no position to entertain such elaborate ambitions. If we are correct in surmising that Cardinal Hyacinth's actions referred to above are to be placed in 1172-3 it can hardly have happened before then. On the other hand, the claims of Compostela were sufficiently frightening—at the least; they may already have received papal recognition—in 1175 to cause the archbishop of Braga to take special precautions over the consecration of Esteban's successor Guillermo:[5]

ex mandato Bracarensis. . .episcopus Lucensis consecravit episcopum Zamorensem Willelmum qui nunc sedet et timuit eum consecrare in Salamantica neque in Zamora ne ibi aliquis episcoporum Compostellane ecclesie obedientium (MS. *illegible here*) sed apud Legionem convocatis Legionensi et Ovetensi episcopis qui sunt speciales domni pape eum consecravit.

It is not therefore unreasonable to suppose that Alexander's

---

[1] *MHV* I, no. 96.
[2] Rivera, *La Iglesia de Toledo,* p. 312, n. 55. Innocent III's comments are in *MHV* I, no. 199, at pp. 224-5.
[3] JL 14160, which is to be dated to Hyacinth's second legatine visit.
[4] *MHV* I, no. 199, at p. 222.
[5] ANTT, Colecção Especial, Corporações Diversas, Mitra de Braga, caixa 1, no. 2, at lines 19-22.

change of mind took place in about 1174 or 1175, but these dates must be regarded an extremely tentative. Innocent III's letter on the subject proves that Compostela grounded her claims on the argument that Braga had never had 'possession' of the church of Zamora in the canonical sense of the word: what she could not keep, she ought to give up.[1]

Alexander III was a scrupulous but also a busy man. Heedful of, though perhaps unconvinced by Compostela's argument, he commissioned three bishops as judges-delegate to look into the affair: these were the bishops of Porto, of Avila and of Tarazona, who were suffragans respectively of Braga, Compostela and Toledo. Braga was later to refer to this action of Alexander's, rather tactlessly, as *commissionem cui similis alia ab hac curia numquam emanavit.*[2] We do not know precisely when this occurred, but there are indications that it was late in 1180 or early in 1181.[3]

The delegates were slow to act, it seems that nothing was done during 1181, and Lucius III renewed the commission in September 1181, soon after he became pope.[4] Sancho II of Avila died between December 1181 and May 1182, and his place among the delegates was taken by Vidal bishop of Salamanca. The delegates gave their judgement on 16 January 1184, at Coria.[5] Since the bishop of Porto could not attend, the bishops of Tarazona and Salamanca acted without him. The archbishop of Braga failed to appear, and sent to representative, but the delegates and the parties were prepared to proceed without him. Compostela stated her case; it was accepted; and Zamora was declared a suffragan of Compostela.

The Braga party was later to tell a rather different story. According to this, it had been arranged that the delegates

---

[1] *MHV* I no. 199, at p. 223: 'Suggesserat enim Compostellanus archiepiscopus quod non habueras possessionem ecclesie Zamorensis', This explains why all Braga's arguments were designed to prove that she *had* had such possession.

[2] ANTT, Colecção Especial, Corporações Diversas, Mitra de Braga, caixa 1, no. 1, at line 21.

[3] Presumably at the same time as the other commissions to the same bishops, *PUP* nos. 78, 82. Erdmann incorrectly gave the bishop of Avila's name as Diego: it was Sancho II, still traceable as bishop in early December 1181, over three months after Alexander III's death.

[4] *PUP* no. 86.   [5] *PUP* no. 99, dated 24 January 1184.

were to hold their court at Alcañices, a place *utrique parti conveniens*. But this was suddenly changed, without any consultation of Braga's wishes, to Coria, a place which was 'fere inaccessibilem. . .cum esset in Sarracenorum faucibus constitutus et per decem dietas distaret ab ecclesia Bracarensi', and, 'propter regum discordias et alia multa impedimenta illuc ire non potuit archiepiscopus Bracarensis'. It is implied moreover that the exclusion of the bishop of Porto, Braga's suffragan, from the counsels of the other two delegates was deliberate.[1]

It is impossible to tell how much truth there may have been in these assertions. Coria was certainly a singular place to hold such a hearing. The *regum discordias* are a little puzzling, since there was peace between León and Portugal, albeit uneasy peace, between 1180 and 1188. At some point, claimed Braga, Fernando II of León had ordered those suffragans of Braga within his kingdom not to obey their archbishop,[2] and it may be that the reference is to this.

Eagerly, Compostela sought a papal confirmation of this ruling: but Urban III, who had succeeded Lucius in 1185, was curiously reluctant to give this. Instead he appointed John, *vidame* of Brescia, and Master John of Bergamo to visit Spain to look into the matter, but with a limited brief,[3] 'super sola sententia confirmanda vel infirmanda in ea si quid existeret infirmandum'. But Braga disregarded the terms of reference and re-opened the whole question, while Compostela simply continued to press for a confirmation of the sentence already given, as might have been predicted. John of Brescia made his report to the pope.[4] And the popes simply sat on it: Clement III and Celestine III took no further action that we know of.

And so at long last the whole question came before Innocent III in 1199. His handling of it was masterly. First of all,

[1] ANTT, Colecção Especial, Corporações Diversas, Mitra de Braga, caixa 1, nos. 1 and 2.
[2] ANTT, Colecção Especial, Corporações Diversas, Mitra de Braga, caixa 1, no. 2, at lines 70-74; note in particular that it was said that Fernando II 'persuasisse Zamorensi episcopo ut pocius obediret Compostellano quam Bracarensi archiepiscopo'.
[3] *PUP* no. 104; *MHV* I, no. 199, at p. 225.   [4] *PUP* no. 110.

the archbishop of Braga requested a confirmation of Eugenius III's sentence of 1153 in favour of Braga. Innocent confirmed the authenticity of the bull, but not the binding force of its contents.[1] But this was clearly not enough. On 5 July 1199 Innocent issued a bull in which, after a long and characteristically incisive review of the whole dispute, he merely declared that John of Brescia's ruling in favour of maintaining the earlier sentence in favour of the claims of Compostela was not to constitute any impediment to the church of Braga; he did not confirm the rights of Compostela over Zamora; but neither did he deny them.[2] A few days later, as a further sop to Braga, he appointed three more delegates—the bishops of Osma, Porto, and Plasencia—to hear the whole suit, should Braga wish to pursue it.[3] Nothing further is known of it, so it is to be presumed that Braga gave up the struggle at this point. During the thirteenth century Zamora was incorporated *de facto* among the suffragans of Compostela.

At this, the end of the story, a few reflections upon it may be permissible. First, then, the issue was one of fundamental importance. However wearisome the details may seem to us now, this is something which we cannot and should not shirk. We can attempt to make it more comprehensible to ourselves by saying that the issue was in part a political one— Fernando II's action is eloquent proof of that. But in part only, for it is more important to realize that this was a great constitutional issue in the life of the church, not merely in Spain but all over twelfth-century Europe; for the dispute over Zamora can be closely matched by similar disputes elsewhere. It was moreover an issue with far-reaching consequences: Zamora is still in the province of Santiago de Compostela.

But, secondly, it was a dispute which could not be settled within Spain. Feeling ran far too high between the three metropolitans concerned, and, more importantly, the 'proofs'

---

[1] *PUP* no. 52.

[2] *MHV* I no. 199, at p. 226. Mansilla suggested that because Innocent III had recently declared the bishoprics of Lisbon, Evora, Lamego and Idanha to lie within the province of Compostela, he did not wish to appear 'excesivamente duro a Brago' by giving 'una rotunda negativa en la cuestión de Zamora'.

[3] *MHV* I no. 216.

upon which a judgement might rest did not exist. By the accident of preservation it so happens that we have in our hands today far more material from the Braga party than from either of the others: the *dossiers* of Compostela and of Toledo, which must have existed, have been lost, perhaps irretrievably. But there is no indication in Innocent III's bull of 5 July 1199—the fullest, most serious, and most perceptive account of the quarrel—that they differed in kind from that prepared by Braga. Essentially, the historian is in the same position as Innocent III. And we can appreciate, as clearly as he did, the intractable nature of the problem, which arose from the lack of early and authoritative documents.

Finally, and especially relevant to our purpose, we should note the significance of the decision taken by Bishop Alo of Astorga in 1123—to lay his grievance before Cardinal Deusdedit. There is an irrevocability about the course of action thus entered upon which deserves special emphasis. What a legate had done, only a pope could undo. What one pope had decided could be reversed only by another. The lessons of this are obvious.

COUNCILS, LEGATES AND DECRETALS

Our concern so far in this chapter has been with ecclesiastical organization and administration. Important as these matters are, they form only a part of our story. Bishops looked also to Rome for guidance in the task of what is loosely and unsatisfactorily called 'reform'. The word is used here to denote concern with issues of a moral, pastoral, spiritual or intellectual nature, in distinction (though sharp dividing lines cannot be drawn) from matters of an institutional kind. Did the Leonese bishops strive to be *au fait* with papal legislation? Did they actively seek papal guidance? As usual our answers to these questions can be only hesitant.

The record of Leonese attendance at papal councils will tell us something. Ecclesiastics who attended councils would have heard the discussions which took place, received copies of the conciliar *acta*, had the opportunity to meet bishops from other parts of Christendom and, by the mere fact of travel, have been enabled to see for themselves something of the life of the church in other and different places. Sometimes

we have direct evidence of attendance, for instance in the
acta of the council itself, or in a chronicle such as the *Historia Compostellana*. Sometimes the evidence is indirect: where
we have papal bulls issued to a Leonese beneficiary and dated
during or very close to the period of time in which a council
sat it may be regarded as reasonably certain that that ecclesiastic, or his representatives, attended the council in question.
We have no hint of Leonese attendance at any papal council before the year 1095. In that year Bishop Dalmatius of
Compostela attended the council of Clermont *cum quibusdam comprovincialium episcoporum*, among them the bishop
of Lugo.[1] The abbot of Sahagún may also have attended.[2]
Paschal II summoned the archbishops of Toledo and Braga,
and the bishop of Compostela, to the Lenten council in
1102; a bull issued on 15 March 1102 suggests that some
Leonese ecclesiastics did attend.[3] Representatives from the
church of Compostela and the Castilian bishopric of Burgos
seem to have attended the council of Benevento in 1108.[4] A
letter of summons to the council held at Benevento in 1113
was carried to north-western Spain, possibly by the abbot of
Cluny, but there is no certain evidence that any ecclesiastics
from the area did attend it.[5] Another such summons, to the
Lateran council of 1116, has survived; the council was attended by Bishop Hugo of Porto, and perhaps by the abbot
of Sahagún.[6] Representatives of the bishop of Compostela
attended the council of Toulonse in 1119, but just missed
that of Rheims in the same year.[7] At the general council of
1123, Lateran I, Spanish business was discussed; representatives of the bishop of Lugo, but not the bishop in person,
were at the curia shortly before the council opened and may
have stayed on to attend it. There is no certain evidence of

---

[1] *HC* p. 20; AHN cód. 1043B, fol. 38ᵛ.
[2] JL 5597.
[3] JL 5882, 5901.
[4] JL 6208, 6209. It may be noted here that the *G.Legionensis* who attended
papal councils in 1106 and 1112 was the bishop of St.-Pol-de-Léon in Brittany:
Mansi, *Concilia,* XX, col. 1212; XXI, col. 67.
[5] *HC* pp. 139–40; cf. also C.J. Bishko 'The Spanish journey of abbot Ponce of
Cluny' *Ricerche di Storia Religiosa* i (1957), 311–19.
[6] JL 6462, 6513, 6515; Mansi, *Concilia,* XXI, col. 150.
[7] *HC* pp. 276 (274), 278–83.

attendance from León; from Castile, the bishop of Segovia may have been present.[1] Diego Gelmírez was summoned to attend the council of Rheims in 1131 but did not do so; the bishop of Lugo or his agents may have attended; Alfonso Pérez of Salamanca certainly did.[2] Three Castilian bishops attended Lateran II in 1139, from the sees of Osma, Avila and Segovia. The only possible Leonese attender was the abbot of Carracedo in the diocese of Astorga.[3] Summonses to the council held at Rheims by Eugenius III in 1148 certainly reached western Spain, for they were discussed at meetings held at Braga and at Palencia, as we have already seen; the bishop of Coria attended, and perhaps the bishop of León.[4] The same bishop of León, Juan, would seem to have attended, or sent representatives to, the council of Tours in 1163.[5] Someone from the church of Salamanca attended the council of Venice in 1177.[6] At Lateran III, in 1179, the archbishop of Santiago de Compostela was present, with two of his suffragans, Sancho of Avila and Pedro of Ciudad Rodrigo; from the province of Braga, Bishop Juan of Lugo and apparently Guillermo of Zamora attended.[7] Lateran IV in 1215, was attended by the archbishop of Compostela, and the bishops of Oviedo, Astorga, Orense, Ciudad Rodrigo and perhaps Mondoñedo.[8]

Our record is doubtless incomplete. Even so, no-one could describe the Leonese bishops as assiduous attenders at papal councils. The brute obstacle of distance must surely have been one of the main reasons for this. The limited attendance that we can trace did bear some fruit; a decretal letter of 1206 addressed to the bishop of Orense shows us that he did at least know what canons had been passed at Lateran III in

---

[1] Mansi, *Concilia,* XXI, col. 284; JL 7020; AC Lugo, Leg. 3, no. 2; AC Segovia, D/3/8 (= JL 7061, where incorrectly dated).
[2] JL 7475; AC Lugo, Libro de Bulas Apostólicas, no. 1; above, p. 39.
[3] AHD Astorga, Cartulario de Carracedo, fol. 74.
[4] JL 9255; AC León no. 1267; cf. above, ch. 4, p. 138.
[5] JL 10859; AC León, nos. 1269, 1271.
[6] AC Salamanca, nos. 45, 49, 50.
[7] Mansi, *Concilia,* XXII, coll. 216, 465.
[8] J.F. Rivera, 'Personajes hispanos asistentes en 1215 al IV Concilio de Letrán', *Hispania Sacra* iv (1951), 335-55.

1179 and that he was trying to put them into effect in his diocese.[1] But there was clearly a need for local councils to be held, which might diffuse papal legislation. This need was met by a series of ecclesiastical councils presided over by legates *a latere*.

The first such council was that held at Burgos in 1080, presided over by Cardinal Richard of Marseilles. Its *acta* are lost, and all we know for certain about it is that it decreed the abolition of the so-called Mozarabic Rite, but it has seemed to the most acute modern investigator that 'les décrets habituels de la réforme grégorienne y furent certainement promulgués, contre le simonie et le mariage des clercs'. It was attended by all the Leonese bishops.[2] Richard of Marseilles held a further council at Husillos in 1088—strictly speaking, not a legatine council, for his legation had lapsed— and Cardinal Rainerius, later Pope Paschal II, held one at León in 1090. No *acta* have survived and we know only that the councils were concerned with matters of ecclesiastical organization, for example the delimitation of diocesan boundaries between the sees of Osma and Burgos at the council of Husillos.[3] Here again, however, it is hard to believe that 'reforming' legislation was not promulgated at these two councils. The first legatine council of which the *acta* have been preserved was that held by Cardinal Boso at Burgos in 1117. Decrees were passed, among others, forbidding lay investiture (c.8), clerical marriage (c.2), nepotism (c.16), the alienation of church lands *in feodum, quod in Ispania prestimonium vocant* (c.5) and the taking of disputes between ecclesiastics to secular tribunals (c.10). It was attended by four Leonese bishops, Jerónimo of Salamanca, Pelayo of Oviedo, Diego of León and Nuño of Mondoñedo.[4] Boso held another council at Sahagún, on his second legatine visit in 1121. The familiar decrees against simony, lay investiture and

---

[1] *MHV* I, no. 334.
[2] F.Fita, 'El Concilio Nacional de Burgos en 1080. Nuevas ilustraciones', *BRAH* xlix (1906), 337–84; P.David, *Études historiques sur la Galice et le Portugal*, p. 418. The exact date of the council is uncertain; it may have met early in 1081; see J.F. Rivera, *La Iglesia de Toledo*, pp. 131–2.
[3] F.Fita, 'Texto correcto del Concilio de Husillos', *BRAH* li (1907), 410–13.
[4] F.Fita, 'Concilio Nacional de Burgos', *ibid.*, xlviii (1906), 387–407.

clerical marriage were passed (cc. 1, 10), and other matters received attention—the problem of sacrilege and lay usurpation of church property (c.6), episcopal connivance at adultery (c.5), penitents (c.12), apostates (c.9), rebellious monks (c.8) and the protection of the persons of ecclesiastics and pilgrims (c.11). Six Leonese bishops attended, Geraldo of Salamanca, Diego of León, Nuño of Mondoñedo, Pelayo of Oviedo, Diego of Orense and Alfonso of Tuy.[1]

No *acta* have been preserved from the succeeding four councils held by visiting legates. The first of these was celebrated by Cardinal Deusdedit at Valladolid in 1123. It is possible that initiatives taken there were copied by Diego Gelmírez in the council which he held shortly afterwards at Santiago de Compostela—a council in which he boldly proclaimed the *Pax Dei. . .in toto Hispaniae regno.*[2] At Carrión de los Condes in 1130 Cardinal Humbert together with three archbishops, at least twelve bishops of whom six were Leonese, and an unknown number of abbots, decreed *multa ad honorem et utilitatem sanctae ecclesiae et Hispani regni pertinentia*, but we do not know what they were.[3] A council appears to have been held by Cardinal Guido at León in 1133, but it is completely obscure.[4] He certainly presided over one at Burgos in 1136; we know something of its business—the confirmation of the *cofradía* of Belchite, the settlement of a boundary dispute between the sees of Sigüenza, Osma and Tarazona—but no formal decrees have come down to us.[5]

Guido returned to Spain in 1143 and held a council at Valladolid. The *acta*, which have survived, are patterned on the canons passed at Lateran II in 1139, which, as we have seen, was attended by no bishops from the kingdom of León. A full complement of ten bishops was present at Valladolid, and an eleventh was elected there, a new bishop

---

[1] *PUP* no. 22.
[2] *HC* pp. 416–19; *PUP* no. 25.
[3] *HC* p. 498; AHN 1326B/24; AC Segovia A/3/9.
[4] *HC* pp. 557, 564–5.
[5] *HC* p. 578; P.Rassow, 'La Cofradía de Belchite', *AHDE* iii (1926), 200–26; Minguella, *Historia de Sigüenza*, I, p. 358; AHN cód. 1044B fols. 78ʳ–79ʳ; JL 7952.

for the see of Oviedo.[1] Twelve years later, the decrees promulgated once more at Valladolid, this time by Cardinal Hyacinth, later Pope Celestine III, were again modelled on those passed at Lateran II. Eight Leonese bishops attended; a ninth was deposed (whether in his absence or not we do not know); and a tenth, who was not among his attenders, Pelayo Menéndez of Tuy, certainly received the text of the decrees, for they have survived copied in a crabbed little hand on the dorse of a private charter of 1154 in his archives.[2]

This completes our evidence for the holding of councils by papal legates. It is possible that Hyacinth held a council during his second legatine visit to Spain, for he was in the peninsula for nearly two extremely active years, but there is no certain evidence of it.[3]

There is, then, a fair amount of evidence for the reception of papal legislation in the kingdom of León during the first half of the twelfth century. There was perhaps less need for legates to transmit such legislation to Spain in the course of its second half, seeing that papal councils like Lateran III and IV were reasonably well-attended by the Spaniards. Obviously, the foregoing discussion contains nothing like a complete list of papal legates, of one sort or another, to the kingdom of León in the course of the century. It would be a laborious and perhaps not very rewarding task to compile such a list.[4] What it would show is that there were few years in the course of the century when papal agents were not to be found in the kingdom of León, or León-Castile, engaged on some piece of business, great or small. Diego Gelmírez believed that a secret legate had been sent to spy on him by Pope Honorius II.[5] Bishop Guy of Lescar was sent to

[1] *PUP* no. 40; BN MS. 1358, fol. 4ᵛ: F.Fita, 'El Concilio Nacional de Valladolid en 1143', *BRAH* lxi (1912), 166–74; cf. also the dating-clause of AHN 3548/11.

[2] This testimony to the scarcity of parchment in the far north-west, or to the poverty of the see of Tuy (or both), is now AC Tuy 10/24. The decrees were published by Carl Erdmann, *O Papado e Portugal,* ap. V.

[3] Aguirre believed that Hyacinth held a council at Salamanca, but Mansi showed long ago that the evidence had been misinterpreted: *Concilia,* XXII. coll. 145–6, 320; cf. JL 14160, which is misleading.

[4] Perhaps it has been done. I have been unable to track down a copy of G. Säbekow, *Die päpstlichen Legationen nach Spanien und Portugal bis zum Ausgang des XII Jahrhunderts* (Berlin, 1931).

[5] *HC* pp. 489–90.

summon the Spanish bishops to Lateran II—and as we have seen they paid him scant attention.[1] Alexander III sent fundraisers during his struggle with Barbarossa.[2] We have already met the two Italian experts who were sent out by Urban III to look into the Zamora dispute.[3] Celestine III sent his nephew Cardinal Gregory in the 1190s with the difficult and delicate task of bringing about peace between the warring kings of Christian Spain.[4] Dozens of further instances could be cited, but this is not the place to do so.

Bishops sometimes took the initiative, seeking papal advice about particular problems as they encountered them, when the custom of the church spoke dubiously or ambiguously or not at all. Few such occasions are recorded. This does not necessarily mean that the bishops did not meet problems, nor that when they did they were well-informed, or indifferent. It is more likely to reflect the fact that there were few decretalists at work in Spain, to collect the letters and so to preserve them for us.[5] Early in the century Geraldo of Braga had asked Paschal II whether ordinations carried out according to the so-called Mozarabic-Rite were valid. The pope's answer, that they were, has come down to us because it was copied into the cathedral cartulary of Braga, the *Liber Fidei*, in the thirteenth century.[6] Much later on, Bishop Juan of Lugo received two decretal letters from Alexander III, while Manrique of León received one from Urban III and a bishop of Astorga, either Fernando II or Lope, got one from Clement III.[7] The evidence is fuller from the pontificate of Innocent III, with the beginning of a complete series of papal registers. We have already encountered a decretal letter sent

---

[1] HC pp. 597–8. He was at Compostela in October 1138, when he executed the very splendid autograph subscription which adorns AHN 526/7.
[2] AC Lugo leg. 3, no. 9.
[3] Above, p. 201.   [4] Below, p. 219.
[5] Some collections have come to light recently, and more may be expected to follow when Spanish libraries have been systematically explored. See A.Garcia y Garcìa, 'Una Colección de Decretales en Salamanca', *Proceedings of the Second International Congress of Medieval Canon Law*, ed. S. Kuttner and J. J. Ryan (Vatican City, 1965), pp. 71–92; F. Marcos Rodríguez, 'Tres manuscritos del siglo XII con colecciones canónicas', *Analecta Sacra Tarraconensia* xxxii (1960), 35–54.
[6] PUP no. 8.
[7] JL 14005, 14006, 15735, 16558.

to the bishop of Orense in 1206.[1] Two years earlier, Innocent had replied to a query of bishop Martín of Zamora; a
young man who had accidentally been the cause of another's
death might receive holy orders.[2] He tells the archbishop of
Compostela that canons regular may not act as advocates in
secular lawsuits. He even finds time to write him a long letter
about the names of the divine Persons, in reply to a question.[3]
To his successor he replies that the church of the Apostle
need not be reconsecrated after the brawling of pilgrims near
the shrine—purification by water, wine, and ashes will do.[4]

The issue about which we hear most concerned the law of
marriage. This was an area of canon law where much was
vague, at least until towards the end of the century; one
therefore, which generated controversy. There were special
reasons why it should have raised difficulties in Spain. The
earliest in time of these issues—according to our surviving
sources—arose, predictably, from the change in the liturgy.
Were children born of marriages celebrated according to the
Mozarabic liturgy legitimate or not? The question was put
to Paschal II by Diego Gelmírez in 1101, and the pope decided that they were.[5] It is possible that this issue lay behind
the case of Bishop Pedro of León in 1089, referred to at the
beginning of this chapter.

The second problem was that of incestuous marriages,
marriages within the prohibited degrees. This issue, keenly
debated throughout Europe, was of no particular moment in
Spain for political reasons. Queen Urraca's marriage to
Alfonso el Batallador was incestuous according to the canon
law; Aflonso VII's to Berenguela probably was; Fernando II's
to Urraca of Portugal certainly was; both Alfonso IX's
marriages flagrantly were—that is to say five marriages of
reigning monarchs of León out of a total of eight such
marriages in fewer than ninety years. Marriages with neighbouring royal families were highly desirable in the conduct
of diplomacy. And if they had to be eschewed, rulers had

[1] Above, p. 205.   [2] *MHV* I no. 298.
[3] *MHV* I nos. 237, 332.   [4] *MHV* I no. 369.
[5] JL 5881.

either to marry outside royal houses, as Fernando II was compelled to do after his first marriage had been dissolved by a papal legate, or to look very far afield indeed—Alfonso VII's second wife was the daughter of a duke of Poland. It was extremely trying. Sometimes the ecclesiastical authorities were prepared to connive: Alfonso VII and Berenguela got away with it—though at a heavy price[1] —and it was whispered that Celestine III was willing to say nothing about Alfonso IX's second incestuous marriage.[2] But this, apart from being probably humiliating and certainly expensive, could never be relied on. Paschall II stood out against Urraca's marriage, backed up by most (it would seem) of the bishops of León-Castile.[3] Alexander III stood out against Fernando II's first marriage,[4] and Innocent III against Alfonso IX's second marriage (when to do so was against his own immediate interests).[5] Humbler people were concerned in this sort of trouble too. Diego Gelmírez consulted Calixtus II in 1121 over the case of one Geraldo, who had married a wife who was related to the woman who had previously been his mistress.[6] There is also some evidence of concern with the issue in Spanish conciliar decrees.[7]

The third reason why the law of marriage was a specially contentious matter in Spain was the presence there of different religious groups. The diverse nature of Christian, Jewish and Moslem matrimonial customs must have caused grave difficulties for churchmen whose dioceses included settlements of infidels, especially if intermarriage between Christian and Jew, or Christian and Moslem, took place.

---

[1] The grant of Cacebelos to the church of Compostela, dated 22 February 1130: *LFH* IV, ap. vii, pp. 19–21. This was almost certainly part of the bargain made between Alfonso VII and Diego Gelmírez before the council of Carrión: *HC* p. 497.

[2] Innocent III had to issue a vigorous denial of this: *MHV* I, no. 196.

[3] JL 5987, if it really is of 1104, as Jaffé held, shows that concern for the subject was lively in the years before Urraca's marriage took place. But it could be of 1109 or 1110, and thus perhaps the most discreet of references to that marriage itself.

[4] *GRF* pp. 111–12.

[5] The most recent discussion of this is that of Rivera, *La Iglesia de Toledo*, pp. 237–41.

[6] JL 6912. Note the 'quem ad nos misisti'.

[7] Councils of Compostela 1114, c.5; Sahagún 1121, c.6; Valladolid 1155, c.19.

(How frequent was this in twelfth-century Spain? We still do not know). Clement III replied to a query on the problem, sent either by the bishop of Segovia or the chapter of Ciudad Rodrigo.[1] In his decretal he spoke in a sensible and tolerant way. But it is to be regretted that we know no more of this important question.

THE RECIPROCAL PROCESS

If bishops sought privileges, assistance and advice from the curia, the popes in their turn wanted certain things from the bishops; and it is impossible to understand the closer links that were forged during the twelfth century between episcopate and papacy without saying something of these. Most prominently, the popes wanted cash. The period from the middle of the eleventh century onwards was one of mounting expenditure for the papacy. This expenditure could not be supplied from the patrimonial lands in Italy, over which papal control was intermittent and which in any case were of no great economic value. Money had therefore to be raised elsewhere. But no systematic papal taxation was devised before the thirteenth century. The twelfth witnessed a variety of expedients used by the popes, some of which proved lucrative and some of which did not.

Kings could be exploited. The king of Aragon became a tributary of the papacy in 1089, the king of Portugal in 1143-4. The payments made by these rulers were small, but attempts were made to exact them with regularity.[2] No tribute was exacted from the king-emperors of Leon-Castile by the popes, presumably because Cluny had got in first; even so late as 1142 the abbot of Cluny was still insisting upon payment either of the annual *census* promised by Alfonso VI or of some commutation in lieu of it.[3] Monasteries which sought papal privileges commonly had to agree to pay a small annual tribute. Thus, for example, the canons of San Isidoro de León had to agree to pay one gold piece

---

[1] JL 16595.
[2] E.g., *MHV* I, no. 170, for a Portuguese payment of arrears in 1198.
[3] C.J. Bishko, 'Peter the Venerable's journey to Spain', *Studia Anselmiana* xl (1956), 163-75.

(*aureus*) every year in return for their privilege of 1163.[1] An interesting document has survived from the priory of Sta. Crux de Coimbra in which were jotted down notes on when and where the payments that it owed to the papacy were made, and copies of the receipts given by the papal *camerarii*. It shows, significantly, that such payments of tribute were nearly always accompanied by payments of equivalent size *pro benedictione*—a warning that documents do not always allow us to glimpse the realities of papal finance.[2]

No such tributes were demanded of any of the bishoprics in the kingdom of León, but in two ways the bishops also were mulcted. First, privileges themselves cost money, and profited not only the pope himself but also the whole phalanx of officials, courtiers and servants about him who had to be bribed. We have seen evidence that Diego Gelmírez had to spend enormous sums of money for the prize of the archbishopric, and the pages of the *Historia Compostellana* are studded with references to the sending of money to the popes *pro benevolentia*. We even have a letter of Cardinal Deusdedit asking in pointed terms for a chasuble he had seen at Compostela and which had caught his fancy.[3] It is only reasonable to assume that comparable privileges cost comparable amounts. How much did Oviedo and León have to pay for their privileges of exemption? We shall never know, but we may be sure that it was no small sum. As with privileges, so with justice. What did the contending parties have to spend in the Zamora dispute? Again we shall never know, but again we may be sure that it was not a little.

Intimately linked with the popes' need for cash was their need for loyalty and moral support—so intimately that it is perhaps unrealistic to try to untangle the web that resulted. A good instance of these interlocking needs is furnished during the early years of Alexander III's pontificate. Fernando II and his bishops appear to have recognized Alexander

---

[1] León, Archivo de San Isidoro, no. 1.   [2] *PUP* no. 159.
[3] *HC* pp. 422-3.

as the rightful pope without too much hesitation.[1] On 13 March 1161 the pope addressed the bull *Illa devotionis* to Archbishop Martín of Santiago de Compostela, exposing the needs of the papacy, threatened by Frederick Barbarossa, and urging him to be loyal. He then asked for financial help from him and from his suffragans; the proceeds of the appeal were to be given to the bearers of the letter, Theodinus and Leo.[2] The request is given added interest because we happen to know that it was successful. A document survives at Compostela which shows us the chapter selling land to the priory of Sar in order to raise some of the money which they intended to send to the pope *in signum obedientie et sincere devotionis.*[3]

Earlier instances of the same anxiety to retain a hold on the loyalties of the Leonese bishops can be found. When Maurice Bourdin, archbishop of Braga, became antipope in 1118 he turned immediately to his old suffragans. The first letter of his that we possess is dated 22 March 1118, a mere fourteen days after his election, and is an appeal to Gonzalo bishop of Coimbra for support.[4] But the rightful pope, Gelasius II, was almost as quick to warn Spanish bishops against the new antipope, in two letters of 25 March 1118.[5] We learn too of his solemn warning against the antipope delivered to the two *clerici* of Diego Gelmírez, Pedro Díaz and Pedro Anáyaz, when they visited the curia early in June.[6] And in the letter which they carried back to Diego the pope besought him, *rogantes et monentes. . .caritate subvenias.*[7] The request was scarcely veiled, and Diego obediently set himself to answer it. Gelasius II died on 29 January 1119, and the antipope remained at large until April 1121. This

---

[1] See the letter in S. Tengnagel, *Vetera Monumenta contra Schismaticos* (Ingoldstadt, 1612), p. 412, ep. LIX, a reference which I owe to Mrs. C. R. Cheney. It is undated, but unlikely to be later than the earliest weeks of 1161. JL 10629, of 4 April 1160, might imply that the province of Toledo had already by that date recognized Alexander III.
[2] AC Lugo, leg. 3, no. 9.
[3] *LFH* IV, ap. xxxiii, pp. 84–6.   [4] *PUP* no. 20.
[5] JL 6637, 6638.   [6] *HC* pp. 258–9.
[7] JL 6645.

helps to explain the urgency of Calixtus II's early appeals for help addressed to Diego Gelmírez in 1119 and 1120.[1]

A similar situation arose at the time of the schism between Innocent II and Anacletus II. Diego Gelmírez was courted early on by Anacletus, within two months of the latter's election.[2] Innocent did not write until rather later, until 2 August 1130—but when he did write, how much that Diego most wanted was he prepared to give![3] But Anacletus had by no means given up hope: he was still writing to Diego in the spring of 1134.[4] How near Alfonso VII, or Raimundo of Toledo, or Diego Gelmírez himself, ever were to throwing themselves behind Anacletus we shall never know. But it is not without significance that Diego troubled to keep the bulls that came from him. Innocent II, for his part, seems to have been by no means sure of his friends; at any rate, his surviving letters show him acting warily. He kept Diego informed of his progress in long bulletins.[5] He thanked him and the bishops of Lugo and León for their support of him.[6] He fretted that he might lose that support.[7] He was deferential to Alfonso VII.[8] He did not ask any favour of Diego until the threat of Anacletus was declining.[9]

This assiduous wooing seems, over the century, to have been fruitful. By the end of Innocent III's pontificate the Leonese churches were well under the thumb of the pope. One indication of this may be found in the history of papal provisions in León in our period. The first of them happens to be the earliest papal provision of which we have knowledge. In March 1137, Innocent II wrote to Diego Gelmírez requesting that he should grant an *ecclesiasticum beneficium cum prebenda in Compostellana ecclesia* to Arias, *filius noster et clericus*.[10] This begging letter was accompanied and

---

[1] JL 6711, 6877.
[2] JL 8374.
[3] JL 7415–7419.
[4] JL 8426.
[5] JL 7449, 7653.
[6] JL 7610.
[7] JL 7665 (not necessarily of 1134, as Jaffé suggested).
[8] AC Orense, Privilegios I/8; T. Minguella, *Historia de la diócesis de Sigüenza y de sus obispos* (Siguenza, 1910), I, p. 361.
[9] JL 7831.   [10] JL 7831.

reinforced by two others, from the papal chancellor Aimeric, an old correspondent of Diego's, and from Cardinal Guido, whom Diego had met in the recent past, during his two legatine visits to Spain in 1133 and 1136.[1] These letters make clear, what the pope's does not, that Arias was returning (*redeuntem*) to Compostela, and that he had in fact been *in vestra enutritus ecclesia*. So Innocent was not asking a favour for a complete stranger; nonetheless he was asking for more than a pope had, to our knowledge, asked for before.

Our second provision comes from a generation later. In 1173 or 1174 Alexander III wrote to the members of the chapter of Salamanca requesting them to give the first vacant canonry to a certain clerk *R*.[2] At some point towards the end of the century we hear of a man provided by the pope to a prebend at Astorga.[3] Innocent III provided a relative of his to a prebend at Compostela, which had previously been held, it may be noted, by the papal Chancellor.[4] He also provided to Toledo, and possibly to Zamora.[5]

Favours of this sort, papal provisions, are not asked by those who expect to see their requests denied or flouted. It is for this reason that they may be seen as evidence of the confidence of the popes in their hold over the church in León by the end of the twelfth century. But it would be more than unjust to suggest that the popes were interested only in material things. They were also moved by idealistic considerations. Only a cynic would deny that their desires to reform the organization of the Spanish church, to stamp out the last traces of the so-called Mozarabic liturgy, to bring about peace between monasteries and bishops, and so forth, were not so motivated, at the least in part. Of these matters enough has already been said. But one further topic remains,

---

[1] *HC* pp. 584–585.
[2] AC Salamanca, no. 54. *R.* cannot be identified with certainty.
[3] Referred to in a bull of 31 May 1188, summarized in A. Quintana Prieto, 'Registro de documentos pontificios de la diócesis de Astorga (1139–1413)', *Anthologica Annua* xi (1963), 189–226.
[4] *MHV* I no. 506.
[5] *MHV* I nos. 134, 420. It should be pointed out here that AC Salamanca no. 124, an interesting bull dealing with the nefarious activities of unscrupulous provisors, is incorrectly entered in the printed catalogue; it belongs to the pontificate of Innocent IV, not to that of Innocent III.

the desire of the popes to ensure the safeguarding and expansion of Christendom by encouraging the war against the Moslems.

Papal thinking in these matters followed four lines. In the first place, it became quickly necessary in the years after 1096 to prevent able-bodied fighting men from going crusading in the Holy Land, or at least to discourage them from doing so. This action was first taken early in Paschal II's pontificate.[1] A necessary corollary soon appeared: those who fight in Spain must enjoy the same privileges as those who fight in the Holy Land. Such a doctrine was accepted formally at the first Lateran council in 1123.[2]

In the third place the popes encouraged the foundation of confraternities and orders devoted to fighting the infidels. The institution of the *cofradía de Belchite* was confirmed by the papal legate Cardinal Guido at the council of Burgos in 1136.[3] The origins of the Order of Calatrava are to be sought in 1158, and in 1164 its foundation was confirmed by Alexander III. The Order of San Julián del Pereiro, later of Alcántara, started in about 1163 or 1164, and received papal recognition in 1177. In 1170 the 'Friars of Cáceres' were founded, becoming the Order of Santiago in 1171; they were received as sons of the Roman church by Cardinal Hyacinth in 1173, and their institution was confirmed by Alexander III in 1175.

The kind of papal activity concerned with the *Reconquista* which has left most trace upon our records is that concerned with the effort to bring about peace among the Christian kingdoms. This can first be seen between the years 1109 and 1126, when it was with papal encouragement that the Leonese and Castilian bishops held their series of councils which was concerned, perhaps primarily concerned, to prevent the warfare between Castilians and Aragonese which was tearing Christian Spain apart and leaving the southern frontiers almost undefended. To give but one example, the

---

[1] JL 5839, 5840, 5863.
[2] Mansi, XXI col. 284; JL 7111 (which appears to be spurious) and 7116, which is explicit, and perhaps also of 1123.
[3] P. Rassow, 'La cofradía de Belchite', *AHDE* iii (1926), 200–26.

council of Burgos in 1113 was held at the instance of Paschal II.[1] A generation later, one of the concerns of the legate cardinal Guido in 1143 was to bring about peace between Alfonso VII of León-Castile and Afonso Henriques of Portugal.[2] A few years afterwards, we find Eugenius III insisting upon the maintenance of peace with Portugal when writing to Alfonso VII in 1148.[3] Cardinal Hyacinth's second legatine visit in 1172-4 was also, among much else, concerned to ensure political peace.

Papal peace-making activity was at its most intense in the years from 1188 to 1209. This was owing, first of all, to the loss of Jerusalem in October 1187. Christendom was threatened, and a new urgency entered into papal entreaties for peace. This can be most vividly sensed in two bulls despatched to Spain by Clement III in 1188, especially when they are contrasted with the more leisured plea for peace contained in the last bull concerned with this subject sent *before* the fall of Jerusalem, that of Urban III dated 27 August 1186 or 1187.[4] The mounting Almohade attack on Spain which culminated in the disastrous defeat of Alarcos in 1195 only served as fuel to urge the popes on to efforts yet more intense.

As far as the kingdom of León was concerned, the problem was twofold. In the first place, the popes had to reckon with the inveterate hostility between Alfonso IX of León who came to the throne in 1188, and Alfonso VIII of Castile. There is some indication that the Leonese bishops shared the feelings of their king, or were too frightened to oppose his will, or were simply not interested in fighting the Moslems. One or more or all of these possibilities is suggested by their reply to Archbishop Gonzalo of Toledo's attempt to

---

[1] *HC* 167; JL 6350.
[2] A. Herculano, *História de Portugal* (9th ed., Lisbon, n.d.), II, p. 188; C. Erdmann, *O Papado e Portugal,* p. 47.
[3] JL 9255.
[4] These documents are to be found in Rivera, *La Iglesia de Toledo,* p. 220, n. 71; pp. 222-3, n. 74, and p. 225, n. 75. Rivera's discussion of this facet of papal diplomacy is excellent; see especially pp. 219-37.

carry out Clement III's suggestions.[1] This letter, which must
be dated late in 1188 or early in 1189, effectively halted any
attempt that might have been made during the remainder of
Clement III's pontificate to turn the uneasy truce between
León and Castile into a permanent peace.

Cardinal Hyacinth, aged nearly ninety, ascended the papal
throne as Celestine III at the end of March 1191, and among
the earliest letters he despatched was one to the archbishop
of Toledo scolding him for his feeble response to Clement's
scheme for peace and urging him to greater efforts.[2] But this
bull must have arrived just as the uneasy truce fell to pieces.
In May 1191 the kings of Aragon, León and Portugal agreed
on common military action against Castile, and in July or
August Alfonso IX entered into alliance with the Almohades
to protect his southern frontier. He was excommunicated,
and his kingdom interdicted, soon afterwards—it is not
known exactly when—and Gregory, cardinal-deacon of Sant'
Angelo, was sent to impose a peace upon the kings. This is
precisely what he did. Neither of the kings wanted the treaty
of Tordehumos (April 1194), and it lasted only a short time.
The Castilian forces were shattered at Alarcos, and a new
rupture between León and Castile took place. Alfonso IX
renewed his alliance with the Almohades, and was condemned for this in the strongest terms by Celestine III in
October 1196.[3] War between León and Castile dragged on
through 1196 and 1197, until finally a peace was arranged
through the mediation, once more, of cardinal Gregory. To
strengthen it, Alfonso IX was married to the Castilian Berenguela, daughter of Alfonso VIII, in the autumn of 1197.

There is every indication that the magnitude of the Almohade threat, the Leonese defeats at the hands of Castile, and
general war-weariness, had combined to persuade the kings
to accept the peace of 1197 as definitive. But it was at this
point that the second problem arose. Berenguela was related
to Alfonso IX within the prohibited degrees. It appears that

---

[1] AC Toledo, A.6.F.I.8. I have to thank Father Rivera for sending me a summary
of this document, which was not to be found when I worked in the Toledo
archives in September 1967.
[2] *Non sine causa* of 25 April 1191: Rivera, *La Iglesia de Toledo*, p. 228, n. 79.
[3] JL 17433.

cardinal Gregory—and even Celestine III himself—were prepared to connive at this.[1] But Innocent III, who succeeded as pope a few months after the marriage, was not.[2] His insistence that the marriage be dissolved only gained its end in the spring of 1204. And the separation at once brought on further quarrels between León and Castile, this time over the issue of the restitution of Berenguela's dowry. The upshot was that a full, final and definitive peace between the kingdoms did not come until 1209, and after insistent papal pressure. It was only then that Innocent III could turn to the great crusade he had in mind, which at Las Navas de Tolosa in 1212 was so strikingly successful.

[1] This is indeed implied by Rodrigo, *De Rebus Hispaniae*, VII, 31; cf. also above, p. 211, n. 2.

[2] A lucid guide to Innocent's relations with the Spanish kingdoms is given by A. Luchaire, *Innocent III: les royautés vassales du Saint-Siège* (Paris, 1908), pp. 1–58: some detail is added by D. Mansilla, 'Inocencio III y los reinos hispanos', *Anthologica Annua* ii (1954), 9–49.

6

CONCLUSION

That the popes exercised supervision over Spanish ecclesiastical affairs is but one of the indications that Leonese churchmen were subject to the same constraints as their contemporaries in other kingdoms. Other similarities abound, as will by now be evident. To claim that there was little that was unusual about the Leonese church in the twelfth century may seem a lame conclusion. It will appear less so to those who are acquainted with the work of Spanish ecclesiastical historians. Much of their writing has been underpinned by the assumption that there was something special or unusual about the church in Spain, an assumption explicable in part by the tendency to study it in isolation, rather than as a member of the community of western Christendom. It is to be hoped that this essay will go a little way along the road to correcting this misapprehension.

Of course, no two members of this community were or are exactly alike; so it may not be inappropriate to conclude with some reflections about those features of the secular church in the kingdom of León which do seem to be distinctive. The most striking of them is the awkwardness of its structure in relationship to historical and political realities. The kingdom of León had a historical coherence fashioned in the tenth and eleventh centuries which survived the union with Castile and re-emerged in the form of a distinct political unit on the death of Alfonso VII in 1157. But the notion of a 'Leonese church' makes little sense; as an ecclesiastical unit it had scarcely any identity in the twelfth century, seeing that its bishops owed loyalty to metropolitans variously at Braga, Toledo or Compostela, and in two instances to no metropolitan below the pope.[1] This sort of muddle did not

---

Perhaps therefore a book about the Leonese episcopate should not have been written. But a part of my purpose, lurking in the background, was to suggest that there were reasons other than the purely political for the failure of the independent kingdom of León to survive after 1230.

occur at other places in Europe where ecclesiastical organization was being overhauled in the course of the twelfth century, in Ireland, for example, or Norway, or Sweden. Why
did it happen in Spain? Naturally we can only guess. Was it
because the reformers were too little respectful of a recent
Leonese past, too much respectful of a distant Visigothic
one? Was it because they were outsiders who took little
trouble to understand Spanish conditions before they imposed their administrative network? Or perhaps it was not
like this at all. The organization we find in the twelfth century was the outcome of a multitude of decisions taken by
many different people over a long period of time; compro-
mises, sometimes, reached in weariness of spirit after long
expense of rancour. It is too easy for us to say that the result
was a mess, and that by the time it was apparent as such it
was too late to do anything about it. A mess is what reformers
often produce.

Supposing that the kingdom of León had been formally
an ecclesiastical unit—a single metropolitan province, let us
say—this would still have had little coherence. The kingdom
was uneasily divided between Galicia, the old-settled lands
of the central plateau and the new frontier territories. The
concerns of ecclesiastics were necessarily as diverse as those
of secular men. We may doubt whether a bishop of Ciudad
Rodrigo or Coria had much in common with a bishop of
Astorga or León, let alone with a bishop of Tuy or Mondoñedo. Such a state of affairs was not peculiar to León; as
foolish to suppose that an archbishop of Magdeburg had
much in common with a bishop of Riga, or an archbishop
of York with his suffragan of the Orkneys. Such diversity of
interests and concerns, however, may have mattered in a
small and poor kingdom like León in a way that it did not
elsewhere, for example in the larger and richer *Corona de
Aragón*. The bishops of the southern sees—like their Castilian or their Portuguese neighbours (Sigüenza, Segovia,
Avila, Plasencia, Idanha, Lisbon)—were trying to refound a
Christian church in new territories, in much the same way as
their contemporaries the bishops in Outremer. The churchmen of the north presided over an old-established church
and were probably little, if at all, interested in the progress

of the *Reconquista*. There was little point of contact between them.

Like branches of the church elsewhere in the twelfth century—Ireland is a good example—the Leonese church was undergoing organizational reform at the hands of outsiders. The impulse towards change seems to have slackened in the second half of the century, perhaps because the administrative changes had been effected by then, perhaps because foreign reformers were no longer entering the kingdom in such numbers as they had done hitherto. But were the reforms 'followed up'? Organization is one thing, pastoral practice quite another.

We come back to the bishops themselves. How little we know about them, and how difficult therefore to come to any sort of judgement on them. In general they seem not to have been a very distinguished lot. It may be illuminating to compare them with their English contemporaries. In one respect the lack of distinction of the Spaniards is at once apparent. They were singularly deficient in intellectual attainment. Of course, an Anselm or a Stephen Langton is a rarity in any age or country. Yet throughout the twelfth century there were among the English bishops men who had at their command a body of solid and respectable learning such as did them credit. There were several who if not themselves scholars were patrons of scholarship. There were others whose intellectual vitality found expression in discerning patronage of the arts. There were others again whose qualities of mind can be seen not in ecclesiastical learning but in the practical arts of government and administration. We look in vain for these qualities among the Leonese bishops. Pedro Suárez de Deza and Martín of Zamora may have been competent canon lawyers, but they cannot bear comparison with a Bartholomew of Exeter or a Roger of Worcester. The latinity of Pelayo of Oviedo or Arnaldo I of Astorga—if the latter did indeed compose the *Chronica Adefonsi Imperatoris*—is poor weak stuff when set against that of a Herbert Losinga or (a native of England but a bishop in France) a John of Salisbury. No Leonese bishop at any time during the century encouraged scholarship as did Archbishop Theobald of Canterbury. Leonese bishops certainly patronized the arts. But here too they were curiously hesitant and slow to respond to new ideas. The cathedral of Santiago de Compostela is a magnificent building, but it is in no sense original as its contemporary Durham was; heavily dependent on French models, it belonged to an architectural tradition that was already outmoded.[1] The very few surviving illuminated manuscripts from León show this same reluctance to follow new trends and fashions.[2] Questions of scale apart, no Leonese bishop showed the discernment in artistic patronage of an Alexander the Magnificent or a Henry of Blois. It was the same with the skills of practical affairs. Royal servants who acquired bishoprics in the kingdom of León—a Nuño of Mondoñedo or a Berengar of Salamanca—were not men with the forceful ingenuity of the great civil-servant bishops of Norman and Angevin England—a Flambard, a Roger of Salisbury, a Hubert Walter.

Intellectual attainment, though desirable, is not an essential prerequisite in a bishop. Were the Leonese bishops good pastors of their flocks? Did they adopt those administrative practices which might have assisted them in their pastoral mission? In our earlier consideration of surviving episcopal *acta* and of the other evidence relating to diocesan administration, we saw that the Leonese bishops were slow to adopt new instruments and techniques, and that the machinery of episcopal government seems to have worked sluggishly. This is in itself suggestive. Administrative efficiency is not pastoral efficiency: but the two often go hand in hand. It is probably fair to say that the Leonese bishops were less active pastors than they might have been. Of course, such a thing could be said of many bishops at any period in history; a Grosseteste is a rare phenomenon indeed. But men like him did exist in the twelfth century; in England, Foliot was such a one. We know of no such in the kingdom of León.

An air of mediocrity, then, hangs over these bishops. It would be possible to argue that they were more reprehensible

---

[1] G.E. Street, *Gothic Architecture in Spain* (2nd ed., London, 1869), ch. 7; K.J. Conant, *The Early Architectural History of the Cathedral of Santiago de Compostela* (Cambridge, Mass., 1926).
[2] C.R. Dodwell, *Painting in Europe 800–1200* (Harmondsworth, 1971), chs. 6 and 11.

than this. Is it not surprising that there is no certain evidence for the holding of ecclesiastical councils after 1155? Is it not somewhat disconcerting to find that visitations and synods tend to have the look of occasions when fund-raising was uppermost in episcopal minds? Is it not distinctly odd to find a bishop of Lugo in the year 1189 leasing a church to a lay-woman for an annual money rent?[1] We must reiterate yet once more that our body of source material is extremely small. It may be a proceeding of questionable honesty to select evidence for malpractice from that tiny *corpus* in order to paint these bishops in darker colours. Yet it would be equally dishonest to gloss over the evidence that all was not well with the Leonese church. How harshly we choose to judge these bishops will depend in the last resort upon the subjective judgement about how far we think we can go in our interpretation of scanty evidence.[2] The historian of a dark age can state problems but he cannot solve them.

The heart of the matter may be that the Leonese bishops were poor bishops, and it is arguable that they were poor because they were under the thumb of their rulers. Here once more we need to tread with circumspection. The nature of twelfth-century records makes it notoriously difficult to say anything with confidence about episcopal finances in any country. Yet it is hard to resist a sense forced in upon one after long acquaintance with the evidence that Leonese bishops were worse off at the end of the century than they had been at its beginning. It must be frankly admitted that this is an impression, not an assertion susceptible of proof; the means are not yet to hand which would enable us to say anything with confidence about the material resources of any one of these bishoprics. But even an impression may have its uses. Take the see of Santiago de Compostela: in the time of Diego Gelmírez it was clearly very rich; he could initiate an enormous building programme, establish a chapter with no fewer than seventy-two canons, lavish bribes on popes and cardinals, build castles and a fleet. Pedro Suárez, on the other hand, looks like a man operating on a more restricted budget;

[1] See below, Appendix, no. XXI.
[2] In my doctoral thesis, which represents a first draft of the present work, I was disposed to judge these bishops rather more harshly than I am now.

he tried to limit capitular growth, undertook no new building, and made a determined attempt to tap new sources of revenue like the famous levy known as the *votos de Santiago*.[1] Is it purely coincidental that the archbishopric should display these signs of financial strain not long after the troubled years of royal intervention between 1140 and 1173? The case of Oviedo is more dramatic. The Oviedo of Bishop Pelayo was certainly wealthy; he could offer Queen Urraca an astounding sum for the *señorío* of the town in 1112. But a century later the see was in desperate straits; the bishop could not pay the 15,000 *aurei* he owed for *tercias* and had had to borrow from the king to redeem property from usurers.[2] We do not know how the situation had arisen. It is worth noting, however, that there was one period in the century when the church of Oviedo had passed out of the control of its bishops for no little time, into the hands of one who was not well-disposed towards it; and that was during the exile of bishop Juan when the see was in the hands of Alfonso IX, a period of over seven years, from at latest March 1191 to at earliest May 1198. At Lugo, Cardinal Hyacinth effected in 1173 a reduction in size of the cathedral chapter, because the resources of the see could no longer support such a big one.[3] At Tuy, like Mondoñedo never a rich see, the upheavals of 1170 led to heavy temporary and perhaps some permanent financial loss. The southern sees of the kingdom fared rather better, but of course they faced a different problem; as 'new' sees they had started with nothing. The signs are that Salamanca's and Zamora's endowments steadily grew. Coria, on the other hand, was so modestly endowed by Alfonso VII in 1142 that its bishop took the matter to Pope Eugenius III in 1148, who appealed to the king to be more generous.

Individually these scraps of evidence amount to very little. They may be no more than straws in the wind—but it is significant that they all seem to be blown in the same direction. It may also be significant that royal exactions, or royal

---

[1] On the date of the forgery of the 'diploma of Ramiro I' which provided justification for the levy, see T.D. Kendrick, *St. James in Spain* (London, 1960), chs. iii and xiv.

[2] *MHV* II, nos. 477, 494.

[3] AHN 1325F/9, inaccurately ptd. *ES* XLI, ap. xvii, pp. 326–8.

failure to provide, seem often to have been at the back of the financial difficulties experienced by Leonese bishops. Possibly material poverty was in part at least brought about by the general sluggishness of the episcopate in matters of ecclesiastical reform. We have already commented upon the lack of church councils during the second half of the century. Churchmen gathered in councils can stand up to kings in a way that a churchman on his own cannot. But no councils were held.

For the twelfth century we have only hints and we can make only guesses. The historian of the thirteenth century can set his sights a little higher, for the surviving source-material is vastly greater in bulk than that relating to the twelfth century. A recent study has used this material to advantage.[1] It is now plain that during the thirteenth century the Leonese-Castilian churches were very poor; that they were closely controlled by the kings (who must therefore be held responsible for at least the perpetuation of this poverty); and that, judged by the moral, pastoral and intellectual standards set at the Fourth Lateran Council, their condition was deplorable. It is not to be believed that these characteristics developed in the years after 1215. The roots of decay lay deeper.

We should not forget that the men who made up the Leonese episcopate in the twelfth century had much to contend with. Their land was ill-endowed by nature. It was isolated from the main currents of European culture. It was a prey to external enemies. It experienced periods of civil war. Kings and nobility were predatory. The church over which the bishops presided was a various one: an old church had to be adapted to new standards, had with difficulty to be reconciled to change; a new church had to be constructed in newly-won territories, had to be endowed, organized, supervised. These tasks demanded time and money; they demanded a whole range of human qualities, tact and flair, energy and vision, moral authority and administrative expertise. The complicating factors of kings who wanted a

[1] P.A. Linehan, *The Spanish Church and the Papacy in the Thirteenth Century* (Cambridge, 1971).

Reichskirche, of political rivalries between León, Castile and Portugal, of metropolitans wrangling over suffragans, of a papal curia increasingly assertive but not always sympathetic nor well-informed, of incoming ecclesiastical empire-builders from France—all served to compound the bishops' difficulties. These bishops may have been by and large a rather dim lot; but how many twelfth-century bishops measured up to ideal standards? In the years after 1215 their work was weighed in the balance; that it was found wanting may not have been altogether their own fault.

APPENDIX

SELECTED EPISCOPAL ACTA

The documents here printed are primarily intended to illustrate the remarks made in chapter 3 about the diplomatic of Leonese episcopal *acta*. With two exceptions (nos. IV and XV) they have not previously been published. All abbreviations have been extended, unless the exact form intended by the writer is in doubt. Conjectural readings have been given in round brackets. The punctuation and spelling of the originals have been retained, but not the capital letters.

The Latin of the documents is sometimes extremely bizarre. The written Latin of twelfth-century Spain was fast turning into the vernacular and on the whole the scribes of official documents were not resisting the trend. On occasion, in the charters which follow, this movement towards the vernacular has been carried far, e.g., in nos. VII and XII. To have peppered the documents with the customary '(*sic*)' would have served little useful purpose, so it has been used only sparingly. Sticklers may be comforted by the assurance that strenuous efforts have been made to ensure fidelity of transcription.

I

Profession of obedience by Pedro, bishop of Mondoñedo, to Maurice, archbishop of Braga, *c*.1109.

AD Braga, Liber Fidei, no. 572, fol. 151^r, ^{v}. Cartulary copy of the thirteenth century.

Ego Petrus sancte Minduniensis ecclesie nunc ordinandus episcopus. subiectionem et reverentiam et obedientiam a sanctis patribus constitutam secundum precepta canonum ecclesie Bracarensi rectoribusque eius in presentia domni archiepiscopi Mauricii perpetuo me exhibiturum promitto. et super sanctum altare propria manu firmo.

II

Notitia of lawsuit and agreement between Diego, bishop of León, and the lay proprietors of the *monasterium* of San Tirso, 26 April 1117.

AC León, no. 1382. Original, 22 cm × 19 cm. Half of a polled chirograph. The script is *francesa*, without a trace of Visigothic left in it. The document is damp-stained in several places and some of the readings are conjectural.

Orta fuit intencio inter episcopum Legionensem domnum Didacum videlicet. et inter Pelagium Froilaz cum suis iermanis et cum filiis de Martino / Cidiz.et inter Petrum Vermudiz cum suis iermanis.et cum filiis Micahelis Rodriquiz.et inter filios Roderici Ciprianiz cum filiis Petri Sarraquiniz / super monasterium sancti Tirsi quoniam ipsi iudicabant sibi hereditates ipsius monasterii. et episcopus domnus

Didacus dicebat eum esse proprium sancte Marie. / Postremo invenerunt quod episcopus domnus Didacus debebat habere medietatem ipsius monasterii cum filiis de Roderico Ciprianiz et de Petro Sarraquiniz. / et aliam medietatem Pelagius Froilaz cum suis iermanis et cum filiis Martini Cidiz.et Petrus Vermudiz cum suis iermanis et cum filiis Micahelis / Rodriquiz. Denique convenerunt in concilium et fecerunt inter se pactum simul et placitum tali videlicet pactione.quod ipsi hereditarii dimittant / hereditates ipsius monasterii quas retinent. et episcopus domnus Didacus construat et populet illud monasterium.et per consilium eorum preponat / et deponat abbatem.et quod ipsi hereditarii semper auxilientur suis rebus abbati ipsius monasterii. et defendant pro posse suo.et amplificent illud / monasterium suis hereditatibus.et quicumque illorum pertransiens in monasterio hospitari voluerit.recipiatur sicut hereditarius.nec (aggraventur) / sed pro posse abbatis.et si forte aliquis illorum ad inopiam devenerit.atque in monasterio morari et ibidem Deo deservire voluerit. / recipiatur et honeste teneatur pro posse abbatis qui eo tempore monasterio prefuerit. /

Si ergo predictus episcopus domnus Didacus vel aliquis successorum eius hoc placitum confringere et ab hac (*here a word illegible*)[1] exire presumpserit.exsolvat / supra scriptis hereditariis D.^{os} solidos.et observat placitum. Similiter siquis ex hereditariis a diffinito placito deviare temptave / rit.persolvat Legionensi episcopo D.^{os} solidos et observat descriptam conventionem. /

Facto placito VI.º Kalendas Maii in Era M.ª C.^a L.^a V.^a

III

Pedro III, bishop of Lugo, grants the church of Sta. Eulalia to Miguel Peláez for the term of his life, 21 August 1119.

AHN 1325C/9. Original, 17 cm × 28 cm. Authenticated by the *signa* of the bishop and the scribe, both drawn by the same hand, presumably that of the scribe. The remainder of the document is in a different hand, and the script is transitional, still fundamentally Visigothic but with strong traces of *francesa* influence.

In Dei nomine. Ego.P.III.Dei gratia Lucensis episcopus una cum conventu eiusdem / ecclesie clericorum.tibi Michael Pelaiz facio placitum de una ecclesia / de illa canonica videlicet que cognominatur sancta Eulalia Alta / et est sita in territorio Flammoso super flumen quod dicitur Tordeia. / Do tibi ipsam ecclesiam cum omni sua hereditate quanta ad ipsam pertinet et / cum tota sua pertinencia ut habeas et possideas edifices et plantes / et popules omnibus diebus vite tue.post obitum vero tuum remaneat ad / illum canonicum cum sua populacione et edificacione. Si quis vero inrumpere factum / hoc meum temptaverit nisi penituerit sit maledictus et excommunicatus / et cum Iuda Domini traditore penas lugeat in eterna damnatione.insuper / hoc meum factum non disrumpatur. / Facta karta donationis era.I.C.LVII. XII.Kal'.

---

[1] Probably either *conventione* or *pactione*.

Septembris. / Ego Petrus episcopus cum reliquis beate Marie clericis hanc cartam fieri iussi firmavi et roboravi. (*Signum*)

1st column:
Bernardus eiusdem canonice archidiaconus conf.
Iudex Pelagius et archidiaconus conf.
Item Pelagius archidiaconus conf.
Nunnus archidiaconus conf.
Munio archidiaconus conf.
Veremudus Pelais prepositus civitatis conf.
Martinus Citiz conf.
Michael Citiz conf.
Petrus testis.
Iohannes testis.
Menendus testis.

2nd column:
Pelagius Iohannis conf.
Gundesindus presbiter conf.
Guimara Aspaiz conf.
Martinus sacrista conf.
Petrus Didaz conf.
Suarius albergarius conf.
Pelagius Citiz conf.
Rubert conf.
Liger conf.
MARTINUS NOTUIT (*Signum*)

IV

Diego, bishop of León, grants to the canons of his cathedral the right to hold their prebends in the future without any interference from the bishop, 29 June 1120.

AC León, no. 1384. Original, 71 cm X 42 cm. Authenticated by the bishop's *signum*, 'pictorial' type, a hand grasping an episcopal crozier. The script is a neat *francesa*. The document has been published before, by Risco, in *ES* xxxv, ap. iv, pp. 417–21—a version of startling inaccuracy. The text is a complicated one. Before describing the nature of the present edition, it will be as well to give in schematic form, though not to scale, the layout of the text:

	Text (9 lines)	
1st column	2nd column ORDO DIACONORUM	3rd column ORDO SUBDIACONORUM
	Additions to Text, and Sanction	
Clerical subscriptions	Lay subscriptions	Dating-clause and episcopal subscription

The special interest of this text lies in the number of erasures and additions that have been made, which suggest that it was, so to say, kept up to date in the years after 1120. In the version given here, additions over erasures have been indicated by italics, additions not over erasures by square brackets; where additions appear to have been made to the original text but have in their turn been erased to be replaced by secondary additions, this is indicated both by italics and by square brackets. Some of the additional material is in the same ink and by the same hand, some in a different ink and by the same hand, as the original; some in a different ink and by a different hand. It may be doubted whether even a very good photograph would reveal the full palaeographical complexity of this document. (In fairness to Risco, it should be pointed out that he may have been working from the cartulary-copy in the *Tumbo de León*. I have not myself collated the original with the cartulary-copy; so that the present edition, though it may (I hope) be regarded as a definitive version of the original charter, is emphatically not a definitive edition of the text in its character as a statement about the constitution and composition of the chapter of León cathedral in the twelfth century.)

XPS. CVM A TEMPORIBVS PRIMI CONCILII LIBERRITANI ECCLESIA LEGIONENSIS QVE SEDES REGIA NVNCVPATVR EO QUOD ANTIQVO MORE REGES IN EA CORONANTVR / et a regibus Yspanie et a principibus plurimas dignitates obtineret. nulli etenim metropolitano. sed tantum romano pontifici subdita. ecclesiasticos tamen honores. et canonicorum prebendas. secundum morem aliarum ecclesiarum canonice dispositarum. non habebat. Quia omnes persone predicte sedis. videlicet archidiacones (*sic*). prior. / precentor. sacrista. atque universi canonici. dignitates suas et honores. non firmiter. necque secundum canonum institucionem possidebant. sed secundum pontificis libitum. et consideracionem obtimam vel pravam. prout amicicia. servicium. amor sui generis. vel ira. et odium. eum preocupabant. ab honoribus / et a prestaminibus. et a sua canonica. et ab omnibus ecclesie beneficiis. sine ecclesiastico iudicio. tam senes quam iuvenes expellebantur. vel in honores ecclesie sublimabantur inordinate; in Dei igitur et individue Trinitatis nomine. ego Didacus Legionensis ecclesie episcopus quamvis indignus. huiusmodi iniusticiam / et controversiam. et clericos non firmo animo ecclesie servire. sed vacillanti et dubio considerans. nostrorum clericorum atque laicorum nobilium consilio. maiorum. et mediocrium. et minorum clericorum. honores. et beneficia. sicuti sancti canones et sancti patres constituere. pro anime mee remedio. et omnium regum Yspanie / christianorum et benefactorum nostre ecclesie. dilectissima voluntate dispono et assero. ut omnes canonici istius nostre ecclesie sancte Marie tam maiores quam minores numero conscripti Χ^{e ta} exceptis archidiaconis (*here some three words have been erased*) canonicas suas scilicet prebendas in hereditate possideant. Et si aliquis ex canonicis / obierit. alius idoneus et persona ecclesie conveniens in locum eius succedat. et in vita sua canonice

possideat. Deinde si aliquis canonicorum culpam gravem vel levem
conmiserit.vel verbis veris vel falsis accusatus fuerit.in capitulo canonice
iudicetur.et secundum canonum precepta salvetur vel dampnetur. /

Ergo ego D.Legionensis episcopus ex auctoritate romane ecclesie et
domni Bernaldi archiepiscopi Toletani.et tocius Yspanie legati. et cum
provincialium episcoporum[1] istis canonicis subscriptis suas hereditates
scilicet prebendas in Dei nomine canonice concedo. Scilicet michi
Didaco episcopo et omnibus successoribus meis in prebenda /
monasterium sanctorum Cosme et Damiani cum suis hereditatibus. *Et
domno Sesnando Vistrarii monasterium sancte Marie de Mazaneda cum
omnibus suis hereditatibus.* Et domno *Bernardo Zamorensi* episcopo
monasterium sancti Iohannis cum suis hereditatibus in urbe Legionensi
et terciam de Val de Eras. /

1st column:
Et dompno Pelagio priori monasterium sancte Leocadie cum suis here-
ditatibus et medietatem de Villa Cidre.
Et Martino precentori villam sancti Iohannis de rivo Porme fluvii et
terciam de Villa Roan et terciam de Navis et terciam de Centum
Fontibus.
Et Petro Arie hereditatem de Morales et terciam de Fonte Foiolo et
terciam de Arcello et terciam de Bustello de Flavio.
Mauricio archidiacono (*here some five words have been erased*) et
terciam de ecclesiis de Graliare.
Pelagio archidiacono *Rozola cum suis hereditatibus et tercias Campo
Villa* Viader (?) Levanega.Corvellos.Rebollar.
Dominico archidiacono Mata Plana cum suis ecclesiis et terciam de
Villa Alba.
Pelagio Citiz.*Villa Froila.* et illo foro de Castrello de Porma [*monasterium
sancti Christofori de Curonio.Moral.Barrio.*]
Andree Dominici Villa Savarigo.Sancto Cipriano. Villa Frida. Vallizello.
Tebaldus Graliarello.Vegas.Ceresales (?). Orcenaga (?) Valparadiso.
Oterolo.
Martin Lazari Villa Gontille.Sanctus Victor. Sanctus Martinus de Super
Ripa.
Mames Pelaiz Val de Savugo. Sancta Eugenia. Quintanilas de Paramo.
Carvaliare. Villa Mizar (?).
Dominicus Cidiz Villa Burgala. Roveredo. Quintana.Tendabale. Villa
Seca Foro.
Petro Guterriz Sancto Petro cum suis hereditatibus.Villa Paderna. Val
Denanne (?).
Petro Dominici Masella. Villa de Biera. Otero.Pedrun Foros.
(*the name erased*) Villa Grat. Veiga de Fernando Veremudi. Castro
Maior.
Michael Floridiz monasterium sancti Tirsi cum suis hereditatibus.

---

[1] Here some such word as *consilio* or *consensu* needs to be supplied.

Pelagio Pelaiz terciam de Matavaiu.Marin cum suo monasterio.
Lormano presbitero terciam de Villa Vellaco.
Dominico Falconiz Veiga monasterium cum suis villis et cum suis hereditatibus.
Domno *Guistrario* Villa Cresces.Melgar de Abduce et Fontezellas.
Petro Flores Golpeliones. *Soto Noval.*
Fernando Petriz Monasterium sancti Micahelis de Veiga quod est iuxta monasterium sancti Claudi cum omnibus villis molendinis et hereditatibus suis.

2nd column:
ORDO DIACONORVM
Fernando Dominici tercia de Barrio.Villa Martin. Veiga et Garfin. Valdesalze.Villa Volezar.
Arie Martini Villa Fateme.Vane Celia.Fontes de Veroz.Villa Vascon.
Pelagius Felix Mazelleros.Lagartos.Rebollar.Sancto Felices. Tonros II^{os}.
Petro Xabiz Vacella.Villa Davi.
Petro Fernandiz Villa Arent.Villa Moros.Villa Olquit. Illa ponte et Scalada. Foros II^{os}.
Pelagio Stephaniz Valle Castro. Roda.Castrello. Maria Alba.Alixa.
Iohanni Michaeliz Castronuidaraf. Castro de Martino. Carisac.
Tirso.Berrianos.Castro Vaia.Villa Alvobu (?) [*Sancto Martino de Gordaliza. Val Fartel. Bustello.*]
Martino Moniz Granietas. Villa Nanin.
(*the next line completely erased*)

3rd column:
ORDO SUBDIACONORVM
Martino Xabiz Furones. *Villa Grat.* [*Vezella.*]
Fernando Pelaiz Villa Ciz et illos foros de Cervera [*Et terciam sancti Romani Cubas* (?).]
Iohanni Petriz Cornelios. Nogales. Reto (?) de Coronio.
Iohanni Petriz Sotello (*here two words erased*) Sancta Maria de Annaia Velaz. Aviados.
Stephano Iohanniz Gadrefes. Ravanal.
Martino Pelaiz Villa Mudarafe.Sancta Columba.
Vilielmo Sanctus Martinus de illa Fonte.
Iohanni Pelaiz Villa verde.
Domno Arvio
Martino Gualterio Villa Moratelle.
Isidorus Guterrii
Fafila Fernandiz Sanctum Iacobum de Cellerolo cum suis hereditatibus et terciam de Villa Torel.
[*Magistro Ivoni.Monasterium sancti Michaelis cum suis hereditatibus.*]

Item in Dei nomine decrevimus ut quicumque monasterium.vel villas. vel hereditates.tenuerit.si in vita sua vel causa sue mortis dimiserit. omnia bona sua recipiat et voluntatem suam inde faciat. preter boves arantes necessaria bovum et preter torcular.et preter mensam.et dolia. et preter cetera que sunt necessaria in domo que superlectilia vocantur. De pane eciam et de vino medietatem accipiat.et medietatem monasterio dimittat.et si panis et vinum sunt in agris ad colligendum'.medietatem similiter accipiat' et clericus qui post mortem canonici in prebendam successerit. et beneficio eius usus fuerit'.missam pro anima eius per annum integrum celebret si est sacerdos.et si non celebrare faciat.

[Recepimus Xemenonem Lupiz in canonicum et damus ei in preben-dam monasterium sancte Marie de Valle de Umane (?) cum suis villis et hereditatibus.]

Quicumque igitur contra kartam istam insurrexerit et contrariare et confringere conatus fuerit'.sit anathema maranata et sicut Iudas periit cuius corpus terra recipere noluit'.et sicut Dathan et Abiron quos terra obsorbuit perierunt.ita ut omnes adversarii istius pagine'.tam clerici quam laici pereant.et de libro vite deleantur.

Clerical subscriptions:
Archiepiscopus Toletanus et Yspanie legatus conf.
Palentinus episcopus conf.
Astoricensis episcopus conf.
Ovetensis episcopus conf.
Compostellanus episcopus (*sic*) sancti Iacobi conf.
Bragarensis episcopus (*sic*) cum suis provincialibus conf.

Lay subscriptions:
Domna Urracha Yspanie regina conf. (*Signum*)
Suerius comes conf.
Fernandus comes conf.
Rudericus Martiniz conf.
Petrus Diaz conf.
Xemenus Lupiz maiordomus regine et princeps turrium Legionis conf.

Quando Didacus episcopus Legionensis ad utilitatem sancte ecclesie et ad clericorum honorem hanc kartam composuit fuit ERA.I^a.C^a.L^a. VIII^a. et quod III°. Kal'. Iulii.

Ego Didacus Dei gratia Legionensis ecclesie episcopus hanc institutionis mee kartam quam fieri iussi et legi.ilari animo confirmavi et roboravi. (*Signum.*)

V

Diego Gelmírez, archbishop of Santiago de Compostela, grants a share in the water-supply piped to his cathedral by its treasurer Bernardo to the monastery of San Martín Pinario, in return for the prayers of the monks, 1122.

AHN 512/9. Original, 58 cm × 41 cm. Authenticated by autograph sub-scriptions and *signa*. The script is a late but pure Visigothic hand. The document has suffered severely in the course of the centuries; its edges are ragged all the way down the right-hand side, with one large chunk missing, it is much spotted by damp in the centre, and at the bottom-left it has faded badly and lost another chunk. But the feat of engineering to which it refers was famous in its day (cf. *Le Guide du pèlerin de Saint-Jacques de Compostelle*, ed. J. Vielliard (4th ed., Mâcon, 1969), p. 94), and since the document has never before been printed it seemed worth finding a place for it in the present collection.

XPS. CATOLICORUM EST et presertim pontificum honestati et quieti providere monasteriorum. Quo circa. . . / digna opera.luce scripture presentibus et posteris nota fieri opere precium est et enim sole in huiusmodi irripere oblivionis nebula.diutina. . . / distancia. Quam ob rem ego Didacus ecclesie sancti Iacobi archiepiscopus et sancte romane ecclesie legatus.et universa plenitudo canonicorum nostre ecclesie. nostr. . . / acensam lucernam ponere sed super candelabrum.et in lucem memorie scripture titulo aperire.quod ope nostra necnon et artificiali ingenio dompni B.ecclesie (beati Iacobi the) / saurarii per subterraneos meatus aque habundanciam in claustro monasterii sancti Martini sicut res evidenter indicat (?). fecimus egredi.et per plumbea et area cornua prosilire . . . (reme) / dium animarum nostrarum et parentum nostrorum.ea semper racione servata ut in claustro (iamdic) ti monasterii. ipsa aqua in tres partes dividatur. et terciam inde habeant . . . / II^{as}. ecclesia sancti Iacobi.et ita dum mundus steterit inmobiliter permanere decernimus eo semper tenore servato. ut usque ad . . . (ora) ndi pro nobis in letania ad premam.et in missa s (olemni) . . . / orationem.et ad terciam psalmum *Levavi oculos meos* recitent. Post obitum vero nostrum.septenarium duplicatum . . . et tri . . . arium pro nobis faciant. Et in unoquoque anno imp (erpetuum) faciant anniversarium. Et in unaquaque semana (?) quantam comemoracionem pro defunctis canonicis ecclesie beati Iacobi plenarie perfeciant (*sic*). et usque ad finem mundi complere non desinant. De cetero nulli . . . / successorum sive canonicorum liceat aliqua occasione seu violencia aut temeritate hoc beneficium quod monasterio sancti Martini concedimus inperpetuum infringere. aut aquam illam . . . / seu machinacione subdola transmutare studuerit.auctoritate Dei omnipotentis et beatorum apostolorum Petri Pauli et Iacobi.et omnium sanctorum.sit maledictus et excommunicatus. et cum Iuda traditore / Domini.et cum Datan et Abiron quos pro suis sceleribus terra vivos absorbuit in inferno sulfureas penas irremediabiliter sustineat.et a corpore et sanfuine Domini in die iudicii expers existat . . . / temeritatis.I^c. auri libras. monachis et monasterio regali imperio. . . exsolvat.et hoc nostrum voluntarium beneficium incon. . . .permaneat in secula seculorum. . . / Facta serie scripture in Era I^a.C^a.LX^a. et quot III°. Nonas . . . /

The witnesses are not arranged in columns, but scattered in apparently random fashion over the generous area of parchment—exactly half the total area—left after the end of the text. All the subscriptions are autograph: all are in Visigothic script except the three marked with an asterisk.

EGO DIDACUS COMPOSTELLANE ECCLESIE ARCHIEPISCOPUS

SANCTE ROMANE ECCLESIE LEGATUS HOC FACTUM. . . (*Here a large area of parchment is missing; it probably contained the archbishop's Rota.*)

Munio Adefonsi Vallibriensis episcopus. . .
Petrus Gundesindiz cardinalis et primi. . .
Adefonsus Cardinalis conf. (*Signum*)
Petrus Anaides conf.* (*Signum*)
Petrus Danieliz clericus et iudex conf. (*Signum*)
Petrus Elie archidiaconus conf.* (*Signum*)
. . .Didaci kardinalis sancti Iacobi conf. (*Signum*)
Petrus Cresconides archidiaconus kardinalis conf.* (*Signum*)
Pelagius Gudestei iudex. . . (*Signum*)
Petrus ecclesie sancti Iacobi kardinalis notuit (*Signum*)

VI

Pedro Daniélez, priest, swears an oath of fealty to Pedro III, bishop of Lugo, as his *vasallus*, for a church held of him, 24 October 1130.

AHN 1325C/20. Original or contemporary copy, 12 cm X 23 cm. This is not, strictly speaking, an episcopal act, but the document as we have it was written by one whom we may presume to have been an episcopal scribe (cf. above, p. 118, n. 5): it was in the bishop's interests that the terms of the oath should have been committed to writing, and it is reasonable to assume that this was done in whatever episcopal 'chancery' existed. There are no signs of authentication. For a very similar document, dated 5 August 1130, see AHN 1325C/18.

Domno meo pontifici et spirituali patri domno Petro III°. Lucensi. ego Petrus Danalaci qualiscumque presbiter promitto vobis et Lucensi ecclesie cui vos auctore Deo presidetis per presentis placiti seriem quod sim vester vasallus sine alio domino et serviam vobis cum illa ecclesia sancti Ieorgii de Turre quam vos datis mihi ad tenendam populandam et edificandam atque plantandam et ut pro posse meo et nosse regam illam studiose. destructa restaurem.perdita adquiram. adquisita modis omnibus conservem. atque ut prudens agricola labores in ea necessarios exercere studeam. De omnibus autem frugibus quas collegero inde vel aliunde ubicumque laborare potero ac de decimis et arborum fructibus in unoquoque anno dem vobis fideliter terciam partem. Si autem quod absit aliter egero.pariam vobis vel voci vestre. CCC^{tos}. solidos et sit vobis licitum vestra accipere et in me plenariam iusticiam exercere. Factum est era M.C.LXVIII^{a}. VIIII°. Kal'. Novembris. Qui presentes fuerunt. Iohannes testis.Suarius testis. Adefonsus testis. Didacus notuit.

VII

Bernardo, bishop of Zamora, grants a *fuero* to the *pobladores* of Fuentesauco, March 1133.

AC Zamora, Libro Negro, fol. 15^{v}. Cartulary copy of the thirteenth century.

XPS. In nomine domini nostri Iesu Christi. Ego B.Zemorensis ecclesie
episcopus facio kartam ad populatores de Fonte de Savugo ut nullus
homo habeat ibi vassallum nisi suum iugarium vel suum ortulanum qui
moratus fuerit in sua propria kasa. Et qui fecerit ibi homicidium vel
calumpniam vel rausum pectet illum per foro de Zemora. Et homines
de Fonte de Savugo faciant sernam ad suum episcopum unum diem
arrelvar et alium ad bimar et tercium ad seminar et episcopus det eis
panem et vinum et carnem et alios duos dies panem et vinum et de
cozinas. Et homines de la Fonte quos habuerunt asinos dent unum diem
ad karreiar cibariam ad Taurum vel ad Zamoram et episcopus det eis
panem et civada. Ego Bernardus Zamorensis pro remedio anime mee
laxo ad homines de la Fonte nuntium et manariam et de osas de aliqua
mulier per foro de Zamora dent eas. Et si aliquis de populatoribus
voluerit vendere suam hereditatem vendat cui voluerit, et ille qui eam
comparaverit faciat forum ad episcopum quod ipse faciebat, id est
unum denarium et unum panem et una octava de civada. Et quantos ibi
laboraverint dent suum decimum de quanto laboraverit ad ecclesiam
episcopi. Et qui non habuerint asinum dent unum diem apodar. Et de
fossado et de fossadera per foro de Zamora. Et kavaleiro non faciat
serna. Et si aliquis homo venerit ad inrumpendum hunc factum nostrum
sedeat excommunicatus et cum Iuda traditore habeat participium.
Facta karta populationis noto die quod est XXIII (sic) Kal'. Aprilis,
Era MCLXXI. Ego Bernardus Zamorensis episcopus in hanc kartam que
fieri iussi manus meas roboravi. Mandante Zamora rex Adefonsus et
comite domno Roderigo sub manu eius. Episcopus in Zamora
Bernardus, sub manu eius archidiaconus domnus Willelmus. Qui
presentes fuerunt et audierunt. Roman Cidiz conf. Cidi Hoderriz conf.
Petro Xabiz conf. Petro Pelaiz conf. Fernandus Iohannis conf. Petro
Cidiz conf. Pelagius notuit.

VIII

Notitia or record of a lawsuit between Arias, bishop of León, and
Count Rodrigo Martínez over the property of Pedro Peláez, 1130–5.

AC León, no. 1410. May be either original or a closely contemporary
copy. 15 cm × 29 cm. No signs of authentication. The script is *francesa*.

Orta fuit intentio. (sic) inter Legionensem episcopum domnum Ariam.
et comitem Rodericum Martini.super he / reditates Petri Pelaiz. Petrus
Pelaiz siquidem pro rapinis et maleficiis que fecerat in possessionibus et
/ hominibus sancte Marie.Legionensis scilicet ecclesie.dederat omnes
hereditates suas quas habebat in / campo de Tauro.et in terra Legionis.
a flumine Dorio.usque ad portus Asturiarum. tam de parentum suorum
/ successione.quam de sua adquisitione vel comparatione.episcopo
domno Didaco et canonicis eiusdem ecclesie.tali / scilicet pacto quod si
sine filiis mortuus fuisset.istas supradictas hereditates.episcopus
Legionensis. et / canonici eius post partem sue ecclesie obtinerent. Si
autem filios habuisset medietatem harum heredita / tum filii eius
habuissent.et aliam medietatem ecclesia sancte Marie pro rapinis et

iniuriis quas ab / ipso Petro Pelaiz perpessa fuerant.per scriptum firmitatis in perpetuum obtineret. Quia vero isdem / Petrus Pelaiz res comitis Roderici rapuerat.impetitus super rapina ab ipso comite coram rege.co / actus a rege quod rapinam comiti restitueret.has predictas hereditates post prime donationis pac / tum comiti in vadimonio posuit. ea videlicet conventione.ut comes eas teneret.donec peccu / niam taxatam pro rapina Petrus Pelaiz sibi persolveret. Super his memoratus episcopus domnus Arias simul / cum clericis suis. et predictus comes in Legione coram electis iudicibus ratiocinacionem habuerunt. Iudices vero / decreverunt quod episcopus exsolveret peccuniam illam comiti pro qua Petrus Pelaiz predictas heredita / tes in vadimonio posuit. et sic hereditates illas reciperet. Episcopus itaque domnus Arias suscepto iu / dicio dedit comiti Roderico Martini.II^{as} scutellas argenti.et aliud quod comiti pla / cuit.et sic hereditates ipsas sue ecclesie vendicavit. et est manifestum. In concilio etenim Legio / nis coram Roderico Vermudi et Petro Bravolionis.et aliis baronibus civitatis.et coram cano / nicis sancte Marie fuit factum. Rodericus Vermudi conf. Petrus Bravolionis conf. Orodnius Sesnandiz clericus conf. / Rabindaldus Nuni maiordomus episcopi conf. Archidiaconi et reliqui canonici qui interfuerunt confirmant. /
Petrus testis. Dominicus testis. Munio testis.
Arias archidiaconus qui notuit conf. (*Signum*)

IX

Pelayo Menéndez, bishop of Tuy, grants land in Pesegueiro to two brothers, Pedro and Lucio, in return for an annual render of two *solidi* to the canons of Tuy, 31 August 1152.

AC Tuy, 10/10. Original, 53 cm × 39 cm. Authenticated by the *signum* of Alfonso VII. The script is a very neat *francesa*, strongly reminiscent of the royal chancery hands during the reign of Alfonso VII. Was the charter drawn up in the royal chancery? Quite probably it was. Its most puzzling feature is the inclusion of 'Bernandus' of Sigüenza in the witness lists. At this date Bishop Bernardo had been in his grave for at least four months—and he had died not as bishop of Sigüenza but as archbishop of Compostela. His successor at Sigüenza was his nephew Pedro. It is scarcely credible that a scribe in the royal court where Bernardo had spent so much of his life should have made such a mistake; it is equally difficult to believe that a scribe at Tuy—a mere fifty miles from Compostela—could have made the mistake. Slips will happen; and Bernardo had been bishop of Sigüenza for thirty years. This feature alone is not sufficient to ensure the rejection of the document as a forgery.

Oblivio mater errorum plerumque discordie fomitem parere consuevit. ob hoc quodlibet negotium per scripture seriem necessarium est declarare. Idcirco ego sub Christi / nomine.Pelagius Dei gratia Tudensis episcopus una cum conventu canonicorum suorum.tibi Lucio et fratri tuo Petro scriptum donationis et confirmationis facere decrevi super here / ditate. (*interlined* videlicet casal de Bera Mido.) que habet iacentiam in territorio Pessegarii in loco qui vocatur de Iscaria.et est iuxta rivum qui vocatur Malones prope ecclesiam sancti Michaelis sub monte Alogie non longe ab urbe / Tude civitatis. Do vobis illam cum suis terminis sive exitibus necnon inter et foris suisque adiunctionibus in omnibus locis cum sua voce. tali tenore ut neque ego dum ista tripalis vita mihi fuerit / comes.neque alius successor ecclesiam regens aliud petat vestre propagini moranti in illa hereditate.nisi in unoquoque anno canonicis sancte Marie norman beati AUGUSTINI. degentibus. / duos solidos bone monete in festivitate sanctorum Cornelii et Cypriani pacatos dare non diferrat. et hoc scriptum donationis maneat inconcussum et inviolatum. Facta carta donationis.sub / ERA.M.C. LXXXX^a. et quod II.Kal'. Septembris. Ego Pelagius episcopus hoc scriptum quod cum canonicorum conventu tibi L.et fratri tuo Petro fieri iussi in curia domini Adefonsi imperatoris. proprio / robore confirmo. Ego Adefonsus Ispanie imperator hoc scriptum concedo et proprio robore confirmo. /

1st column:
Qui presentes fuerunt.
Petrus testis.
Iohannes testis.
Pelagius testis.

2nd column:
Didacus scripsit et conf.
Nunus canonice prior conf.
Pelagius archidiaconus conf.
Pelagius secundus archidiaconus conf.
Sisnandus archidiaconus conf.
Ceteri canonici laudant et conf.

3rd column:
This contains Alfonso VII's signum, and the explanatory words
SIGNÚM IMPERATORIS.

4th column:
Ego Sancius rex hoc factum Tudensis episcopi proprio robore conf.
Fernandus eius (*sic*) imperatoris filius propria manu firmiter laudat et conf.
Pontius comes totius curie imperatoris laudat et conf. existente maiordomo.
Bernandus Seguentinus episcopus conf.
Iohannes Segobiensis episcopus conf.
Raimundus Palentinus conf.

Beneath the columns:
Pelagius archidiaconus atque abbas monasterii Pessegarii laudat et conf.
Abbas Gunsalvus et ceteri clerici confirmant.
In tempore illo ex parte episcopi erat vicarius Martinus Sisnadiz. et ex

parte canonicorum Mitus Ruderici et Martinus Luci. Sed inter cetera domno episcopo alacriter in fialas obtuli.XX^{ti} solidos.

X

Fernando I, bishop of Astorga, grants a *fuero* to the *pobladores* of Quintanilla y Castro, 7 June 1157.

AHD Astorga, Cámara Episcopal, I/11. Original, 29 cm × 12 cm. Half of a polled chirograph. The script is a remarkably neat *francesa*. Endorsed in a contemporary hand *Karta de Quintanella de Somoza.*

XPS. In nomine sancte Trinitatis Patris et Filii et Spiritus Sancti. Ego Fernandus Dei gratia Astoricensis episcopus una cum consilio et consensu totius conventus canonicorum / do vobis Monioni Pelagii Martino Iohannis Isidoro Romaniz Petro Ciprianiz populatoribus de Quintanella. et aliis omnibus qui populaverint ibi tale forum / ut unusquisque vestrum persolvat mihi vel successoribus meis annuatim ad festum sancti Martini. XX^I. triticeos panes bonos et unum cannatum vini.et arietem / unius anni. et semel in anno asinum suum ad deferendum cibariam aut vinum ad Austoricam. et pro remedio anime mee aufero vobis nuncium et manne / riam.et calumpniam.que non fuerit conquestam a vobis. non sit expechata. Dono vobis et concedo ut quantumcumque laborare poteritis in terminum de Quintanella et de / Castro. laboretis et sit vestrum.per terras.et per divisas moncium. exceptis iugariis cellarii mei quas ibi habeo aut voluero facere. Siquis vero ex successoribus meis / hoc vobis corrumpere voluerit. sit a Deo maledictus et excommunicatus et cum Iuda Domini traditore in inferno dampnatus.et ad partem illius qui vocem vestram pul / saverit. pectet.C. morabitinos.et hoc supradictum forum quod spontanea voluntate ego Fernandus episcopus facere decrevi. maneat.ratum.et firmum. per secula cuncta amen. / Adicio etiam aliud vobis populatoribus de Quintanella ut de vobis maiorinum et saionem super vos habeatis. Facta kartula die quo fuit.VII.^oIdus Iunii. / ERA.M.^aC.^aLXXXX.^aV^a Imperante domno Aldefonso imperatore cum imperatrice Rica in Hispania. Comite Ramiro et imperatrice Rica tenentibus / Astoricam. Ego supradictus Fernandus episcopus hanc kartulam quam facere cum voluntate et iussu canonicorum Astoricensium decrevi vobis populatoribus de / Quintanella et ceteris supervenientibus ibi populare propria manu roboro et confirmo. /

1st column:
Pelagius Fernandiz prior conf.
Iohannes archidiaconus conf.
Mattheus archidiaconus conf.

2nd column:
Nunnus archidiaconus conf.
Petrus archidiaconus conf.
Garcias cantor conf.

3rd column:
Martinus Goestiz conf.
Petrus Bezerro conf.
Conventus canonicorum conf.

4th column:
Petro teste.
Iohanne teste.
Martino teste.

5th column:
Stephanus notuit. (*Signum*)

XI

Agreement between Esteban, bishop of Zamora, and Domingo Martínez, Martín Peláez and others over episcopal rights in the church of Villardondiego and related matters, 30 January 1158.

AC Zamora, Libro Nego, fol. 5^v. Cartulary copy of the thirteenth century.

Hec est convenientia quam facit domnus Stephanus episcopus cum Dominico Martiniz et suis iermanis et Martino Pelaiz et suis iermanis cum don Juliano et suis iermanis et don Xemeno et suis iermanis et Petrus Iohannis super ecclesiam sancte Eulalie Vilar Don Didaci, quod episcopus non mittat clericum in ipsa ecclesia sine illis neque illi sine episcopo, sed conveniant in unum sicuti heredes et mittant ibi clericum, et quod non fuit unquam alia ecclesia in Vilar et quod episcopus habeat terciam decimarum iuste. Et domnus Stephanus episcopus dat eis pro ista conveniencia et pro concambia duas sernas, una iacet al portelo de Vilar, et alia in Vilar circa illa villa que fuerat regalengas. Et si in alico tempore rex terre illis fecerit iurtu (?) aut forcia ipse episcopus qui fuerit in Zamora et in Tauro auctorizet,et si non potuerit auctorizare ipsas sernas det eis LX^a morabitinos sine alio interdictum,et ipse episcopus sit heres in ipsa ecclesia et quantum ad illam pertinet. Hec convenientia facta est in ERA MCLXXXXVI,noto die quod erit III Kal'.Februarii,regnante rege Fernando in Legione et in Gallecia,Poncio comite mandante Zamora et Tauro,Stephano episcopo in Zamora et in Tauro. Qui viderunt et audierunt. Iohannes archidiaconus conf. Raimundus Pisano conf. Iohannes Gondisalviz conf. Petrus Christovalis conf. Fernando Gonzaliviz conf. Romano Velidi conf. Fructuoso Pelaiz conf. Iohannes Cidiz conf. Gonzalvo Cidiz conf. Michael Petriz conf. don Guilelmo conf. Michael Salvatoriz conf. Gonzalvo Ovequiz conf. Pelagio Michael conf. Andres Pelaiz conf. Petrus indignus qui notuit.

XII

Agreement between Fernando I, bishop of Astorga, and the abbot and monks of Eslonza over episcopal rights in the church of Villafáfila, 4 July 1160.

AHN 963/20. Original, 16 cm × 13 cm. Half of a polled chirograph. The script is *francesa*.

Mota fuit dissensio inter abbatem domnum Petrum.et monacos sancti Petri Deslonza.et domnum.F. / Astoricensem episcopum et suos! super ecclesia sancte Marie de Villa Fafila. In presencia tandem. J. venerabilis episcopi Legio / nensis.utrique convenientes! de communi beneplacito ibidem concorditer diffinitum fuit. ut semper singulis / annis monachi sancti Petri de prefata ecclesia pro tercia quam dare debebant! persolvant sedi sancte Marie Asto / ricensi.IIII.modios salis. et pro ariete! unum solidum. et recipiant archidiaconum terre.preter hospites cum.X.hominibus / et.VI. equitaturis. Quod si peccatis exigentibus. ad tantam paupertatem iam dicta ecclesia devenerit. ut predictos modios / monachi graventer persolvere! dismissis ipsis.IIII^{or}.modiis ab episcopo. persolvant episcopo! integre pro ipsis semper terciam / partem omnium decimarum. De medietate vero ecclesie sancti Iacobi! prefati monachi persolvant terciam / partem omnium decimarum similiter ecclesie sancte Marie Astoricensi. Facta conveniencia in Legione / .IIII^{to}. Nonas Iulii.ERA M^a.C^a.LXXXX^a.VIII^a.

1st column:
Fernandus Astoricensis episcopus conf.
Iohannes archidiaconus conf.
Olivarius archidiaconus conf.
Nunnus archidiaconus conf.
Conventus canonicorum conf.

2nd column:
Petrus abbas sancti Petri conf.
Petrus prior conf.
Iohannes Spora conf.
Gonzalvus conf.
Petrus Villanus conf.
Et omnis conventus monacorum conf.

3rd column:
Qui presentes fuerunt et audierunt.
Iohannes episcopus Legionensis.
Wilelmus archidiaconus.
Thomas archidiaconus.
Petrus archidiaconus.
Veremudus Didaci et ceteri canonici Legionenses.

Beneath the colums:
Hec conveniencia tali conditione facta est! ut monachi nullatenus deinceps parrochianos predicte ville! promissione vel precio sibi attrahere presumant.

XIII

Esteban, bishop of Zamora, licences the building of a church by Pedro

Díaz and other merchants of Zamora to serve the hospital they have founded for the poor, and lays down regulations concerning its incumbent and endowments, 29 April 1167.

AC Zamora, leg. 13 (= D-3), no. 26. Original, 45 cm × 18 cm. Lower half of a polled chirograph. Clear, rather elaborate *francesa* charterhand, somewhat similar to that characteristic of the royal chancery of León.

In nomine sancte et individue Trinitatis. Ego Stefanus Zamorensis episcopus.vobis Petro Didaci et ceteris mercatoribus zamorensibus. pro Dei amore ad relevandam pauperum inopiam.et divine miserationis beneficium promerendum. / in domo illa quam ad usus pauperum Christi iuxta pontem novum hedificastis ecclesiam construere.et in eadem clericum statuere. concedo. Hoc videlicet modo.ut clericus qui in ipsa ecclesia cantare debuerit.sit bone vite et / honeste conversationis. qui semper ingrediatur per manum et voluntatem zamorensis episcopi. et eius semper teneat obedientiam. Sit autem ipsa ecclesia contenta helemosinis quas ipsi mercatores vel alii boni viri aut bone femine de suo / proprio ad usus pauperum ibi dare voluerint. Decimas seu primicias ad alias ecclesias pertinentes. minime recipait.nec eis in aliquo noceat. Ecclesia quoque Sepulchri Domini que iuxta est.sua auferendo non molestet. Que omnia nisi / iuste observaverit.ab episcopo supradicto proprie subversionis periculum incurrat.si tamen quod absit iusticie exinde stare neglexerit. Si vero aliqui populatores sub nomine ipsius ecclesie sancti Iuliani de novo ibi populare voluerint. / et ab ipsis vel ab aliis sine dampno aliarum ecclesiarum decimas vel primicias adquisierit.tercia pars ipsarum decimarum ac primiciarum absque omni diminutione iamdicto detur episcopo. Facta carta tertio Kalendas Maii / sub Era Mᵃ.CCᵃ.Vᵃ. REGNANTE REGE FERNANDO./ Archipresbiter W.conf. Pelagius Francie conf. Domnus W.conf. Petrus Franciscale conf. Petrus Christoforiz conf. Pelagius Gunzalviz conf. Abbas Fernandus Micaheliz conf. Abbas W.conf. Petro Dominico conf./ Abbas Menendus conf. Laurencius conf. Salvator Petriz conf. Salvador Ramiriz conf. Munio Sendiniz conf. Petro Salvadorez conf. Fernandus Stefaniz conf. Pelagius Pelaiz conf. Elias conf./ Petrus Petriz conf. Romanus Petriz conf. Didagus Romaniz conf. Xemenus Caiata conf. Romanus Sesnandiz conf. Romanus Rauperiz conf. Pelagio Tedoniz conf. Pelagio Iohannis conf. Petro Didaz conf. / Eliam notuit.

XIV

Agreement between Esteban, bishop of Zamora and the *concejo* of Sta. Eulalia over the appointment of chaplains in the church of Sta. Eulalia and over the custody of its movable endowments, 19 July 1170.

AC Zamora, leg. 13 (= D-3), no. 4. Original, 46 cm × 28 cm. Half of a polled chirograph. The script is a formal and elaborate *francesa.*

Rerum omnium munimenta maiorem sui procul dubio obtinent certitudinem. si scriptis veridicis.testibusque legitimis.firmata esse dinoscantur. Proinde notum / fieri volumus.ego Stefanus Dei permissu Zamorensis episcopus.omnisque sancti Salvatoris conventus.Helias videlicet archidiaconus.W.decanus.ceterique eiusdem ecclesie can / onici.tam presentibus quam futuris in perpetuum.talem nos concordiam fecisse cum concilio sancte Eulalie.super ordinatione ipsius ecclesie.ut nos inibi unum / capellanum vel duos.qui grati sint concilio ponamus. Volumus insuper ut thesaurum ipsius ecclesie ad honorem Dei et salutem animarum suarum concilium / fideliter custodiat. Ita tamen ut absque consilio nostro donandi vel vendendi potestatem minime habeat. Statuimus etiam ut vel nobis vel successoribus nostris./ thesaurum illius ecclesie absque eorum consilio quoquo modo diminuere minime liceat. Ut autem hec firma illibataque permaneant.kartulam istam ad noticiam posterorum / conscribi voluimus. Actum est hoc apud Zemoram. XIIII.º kalendas Agusti. (sic) ERA.Mª CCª VIIIª Regnante in Legione rege F. Sub potestate illius regente Zamoram Fernando / Roderici. Ego Stefanus Zamorensis episcopus.kartulam istam episcopali auctoritate roboro. propriaque manu subscribo. Viderunt et audierunt hec. Petro Salvadoriz conf. Don Matheus conf. Iohanne Iulianiz conf. Don Gil conf. Salvador Salvadoriz conf. Domingo Stefaniz conf. Fernando Petriz conf. Menendo Monuz conf. Menendo Gutteriz conf. Salvador Crespo conf. Petro Cidiz conf. Cidi Cidiz conf. Petro Cidiz conf. Cidi Vermuniz conf. Petro Mauro conf. Petro Salvadoriz de Flores conf. Anaia Isidriz conf. Iohanne Petriz conf. Petro Alfonso conf. Petro Ramon conf. Fernando Fernandiz conf. Monio Pelaiz conf. Velaso (sic) Vermuniz conf. Fernando Cidiz conf. Fernando Vermuniz conf. Petro Iohannis conf. Don Rodrigo conf. Roman Petriz conf. Iohanne Pelaiz conf. Iohanne Gonsendiz conf. Pelagio Pelaiz conf. Petro Iohannis conf. Didago Romaniz conf. Fernando Stefaniz conf. Lop Romaniz conf. Iohanne Petriz conf. Petro Guterriz conf. Petro Vermuniz conf. Garcia Garciaz conf. Petro Testa conf. Petro Petriz conf. Roman Sesnandiz conf. Petro Cidiz conf. Roman Petriz conf. Vidales Guterriz conf. Fernando Monuz conf. Petro Velasquiz conf. Iohanne Petriz conf. Anaia Stevaniz conf. Rodrigo Infante conf. Iohanne Fructuoso conf. Xemen Caida conf. Garcia Xemeniz conf. Didago Xemeniz conf. Martin Petriz conf. Pelagio Senleiro conf. Stefan Cidiz conf. Xemen Petriz conf. Roman Rouperiz conf. Salvador Pedrez conf. Don Xaino conf. Velasco Velaz conf. Domengo Domenguiz conf. Didago Petriz conf. Gunzalvo Menendiz conf. Pelagio Canto conf. Arias Centeno conf. Petro Arias conf. Didago Alvarz (sic) conf. Pelai Baldron conf. Iohanne Honoriguiz conf. Petro Lobo conf. Gunzalvo Petriz conf. Petro Falcon conf. Petro Menendiz conf. Betegon conf. Iohanne Campaneiro conf. Tomei Nano conf. Don Nicolao conf. Petro Alvitiz conf. Pro testes. (sic) Xab testis. Cidi testis. Vilidi testis. Pelagius notuit.

XV

Pedro Suárez de Deza, archbishop of Santiago de Compostela, acting as a papal judge-delegate, decides the boundary dispute between the dioceses of Salamanca and Ciudad Rodrigo, 14 January 1174.

AC Salamanca, no. 61. Original, 26 cm × 46 cm. The document is authenticated in four ways.

1. By the autograph subscriptions of the archbishop and many, though not all, of the witnesses.
2. By chirograph; the parchment forms the lower half of a polled chirograph.
3. By the archbishop's *rota*.
4. By the archbishop's seal; pendent from cords of red and yellow silk, wax seal, one-sided, oval in shape; the device, a figure of an archbishop with pastoral staff in his left hand, with the legend 'PETRVS COM(POST) ELLANVS ARCHIEPS III'.

The script is a neat *francesa*, similar to that used in the Leonese royal chancery at the time. This document has twice previously been edited, most recently by F. Fita, *BRAH* lxii (1913), 145–8.

PETRUS Dei dignatione sancte Compostellane metropolis humilis minister. dilectis fratribus.M.Salamantino decano.et.A.ecclesie Civitatis Roderici priori.atque universis ecclesie utriusque capitulis. salutem et debitam in Christo dilectionem. Ex iniuncto parvitati nostre / archiepiscopatus officio. tenemur ecclesiis nobis commissis pacem querere.et discordantes ad concordiam revocare. Eapropter ecclesiarum vestrarum diuturnam fatigationem.et laborem importabilem.super causa que inter vos de terminis vertebatur attendentes. libenti animo / assensum nostrum et studium illi impendimus transactioni.que inter vos de utriusque partis beneplacito celebrata est. Videlicet ut inter fluvios qui dicuntur Heltes et Opera. ville que quasi in communi limite Salamantice et Civitatis Roderici hinc inde site sunt. / secundum ius diocesanum ab utraque ecclesia pro indiviso possideantur. Et ecclesie que in fine termini Salamantice ab antiquo constructe sunt.contra quas ville alie in fine termini Civitatis Roderici de novo surrexerunt. videlicet Aguseio. Sotel de Leon.Sotel de Arrago. Cabreias. / et Bovadella. tam iste quam que infra earum terminos de cetero constituentur ecclesie.communiter ab utraque possideantur ecclesia imperpetuum.et fructus ex equo dividantur. Ita quod si Salamantinus episcopus vel eius minister.in aliqua earum clericum voluerit instituere. / non ante eius administrationem recipiat. quam episcopo Civitatis Roderici. vel eius vicario eat obedientiam promittere. Et ex altera parte similiter fiat. Interdictum. suspensionem.vel excommunicationem quam unius partis prelatus fecerit. alter non solvat.et quem / unus deposuerit. alter non restituat.sed siquid super hoc questionis habuerit. ad superiorem iudicem referat. Uno anno oleum et crisma ab una ecclesia recipiant. altero ab altera. semper vicissim. Ecclesiarum dedicationes.et clericorum ordinati / ones.ab uno cum alterius conscientia salvo eius iure celebrentur. Et christianissimus rex domnus.FERNANDUS. qui huic paci studiosam adhibuit devotionem. in recompensatione laboris et fatigationis vestre fratres Salamantini. de regalibus / suis duas villas dedit ecclesie vestre in ripa fluminis Tormes.scilicet Balneos et Iusuadem. Et vos adrenunciastis illi questioni.quam habebatis adversus predictam ecclesiam Civitatis Roderici.de diocesi eius cum omnibus terminis suis / quam dicebatis ad ecclesiam vestram pertinere.ut de cetero non impediatur propter causam vestram illa ecclesia pastore proprio decorari. Nequis igitur contra hanc tam concordem et ecclesie utrique necessariam pacis compositionem venire presumat. nos eam / auctoritate nobis ab apostolica sede concessa confirmamus. et sigilli nostri impressione munivimus.

+ Ego Petrus sancte Compostellane metropolis minister subscripsi.

1st column:
+ Ego M.decanus Salamantinus subscripsi.
+ Ego C.Albensis archidiaconus subscripsi.
+ Ego A.archidiaconus Ledesme subscripsi.
+ Ego P.magister scolarum subscripsi.
+ Ego J.canonicus subscripsi.
+ Ego M.capellanus subscripsi.
+ Ego P.canonicus subscripsi.
+ Ego Didacus canonicus subscripsi.
+ Ego W.canonicus subscripsi.
+ Ego M.canonicus subscripsi.
+ Ego J.canonicus subscripsi.
+ Ego B.canonicus subscripsi.

2nd column:
+ Ego Vilielmus Salamantinus archidiaconus subscripsi.
+ Ego X.^{o} cantor subscripsi.
+ Ego W.tesaurarius subscripsi.
+ Ego O.canonicus subscripsi.
+ Ego G.canonicus subscripsi.
+ Ego F.canonicus subscripsi.
+ Ego B.canonicus subscripsi.
+ Ego A.canonicus subscripsi.
+ Ego M.canonicus subscripsi.
+ Ego W.canonicus subscripsi.

3rd column:
(*This contains the archbishop's rota, beneath his subscription*).

4th column:
+ Ego A.prior Civitatis Roderici subscripsi.
+ Ego J.archidiaconus subscripsi.
+ Ego Cornelius canonicus subscripsi.
+ Ego J.cantor subscripsi.
+ Ego J.archipresbyter subscripsi.
+ Ego P.canonicus subscripsi.
+ Ego I.canonicus subscripsi.
+ Ego J.canonicus subscripsi.

Dat'.Salamantice.XVIIII.Kalendas Februarii.ERA.I^{a}.CC^{a}.^{XII}
Archiepiscopatus autem domni Petri.III.anno primo.

XVI

Pedro Suárez de Deza, archbishop of Santiago de Compostela, announces to the chapters of Salamanca and Ciudad Rodrigo that he will retain in his own hands for an indefinite period certain of the territories disputed between them, 14 January 1174.

AC Salamanca, no. 62. Original, 21 cm × 16 cm. The document is authenticated in three ways.
1. By the autograph subscriptions of all the witnesses.
2. By chirograph; the document forms the upper half of a polled chirograph.
3. By the archbishop's seal, as in no. XV above.

This act was not written by the scribe of no. 7, though these two documents were issued on the same day and by the same archbishop: the script is *francesa*, but with some slight remnants of Visigothic elements —e.g., in the form of the 's'—and is much less neat.

Petrus Dei dignatione sancte Compostellane metropolis humilis minister. dilectis fratribus.M.Salamantino decano. et.A.Civitatis Roderici priori./ atque universis utriusque ecclesie capitulis.salutem et debitam in Christo dilectionem. In transactione que super causa que inter vos de terminis vertebatur. / concorditer est celebrata.dominus rex.F.intuitu laboris et fatigationis vestre fratres Salamantini.de regalibus suis duas villas ecclesie vestre heredita / rio iure possidendas assignavit.scilicet Balneos et Iusuadum. quas quia detentat adhuc Michael Sesmiri.et ab eo sunt redimende.ego de / assensu vestro fratres de Civitate Roderici. retinui totum terminum illum diocesanum.qui est a terminis Salamantice usque ad fluvium Eltem. / ut ego instituam ibi archipresbiterum qui mihi tamen teneatur.et ego tenear ecclesie Salamantine fructus inde provenientes in renpensatione (*sic*) fruc / tuum predictarum villarum persolvere.quousque eidem ecclesie predicte ville libere conferantur.quibus collatis.predictus terminus ad ecclesiam vestram sicut in / scripto transactionis resonat. revertatur. Interim tamen ville que per transactionis formam secundum ius diocesanum pro indiviso debent possideri. / videlicet Agusejo.Sotel de Leon.et Sotel de Arrago. Caprejas.et Bovadela.nicholiminus ab ecclesia Salamantina et archipresbitero nostro.modo / statuto teneantur. Si autem predicte ville tempore nostro redempte non fuerint. vos fratres de Civitate Roderici. successoribus nostris predicto modo / teneamini.et vobis fratres Salamantini.successores nostri predictam pignoris rationem predicto modo ŏbservaturi succedant. Dat'.Salamantice.

1st column:
+ Ego M.decanus subscripsi.
+ Ego X.⁰ cantor subscripsi.
+ Ego P.magister scolarum subscripsi.
+ Ego Didacus canonicus subscripsi.
+ Ego W.canonicus subscripsi.
+ Ego M.capellanus subscripsi.

+ Ego I.canonicus subscripsi.
+ Ego G.canonicus subscripsi.

2nd column:
+ Ego A.prior subscripsi.
+ Ego I.archidiaconus subscripsi.
+ Ego I.cantor subscripsi.
+ Ego I.archipresbiter subscripsi.
+ Ego P.canonicus subscripsi.
+ Ego Isidorus canonicus subscripsi.
Dat'.Salamantice.XVIIII.Kalendas Februarii.Era.I^a.CC^a.XII^a. Archie-
piscopatus autem domini Petri.III.anno primo.

XVII

Vidal, bishop of Salamanca, grants the church of San Bartolomé to
Berengar, who has built it with the consent of Pedro Suárez, archbishop
of Compostela, and his two sons, 16 June 1181.

AC Salamanca, no. 78. Original, 32 cm × 32 cm. Half of a polled chirograph. Originally sealed in two places: to the left—presumably for the
episcopal seal—only the leather tags remain from which the seal de-
pended; to the right, the capitular seal remains; wax seal, one-sided,
oval in shape, pendent on leather tags; the device on the seal is the
Virgin with hands open to receive the Child, and the legend 'SIGILLVM
SALAMANTINI CAPITVLI'. On this seal see M. Gómez Moreno,
'Sellos cereos salmantinos', *Revista de Archivos, Bibliotecas y Museos*
x (1904), 51–2. The document is written in a neat and rather elaborate
charter-hand. There is a second 'original' of this document in AHN
902/16.

In nomine sancte et individue Trinitatis. Ego Vitalis Dei dignatione
Salamantine sedis humilis minister rogatu domini regis una / cum
consensu nostrorum canonicorum tibi Berengario et filiis tuis.R.et.M.
super illa ecclesia sancti Bartolomei quam consensu predecessoris nostri.
P.Compostellani archiepiscopi honorifice construxisti.cartam facio
donationis et libertatis in perpetuum valituram.eo pacto ut in signum
obedientie / annuatim ecclesie Salamantine unum aureum persolvatis.
Si autem ibi parrochiani extiterint.et eorum decime et primicie
servientibus ibi Deo / habite fuerint. III.aurei absque ulla contradictione
per singulos annos persolvantur.et si tota villa posita sub interdicto
fuerit.idem interdictum / quicumque ibi celebraverit modis omnibus
observet. nec excommunicatos nec nominatim interdictos presumat
aliquo modo ibidem recipere. Si vero tu vel / filii tui predictam
ecclesiam religioni donare volueritis.liberam habeatis potestatem in
illam cononicos de novo constituendi.et in eam / mittendi tam vos
quam successores vestri qui ibi Deo canonice servierint ita quod
canonici illius ecclesie nullis aliis monasteriis obedientes sint.set tam /
ipsi quam ecclesia illorum exempti sint a iurisdictione omnium exceptis
his quos supra memoravimus. Insuper nec episcopus Salamantinus nec

eiusdem ecclesie / canonici.in prefata ecclesia neque in rebus eiusdem ullam habeant potestatem accipiendi vel aufferendi aliquid sine voluntate illius patroni.et ibidem / Deo servientium. nisi tantum prenominatum censum. Siquis de progenie tua vel aliorum hoc nostrum spontaneum factum infringere temptaverit.iram Dei / omnipotentis incurrat.et cum Datan et Abiron quos terra vivos absorbuit. et cum Iuda traditore penas inferi (*sic*) luat.et insuper regie magestati.M.et / episcopo Salamantino alios.M.morabitinos persolvat. Facta karta Medine.XVI.kalendas Iulii. sub.ERA.M.ªCC.ªXVIIII^a Regnante rege.A. / in Castella. Toleto.et Stremadura.Senior in Medina.P.Fernandez.Iudex.M.Moro.Sayon.P. Ferron.

1st column:
Ego Aldfonsus (*sic*) decanus subscribo.
Ego Willelmus archidiaconus subscribo.
Ego Ciprianus archidiaconus subscribo.
Ego Iohannes precentor subscribo.
Ego Willelmus thesaurarius subscribo.
Ego Petrus Franco subscribo.
Ego Iohannes Cormanus subscribo.
Ego Willelmus Ricartus subscribo.

2nd column:
Ego Micahel Sancius subscribo.
Ego Sancius subscribo.
Ego Arnaldus subscribo.
Ego Gomicius subscribo.
Ego Martinus subscribo.
Ego Randulfus subscribo.
Ego Petrus subscribo.
Ego Munio subscribo.

3rd column:
Ego Petrus subscribo.
Ego Bartolomeus subscribo.
Ego Vincenius subscribo.
Ego Bricius subscribo.
Ego Dominicus subscribo.
Ego Blasius subscribo.

XVIII

Manrique, bishop of León, acting as a papal judge-delegate, decides a dispute between Juan Martínez, priest, and Jimeno, clerk, over their rights in the church of Genestal, 18 April 1182.

AC León, no. 1397. Original, 7 cm × 12 cm. Half of an indented chirograph. The script is *francesa*.

Anno ab incarnatione Domini M.º C.º LXXX.º II.º Men / se Aprili XIIII.º Kalendas Maii. Ego Manricus Legionensis / episcopus a domino papa L.III.º iudex delegatus inter Iohannem Mar / tini presbiterum et

Xemenum clericum super ecclesia de Genestal./ auditis utriusque partis allegationibus et attestationibus./ inquisita rei veritate diligenter et cognita. commu / nicato consilio fratrum.talem profero sententiam. videlicet / quod Iohannes Martini habeat in ecclesia de Genestal totam / illam partem quam dederunt ei Iohannes Pelagii.Petrus Bezer / ra. Pelagius Martini. Dominicus Martini. Dominicus Petri. Pelagius Romeo./ cum concessione capituli Astoricensis. et Xemenus habeat illam partem. quam Michael Petri sacerdos tenuit ex parte Fernandi / Xemeni. Addo etiam in sententia.quod Iohannes Martini res / tituat Xemeno.quicquid de decimis per triennium laicali / violentia amisit.

XIX

Rodrigo II, bishop of Lugo, grants the church of San Salvador de *Monseti* to Urraca Adefonsi *in beneficio* for life, making various stipulations about the building and endowment of the church, and receiving her as a *vasalla* of the church of Lugo, 30 September 1182.

AHN 1325G/13. Original, 30 cm X 37 cm. Half of an indented chirograph. Autograph subscriptions and *signa* of all witnesses except the bishop and the dean. The hand is a neat and regular *francesa*. Endorsed in a contemporary hand *Sancti Salvatoris de Monseti*.

Nec iuri nec rationi contrarium invenitur.si a prelatis sancte ecclesie femine vidue et maxime religiose defendantur.et de patrimonio pauperum Christi.in suis necessitatibus / sustinentur. Inde est quod ego Rudericus II.^{us} Dei gratia Lucensis episcopus. cum consensu J.decani et totius capituli.vobis domna Urraca Adefonsi.iusto desiderio vestro faventes.et vestris / iustis petitionibus assensum prebentes.damus in vita vestra ecclesiam nostram sancti Salvatoris de Monseti.et servicialias quas habemus in Uliola.in beneficio.et ad me / liorandum.ut scilicet faciatis ipsam ecclesiam.in qua ad servitium et honorem Dei omnipotentis divina officia a fidelibus celebrentur. Vbi omnes qui adiutorium / dederint.et de suis facultatibus aliquid ministrari fecerint. remissionem peccatorum suorum consequantur. Ita quidem predictam baselicam construatis.quod absidam eius de cesis / et quadratis lapidibus cum portali eius faciatis. Ceteros vero parietes de minutis lapidibus cum calce compositis construatis. sub ea videlicet celeritate.quod a Kalendis / proximi Marcii.usque ad finem trium annorum.predictam ecclesiam totam perficiatis. Circa quam ecclesiam.domum etiam in qua honeste recipiatur Lucensis episcopus cum dio / cesim suam visitaverit.in proxima estate vos promittitis constructuram. Sed si interim vos premori contigerit. tantum de vestris rebus eidem ecclesie relinquatis. unde / idem opus ad quod perficiendum vos tenemini.suficienter possit consummari. Cui ecclesie vos datis in presenti.duas servicialias bonas et populatas nominatas.Villam / Tesam.et Romariz Inferiorem.XII.^{m} vaccas. C.^{m} de capris et ovibus.duo iuga boum. Quoniam sicut eam in presenti de manu et iure nostro accipitis.in vita vestra quiete / possidendam.ita post mortem vestram.predicto modo a nobis et vobis ditata. et populata.sicut eam in presenti recipitis.ad dominium et ius Lucensis ecclesie quiete et sine omni calumpnia / revertatur. Quoniam interim in vita vestra.de his que vobis damus.nobis vel successori nostro.et his quibus ex parte sedis cura ipsius terre commissa fuerit.in iure suo servietis. Quoniam nos / etiam promittimus vobis.tam in his que a nobis recipitis.quam etiam in omnibus aliis vestris rebus et negotiis.consilium. et auxilium.et defensionem. tam nostram quam successorum nostrorum./ Quoniam vos excepto debito religionis vestre.conceditis vos pro vasalla sancte Marie.et nostra. Hec itaque omnia que predicta sunt.sicut statutum est.vobis amodo concedimus et confirmamus./ Et quicumque sive ex parte nostra sive ex parte vestra. contra hoc venire temptaverit. vel infringere voluerit.persolvat parti altaris.C.aureos. et mendacii et levitatis reus / habeatur. Quoniam ego Vrraca Adefonsi recipio a vobis domno R.II.° Lucensi episcopo.cum consensu J.decani.et totius capituli in vita mea ecclesiam vestram sancti Salvatoris de / Mon Seti.et servicialias quas habetis in Uliola.in benefitio et ad meliorandum ut scilicet. . . . (*Urraca recites the terms of the arrangement from her own point of view in the same wording as hitherto*). . . et mendacii et levitatis reus habeatur. ERA M.ᵃ CC.ᵃ XX.ᵃ et quot II.ᵉ Kal.Octobris./ Ego R.II.ᵘˢ Lucensis episcopus hoc scriptum quod fieri iussi propria manu roboro et confirmo./ Iohannes Lucensis decanus conf./

1st column:
Petrus Lucensis cantor ss.
Iohannes Lucensis iudex ss.
Iohannes Lucensis prior ss.
Iohannes tesaurarius ss.

2nd column:
Archidiaconus Suerius ss.

3rd column:
J.archidiaconus ss.
Pelagius Benenatus archidiaconus ss.
Pelagius notuit.

XX

Pedro Suárez de Deza, archbishop of Santiago de Compostela, orders the archdeacon, clergy and people of Plasencia to be obedient to the bishop of Avila, *c*.1188-9.

AHN 18/4 (6), a closely contemporary copy. The text is evidently truncated.

.P.Dei dignatione sancte Compostellane ecclesie archiepiscopus karissimis in Christo filiis.archidiacono et clero. ac populo Placentino salutem in Domino. Preter comune / debitum quo cunctis ecclesie Compostellane filiis per provintiam eius in beatissimi apostoli devotione manentibus tenemur. speciali quodam caritatis vinculo / connectimur vobis.quod tempore nostro pars illa vestre habitationis accrevit intra fines nostros cultui Christianitatis. et velut novelle plantationis gratissi / mum incrementum. inserta est sollicitudini nostre atque dilectioni. Ut fixum nobis sit in corde propositum.quantum cum Deo possumus vestris invigilare / utilitatibus et honori. Significamus autem vobis per alias iam litteras. nos domini pape recepisse mandatum.ut vos monitis nostris induceremus.episcopalia iura / Abulensi episcopo persolvere. quorum possessionem.eius antecessor usque ad exitum vite dinoscitur habuisse. Et nos secundum quod saluti vestre atque utilitati intelle / ximus expedire.diligentius vos monuimus.ut nil contra hec vestra usurparetis auctoritate. Sed siquid amplius curaretis impetrare in bona mansue / tudine.et humili suplicatione.sedis apostolice expectaretis auctoritatem. Sed quia nostra apud vos monita efficatiam nondum obtinuerunt. . .(*The copy ends here*).

XXI

Rodrigo II, bishop of Lugo, grants the church of St. Eusebius to Teresa Peláez, *in prestimonium*, for life, at an annual money rent, 18 January 1189.

AHN 1325H/8. Original, 31 cm × 23 cm. Half of an indented chirograph. Script, an elaborate *francesa* charter-hand.

In Dei nomine. Ego. R. Dei gratia Lucensis episcopus.cum consensu .J.decani totiusque capituli damus in prestimonium vobis dompne. Te / rasie Pelagii ecclesiam sancti Eusebii cum suis pertinentiis. intuitu dilectionis quam novimus erga nostram ecclesiam vos habere. et intuitu / etiam illius beneficii quod nostre contulistis ecclesie. in eo quod ei dedistis iure hereditario inperpetuum possidendam villam que dicitur Paacios de / Maurelos. cum omnibus directis suis.sicut eam in dotem habuistis a viro vestro domno. M.Fernandi. et medietatem de Envoadi. et sex / tam partem de sancto Martino Doscondes. Set tali modo eam vobis damus in prestimonium.ut in vita vestra eam teneatis.et in pace / possideatis.et senper sitis cum ea vassalla fidelis ecclesie Lucensis. senperque vos ipsa pro posse suo cum predicta ecclesia manuteneat et defendat.et persol / vatis singulis annis.X.morabitinos legitimi ponderis nobis vel voci nostre.et quandocumque contigerit nos vel aliquem de nostris canonicis ad / hanc venire ecclesiam.eum recipiatis tamquam ipsius ecclesie dominum.et eum splendide procuretis. Cum autem contigerit vos in fata decedere.nostram nobis ecclesiam / vestro pro posse melioratam.cum omnibus suis directuris in pace resignetis. Quicumque nostrum hoc pactum non compleverit.quantum defuerit in duplum comple / at.et pectet alteri.C.morabitinos. Facta carta sub ERA. M^a.CC^a.XX^a.VII^a et quot XV°.Kal'. Februarii.

Ego R.Lucensis episcopus hoc pactum quod fieri feci propria manu confirmo.
Ego.J.Lucensis decanus conf.
Ego.P.Bermudi (?) Lucensis archidiaconus conf.
Eg.L.Lucensis tesaurarius conf.
Totum capitulum approbat et conf.
Ego.M.Fernandi hoc pactum mee coniugis conf.

Ego.T.Pelagii hoc pactum quod fieri iussi conf.
Et qui presentes fuerunt. Pelagius Munionis.
P. Iohannis.
Arias Iohannis.

XXII

Pedro, bishop of Ciudad Rodrigo, grants houses in Zamora to the monastery of Sobrado, 7 March 1189.

AHN cód. 976B, fol. 29^r. Cartulary copy of the thirteenth century.

Sub Christi nomine. Ego Petrus Dei gratia Civitatensis episcopus dono Deo et monasterio de Superado et vobis domno Fernando loci ipsius abbati et successoribus vestris pro remedio anime mee illas meas domos quas emi in Zamora de abbate de Morerola nomine Gundisalvo et de conventu suo ut eas in perpetuum habeatis. Retineo tamen michi in vita mea integram medietatem usus fructus illarum, post mortem vero meam libere et quiete eas possideatis ab integro cum omni suo usu. Sunt autem predicte domus in burgo Cemore in parrochia sancti Andree iuxta domos monasterii Despina. Facto scripto donationis Nonae Marcii sub era millesima CC^a.XX^a. VII^a, regnante rege domno Adefonso in Legione,Gallecia,Asturiis et Extremadura. Siquis igitur contra hoc pietatis factum venire presumpserit iram Dei omnipotentis incurrat. Iterum atque iterum omnibus innotescere volumus quod ego iamdictus episcopus retineo michi medietatem usus fructus in domibus pretaxatis. Qui presentes fuerunt. W.Cemorensis episcopus conf. Stephanus archidiaconus conf. Magister Pelagius conf. Magister Petrus conf. Rodericus Martini conf. Petrus Adriani conf. Petrus testis. Adefonsus testis. Fernandus testis.Pelagius testis. Ego Petrus Dei gratia Civitatensis episcopus hoc scriptum quod fieri iussi propriis manibus roboro et confirmo. Ego Nuno qui scripsi.

XXIII

Composition between Rodrigo II, bishop of Lugo, and M., abbot of Ribas del Sil, over the disputed right to exact *iantar* from the church of San Juan de Barantes, 17 August 1191.

AHN 1325H/17. Original, 9 cm × 24 cm. Half of an indented chirograph. *Francesa*. Endorsed in a contemporary hand *Karta de prandio de Varantes*.

Era M.^{a}CC.^{a}XX.^{a}VIIII.^{a} et quot XVI.º Kalendas Septembris. Notum / sit omnibus hominibus.tam presentibus quam futuris.quod do / minus R. Lucensis episcopus. et M.abbas sancte Christine / de Ripa de Sil. super questione que inter ipsos ver / tebatur de persolvendo iantar ecclesie sancti Iohannis / de Varantes.quod dominus episcopus iure episcopali in ipsa ecclesia / sancti Iohannis.que ad ipsum abbatem iure fundi spec / tat.querebat.talem fecerunt compositionem / et diffinitionem.scilicet quod ipsa ecclesia sancti Iohan / nis de Varantes.in pace et sine omnis calum / pnie scrupulo.persolvat semper in quolibet / anno ecclesie

sancte Marie de Luco.vel eius episcopo / X.^{em} solidus probate monete.
Et istud fatiendo./ ab hac quatione.de cetero libera sit.et / absoluta.iam
dicta ecclesia sancti Iohannis.

Abbas Samanensis testis.
Abbas de Pinu testis.
Abbas de Sancti Antonini de Tocas testis.
Pelagius Sebastiani notuit.

XXIV

Martín I, bishop of Zamora, makes a grant of tithes to the canons of
San Miguel de Grox, 30 May 1195.

AC Zamora, leg. 12 (= D-2), no. 2. Original, 27 cm × 33 cm. Half of
an indented chirograph. Pierced for sealing at the centre, leather tags
remain, seal missing. The episcopal *signum*, of the type described above,
p. 110, may be autograph. Most of the witnesses subscriptions appear to
be autograph. The script is *francesa*.

In nomine domini nostri Iesu Christi amen. Ego Martinus Dei gracia
Zemorensis episcopus una cum consensu / et voluntate capituli nostri
dono et concedo vobis domno Ysidoro abbati sancti Michaelis de Grou
/ et capitulo eiusdem monasterii necnon et successoribus vestris
canonice instituendis ut habeatis plene / et integre decimas de terris et
vineis quas Matheus mercator dedit vel daturus est vobis ad opus /
capelle sancti Thome Cantuariacensis quam ipse edificavit in Tauro.^{1}
De reliquis vero possessionibus quas / intuitu illius capelle adquisierit.
tertiam partem decimarum ecclesie sancti Salvatoris sicut cetere ecclesie
/ de Tauro persolverint vos absque contradictione cessante omni
privilegio persolvetis.et eam obedienciam et / reverenciam quam alie
ecclesie Zemorensis episcopatus cuiuscumque religionis sint episcopo et
vicariis eius / impendere debent.clerici impredicta (*sic*) capella
deservientes similiter impendent. Facta carta.Era. / millesima. CC.^{a}
XXX.^{a}III.^{a} et quoddum.III.º Kalendas Iunii. /
Ego Martinus Zamorensis confirmo. (*Signum*) Ego Iohannes eiusdem
ecclesie decanus subscribo. /

1st column:
Ego Stephanus Zemorensis archidiaconus subscribo.
Ego Albergans magister scolarum subscribo.
Ego Egas cantor subscribo.
Ego Munio Longus subscribo.
Ego Petrus Garsie subscribo.
Ego magister Martinus subscribo.
Ego Micael Giraldi subscribo.
Ego sacrista Pelagius subscribo.
Ego domnus Pedruche subscribo.
Ego Petrus Ordonii subscribo.
Ego capellanus subscribo (*sic*)
Ego magister Pelagius subscribo.

^{1} This is among the earliest references to the cult of Becket in Spain.

2nd column:
Ego Isidorus abbas sancti Michaelis de Grou confirmo.
Ego frater Martinus prior subscribo.
Ego frater Dominicus subprior subscribo.
Ego frater Andreas subscribo.
Ego frater Pelagius subscribo.
Ego frater Michael subscribo.
Ego frater Dominicus subscribo.

XXV

Martín I, bishop of Zamora, licences the building of a church at *Lacuna Toral*, 8 January 1199.

AC Zamora, leg. 33 (= L–1), no. 2. Original, 37 cm X 20 cm. Lower half of polled chirograph. Turn-up pierced, but seal and cords are missing. The bishop's *signum*, which may be autograph, is of the stylized type described above, ch. 3, p. 110. The subscriptions of some of the witnesses appear to be autograph. The script is a neat *francesa*.

Martinus Dei gratia Zemorensis episcopus dilecto suo Ramiro salutem in Domino. Notum sit omnibus quod de voluntate mea et canonicorum ecclesie mee licencia tibi concessa est edificandi / ecclesiam in loco qui dicitur Lacuna Toral.sub modis in carta pernotatis.videlicet ut ecclesia sancti Salvatoris terciam partem decimarum integre de ea percipiat et / clericus in ea deserviens tibi vel alicui de genere tuo nullum servicium exibeat nisi munus orationum. Ipsam autem terciam que ecclesie nostre debetur pro amore tuo tibi concedimus / ut eam diebus vite tue habeas non ad opus tuum sed ad predicte ecclesie fabricam tuo tempore feliciter consumandam. Te vero sublato de medio Iohannes ecclesie nostre decanus / si supervixerit de concessione quam ei fecimus predictam terciam habeat. et deinceps ad ius ecclesie nostre perpetuo et sine aliqua contradictione pertineat. Facta carta apud Ze / moram. VI.º Idus.Ianuarii. Era.M.^{a} CC.^{a} XXX.^{a} VII^{a} /

1st column:
Ego M.Zamorensis episcopus confirmo. (*Signum*)
Ego Iohannes Zemorensis decanus subscribo.
Ego Stephanus Zemorensis archidiaconus subscribo.
Ego Albergans magister scolarum subscribo.
Ego Pelagius sacrista subscribo.

2nd column:
Ego Iohannes Didaci Zemorensis canonicus subscribo.
Ego Monio Longo Zemorensis canonicus subscribo.
Ego Martin Constanz subscribo.
Ego Petrus Garcie subscribo.
Ego magister Pelagius subscribo.
Ego Mamens subscribo.

3rd column:
Ego magister Rodericus subscribo.

XXVI

Pedro, bishop of Tuy, awards certain rights over the church of Sta. Marina *de Rosal* to the abbot of Oya, after a suit between the latter and the heirs of the church, 30 June 1200.

AHN 1796/4. Original, 13 cm × 11 cm. Leather tags for sealing remain, seal missing. The script is *francesa*, charter-hand.

P. Dei gratia Tudensis sedis episcopus.dilecto in Christo fratri.B.eadem abbati de Oia / omnique eius conventui. salutem in domino. Quoniam in presencia nostra vos vidimus sepe.immo / sepissime.de heredibus ecclesie sancte Marine de Rosal conquerentes.qui quartam partem / ipsius ecclesie vos ut dicebatis violenter vobis retinebant. nos prout ius dictat / primo. et secundo. et tercio conveni sub peremptorio eos citavimus.ut in presentia nostra vel / responsalem sufficientem mitterent. vel die et loco competenti quem eis assig / navimus. comparerent. vobis responsuri et satisfacturi. Et licet ad mandatum / nostrum venire neglexissent. nos tamen habito prudentium virorum consilio. eos / per.XX.dies.et eo amplius.expectavimus. Cumque nec comparuerint in nostra presen / tia nec pro se responsalem sufficientem miserint. nos eos de contumacia condemp / namus.supradictam partem ecclesie super qua eos prepetebatis. auctoritate qua fungimur / vobis in perpetuum adiudicamus. illos autem excommunicantes. qui factum nostrum impe / dire temptaverint. Dat'. Tude.sub era M.ªCC.ªXXX.ª VIII.et quotum pridie / Kalendarum Julii.

XXVII

Martín, bishop of Zamora, rules that the clergy of the town of Zamora are required to provide two priests for service in royal *expeditiones*, but that they are to be paid for in part by the bishop and chapter; undated, but of *c.*1200.

AC Zamora, Libro Negro, fol. 85ʳ. Cartulary copy of the thirteenth century, with explanatory rubric *Quod clerici civitatis debent mittere duos presbiteros in exercitu.* This certainly belongs to the episcopate of Martín I (1193–1217), not Martin II (1217–47): the reference to the Pinhel campaign of 1199 suggests a date soon afterwards (cf. A. Herculano, *História de Portugal* (9th ed., Lisbon, n.d.), III, 243–4) and the names of the three dignitaries mentioned are consistent with a date of *c.*1200.

In nomine Domini nostri Iesu Christi amen. M.Dei gratia Zemorensis episcopus canonicis Salvatoris sancti et universo clero de Zemora et de termino eius, salutem in Domino. Notum facimus tam presentibus quam futuris per presentis pagine seriem quod nos questionem que vertebatur inter canonicos ecclesie nostre et clerum civitatis et termini de Zamora de clericis mittendis ad expeditionem regis, si contingeret populum Zemorensem ibi adesse, semel amicabiliter terminavimus. Accidit autem postea quod predicta questio iam sopita tempore exercitus de Pinel ad dubitabilem contentionem coram nobis rediit, tandem clerici civitatis ad testimonium canonicorum ecclesie nostre decurrentes per J.decanum et E.cantorem et M.magistrum scolarum et M.Longum et per S.huius civitatis archipresbiterum rei veritatem ad certitudinem reduxerunt, videlicet quod ipsi duos ex se perpetuis temporibus ad exercitum regis mittere tenerentur, ita tamen quod de ecclesiis ad nos et ad canonicos nostros in Zemora et eius termino specialiter pertinentibus contributionem expensarum sicut de ceteris percipere debeant. Et ad comprobandam huius facti certitudinem predicti clerici duos ex se scilicet P.Gundisalvi et B.presbiterum ecclesie sancti Petri ad exercitum de Pinel transmiserunt.

XXVIII

Rodrigo II, bishop of Lugo, and Juan, archdeacon of Lugo, acting on the orders of the archbishop of Braga, judge a dispute between Juan Arias, dean of Lugo, and Pedro Ibáñez, deacon, over dues owed from the church of Pedraza, 7 September 1202.

AHN 1326D/3. Original, 14 cm × 19 cm. Pierced for sealing in two places at foot, seals and cords missing. The subscriptions are not in the same hand as the text, but they are not autograph; they are all in the same hand, and were presumably added later. The *signum* is in the same hand as the subscriptions, and it is not clear whose it is meant to be. The script is a rather careless *francesa* bookhand.

Rudericus Dei gratia Lucensis episcopus.et Iohannes eiusdem ecclesie archidiaconus.ad quoscumque lit / tere iste pervenerint.salutem. Notum sit tam presentibus quam futuris.quod nos de mandato / domni Bracarensis archiepiscopi determinavimus negocium quod inter Iohannem Arie Lucensem de / canum et Petrum Iohannis diaconum sancti Laurencii de Pedraza super directis ipsius ecclesie diu / fuerat ventilatum. Auditis etenim allegationibus utriusque.iamdicto clerico dedimus / in mandatis.quod duos modios de tercia iamdicto decano persolvet per quartari / um palatii.et tercium modium de decima per talegam illam per quam vicine / ecclesie illi persolvere consueverunt. vinadariam vero et arietem illi dari / precepimus sicut dare solent ea ecclesie in Lucensi cauto constitute.scili / cet pro vinadaria.III.solidos. pro ariete.I.solidum. et hoc totum iccirco scrip / ture commisimus et sigillis nostris munivimus. ne inde amplius inter eos / vel eorum sequaces ulla questio vel controversia oriatur. Facta carta Luco / sub era Mª.CCª.Xᵉª. et quot VII.Idus Septembris.

Rudericus episcopus Lucensis   Iohannes archidiaconus Lucensis
(*Signum*)
Lupus notarius fuit presens.

XXIX

Martín I, bishop of Zamora, grants a church near Toro which has been built on his orders to Domingo Menéndez for life, and ratifies the arrangements which have been made for its endowment, 1203.

AC Zamora, leg. 13 (= D–3), no. 39. Original, 22 cm X 16 cm. Lower half of a polled chirograph. The bishop's *signum*, which may be autograph, is of the stylized type described above, ch. 3, p. 110. All the witnesses' subscriptions are autograph. The script is a careful *francesa*.

In Dei nomine. Notum sit omnibus presentibus et futuris quod ego M. Dei gratia Zemorensis episcopus una cum / capitulo sancti Salvatoris dono et concedo canonice vobis Dominico Menendi illam ecclesiam quam iussi facere in illa mea / hereditate circa villam Tauri iuxta viam de Puteo Antico.ut vivatis in ea et possideatis eam cum duabus / terciis omnibus diebus vite vestre. Et ego Menendus nutritus ecclesie sancti Salvatoris atque vasallus vester dono / Deo et predicte ecclesie IIII.^{or} aranzadas bone vinee. in loco cognominato Balesteros.et medium quinonem de / azenia quam habeo in Villgraver. ita tamen quod Dominicus Menendi teneat et possideat in vita sua post mor / tem autem suam integre remaneant ecclesie. Et adhuc amplius illas domos quas facio circa populationem vestram / tali convenientia ut ego Menendus et uxor mea Maria Fernandi vivamus in illis domibus omnibus diebus / vite nostre.et post obitum nostrum remaneant libere ecclesie iam dicte. Facta carta ERA.M.^{a} CC.^{a} XXXX.^{a} I.^{a} Reg / nante rege A.cum regina Berengaria in regno suo./
Ego Martinus Zamorensis episcopus confirmo. (*Signum*)

1st column:
Ego Iohannes dechanus subscribo.
Ego M.Longo canonicus subscribo.
Ego A.canonicus subscribo.
Ego Petrus Garcie canonicus subscribo.

2nd column:
Ego E.Zemorensis cantor subscribo.
Ego G.canonicus subscribo.
Ego magister Richardus canonicus subscribo.
Ego magister Bernardus canonicus subscribo.

XXX

Composition between Manrique, bishop of León, and Pedro Monacino over the church of Sta. María del Azogue, in Mayorga, July 1203.

AC León, no. 1428. Original, 24 cm X 19 cm. Half of an indented chirograph. The script is a rather elaborate *francesa* business-hand.

Era M.^{a} CC.^{a} X^e.^{a} I.^{a} et mense Iulio. In Dei nomine. Notum sit tam presentibus quam futuris. quod orta fuit intentio inter Petrum Monacinum. et episcopus dompnum Man / ricum.super ecclesiam sancte Marie del Azogue. que est in Maiorica.et tandem venerunt ad talem conposicionem.quod Petrus Monazino una cum suis pa / rentibus dimittat iam dictam ecclesiam episcopo dompno Manrico.et ecclesie sancte Marie Legionensis.in pace. et episcopus dompnus Manricus dat predictam ecclesiam sancte Marie / del Azogue de Maiorica. in prestimonium et propter amorem Dei.Petro Monazino. ut vivat in illa in omni vita sua.et post obitum suum. teneat eam Iohannes / Martini nepos Iohannis Scribani filius Martini Stephani. et Petrus Monazino vel Iohannes Martini nepos Iohannis Scribani filius Martini Stephani qui ipsam ecclesiam tenuerit. / persolvat singulis annis in festo sancti Martini. II aureos opere sancte Marie pro incenso.et si aliquis supradictam ecclesiam contrariaverit.ecclesie sancte Marie Legionensis sedis./ Petrus Monazino.et Iohannes Martini filius Martini Stephani nepos Iohannis Scribani.tenentur removere eum.et liberare eam.ab omni inquietante. Decetero / episcopus dompnus Manricus. facit mercedem Petro Monacino. pro redempcione anime sue.et quitat se de omnibus rebus.quas adversus eum requirebat.tam / de casis.quam de hereditate.et si predictos morabitinos bonos non dederit ad predictum festum sancti Martini.det IIII.^{or} morabitinos bonos. Siquis igitur hanc cartam infrin / gere temptaverit.sit maledictus et excommunicatus.et vocem huius carte pulsanti CC.morabitinos pectet. et careat voce.et hec carta sit firma.

1st column:
Archidiaconus dompnus Rodericus testis.
Archidiaconus dompnus Pelagius testis.
Archidiaconus dompnus Ysidorus testis.
Dompnus Benedictus Garin testis.

2nd column:
Dompnus Grimaldus iudex testis.
Dompnus Lupus de Ordax testis.
Martinus Calvus testis.
Dompnus Scutarius testis.

3rd column:
Petrus Lambert canonicus.
Dompnus Reimundus canonicus.
Petrus cantor.
Dompnus Florencius.
Martinus Roderici.
Martinus de Cumanes.
Dompnus Gallecus.
Dominicus Tisova.

4th column:
Verzas Bonas conf.
Fernandus Salvatori conf.
Petrus Maiorica conf.
Garcia Iohannis conf.

5th column:
Petrus Gorcha conf.
Ioan Montero conf.
Martin Rocia conf.
Petrus Iuliani conf.

6th column:
Martin Fogaza conf.
Fernandus Micaelis conf.
Guterius Petri conf.
Iohannes Scribani conf.
Petrus Lupi conf.

Beneath columns 3, 4 and 5:
Dompnus Helias. Ioan Rosa. Guterius presbiter. Dominicus Vincencii.

Scribal subscription:
Dominicus notuit. *Beneath this* Iohannes Felix. Petro Anncio.
                                                    Vilielmo de Gofac.

XXXI

Lope, bishop of Astorga, promises an indulgence of forty days to all
those who contribute to the building of the monastery church of
Carracedo. 19 January 1204.

AHD Astorga, Cartulario de Carracedo, fols. 58^V–59^V. A copy of the
seventeenth century. The original was authenticated by a seal since the
copyist noted 'Cayosele el sello'.

Lupus Dei gratia Astoricensis ecclesie episcopus, omnibus Christi
fidelibus per episcopatum suum constitutis ad quos littere iste per-
venerint, salutem et gratiam. Quoniam ut ait apostolus omnes stabimus
ante tribunal Christi recepturi prout gessimus in corpore sive bonum
sive malum, oportet nos diem iudicii extremi beneficiis et elemosinis
ac bonis operibus prevenire, ut dantes temporalia, caduca et transitoria,
eterna premia mereamur adipisci. Eapropter universitati vestre notum
facimus monasterium de Carracedo esse situm in sancto et religioso
loco ubi Dei gratia largiente tam divitibus quam pauperibus quam in
elemosinis multa beneficia conferuntur. In quo quedam ecclesia ad
honorem beate Marie semper virginis lapide (*sic*) opere construitur ut in
ea tantum collegium Deo et matri sue possit honorabilius deservire.
Verum quia predictum monasterium plus habundat religionis devotione
sincera quam pecunia vel divitiis temporalibus, sine vestro auxilio et
aliorum fidelium subsidiis inceptum opus potest nullatenus consummari.
Vestram igitur caritatem monemus et exhortamur in Domino, atque
in remissionem peccatorum vestrorum vobis iniungimus quatenus de
bonis temporalibus vobis a Deo collatis operi predicte ecclesie vestras
elemosinas conferatis. Omnibus igitur qui per modum sue possibilitatis
predicto operi aliquid dederint vel cum bobus suis vel cum curru vel
operario in calce vel lapidibus portando vel extrahendis aliquod subsi-
dium prestiterint, quadraginta dies de injuncta sibi legitime penitentia

misericorditer relevamus. Qui autem portatorem ipsarum litterarum benigne et caritative receperit predicte indulgentie particeps fiat. Et qui ei malum vel aliquod impedimentum fecerit, indignatione Dei et beate Marie semper virginis se noverit incursurum. Astorice, Era M.CC. quadragesima secunda, XIIII Kalendas Februarii.

XXXII

Pedro Suárez de Deza, archbishop of Santiago de Compostela, grants to bishop Pedro and the church of Tuy a one-third part of the *votos de Santiago* due from the diocese of Tuy, 16 November 1204.

AC Tuy 10/21. Original. Authenticated in three ways.
1. By autograph subscriptions; presumably the *signa* are also autograph.
2. By chirograph; the document forms the right-hand side of an indented chirograph.
3. By seals; the turn-up is pierced for sealing in four places, two beneath each column of witnesses; cords and seals missing.

The script is a characteristically Compostellan *francesa*, and—as we should expect from the scribal subscription—is strikingly like that of Lope Arias himself.

In nomine domini nostri Iesu Christi. Notum sit universis quod ego Petrus Compostellanus archiepiscopus.III.^{us} et eiusdem ecclesie capitulum atten / dentes sollicitudinem episcopi Tudensis et ecclesie sue nobis esse necessariam in colligendis votis que in episcopatu Tudensi ad ecclesiam sancti Iacobi perti / nere dinoscitur eorundem votorum. terciam partem concedimus predicto episcopo Tudensi et eius ecclesie. exceptis votis de Novua.que integre nobis re / tinemus.ita quod utraque ecclesia auxilium suum fideliter prestet adipisci vota fideliter persolvenda nec una sine altera de his que supradiximus / dividenda. aliquid recipiat. quod cum altera non dividat.sed fideliter per ministros utriusque ecclesie colligantur. et collecta. ut dictum / est fideliter dividantur. et utraque ecclesia tam per prelatum suum quam per capitulum fideliter promittit. quod conventionem istam fideliter et irre / fragabiliter in perpetuum conservabit. Et nos Petrus Tudensis episcopus.et eiusdem ecclesie capitulum firmiter nos obligamus quod sollicitudinem / et diligentiam adhibeamus tam per ecclesiasticam districtionem quam modis omnibus quibus commode fieri potuerit quod vota ipsa / ecclesie Compostellane ac nostre cum debita integritate persolvantur.

1st column:
Ego Petrus Compostellanus archiepiscopus subscripsi.
Ego Fernandus Compostellanus decanus subscripsi.
Ego Petrus Munionis Compostellanus archidiaconus subscripsi.
Ego Petrus Cantel Compostellanus archidiaconus subscripsi.
Ego Adam Compostellanus archidiaconus subscripsi.
Ego Iohannes Cresconii archidiaconus Compostellanus subscripsi.
Ego Martinus Iohannis magister scolarum subscripsi.
Ego Petrus Nunonis cardinalis subscripsi.

Ego Iohannes Pelagii iudex subscripsi.
Ego Martinus Petri canonicus subscripsi.
Ego Ebrardus Iohannis canonicus subscripsi.
Ego Eleazar canonicus confirmo et subscripsi.
Ego Petrus Eugerii Compostellanus canonicus subscripsi.

2nd column:
Ego Petrus Tudensis episcopus. (*Signum, in shape of a fish.*)
Ego Suerius Tudensis decanus confirmo.
Ego Iohannes Tudensis cantor. (*Signum*)
Ego Iohannes canonicus Tudensis confirmo.
Ego Iohannes archidiaconus Tudensis confirmo.
Ego Alfonsus Petri Tudensis archidiaconus subscripsi.

Beneath the columns.
Ego Lupus Arie Compostellanus publicus notarius et iuratus subscripsi.
Ego Pelagius Martini clericus de mandato magistri mei domni Lupi Arie
Compostellani notarii scripsi.sub die. XVI.° Kalendas.Decembris.ERA.
M.ªCC.ªҖ.ªII.ª

XXXIII

Agreement between Martín I, bishop of Zamora, and the Hospitallers
over episcopal rights in certain churches belonging to the latter in the
valley of the Guareña, June 1208.

AC Zamora, leg. 13 (= D-3), no. 13. Original, 60 cm × 31 cm. Authenticated in three ways.
1. All the subscriptions are autograph; episcopal *signum* of stylized
   type described above, p. 110.
2. The document forms the lower half of an indented chirograph.
3. By the seals of the Hospitallers, of the bishop, and of the dean and
   chapter of Zamora. The episcopal seal is pendent from leather tags,
   wax, oval and one-sided; a bishop in pontificals, pastoral staff in the
   left hand, the right hand raised in blessing, with the legend
   'SIGILLVM MARTINI ZEMORENSIS EPISCOPI'; remains of a
   seal-bag.
The script is a large, clear *francesa*.

In nomine domini nostri Iesu Christi amen. Hac presenti scriptura
notum sit omnibus tam presentibus quam futuris quod super controversia que vertebatur inter.M.Dei gratia episcopum.et capitulum
Zemorensis ecclesie ex una parte. et Xemenum / de la Vacca maiorem
commendatorem Hospithalis Ierosolimitani citra mare.et Munionem
Sancii maiorem commendatorem in regno Legionensi.et alios fratres
eiusdem Hospithalis ex altera.super procurationibus quas ratione vi /
sitationum exigebat idem episcopus ab ecclesiis quas habent idem
fratres in valle Garone.mediantibus.J.decano. et.E.cantore Zemorensi-
bus.pro ecclesia Zemorensi.et.M.Sancii maiori commendatore in regno
Legionensi.et Fernando / Sancii commendatore in Ponte de Orvego.de
voluntate et mandato prefati Xemeni de la Vacca.habito apud Fresnum

ubi eo anno celebratum fuit generale capitulum pro bono pacis talis conveniencia et concordia inter / cessit. videlicet quod prefatus episcopus si ei placuerit singulis annis visitet ecclesias de valle Garone.et recipiatur in quatuor villis eiusdem vallis.scilicet Boveda. et Fonte de Penna. et Ordenio.et in Villa Scusa.et frater vel fratres qui in / Boveda pro tempore baliam tenuerint. procurent episcopum honorifice una die in domo Hospithalis. Et si populus eiusdem loci voluerit quod episcopus sequenti die ibi remaneat ad crismandum vel alia Cristianitatis misteria exhibenda. placeat fratri / vel fratribus qui pro tempore ut dictum est ibi fuerint.quod ab ipso populo procurationem recipiat. Si vero populo non placuerit quod ibi remaneat. sequenti die proficiscatus (sic) ad aliam villam de prefatis quatuor.et similiter ut dictum est.de Boveda / una die procuretur ibi a fratribus. et sequenti die a populo.si populus eum ibi fecerit remanere. Simili modo recepiatur episcopus in aliis duabus villis scilicet Ordenio. et Villa Scusa.et eodem modo procuretur a fratribus et a populo ut dictum est in premissis. / Alie vero quatuor ville scilicet Vaello.Castrello.Canizal.Balessa.que pauperes sunt et insufficientes ad singulares procurationes episcopo exhibendas adiungantur prefatis quatuor in adiutorium. De villa que dicitur Ulmus. ita / convenit.quod si divina gratia in tantum excreverit quod equivaleat alicui de numero illarum.IIII.^{or} in quibus episcopus est recipiendus. simili modo recipiatur ibidem. Episcopus vero dum prefatas ecclesias visitaverit. ultra viginti equitaturas / non ducat in suo comitatu.si autem plures duxerit. non teneantur fratres pluribus quam viginti ministrare annonam. Omnibus aliis litteris et instrumentis que de consensu episcopi et fratrum ad decidendam prefatam controversiam / formata vel scripta fuerunt.quasatis et in irritum redactis. hec sola carta valeat in perpetuum. Illud autem instrumentum quod factum fuit inter sepedictos fratres.et ecclesiam Zemorensem super terciariis et decimis ecclesia / rum de Valle Garone valeat in perpetuum.et maneat in robore suo. Facta carta mense Iunii.sub ERA.M.^{a}CC.^{a} XL.^{a}VI.^{a}

Ego.M.Cemorensis episcopus confirmo. (Signum)
Ego.J.Cemorensis decanus confirmo.
Ego.S.Zemorensis archidiaconus confirmo.
Ego.Mames Zemorensis ecclesie magister scolarum confirmo.
Ego.P.sacrista sancti Salvatoris Zemorensis confirmo.
Ego.E.cantor Zamorensis confirmo.

XXXIV

Martín I, bishop of Zamora, grants the right to retain a chaplain in the church of San Juan de Monzón to the brothers Velasco, 1208.

AC Zamora leg. 14 (= D–4), no. 26. Original, 23 cm X 14 cm. Lower half of polled chirograph, hempen cord remaining in turn-up, seal missing. There are copies of this document in AC Zamora, Libro Negro fol. 65^{r} and Libro Blanco fol. 120^{r}.

M. Dei gratia Zamorensis episcopus omnibus presens scriptum videntibus.

salutem in Domino. Notum sit omnibus / quod ego mando et concedo. P.Velasci.et Monioni.Velasci fratri eius quod habeant capellanum in ecclesia sancti / Iohannis de Monzon qui ibi celebret divinum officium. et ipsa ecclesia persolvat singulis annis Zamorensi episcopo / unam faneigam tritici et aliam centeni et aliam ordei ad mensuram Zamore. salvis etiam omnibus aliis direc / turis.quas alie ecclesie episcopatus Zamorensis ecclesie facere consueverunt.et hoc si quid ecclesia pati possit. Dat'. apud Fradexas sub era M.ª CC.ª XL.ª VI.ª

MANUSCRIPTS AND BOOKS CONSULTED

I MANUSCRIPT SOURCES
II PRINTED PRIMARY SOURCES
III SECONDARY AUTHORITIES

I. MANUSCRIPT SOURCES

Archives and libraries which have furnished me with materials are listed here by place, and in alphabetical order. Where published catalogues or guides exist, they have been noted here, rather than in the third section of this bibliographical note.

Astorga
  Archivo Histórico Diocesano,
    (i) Cámara Episcopal
    (ii) Cartulario de Carracedo
    (iii) Tumbo del Fray Lorenzo de Nogales
    (iv) Tumbo de San Pedro de Montes. (An edition of this cartulary has been published recently; see below, 'Printed Primary Sources'.)
  The papal bulls in this archive have been catalogued by A. Quintana Prieto, 'Registro de documentos pontificios de Astorga (1139–1413)', *Anthologica Annua* xi (1963), 189–226.

Avila
  Archivo de la Catedral
  A guide to the contents of the archive is given by G. Ajo, *Avila: Fuentes y Archivos* (Madrid, 1962).

Braga
  Arquivo Distrital
    (i) Liber Fidei Sanctae Bracarensis Ecclesiae. (An edition of this cathedral cartulary is in hand, of which so far one volume has been published; see below, 'Printed Primary Sources'.)
    (ii) Gaveta dos Arcebispos.

Burgos
  Archivo de la Catedral
  See D. Mansilla Reoyo, *Catálogo Documental de Archivo Catedral de Burgos (804–1416)* (Madrid, 1971).

Corunna
  Archivo Histórico del Reino de Galicia
  A guide to the contents of the archive is given by A. Gil Merino, *Archivo Histórico del Reino de Galicia. Guia del Investigador* (La Coruña, 1968).

León
Archivo de la Catedral
    See Z. García Villada, *Catálogo de los Códices y Documentos de
    la Catedral de León* (Madrid, 1919).
Archivo Histórico Diocesano
    (i) Fondo de Sta. María de Otero de las Dueñas
        See R. Rodríguez, *Catálogo de Documentos del Monasterio de
        Sta. María de Otero de las Dueñas* (León, 1949)
    (ii) Fondo de Sta. María de Gradefes.
Archivo de San Isidoro
    See J. Pérez Llamazares, *Catálogo de los Códices y Documentos
    de la Real Colegiata de San Isidoro de León* (León, 1923).

Lisbon
Arquivo Nacional da Torre do Tombo
    (i) Colecção Especial, Corporações Diversas, Mitra de Braga
    (ii) Colecção Basto, nos. 2 (Livro Santo de Sta. Cruz de Coimbra),
        3 (Livro de D. João Theotonio) and 30 (Tombo de casais e
        propiedades deixadas a Sé de Viseu).
The best short guide to the contents of the archive is contained in
A.H. de Oliveira Marques, *Guia do Estudante de História Medieval
Portuguesa* (Lisbon, n.d., *c.* 1965 ?), at pp. 212–45.

London
British Library
    (i) Add. MS. 20787 (Primera Partida)
    (ii) Add. Ch. 71357 (a royal charter of Alfonso VII)

Lugo
Archivo de la Catedral
    (i) Libro de Privilegios Reales
    (ii) Libro de Bulas Apostólicas
    (iii) Legajos.

Madrid
Archivo Histórico Nacional
    (i) Sección de Clero: documents from the following *carpetas* have
        been cited in the course of this book:

18–19	Avila cathedral
180	Las Huelgas
249	Ibeas de Juarros
494	Cines
497–8	Monfero
512	San Martín Pinario
518–9	San Payo de Antealtares
524	Santiago de Compostela cathedral
526–36	Sobrado
556	Tojos Outos
557	San Antolín de Toques
826	Carbajal

893–902	Sahagún
963	Eslonza
1030	Najera
1064	Valvanera
1067	Chantada
1081	Sta. Eulalia de Devesa
1082	Ferreira de Pallares
1107	Lorenzana
1126–30	Meira
1185	Mondoñedo cathedral
1240–1	Samos
1325C–1326G 1334	} Lugo cathedral
1431	Celanova
1437–38	Melón
1506	Naves
1510–12	Osera
1616	Villanueva de Oscos
1749–51	Armenteira
1794–96	Oya
1857	Poyo
1880	Salamanca cathedral
3017	Toledo cathedral
3536	Montamarta
3548–51	Moreruela
3563	San Martín de Castañeda
3576	Toro
3581	Zamora cathedral

(ii) Sección de Códices: I have cited material from the following collections (in each instance the new numbering is given, i.e., 'signatura B'):

15	Tumbo de Osera
60	Tumbo de Oya
63	Colleción de Documentos del Monasterio de San Martín de Jubia
259	Tumbo de Monfero
324–5	Cartulario de Melón
417	Libro-Tumbo (letra B) de la catedral de Lugo
976–77	Tumbo de Sobrado
988	Becerro segundo de Sahagún
1002	Tumbo de Tojos Outos
1040–41	Libros de Aniversarios de la catedral de Lugo
1043	Tumbo Viejo de la catedral de Lugo
1044	Tumbo del Monasterio de San Salvador de Villanueva de Lorenzana

1197   Colección de Privilegios de la Catedral
                        de Astorga
1439   Tumbo de Caabeiro
The guide to certain of these documents which I have found the
most useful (and the least inaccurate) is L. Sánchez Belda, *Documentos Reales de la Edad Media referentes a Galicia* (Madrid, 1953).

Madrid
Biblioteca Nacional
Material from the following MSS. has been cited:
712   (Privilegios varios de Ciudades, Iglesias y
                        Monasterios)
1358   (Corpus Pelagianum)
4357   (Indice de las Escrituras de la Sta. Iglesia de
                        Astorga)
5928   (Noticias de la Sta. Iglesia de Mondoñedo, 1763)
9194   (Privilegios, donaciones, instrumentos varios)
13123   (Indice de las Reales Donaciones. . .sacados. . .
                        en virtud de la Real Comisión de 30 de junio
                        de 1745)

Madrid
Instituto de Valencia de Don Juan
The Archivo Histórico contains a few twelfth-century charters,
mainly from Galicia.

Mondoñedo
Archivo de la Catedral

Orense
Archivo de la Catedral
  (i) Libros de Privilegios
  (ii) Libros de Escrituras
  (iii) Libro del Obispo y Dignidades
  (iv) Pergaminos Monacales
        See E. Leirós Fernández, *Catálogo de los Pergaminos Mona-
        cales de la Catedral de Orense* (Santiago de Compostela, 1951).
  (v) Códices
        See E. Duro Peña, 'Los códices de la catedral de Orense',
        Hispania Sacra xiv (1961), 185–212.

Oviedo
Archivo de la Catedral
  (i) Pergaminos Sueltos
  (ii) Libro Gótico (or Liber Testamentorum)
All the documents down to the year 1200 have been published by
S. García Larragueta; see below, 'Printed Primary Sources'. For
the period after 1200, see the same author's *Catálogo de los
Pergaminos de la Catedral de Oviedo* (Oviedo, 1957).

Pamplona
Archivo de la Catedral
    See J. Goñi Gaztambide, *Catálogo del Archivo Catedral de Pamplona,* vol. i (829–1500) (Pamplona, 1965).

Pamplona
Archivo General de Navarra

Salamanca
Archivo de la Catedral
Archivo Episcopal
    The documents in both these archives have been catalogued by F. Marcos Rodríguez, *Catálogo de Documentos del Archivo Catedralicio de Salamanca* (Salamanca, 1962).
Archivo del Real Capilla de San Marcos
Biblioteca de la Universidad
    The following MSS. have been consulted:
    1964   (Documentos del Archivo de Husillos)
    2348   (Collectio canonum cui nomen Polycarpus)
    2658   (Historia Compostellana)
    The MSS. in the library have been partially catalogued by F. Marcos Rodríguez, *Los MSS. Pretridentinos Hispanos de Ciencias Sagradas en la Biblioteca Universitaria de Salamanca* (Salamanca, 1971)

Santiago de Compostela
Archivo de la Catedral
    (i) Tumbo A
    (ii) Tumbo B
    (iii) Tumbillo
    (iv) Tumbo de Sta. María de Iria
Archivo de la Universidad
    Fondo de San Martín Pinario. A guide to these documents has been published by M. Lucas Alvarez in the *Boletín de la Universidad de Santiago de Compostela* l–li (1948)
Biblioteca del Seminario
    MS. 72 (a collection of single-sheet charters tied in a bundle)

Segovia
Archivo de la Catedral

Sigüenza
Archivo de la Catedral

Toledo
Archivo de la Catedral

Tuy
Archivo de la Catedral

Zamora
Archivo de la Catedral

Archivo de la Delegación de la Hacienda
There is a useful guide to both these archives by A. Matilla
Tascón, *Guia-Inventario de los Archivos de Zamora y su Provincia* (Madrid, 1964)

II. PRINTED PRIMARY SOURCES

Note: This is not a list of all the works consulted, still less is it a systematic bibliography; its purpose is simply to list the works from which citations have been made in the text.

(a) *Chronicles and other literary sources*
   Anonymous Chronicle of Sahagún, in Escalona, *Sahagún*, pp. 297–365.
   Chronica Adefonsi Imperatoris, ed. L. Sánchez Belda (Madrid, 1950).
   Chronicon Conimbricense, ed. E. Flórez, *ES* xxiii.
   Chronicon Sancti Maxentii Pictavensis, ed. P. Marchegay and E. Mabille (Paris, 1869).
   De Expugnatione Lyxbonensi, ed. C.W. David (New York, 1936).
   Historia Compostellana, ed. E. Flórez, *ES* xx (Madrid, 1765); reprinted 1965).
   Liber Sancti Jacobi, Codex Calixtinus. I have cited book IV from the edition by J. Vielliard, *Le guide du Pèlerin de Saint-Jacques de Compostelle* (4th ed., Mâcon, 1969).
   Lucas of Tuy, *Chronicon Mundi*, ed. A. Schottus, *Hispania Illustrata* iv (Frankfort, 1608).
   Ordericus Vitalis, *The Ecclesiastical History*, vol. ii, ed. M. Chibnall (Oxford, 1969).
   Pelayo of Oviedo, *Crónica del Obispo D. Pelayo*, ed. B. Sánchez Alonso, (Madrid, 1924).
   Rodrigo Ximénez de Rada, *De Rebus Hispaniae*, ed. J. de Lorenzana (Toledo, 1793; rptd Valencia, 1968).
   Sampiro of Astorga, *Sampiro, su Crónica y la Monarquia Leonesa en el Siglo X*, ed. J. Pérez de Urbel (Madrid, 1952).
   Sancti Rudesindi Miracula, ed. A. Herculano, *Portugalliae Monumenta Historica, Scriptores* (Lisbon, 1856), pp. 39–46.

   The best guides to this literature are B. Sánchez Alonso, *Historia de la Historiografía Española*, vol. i (Madrid, 1947), and above all M. C. Díaz y Díaz, *Index Scriptorum Latinorum Medii Aevi Hispanorum* (Madrid, 1959). This is perhaps the most appropriate place to mention the translation of the *Historia Compostellana* by M. Suárez and J. Campelo, *La Compostelana* (Santiago de Compostela, 1950): it contains corrections to Flórez's edition, and very valuable notes.

(b) *Collections of Ecclesiastical Documents*
   These are for the most part editions of monastic or cathedral cartularies and *documentos sueltos*.

Belmonte: *Colección Diplomática del Monasterio de Belmonte*, ed.
               A.C. Floriano (Oviedo, 1960).
Braga: *Liber Fidei Sanctae Bracarensis Ecclesiae*, vol. i, ed. A.
               de J. da Costa (Braga, 1965).
Carboeiro: 'La colección diplomática del monasterio de San
               Lorenzo de Carboeiro', ed. M. Lucas Alvarez, *Compos-
               tellanum* ii–iii (1958–9).
Cluny: *Recueil des chartes de l'abbaye de Cluny*, vol. v, ed. A.
               Bruel (Paris, 1894).
Corias: *El Libro Registro de Corias*, ed. A.C. Floriano (Oviedo,
               1950).
Cornellana: *Colección de Fuentes para la Historia de Asturias:* vol. i,
               Monasterio de Cornellana, ed. A. C. Floriano (Oviedo,
               1949).
Eslonza: *Cartulario del Monasterio de Eslonza*, ed. V. Vignau
               (Madrid, 1885).
Galicia: *Galicia Histórica. Colección Diplomática* (Santiago de
               Compostela, 1901). Various editors contributed to this
               work, among whom the most important was A. López
               Ferreiro.
Jubia: 'La colección diplomática de San Martín de Jubia', ed.
               S. Montero Díaz, *Boletín de la Universidad de Santiago
               de Compostela* vii (1935), 5–156.
Orense: *Colección de Documentos de la Catedral de Orense*
               (Orense, n.d.: about 1916 ?)
Oviedo: *Colección de Documentos de la Catedral de Oviedo* ed.
               S. García Larragueta (Oviedo, 1962).
San Martín de Castañeda: 'El Tumbo del monasterio de San Martín de
               Castañeda', ed. A. Rodríquez González, *Archivos
               Leoneses* xxxix–xl (1966), 181–352.
San Millán de la Cogolla: *Cartulario de San Millán de la Cogolla*, ed. L.
               Serrano (Madrid, 1930).
San Pedro de Montes: *Tumbo Viejo de San Pedro de Montes*, A. Quin-
               tana Prieto (León, 1971).
San Vicente de Oviedo: *Cartulario de San Vicente de Oviedo* ed. L.
               Serrano (Madrid, 1929). Not all the material collected
               by Serrano appears in *Colección Diplomática del Monas-
               terio de San Vicente de Oviedo*, ed. P. Floriano Llorente
               (Oviedo, 1968).
Santiago de Compostela: *Monumentos Antiguos de la Iglesia Compos-
               telana*, ed. F. Fita and A. López Ferreiro, (Madrid,
               1882).
Silos: *Recueil des chartes de l'abbaye de Silos*, ed. M. Férotin
               (Paris, 1897).
Val de Dios: 'Copia del becerro del monasterio de Val de Dios', in
               *Colección de Asturias, reunida por D. Gaspar Melchor
               de Jovellanos*, ed. M. Ballesteros Gaibrois, vol. ii,
               (Madrid, 1948).

Of course, a good many books listed among the secondary sources contain primary material, for example Flórez's *España Sagrada* or Galindo's *Tuy*.

(c) *Papal Documents*

The 'Epistolae Vagantes' *of Gregory VII*, ed. H. E. J. Cowdrey (Oxford, 1972).

Monumenta Hispaniae Vaticana, Registros, vol. i, La Documentación Pontificia hasta Inocencio III, ed. D. Mansilla (Rome, 1955).

Monumenta Hispaniae Vaticana, Registros, vol. ii, *La Documentación Pontificia de Honorio III*, ed. D. Mansilla (Rome, 1965).

Papsturkunden in Portugal, ed. C. Erdmann (Göttingen, 1927).

Regesta Pontificum Romanorum, ed. P. Jaffé, revised by S. Loewenfeld (Leipzig, 1885).

Sacrorum Conciliorum Nova et Amplissima Collectio, ed. J. D. Mansi (Florence, 1759).

Vetera Monumenta contra Schismaticos, ed. S. Tengnagel (Ingoldstadt, 1612).

(d) *Secular Documents and Law-codes*

'Chartes royales léonaises, 912–1037', ed. L. Barrau-Dihigo, *Révue hispanique* x (1903), 350–454.

Colección de Documentos Inéditos del Archivo de la Corona de Aragón, ed. P. de Bofarull y Mascaro (Barcelona, 1847–1910).

Colección de Fueros y Cartas-Pueblas, ed. T. Múñoz y Romero (Madrid, 1847).

Documentos para la Historia de las Instituciones de León y de Castilla (siglos X–XIII), ed. E. de Hinojosa (Madrid, 1919).

Documentos Medievais Portugueses: Documentos Regios, vol. i, ed. R. de Azevedo (Lisbon, 1958).

Fueros Leoneses, ed. F. de Onis (Madrid, 1920).

Las Siete Partidas del Rey D. Alfonso el Sabio, cotejadas con varios códices antiguos, ed. Real Academia de la Historia, 3 vols. (Madrid, 1807).

III. SECONDARY AUTHORITIES

Note: Once again this is no more than a list of works cited.

Andrés, A.,	'Suero, obispo de Coria (1156–1168), *Hispania Sacra* xiii (1960), 397–400.
Antonio, N.,	*Biblioteca Hispana Vetus* (Madrid, 1788).
Arias, P.,	'Don Juan I, abad de Samos y obispo de Lugo', *BCM Lugo* iii (1949), 256–63.
Barrau-Dihigo, L.,	'Étude sur les actes des rois asturiens (718–910)', *Revue hispanique* xlvi (1919), 1–192.
Biggs, A. G.,	*Diego Gelmírez, First Archbishop of Compostela* (Washington, 1949).
Bishko, C. J.,	'Peter the Venerable's journey to Spain', *Studia Anselmiana* xl (1956), 163–75.

Bishko, C. J., 'The Spanish journey of Abbot Ponce of Cluny', *Ricerche di Storia Religiosa* i (1957), 311–19.
'Fernando I y los orígenes de la alianza castellano-leonesa con Cluny', *CHE* xlvii–xlviii (1968), 31–135.

Brandão, A., *Terceira Parte da Monarchia Lusytana* (Lisbon, 1690).

Brooke, C. N. L., and A. Morey *Gilbert Foliot and his Letters* (Cambridge, 1965).

de la Calzada, L., 'La proyección del pensamiento de Gregorio VII en los reinos de Castilla y de León,' *Studi Gregoriani* iii (1948), 1–87.

Cheney, C. R., *English Bishops' Chanceries 1100–1250* (Manchester, 1950).

Cocheril, M., *Études sur le monachisme en Espagne et au Portugal* (Paris-Lisbon, 1966).

de Colmenares, D., *Historia de la Insigne Ciudad de Segovia* (Segovia, 1637).

Conant, K. J., *The Early Architectural History of the Cathedral of Santiago de Compostela* (Cambridge, Mass., 1926).

da Costa, A. de J., *O Bispo D. Pedro e a Organização de Diocese de Braga* (Coimbra, 1959).

David, P., *Études historiques sur la Galice et le Portugal du VIe au XIIe siècles* (Lisbon-Paris, 1947).
'Le pacte successoral entre Raymond de Galice et Henri de Portugal', *Bulletin hispanique* l (1948), 275–90.

Défourneaux, M., *Les Français en Espange aux XIe et XIIe siècles* (Paris, 1949).

Deyermond, A. D., *Epic Poetry and the Clergy: studies on the 'Mocedades de Rodrigo'* (London, 1968).

Dodwell, C. R., *Painting in Europe 800–1200* (Harmondsworth, 1971).

Dorado, B., *Historia de Salamanca* (Salamanca, 1776).

Durán Gudiol, A., *La Iglesia de Aragón durante los reinados de Sancho Ramírez y Pedro I* (Rome, 1962).

Duro Peña, E., 'Las antiguas dignidades de la catedral de Orense', *AEM* i (1964), 289–332.

Eitel, A., 'Rota und Rueda', *Archiv für Urkundenforschung* v (1914), 299–336.

Erdmann, C., *O Papado e Portugal no primeiro Século da História Portuguesa* (Coimbra, 1935).

Escalona, R., *Historia del Real Monasterio de Sahagún* (Madrid, 1782).

Escobar Prieto, E., 'Antigüedad y límites del obispado de Coria', *BRAH* lxi (1912), 314–45.

Fernández
Conde, F. J.,
El Libro de los Testamentos de la Catedral de Oviedo (Rome, 1971).
La Iglesia de Asturias en la Alta Edad Media (Oviedo, 1972).

Fernández
Rodríguez, M.,
'La entrada de los representantes de la burguesía en la curia regia leonesa' *AHDE* xxvi (1956), 757-66.

Fita, F.,
'Bernardo de Périgord arcediano de Toledo y obispo de Zamora', *BRAH* xiv (1889), 456-61.
'Primera legación del cardenal Jacinto en Espana', *BRAH* xiv (1889), 530-55.
'Concilio nacional de Burgos', *BRAH* xlviii (1906), 387-407.
'El concilio nacional de Burgos en 1080: nuevas ilustraciones' *BRAH* xlix (1906), 337-84.
'Texto correcto del concilio de Husillos', *BRAH* li (1907), 410-13.
'El concilio nacional de Valladolid en 1143', *BRAH* lxi (1912), 166-174.
'La diócesis y fuero eclesiástico de Ciudad Rodrigo', *BRAH* lxi (1912), 437-48.
'El Papa Alejandro III y la diócesis de Ciudad Rodrigo', *BRAH* lxii (1913), 142-57.

Fletcher, R. A.
'An *Epistola Formata* from León', *Bulletin of the Institute of Historical Research* xlv (1972), 122-8.
'Obispos olvidados del siglo XII de las diócesis de Mondoñedo y Lugo', *Cuadernos de Estudios Gallegos* xxviii (1973), 318-25.
'Diplomatic and the Cid revisited: the seals and mandates of Alfonso VII', *Journal of Medieval History* ii (1976), 305-37.

Flórez, E.,
Risco, M., et al.
España Sagrada (Madrid, 1747-1879).

Galindo Romeo, P.,
La Diplomática en la Historia Compostelana (Madrid, 1945).
Tuy en la Baja Edad Media (2nd ed., Madrid, 1950).

García Calles, L.,
Doña Sancha, Hermana del Emperador (León-Barcelona, 1972).

García Conde, A.,
'La escuela catedralicia lucense' *BCM Lugo* iii (1949), 214-27.

García y García, A.,
Laurentius Hispanus (Rome-Madrid, 1956).
'Una colección de decretales en Salamanca', *Proceedings of the Second International Congress of Medieval Canon Law*, ed. S. Kuttner and J.J. Ryan (Rome, 1965), pp. 71-92.

Gómez Moreno, M.,
'Sellos cereos salmantinos', *Revista de Archivos, Bibliotecas y Museos* x (1904), 51-2.

González, J., 'El Fuero de Benavente de 1167', *Hispania* ii (1942), 619-26.
Regesta de Fernando II (Madrid, 1943).
'Repoblación de la extremadura leonesa', *Hispania* iii (1943), 195-273.
Alfonso IX de León (Madrid, 1944).
El Reino de Castilla en la Época de Alfonso VIII (Madrid, 1960).

Grassotti, H., *Las Instituciones feudo-vasalláticas en León y Castilla*, Centro Italiano di Studi sull' alto medioevo, no. 4., 2 vols. (Spoleto, 1969).
'Sobre una concesión de Alfonso VII a la iglesia salmantina', *CHE* xlix-l (1969), 323-48.
'Dos problemas de historia castellano-leonesa (siglo XII)', *CHE* xlix-l (1969).

Herculano, A., *História de Portugal* (9th ed., Lisbon, n.d.)

Higounet, C., 'Un mapa de las relaciones monásticas transpirenaicas', *Pirineos* vii (1951), 543-53.

Kehr, P., *Das Papsttum und der katalanische Prinzipät bis zur Vereinigung mit Aragon* (Berlin, 1926).
'El papado y los reinos de Navarra y Aragón hasta mediados del siglo XII', *EEMCA* ii (1946), 74-186.

Kendrick, T. D., *St. James in Spain* (London, 1960).

King, P. D., *Law and Society in the Visigothic Kingdom* (Cambridge, 1972).

Lacarra, J. M., 'Mandatos reales navarro-aragoneses del siglo XII', *EEMCA* ii (1946), 425-31.

Lévi-Provençal, E., *Histoire de l'Espagne Musulmane* (Paris, 1950-5),

Linehan, P. A., *The Spanish Church and the Papacy in the Thirteenth Century* (Cambridge, 1971).

Lomax, D. W., *La Orden de Santiago 1170-1275* (Madrid, 1965).
'Don Ramón, bishop of Palencia (1148-84)' in *Homenaje a Jaime Vicens Vives* I (Barcelona, 1965), pp. 279-91.

López Agurleta, J., *Vida del Venerable Fundador de la Orden de Santiago* (Madrid, 1731).

López Ferreiro, A., *Historia de la S.A.M. Iglesia de Santiago de Compostela* (Santiago de Compostela, 1898-1911).

Lot, F., and R. Fawtier (eds.), *Histoire des institutions françaises au moyen Age*, vol. iii, 'Institutions Ecclesiastiques' (Paris, 1960).

Luchaire, A., *Innocent III: les royautés vassales du Saint-Siège* (Paris, 1908).

Mansilla Reoyo, D., *Iglesia castellano-leonesa y Curia Romana en los Tiempos del Rey San Fernando* (Madrid, 1945).
'Inocencio III y los reinos hispanos', *Anthologica Annua* ii (1954), 9-49.

Mansilla Reoyo, D., 'Disputas diocesanas entre Toledo, Braga y Compostela en los siglos XII al XV', *Anthologica Annua* iii (1955), 89–143.
'La supuesta metrópoli de Oviedo', *Hispania Sacra* viii (1955), 259–74.
'Orígenes de la organización metropolitana en la iglesia española', *Hispania Sacra* xii (1959), 255–91.

Marcos Rodríguez, F., 'Tres manuscritos del siglo XII con colecciones canónicas', *Analecta Sacra Tarraconensia* xxxii (1960), 35–54.

Martín Postigo, M. de la Soterraña, *Alfonso el Batallador y Segovia* (Segovia, 1967).

Martínez Diez, G., 'El Concilio Compostelano del Reinado de Fernando I', *AEM* i (1964), 121–38.

Mattoso, J., *Le Monachisme ibérique et Cluny* (Louvain, 1968).

Menéndez Pidal, R., *La España del Cid* (7th ed., Madrid, 1969).

Millares Carlo, A., 'La cancillería real en León y Castilla hasta fines del reinado de Fernando III', *AHDE* iii (1926), 227–306.

Minguella y Arnedo, T., *Historia de la Diócesis de Sigüenza y de sus Obispos* (Madrid, 1910–13).

O'Callaghan, J. F., 'The foundation of the Order of Alcántara', *Catholic Historical Review* xlvii (1961–2), 471–86.

Pallares y Gaioso, J., *Argos Divina. Sancta Maria de Lugo de los Ojos Grandes* (Santiago de Compostela, 1700).

Pérez de Urbel, J., *Sampiro, su Crónica y la Monarquia leonesa en el siglo X* (Madrid, 1952).

Portela Pazos, S., *Anotaciones al Tumbo A de la catedral de Santiago de Compostela* (Santiago de Compostela, 1949).

Procter, E.S., 'The judicial use of *Pesquisa* in León and Castille 1157–1369', *English Historical Review*, Supplement 2 (1966).

Rassow, P., 'La Cofradía de Belchite', *AHDE* iii (1926), 200–26.
'Die Urkunden Kaiser Alfons' VII von Spanien', *Archiv für Urkundenforschung* x (1928), 328–467 and xi (1930), 66–137.

Reilly, B. F., 'Santiago and Saint Denis: the French presence in eleventh-century Spain', *Catholic Historical Review* liv (1968), 467–83.
'The *Historia Compostelana*: the genesis and composition of a twelfth-century Spanish *gesta*', *Speculum* xliv (1969), 78–85.
'The court bishops of Alfonso VII of León-Castilla, 1147–1157', *Medieval Studies* xxxvi (1974), 67–78.

Rivera Recio, J. F., 'Personajes hispanos asistentes en 1215 al IV Concilio de Letrán', *Hispania Sacra* iv (1951), 335-55. *La Iglesia de Toledo en el siglo XII* (Rome-Madrid, 1966).

Rodríguez López, P., *Episcopologio Asturicense* (Astorga, 1907).

Russell, P. E., 'San Pedro de Cardeña and the heroic history of the Cid', *Medium Aevum* xxvii (1958), 57-79.

Salazar y Castro, L., *Historia Genealógica de la Casa de Lara* (Madrid, 1694-97).

Saltman, A., *Theobald, Archbishop of Canterbury* (London, 1956).

Sánchez Albornoz, C., *Estudios sobre las Instituciones Medievales Españolas* (Mexico City, 1965).

Sánchez Alonso, B., *Historia de la Historiografía Española* (Madrid, 1941).

Sánchez Belda, L., 'En torno de tres diplomas de Alfonso VII', *Hispania* xi (1951), 47-61.

'La cancillería castellana durante el reinado de Doña Urraca', *Estudios dedicados a Ramón Menéndez Pidal* iv (1953), 587-99.

Southern, R. W., *The Making of the Middle Ages* (London, 1953).

Stenton, F. M., 'Acta Episcoporum', *Cambridge Historical Journal* iii (1929), 1-14.

Street, G. E., *Gothic Architecture in Spain* (2nd ed., London, 1869).

Thompson, A. H., 'Diocesan organisation in the Middle Ages: archdeacons and rural deans', *Proceedings of the British Academy* xxix (1943), 153-94.

Trimingham, J. S., *A History of Islam in West Africa* (Oxford, 1962).

Valdeavellano, L. G. De., *Curso de Historia de las Instituciones españolas* (Madrid, 1968).

Valiña Sampedro, E., *El Camino de Santiago.* (Salamanca, 1971).

Vázquez de Parga, L., *La División de Wamba* (Madrid, 1943).

'La revolución comunal de Compostela en los años 1116 y 1117', *AHDE* xvi (1945), 685-703.

Vigil, C. M., *Asturias Monumental* (Oviedo, 1887).

Villanueva, J., *Viaje Literario a las Iglesias de España* (Madrid, 1803-52).

Villar y Macías, M., *Historia de Salamanca* (Salamanca, 1887).

Watt, W. M., *The Influence of Islam on Medieval Europe* (Edinburgh, 1972).

GLOSSARY

aranzada	an areal measure of land, equivalent to 0·447 hectares or a little over one acre.
arenga	the opening preamble of a charter.
aureus	a gold coin assumed to have been imported from Islamic Spain, where such coins were termed *dirhems* or *mithqals*.
carta abierta	a letter-patent.
chirographum	an indenture; hence, any deed recording an agreement between two or more parties.
chrismon	the Chi-Rho monogram which sometimes precedes the opening preamble of a charter.
concejo	the local community assembled to transact business; hence, a village or urban council; Latin, *concilium*.
dispositio	the matter of a charter (as opposed to its formal diplomatic elements).
duplarius	a member of a cathedral chapter who performed, as a substitute, the duties of one of the principal dignitaries.
fonsadera	a money-payment in commutation of military service.
francesa	the post-Carolingian minuscule script of France (as opposed to the Visigothic script of Spain).
fuero de población	charter issued by a lord to a group of settlers, defining rights and obligations: in an urban context a *fuero* means a borough-charter.
iantar	a lord's right to hospitality at the expense of his tenants; a money-payment in lieu thereof.
levita	a deacon.
pesquisador	one commissioned by the king to conduct a royal *pesquisa*, or inquest.
portionarius	a minor canon (?).
prestimonium	a tenancy, fief or benefice.
privilegio rodado	a royal diploma authenticated by the king's *rueda* (q.v.).
repoblación	re-settlement, normally of lands conquered from the Moors.
repoblador	a settler.

rueda a device in the form of two concentric circles containing a legend, derived from the *rota* of the papal chancery, used in Spain for the authentication of certain classes of beneficial document (cf. *privilegio rodado*).

señorío a territorial lordship, its holder normally enjoying certain fiscal and judicial immunities.

signum a written device occurring in various forms (e.g. a monogram, a *rueda*) used for the authentication of documents.

sur double queue sealing on a parchment tag inserted through a slit in a fold at the foot of the document.

sur simple queue sealing on a tongue of parchment cut horizontally at the foot of the document but not severed from it.

tenente the governor of a territory below the crown; the holder of a *prestimonium* (q.v.).

tercia the third part of tithe.

terciarius an episcopal official charged with the duty of collecting the *tercia* (q.v.) due to the bishop.

votos de Santiago an annual render of produce from throughout Christian Spain, claimed by the see of Santiago de Compostela on the authority of documents forged or interpolated *c.* 1140.

votum any form of offering or render.

INDEX

Abd al-Mū'min, Almohade leader, 18
Abd al-Rahman III, Caliph of Córdoba, 4, 6
Abu-Ya'qub Yūsuf, Almohade leader, 19
Afonso Henriques, King of Portugal, 10-11, 16, 20, 35, 52-3, 67, 134, 143, 212, 218
Aimeric, papal chancellor, 216
Alarcos, battle of, 21, 218-19
Albertino de León, 70
Alfonso III, King of Asturias-León, 163, 181
Alfonso VI, King and Emperor of León-Castile, 7-8, 10-16, 30-1, 37, 46, 54, 61, 65, 68-9, 80, 97, 120 n.1, 149, 181, 183, 193, 212
Alfonso VII, King and Emperor of León-Castile, 10-11, 15-17, 19, 26, 31-2, 39-41, 43, 47, 49, 51, 55, 57-8, 63-4, 66, 68, 70, 74-5, 78, 80-1, 83, 97, 102, 106, 111, 115-16, 120, 126-7, 138, 149, 164, 167, 194, 196, 198 n.3, 210-11, 215, 218, 221, 226, 239-40, 241
Alfonso VIII, King of Castile, 11, 20, 34, 218-19, 250
Alfonso IX, King of León, 11, 20-1, 42, 47, 60, 71, 76, 78, 80-1, 83, 98, 120, 132, 180, 210-11, 218-19, 226
Alfonso I, *el Batallador*, King of Aragon, 11, 15-16, 46, 69, 193-4, 210
Alfonso II, King of Aragon, 64, 82, 219
Al-Hakam II, Caliph of Córdoba, 4, 6
Almanzor, Vizir of Al-Andalus, 4, 6, 37, 43
Almohades, 18-21, 34-5, 134, 218-19
Almoravides, 13-18, 31, 56, 193
Alvito, archdeacon of Braga, 156, 158
Antealtares, abbey of, 82, 178
Archdeacons, 150-8
Archpriests, 155-8
Armengol VIII, Count of Urgel, 84

Astorga, bishopric of, 21, 23, 33, 45-8, 64-5, 79, 83, 136-7, 142, 171, 173, 185, 195
archdeacons, 46-7, 152
archpriests, 93
bishops,
Gennadius, 45
Pelayo, 45-6, 190, 235
Alo, 45-6, 93, 125, 137, 139, 196, 203
Roberto, 45-6, 78
Jimeno Eriz, 45-6, 84
Amadeo, 45-6
Arnaldo I, 45-6, 77, 80, 137, 223
Pedro Cristiano, 45, 47, 79, 126, 129 n.1, 178
Fernando I, 45, 46 n.1, 47, 137, 241-3
Arnaldo II, 45, 47, 107 n.6
Fernando II, 45, 47, 80, 209
Lope, 45, 47, 123, 127, 148, 171, 209, 261
Pedro Andrés, 45, 47-8, 205
chapter, 146, 148, 149, 216
Augustinian canons, 26, 32, 34, 51, 63, 71, 79, 111, 144-5, 149
Avila, bishopric of, 24, 32, 38, 41, 77, 112, 131, 136, 140, 142, 175, 179, 252-3
archdeacons, 151
bishops,
Sancho I, 137, 140, 149
Iñigo, 77, 137, 149, 205
Sancho II, 200, 205
Jaime, 96
chapter, 147, 149

Barrantes, abbey of, 51, 165
Belchite, *cofradía* of, 207, 217, *and see* Military Orders
Berengaria, wife of Alfonso VII, 40, 211
Bermudo II, King of León, 162
Bernard, St., of Clairvaux, 39
Bernardo, canon of Santiago de Compostela, 56, 63, 235-6